# WOMEN IN ENGLAND
## c. 1275–1525

## Documentary sources

*translated and edited by* P. J. P. Goldberg

D0070995

Manchester University Press
Manchester and New York

*distributed exclusively in the USA and Canada by St. Martin's Press*

Copyright © P. J. P. Goldberg 1995

*Published by* Manchester University Press
Oxford Road, Manchester M13 9NR, UK
*and* Room 400, 175 Fifth Avenue, New York, NY 10010, USA

*Distributed exclusively in the USA and Canada*
*by* St. Martin's Press, Inc., 175 Fifth Avenue, New York, NY 10010, USA

*British Library Cataloguing-in-Publication Data*
A catalogue record for this book is available from the British Library

*Library of Congress Cataloging-in-Publication Data*
Women in England, c. 1275-1525 / translated and edited by P. J. P. Goldberg.
        p. cm. — (Manchester medieval sources series)
   Includes bibliographical references.
   ISBN 0-7190-4055-8 (hbk). — ISBN 0-7190-4056-6 (pbk.)
    1. Great Britain—History—Medieval period, 1066-1485—Sources.
  2. Women—England—History—Middle Ages, 500-1500—Sources.
  3. Great Britain—History—Tudors, 1485-1603—Sources.
  I. Goldberg, P. J. P., 1958-. II. Series
  DA170.W655   1995
  942—dc20                            95-1714
                                           CIP

ISBN 0 7190 4055 8 *hardback*
ISBN 0 7190 4056 6 *paperback*

First published 1995

99   98   97   96          10  9  8  7  6  5  4  3  2

Typeset in Monotype Bell
by Koinonia Ltd, Manchester
Printed in Great Britain
by Bell & Bain Ltd, Glasgow

# Manchester Medieval Sources Series

*series advisers* Janet L. Nelson and Rosemary Horrox

This series aims to meet a growing need amongst students and teachers of medieval history for translations of key sources that are directly useable in students' own work. It provides texts central to medieval studies courses and will focuses upon the diverse cultural and social as well as political conditions that affected the functioning of all levels of medieval society. The basic premise of the new series is that translations must be accompanied by sufficient introductory and explanatory material and each volume, therefore, includes a comprehensive guide to the sources' interpretation, including discussion of critical linguistic problems and an assessment of the most recent research on the topics being covered.

# Women in England, *c.* 1275–1525

# Contents

For colleagues and students,
past, present, and to come,
associated with the 'Women' options
of the MA in Medieval Studies,
University of York.

# Acknowledgements

My primary debt is to my colleagues and students working within the Centre for Medieval Studies of the University of York whose questions, discussions, and research have helped further my understanding of the lives of medieval women far beyond the economic and demographic concerns central to my research before arriving in York. In particular I wish to thank to my colleague Prof. Felicity Riddy, an inspirational co-teacher, whose assistance with the translation of Middle English literary material has been invaluable. I am similarly indebted to my wife, Dr Patricia Cullum, whose knowledge on matters devotional and advice on a whole variety of points has been a great boon. I wish also to acknowledge a debt of gratitude to the many scholars whose labours, not always acknowledged, in transcribing records have been freely drawn upon within this present collection. Among these are several distinguished women historians, notably Mary Bateson, Mary Dormer Harris, Maud Sellers, and Lucy Toulmin Smith, whose work demonstrates a pioneering interest in medieval women and a thorough attention to contemporary sources that later historians can only strive to emulate.

I am grateful to the Director of the Borthwick Institute of Historical Research, York, for allowing me to publish in translation material in his care, and likewise to the Dean and Chapter of York for material in their custody. Extracts from D. Oschinsky, ed., *Walter of Henley and Other Treatises*, Oxford, 1971, are reprinted by permission of Oxford University Press. Extracts from A. R. Myers, ed., *English Historical Documents*, IV, London, 1969, published by Eyre Methuen are reprinted with permission of Reed Consumer Books. I am indebted to the following for permission to reprint material from the works specified: the Wiltshire Record Society in respect of R. B. Pugh, trans., *Wiltshire Gaol Delivery and Trailbaston Trials 1275-1306*; Dr Maryanne Kowleski and the Devon and Cornwall Record Society in respect of her *The Local Customs Accounts of the Port of Exeter 1266-1321*; the Canterbury and York Society in respect of J. M. Horn, ed., *The Register of Robert Hallum, Bishop of Salisbury, 1407-17*; the Bedfordshire Historical Record Society in respect of R. F. Hunnisett, ed., *Bedfordshire Coroners' Rolls*; the Sussex Record Society in respect of R. F. Hunnisett, ed., *Sussex Coroners' Inquests 1485-1558*; Harringey Art Gallery and Museum Service, Bruce Castle Museum in respect of R. Oram, trans., *Court Rolls of the Manors of Bruces, Dawbeneys, Pembrokes (Tottenham) 1 Richard II to 1 Henry IV (1377-1399)*. Crown copyright is reproduced with the permission of the Controller of HMSO.

# Foreword

The study of medieval women was a relatively late addition to the proliferation of 'women's studies', perhaps because of a widespread perception that historical sources for such work barely existed. Much early work on women as a group, rather than on powerful individuals, was flawed as a result by too uncritical a reliance on literary or patristic sources, with the latter in particular producing an extreme picture of female oppression. In England, Jeremy Goldberg has led the way in demonstrating that the discussion of non-aristocratic women can be securely grounded in archival documentation, and in exploring, with sensitivity and sophistication, the relationship between the picture which emerges from such sources and the literary and theological perceptions of womankind. He now provides a collection of documentary material, much of it previously unpublished, and guides the reader in the techniques needed to glean rich evidence of contemporary behaviour and assumptions from what can seem, at first sight, unpromisingly austere sources. All aspects of women's life are covered here, and if the surviving sources inevitably have more to say about the victims of life's disasters and upheavals than about the undemonstratively contented, such examples, sensitively analysed, can shed invaluable light on the norms of contemporary behaviour. This book recovers the experience of ordinary medieval women. A few speak with their own voices, for others their actions must speak for them, but it will never again be possible to claim that non-aristocratic women are the invisible people of medieval history.

Rosemary Horrox
*Fitzwilliam College, Cambridge*

# Note on editorial conventions used

All the texts have been translated into modern English from their original form. Frequently this is Latin, but in some instances it is French or Middle English. This I have indicated in the headings. In the majority of cases, and even where the edition used contains a translation, I have created my own. This is indicated by the heading 'translated from'. Where the edition used does not reproduce the original text, however, I have used an existing translation. In these instances the heading reads 'translation by/in', although I have sometimes made minor changes in order to modernise or clarify the text. I have tried at all times to strike a balance between communicating the sense of the original, whilst at the same time retaining something of the original language or structure. The texts have been dated as closely as possible. Minor editorial comments and, in the case of some of the lengthier church court depositions, synopses of omitted text are contained within square brackets. Also so indicated, viz. [ ] and [...], are blanks and gaps due to damage within the manuscript respectively, although where the reading can be guessed at, this is contained within square brackets. Occasionally doubtful readings are indicated by a question mark. Where matter has been omitted from my edition of the text, this is indicated by three or four dots according to the position within the sentence. First names have been modernised and standardised so far as possible, but surnames etc., including place name bynames, have been left in the form found in the source. (Where the same name is repeated under several forms, a common spelling has been adopted.) Occupational bynames, however, have been translated wherever it is apparent that these indicate actual occupations. The Latin prefix 'Dominus', a courtesy title for ordained clergy, has here been rendered as 'Sir' as this represents conventional contemporary usage.

# Introduction

The past decade or so has seen an explosion of writings on English medieval women. Only a proportion of this literature, however, represents the fruit of substantial archival work and there is an inevitable tendency for such studies to be primarily dependent on an individual source.[1] Much writing on medieval women has, moreover, drawn upon literary sources, a reflection of the way in which the field of Medieval Studies has come to be dominated by literary scholars. It follows that although certain texts, for example *The Book of Margery Kempe, Ancrene Wisse*, or even Chaucer's Wife of Bath, are well known and readily accessible, of other sources, and particularly the rich variety of conventional historical sources, only a limited range are generally known.[2] The purpose of this present collection is twofold. The first is to make accessible and thus more familiar a broad variety of sources that can throw light on English medieval women. The second is to stimulate scholarship that makes greater use of a range of sources than has hitherto been normal. In making my selection I have consciously attempted to reflect as many facets of women's lives as the record material will allow. On the other hand I have tried to avoid obviously atypical examples and I claim only to represent something of the different classes of source material available and not the range in its entirety.

Although there exists an abundance of sources for women in later medieval English society, as so often with historical documents, few record women's lives directly and all present their own problems of interpretation. Some aspects of women's lives are better documented than others. Paid employment or death bed piety is comparatively well recorded, education, recreation, beliefs, and emotions scarcely at all.

---

1 E.g. J. M. Bennett, *Women in the Medieval English Countryside: Gender and Household in Brigstock before the Plague*, New York, 1987 (manor court rolls); B. A. Hanawalt, *The Ties that Bound: Peasant Families in Medieval England*, New York, 1986 (coroners' rolls). Much the same is true of individual studies contained in such essay collections as P. J. P. Goldberg, ed., *Woman is a Worthy Wight: Women in English Society* c. *1200-1500*, Stroud, 1992; S. S. Walker, ed., *Wife and Widow in Medieval England*, Ann Arbor, 1993.

2 The sources assembled here have consciously excluded a small number of such very well known texts where they exist in readily available editions and translations.

Certain groups of women are likewise more conspicuous than others. The aristocracy, who largely fall outside the scope of this collection, but who form the focus of another volume in this series, and well-to-do townswomen are readily observed, but the poor, the young, and the married are harder to identify outside certain limited contexts. (Jewish women, whose presence overlaps only with the first fifteen years of this collection, are also not represented.) My concern is not to present a synopsis of current historical knowledge, but a brief guide to the sources illustrated here, their problems, and how they may be used to illustrate a variety of facets of women's lives. My choice of chapters is an attempt to impose some order on what may otherwise appear a rather miscellaneous range of source material, but is in itself partly determined by the relative availability of evidence under different heads. Thus it was possible to offer two chapters on aspects of work together with a separate chapter on prostitution, but my chapter on recreation is noticeably brief, and I have almost nothing to offer on such topics as women's attitudes to sex and sexuality, their experience of pregnancy and childbirth, how they coped with childrearing or bereavement, what were their reactions to the barage of misogyny that reached them from the pulpit, the council chamber, or even perhaps fathers, husbands, or brothers, and whether they ever, like Christine de Pisan, wondered if experience might not constitute a surer foundation for living than authority.

Inevitably my selection of texts is shaped in part by my own interests and knowledge. I have deliberately allowed depositions, that is written records of the responses of witnesses to set questions, from the consistory court of York to feature prominently and have reproduced individual cases in extenso. On the one hand the substance of these cases, be they concerned with disputed marriages, defamation, or debt, is illuminating in itself. On the other hand they allow persons of both sexes, and even teenage maidservants, unmarried mothers, and elderly beggarwomen, to speak across the centuries, and they can throw light upon a range of matters quite unconnected with the substance of the case. Whereas few of these cases have ever been published in their original form, let alone in translation, most other sources represented here have been published in one form or another. Women feature in them infrequently and often only briefly. This is particularly true of manor and borough court rolls or Peace session records. My concern here has been to represent those occasions where women do feature in the record rather than to reproduce any particular document at length. In the discussion that follows I shall attempt to offer some guidance as to how even brief and superficially enigmatic entries may be read and suggest ways in which particular sources may be used to address a range of historical questions. I shall arrange this discussion under the same headings as the chapters that follow. The texts referred to are those contained within the pertinent chapter unless indicated otherwise.

## Childhood

As legal minors, youngsters of either sex are hard to find in medieval sources. For the greater aristocracy proofs of age will sometimes provide evidence relating to the births of heirs, but such evidence is not normally available for persons of lesser rank. A disputed marriage case [3] in the York consistory, however, provides a unique range of depositions relating to the birth of one Alice de Rouclif, a girl of minor gentry rank, but also of a number of village children. The depositions reproduced here throw light on the 'ceremony' of childbirth, on baptism, the churching of the mother, and the associated celebrations among kin, friends, and even tenants. (Baptisms and churchings are also occasionally noted in clerical accounts [4].) There is even a reference, contained in the deposition of Anabilla Pynder, to the use of a writing, perhaps a prayer, as an aid to a safe delivery. Similar customs are implied by the adoption of special girdles in childbirth [2]. The care with which the Rouclif family provided wetnurses for their two children contrasts with the conspicuous silence of other records in respect of lower echelons of society. The implication is that the employment of wetnurses was an essentially aristocratic custom in late medieval England (cf. [5]) and that most mothers suckled their own children, often, as these depositions imply, for extended periods of time. This would have had the effect of reducing maternal fertility and of spacing births. It would also have resulted in healthier mothers, because less burdened by repeated childbearing, and healthier infants. The delivery of infants, as the accounts of the deliveries of both John and Alice de Rouclif indicate, were entirely managed and witnessed by women, though there is the implication, as shown in the depositions of Alice Sharpe and Margaret de Folifayt, that men might intervene when difficulties were encountered.[3] The prevailing philosophy, however, was that the mother's health was valued more highly than that of the child [1b].

3 P. P. A. Biller, 'Childbirth in the Middle Ages', *History Today*, XXXVI, 1986, pp. 42-9.

Infants were swaddled (to keep their limbs straight) and kept safe in cradles [3], though pictorial evidence suggests that babies could be carried on their mothers' backs and there is no reason to suppose that peasant women would not have taken their swaddled babies out with them to work in the fields. Children and infants feature as victims within coroners' rolls. Many accidental deaths were no doubt associated with play or lack of proper supervision [6b], but it may be unwise to draw conclusions about the quality of childrearing from such a loaded source. The same source can demonstrate that parents' made proper provision for the care of children when they were busy elsewhere [6a]. Accidental deaths of girls are, moreover, less commonly recorded than those of boys, probably as much because accidental deaths of girls were less likely to be reported to the coroner than that they were less vulnerable than their brothers; although all accidental and unnatural deaths were supposed to be reported, it is likely that the deaths of women and minors (and particularly female minors) would only be reported where these were sufficiently publicised or sufficiently suspicious that the community needed to make use of the proper channels in order to protect itself from suspicion of wrongdoing.[4] Coroners' rolls can suggest that older girls would assist their parents in a variety of tasks and errands [7]. Older girls, described as the daughters of a named parent, were also sometimes presented in manor court rolls for collecting wood, nuts, or berries.[5]

The ways in which pre-pubescent girls were brought up and socialised as young women is very difficult to reconstruct. Often we find clues only when the relationship between a girl and her parents or guardians became sour [9]. It may be that this was particularly likely to occur in the case of children taken into second marriages following the death of a parent [9a], [10], [11], [12] as folklore traditions imply. That the excessive use of corporal chastisement could become a matter for litigation suggests both that parents thought corporal punishment appropriate, but also that it was to be used only within reason and for good cause. The behaviour of John Raven [9b] is particularly interesting here. His justification for beating his 'cousin' (the Latin term implies a blood relationship, but is not more specific), a girl of 'tender age', was that she 'desired to spend her time among boys and

4 P. J. P. Goldberg, 'The Public and the Private: Women in the Pre-Plague Economy', in P. R. Coss and S. D. Lloyd, eds., *Thirteenth Century England III*, Woodbridge, 1991, pp. 78-80.

5 Hanawalt, *The Ties that Bound*, p. 159; 'Law and custom' [7b].

company improper to her rank'. It is implicit, therefore, that for a girl to play with boys was constructed as tolerable among the lower ranks of society (who knew no better), but not for families of rank, or at least having social pretensions. That John is described as a chaplain (priest) may well have meant that he had particularly rigid ideas about how girls should behave. Although aimed at older children, the didactic poem 'How the Goodwife Taught her Daughter' ('Adolescence' [23]) implies that the primary responsibility for the moral and social education of girls fell to mothers. The popularity in later medieval England of the iconography of the Virgin teaching the child Mary to read/pray further suggests that it was mothers who taught their daughters the rudiments of the faith and in particular the Ave, Creed, and Paternoster (Lord's prayer) and some bourgeois and aristocratic mothers may indeed have handed down skills in basic literacy.[6] A small number of girls, presumably from well-to-do backgrounds, may have boarded at a nunnery and been educated there ([5]; 'Devotion' [2b], [3b]), but it is also possible that a few girls attended grammar school.[7]

## Adolescence

It is apparent from the evidence of the poll taxes of the later fourteenth century ('Husband and wife' [1]; 'Work in the countryside' [22]; 'Work in the town' [28]) that comparatively few girls remained within their natal homes by the time they reached their teens and that this was especially true of urban society. It may well be that the poll tax evidence reflects conditions specific to the later fourteenth and earlier fifteenth centuries and that at periods prior to and subsequent to that time it may have been more common for adolescent girls to remain at home, but this observation must be necessarily speculative.[8] We cannot, therefore, use the point at which girls left home as a simple

6 This theme is developed in W. Scase, 'St Anne and the Education of the Virgin: Literary and Artistic Traditions and their Implications', in N. Rogers, ed., *England in the Fourteenth Century*, Harlaxton Medieval Studies, III (Stamford, 1993), pp. 81-96.

7 P. J. P. Goldberg, 'Girls Growing Up in Later Medieval England', *History Today*, June, 1995, pp. 25-32. Caroline Barron has also argued recently that London records provide shadowy glimpses of small schools after the fashion of early modern 'dame schools', which probably provided some sort of tuition, including literacy in the vernacular, for both girls and boys.

8 P. J. P. Goldberg, *Women, Work, and Life Cycle in a Medieval Economy: Women in York and Yorkshire c. 1300-1520*, Oxford, 1992, pp. 200-2, 261-2, 275-9.

point of demarcation between 'childhood' and 'adolescence'. Nevertheless it would appear that from about the age of twelve years girls were
considered old enough to leave home, physiologically to have reached
or least to be approaching sexual maturity, and to have reached an age
of discretion such that in canon law they were deemed of sufficient age
to consent to marriage or enter a nunnery. Thus, though the concept
of adolescence, if not the term itself, may be essentially anachronistic,
the decision here to treat the years between menarche (sexual maturity)
and the common age at marriage as part of a single chapter is not
arbitrary.

It is much easier to find evidence about girls who had left home than
teenage girls, or even young adult women, who continued to reside at
home. Again the poll tax evidence allows us a series of snapshots of the
institution of service in the later fourteenth century. Female servants,
that is invariably young, unmarried persons supported in the households of their employers in return for their labour, appear then to have
been very common in towns, probably as common as male servants,
but rather less so in rural areas and especially arable regions.[9]
(Asmunderby with Bondgate ('Work in the countryside' [22]), where
a broadly equal number of male and female servants are found, is
characterised by woodland pasture.) The great numbers of servants,
and the consequent frequency with which parents let children leave
the natal home in order to take up positions, found in London at the
very end of the fifteenth century was a cause of shocked comment by
a visiting Venetian [1]. His observations, patently exaggerated for
dramatic effect, have to be understood in the context of the visitor's
native culture. In northern Italy young people normally remained at
home until they married. Only the very poor would send their
daughters (let alone their sons) into service, a course of action that
represented a surrender of paternal authority and which could easily
lead to a loss of 'honour' for the girls concerned. In fact the English
institution seems to have been very different. Female servants below
the age of twelve are hardly to be found (cf. [2], [3]; 'Childhood' [9c];
'Law and custom' [63b]). Similarly, despite the comments of the
Venetian observer, female apprentices, that is servants contracted to a
particular employer for a number of years in order to learn a craft,
were probably comparatively uncommon in London and even rarer
outside (cf. [4]; 'Prostitution' [10]).

9 Ibid., pp. 159-60.

The majority of female servants were employed for a year at a time and seem frequently to have changed employers upon the termination of their contracts ([6], [11], [16]; 'Husband and wife' [11] deposition of William Coke). (The customary minimum term of service of one year was enforceable after 1351 by statute [8b], [9], [10], although acute labour shortage in the later fourteenth century still led to conflict between employers [7], [8a], [11].) Often servants were hired at or around particular hiring dates which were dependent upon custom and the needs of the regional agrarian economy.[10] Hence Martinmas (11 November) and Pentecost were regular hiring dates in Northern England ([8b], [11]; 'Childhood' [3] deposition of Maud de Herthill; 'Husband and wife' [11] deposition of William Coke; 'Widowhood, poverty, and old age' [12] depositions of Agnes Kyrkeby and Isabel Nesswyk), whereas Michaelmas (29 September) was common in the arable Midlands, and Candlemas (2 February) in the pastoral West. The ages of servants and former servants can often be calculated from deposition material and this confirms the impression that girls and young women in service were invariably aged twelve or more, but few women are still observed as servants after their mid twenties. (The pattern for males is not dissimilar.) Again it is deposition evidence that allows most glimpses of female servants' tasks ([24] deposition of Walter de Mellerby; 'Widowhood, poverty, and old age' [12] depositions of Agnes Kyrkeby and Thomas Catton; 'Law and custom' [35] deposition of Joan Scharp), but 'The Serving Maid's Holiday' [5] provides a few clues in respect of rural servants. Poll tax evidence ('Work in the countryside' [22]; 'Work in the town' [28]) suggests, however, that certain types of employer were more likely to employ female servants than others.[11] The implication of this is that female servants also assisted in the workshop or the fields.

Depositions and bequests to servants in wills further show that servants were sometimes related to their employers, and the appearance of servants among the will-making population [21b, c] further indicates that there was no necessary social gulf between employer and servant. In some respects employers stood as guardians to their servants [12a] and owed them duties of care, guidance, and moral instruction in addition to providing for their physical needs by providing clothing,

---

10 Cf. ibid., pp. 173-4; A. Kussmaul, *Servants in Husbandry in Early Modern England,* Cambridge, 1981.

11 This is also apparent from the sex-specific pattern of servant-keeping noted in wills. See Goldberg, *Women, Work, and Life Cycle,* pp. 186-94.

board, and lodging. Money wages, if they were paid at all, tended consequently to be modest ([6]; 'Husband and wife' [11] deposition of William Coke). Employers' interest and concern for the well-being of their servants is reflected in bequests to servants of clothing, monies, household utensils etc. [13], [14], [15]. Occasionally former servants are also remembered [21a], and employers would take responsibility for the burial of any servant who died whilst in their employ [22]. On the other hand the employer's duty to exercise discipline could result in conflict [16], [17], [18], though as so often the record is biased towards such cases. Much the same is true of evidence of sexual abuse of female servants ([19], [20]; 'Prostitution' [10]).

Moral instruction and guidance is something that for the most part we can only guess at, but one of the more obvious uses of the didactic text 'How the Goodwife Taught her Daughter' [23] was for the direction of female servants by their mistresses. The text, which draws upon a paradigm of maternal instruction that would hardly require a textual form if the intended audience still resided at home, is evidently aimed at adolescents for the leitmotif is how girls should behave if they want to make good marriages. Such a marriage is here imagined to be to a burgess or citizen with his own workshop.[12] Manners, deportment, the virtues of moderation and conformity, and a willingness to assist and supervise in the workshop are all demanded. Although such teaching would also have been pertinent to daughters continuing to live at home, and indeed the text could have served as a guide to mothers as to how to bring up their teenage daughters, it should be recognised that this is an essentially bourgeois didactic text. It is neither a simple mirror of actual conduct (indeed we may usefully read against the text), nor is it indicative of the values of peasant society or of the urban labouring poor.

Moral guidance may have been considered particularly necessary in respect of young women on the eve of adulthood and the prospect of matrimony. 'How the Goodwife Taught her Daughter' was clearly concerned to dissuade its audience from anything other than the most circumscribed contact with the opposite sex. In practice many young women lived away from the natal home and enjoyed considerable opportunities to socialise with young men. This would have been especially true of the later fourteenth and earlier fifteenth centuries, but it may also have been more generally true of the lower echelons of

12 For the terms burgess and citizen see below.

society. This is suggested on the one hand by reading against the text
of 'How the Goodwife Taught her Daughter', or by lyrics such as 'The
Serving Maid's Holiday' [5], and on the other by the numerous
presentments within the church courts [27], [28], [30], [31], [32],
[33] of unmarried women for fornication and likewise within the
customary (manor) court [39], [42d, e, f] for leyrwite, the fine for
fornication by villein women. (It is noteworthy that most leyrwite
fines were paid in respect of women from poorer peasant families.[13])
How far mistresses gave advice to their female servants, implicit in the
circulation of 'How the Goodwife Taught her Daughter', or how far
servant girls depended on advice handed down by older and more
experienced fellow servants we cannot know. Certainly employers had
a social obligation to protect the chastity of their female employees
[25] and servants of both sexes were forbidden to marry within their
term of contract without their employers' consent.

Most young women in fact probably abstained from serious courtship
relationships, and certainly risky courtship relationships, until a year
or two of when they might hope to marry. The impression gleaned
from church court records is that few young women would consent to
sex until an agreement to marriage had been made (cf. [25] deposition
of John Gamesby, [27a, b, d], [30d]; 'Widowhood, poverty, and old
age' [13]). This is explicit in a few instances, but is also apparent from
the number of instances where sexual relations commenced immediately following a contract of marriage [24], [26].[14] We know almost
nothing of medieval sex education. There are occasional references to
the use of herbs for contraceptive purposes and likewise as aborti-
facients ([5] note, [32b, e]; 'Childhood' [1b]). Coitus interruptus was
probably also known, but this and the most effective contraceptive
practice, i.e. prolonged breast feeding, were most likely to have been
limited to within marriage.[15]

---

13 L. R. Poos and R. M. Smith, '"Legal Windows onto Historical Populations"? Recent
Research on Demography and the Manor Court in England', *Law and History
Review*, II, 1984, pp. 149-50. A few manor court rolls distinguish leyrwite, fines for
simple fornication, from childwite, fines for actually giving birth outside wedlock.
Leyrwite represented an additional source of seigneurial revenue, but lords
historically had a vested interest in discouraging illicit sex in order to prevent
villeins reproducing themselves outside wedlock; villeinage was hereditary, but
illegitimate offspring could not inherit from their parents.

14 Goldberg, *Women, Work, and Life Cycle*, pp. 248-9.

15 P. P. A. Biller, 'Birth-Control in the West in the Thirteenth and Early Fourteenth
Centuries', *Past and Present*, XCIV, 1982, pp. 3-26.

We can get rather further with the question of how far medieval parents controlled marriages and how far the initiative was left to individuals. Marriage was regulated by the Church according to the rules of canon law. This held that the consent of the parties contracting, so long as they were of sufficient age, viz. fourteen for boys, but twelve for girls (cf. 'Childhood' [3]), not already married ([34b], [36]; 'Husband and wife' [11]), and not related within forbidden degrees, was held to be sufficient to make a binding marriage.[16] Marriages did not need, therefore, to be limited to formal contracts at the church door, though the Church tried to discourage 'clandestine' contracts that fell short of this, nor was parental, familial, or seigneurial consent strictly necessary in terms of making a valid contract. According to canon law, moreover, consent demanded no more than the exchange of words (or if those words indicated only intention to marry, the marriage was held to be immediately binding on consummation of the relationship). Although consent is not actually the same as free choice, a marriage made by force ([25]; 'Widowhood, poverty, and old age' [12]) was deemed to be contrary to the principle of consent and therefore invalid. Where disputes arose as to the validity of a marriage or, as was often the case, a woman sought to enforce an alleged contract of marriage against a recalcitrant man ([24], [26]; 'Widowhood, poverty, and old age' [13]), they were liable to become the subject of litigation within the Church courts. Deposition evidence in respect of matrimonial litigation is consequently an invaluable source, but one that is limited to disputed marriages. A careful reading of these texts, however, can suggest ways in which these necessarily atypical cases may throw light on more general patterns.

Different patterns of litigation variously alleging consummated future contracts ([25]; 'Widowhood, poverty, and old age' [13]), contracts using words of present consent (e.g. [25], [26]) and multi-party contracts, where one party was allegedly contracted to two or more

---

16 The circumstances of 'Childhood' [3] are especially complex. Alice de Rouclif was contracted to marry John Marrays whilst still under canonical age. This was a lawful arrangement so long as the child was over seven years and was permitted to ratify their consent upon reaching their majority, at which point the marriage would become binding. The argument of John Marrays in this case was that Alice had indeed ratified the contract after she had reached her majority by consenting to have sex with him, but the counter-argument was that Alice was still below canonical age at the time of the alleged intercourse and that the marriage was thus not binding. The best introduction to the canon law on marriage, including the issue of forbidden degrees, and the Church courts is R. H. Helmholz, *Marriage Litigation in Medieval England*, Cambridge, 1974.

other parties ('Husband and wife' [11]), may suggest different levels of personal initiative or parental control in the making of marriages. In general disputed consummated future contracts suggest courtship relationships that had gone wrong [25]. Likewise multi-party actions often represent engagement disputes and reflect a high degree of personal initiative.[17] Actual depositions provide more clues and may make reference to marriage tokens, viz. rings, gloves, sums of money etc. ([23] stanza 14; 'Childhood' [3] depositions of Anabilla, wife of Stephen Wasteleyne and Ellen, widow of Gervase de Rouclif), the words used ([25] deposition of Margaret Bown; 'Husband and wife' [11] deposition of William Coke), the witnesses, and the location, be it in bed [27c], at the church porch ([36]; 'Husband and wife' [11] deposition of Adam Roger), or in a garden arbour ('Widowhood, poverty, and old age' [12] deposition of Alice Rayner). The impression is that servants, who feature frequently in matrimonial causes ([25]; 'Husband and wife' [11]) and who lived independently of their natal families, enjoyed considerable freedom of courtship. In contrast, evidence of parental control − reflected in forced marriages, marriages within forbidden degrees, or even under-age marriages ('Childhood' [3]) − is most marked among substantial peasants where dowries might be paid [40] and daughters more frequently lived at home until marriage and, from the later fifteenth century, among well-to-do townsfolk (cf. [29b]).[18] For the minor aristocracy evidence of parental involvement in the bringing together of young people in marriage is apparent from the formality of marriage negotiations culminating in the drawing up of actual contracts ('Childhood' [3] deposition of Anabilla, wife of Stephen Wasteleyne). It is also reflected in pleas for dispensations to marry despite ties of consanguinity or affinity sometimes recorded in bishops' registers [34a] and papal letters [35].

Where the ages and marital status of deponents are recorded, it may be possible to draw some conclusions about customary age at marriage.[19] Evidence from York consistory court depositions suggests that in the century after the Black Death urban women tended to marry in their mid twenties and rural women in their earlier twenties to men two or three years older than themselves, there being some relationship between age at marriage and degree of freedom of

---

17 M. M. Sheehan, 'The Formation and Stability of Marriage in Fourteenth-Century England: Evidence of an Ely Register', *Medieval Studies*, XXXIII, 1971, pp. 228-63.

18 Goldberg, *Women, Work, and Life Cycle*, pp. 243-51, 254-66.

19 Ibid., pp. 225-32.

courtship.[20]   A more mundane source for marriage within peasant
society exists in the record of marriage fines or merchets in manor
court rolls and account rolls [39b, e], [42a, b, c], [43].[21] Although
only the marriages of more prosperous villeins – perhaps those which
saw the provision of a dowry – resulted in a merchet payment, and the
levy of merchet declined markedly after the Black Death, the record of
fines may again provide some clues as to marriage formation. Clearly
merchets were a useful source of revenue to lords (e.g. [39e]), but
there is little evidence of actual seigneurial control of marriages except
in respect of the remarriages of some landholding widows in the land-
hungry years before the Agrarian Crisis.[22] That some women are
recorded as paying their own fines [39b], [42a, b, c], [43a, c] may
suggest personal initiative, but equally the many fines paid by
husbands-to-be [39e] and fathers (or sometimes mothers) may signify
parental involvement. Often the record distinguishes marriages within
the manor [42a], [43a] from marriages outside [42c], [43b] and
even marriages at will [43c].[23] Razi has attempted to calculate age at
marriage by observing the number of years elapsed between the first
recorded appearance of the father in the court rolls and his daughter's
subsequent merchet payment, but this method has not commanded
universal acceptance.[24]

Given the bias of the sources available, it is no surprise that we know
more of courtship relationships that failed and resulted in litigation

20 Ibid., pp. 203–79. For an alternative methodology, using manor court rolls, and
rather different conclusions about age at first marriage and marriage regimes in
rural society before the fifteenth century, see Z. Razi, *Life, Marriage and Death in a
Medieval Parish*, Cambridge, 1980. The differences in age at first marriage between
Razi's data and my own for rural society are not in fact so great given that Razi's
data are biased towards the marriages of heirs and span an earlier period, but his
interpretation that these represent a 'medieval' marriage regime, characterised by
early and near universal marriage, rather than a 'northwestern' regime, characterised by late (i.e. in the twenties), companionate (i.e. at like ages) marriage (and
significant minorities failing to marry), is not so easily reconciled.

21 There has been some debate over the precise origins and purposes of the merchet
or marriage fine, but it is apparent by the later Middle Ages that it represented little
more than an additional source of seigneurial revenue rather than any attempt to
control the marriages of the villein population.

22 R. M. Smith, 'Hypothèses sur la Nuptialité en Angleterre aux XIIIe-XIVe Siècles',
*Annales: Economies Sociétés Civilisations*, XXXVIII, 1983, pp. 124–6.

23 J. M. Bennett, 'Medieval Peasant Marriage: An Examination of Marriage License
Fines in the *Liber Gersumarum*', in J. A. Raftis, ed., *Pathways to Medieval Peasants*,
Toronto, 1981, pp. 193–246.

24 See note 20 above, also Poos and Smith, '"Legal Windows"', pp. 128–52 and the
subsequent debate with Razi in the pages of *Law and History Review*.

than of those that succeeded. In practice it is likely that a number of courtship relations that in canon-legal terms were strictly binding marriages were broken off by mutual consent and hence do not enter the record. (We may, for example, speculate that such was the apparently unconsummated contract between servants noted in one York case ('Husband and wife' [11]), remembered in this instance to obtain a de facto divorce from a subsequent established marriage.) In other instances couples cohabited, but apparently without the intention of marrying [28b, c, d], [30a], [31k], [32e]. Sometimes we may detect a popular resistance simply to the solemnisation of marriage at the church door (a position shared by Lollards) [31e, g] rather than to marriage itself, though this may be a consequence of the Church becoming by the earlier sixteenth century even more insistent that marriages should be so solemnised. By much the same period a more puritanical attitude to pre-marital sex emerges such that women could be presented before the Church courts for having had sexual relations with their husbands to be [30d], [32b], (cf. also [37b]) even though this may previously have been a normal part of courtship. The implication is that marriage was increasingly understood in terms of the solemnisation rather than a simple contract. Before the fifteenth century couples who regularly cohabited could be made to undergo an abjuration *sub pena nubendi* [27a], i.e. that if they continued to cohabit then they would be deemed to be lawfully married, but such a policy seems not to have been pursued after that time.[25]

It seems to have been commonplace for priests to keep female servants or others as mistresses and de facto wives, although some clergy seem to have been much more exploitative of the women for whom they had pastoral responsibility [30b, c], [31c, i]. It may be that the former relationships were often tolerated by parishioners, whereas the latter might be reported at visitation. Sometimes these and other relationships led to the births of unwanted children and even to infanticide, perhaps specifically at the urging of the father who no doubt feared exposure or because there was no father to help maintain the child [30b], [31f, i], [33d]. In (canon) law, however, fathers did have a responsibility to maintain infants [32c]. With a hardening of moral attitudes (cf. the vigilance of the 'honest wives of Windsor and Eton' [30b]), however, coinciding with a decline in economic opportunities from the later fifteenth century, women who engaged in sexual

25 A. Finch, 'Parental Authority and the Problem of Clandestine Marriage in the Later Middle Ages', *Law and History Review*, VIII, 1980, p. 196.

relations as a part of courtship may have been particularly vulnerable to social ostracism and particularly at risk of being drawn into a subculture of petty crime and prostitution. Within this social context it became a work of mercy for the well-to-do to provide help in the form of dowries to facilitate the marriages of 'poor maids' [37]. Such dowries are also found in similar social contexts before the plague and in London for a few decades also after the advent of plague. It should finally be noted, by way of a caution, that not all women who achieved adulthood married. Numbers of 'singlewomen' – a term that merits further investigation – are to be found, for example, in fifteenth-century records, and some of the women living on their own noticed in poll tax returns may have been never married (e.g. 'Husband and wife' [1]), but how numerous such women were or how far any remained unwed of choice must remain matters for further research.

## Husband and wife

The lives of married women, beyond the evidence that will be discussed in respect of work, are not easy to reconstruct. In law husbands were regularly held to be answerable or at least to have some responsibility for their wives' actions since the husband was deemed to have authority over his wife [2] and consequently wives are often invisible in court records. What went on in the marital home was, moreover, regarded as an essentially private matter and not something that would normally impinge upon the public record. The upside down world of marginalia and misericords, for example, regularly depicts wives beating their husbands, but since husbands were alone responsible for disciplining their wives (cf. [16]) – and such imagery may in fact have served to reinforce this notion – no husband had his wife presented within the borough or customary courts for assault. The existence of such a topos, however, which is also reflected in the so-called 'Ballad of a Tyrannical Husband' ('Work in the countryside' [2]), may suggest that gender relations and specifically relations between husband and wife were a matter of debate, particularly by the fifteenth century.

Poll tax evidence ([1]; 'Work in the countryside' [22]; 'Work in the town' [28]) shows that marriage led to the formation of a new household. Very few married couples appear to have co-resided with in-laws or unmarried siblings – a pattern unlike that found, for example, in Tuscany over the same period.[26] Most couples lived with children and/or servants, though children below tax age (fourteen in respect of the 1377 tax, which is generally regarded to be the most satisfactory for demographic purposes) do not appear in the tax returns. It is this world of 'nuclear' households in which, for peasant farmers, artisans or merchants alike, the household was also the labour force. Indeed, for the artisan family, into which the Goodwife's daughter was being socialised ('Adolescence' [23]), the home was also the place of work. Wives thus filled roles not just as mothers and cooks [8], roles that in more well-to-do households might partly have been taken by servants, but as household managers, economic partners, and, in their husbands' absence, acting heads of household able to answer for their husbands vis-à-vis the wider community [2a], [7].

Though evidence of affection and indeed love is sometimes found in matrimonial litigation, there are fewer sources that can show that such feelings lasted through marriage.[27] This, however, is no evidence that such feelings were uncommon within marriages. An Italian visitor writing in 1497 certainly thought that English men showed (unreasonable) love for their wives [3]. For the lesser aristocracy and (substantial) merchant classes of the fifteenth century there is of course material to be gleaned from the Paston, Stonor, Plumpton, and Cely correspondence. These allow occasional insights into marital relationships and can reflect real intimacy and affection.[28] Husbands and wives occasionally used terms of endearment towards their spouses in their wills and husbands regularly named wives among their executors. Wives for their part often asked to be buried beside their predeceased spouses ('Devotion' [14c]).

For most wives marriage would have meant having children and becoming mothers. Unfortunately we have almost no evidence of the support husbands gave their wives during pregnancy, although a chance reference to a man providing for his wife's food craving is found in a collection of model manor court entries [5]. We cannot know how

26 D. Herlihy and C. Klapisch-Zuber, *Tuscans and Their Families: A Study of the Florentine Catasto of 1427*, New Haven and London, 1985, pp. 290-319; C. Klapisch-Zuber, *Women, Family, and Ritual in Renaissance Italy*, Chicago and London, 1985, pp. 23-35; Goldberg, *Women, Work, and Life Cycle*, pp. 333-45.

27 P. J. P. Goldberg, 'Female Labour, Service and Marriage in the Late Medieval Urban North', *Northern History*, XXII, 1986, p. 27.

28 Cf. H. S. Bennett, *The Pastons and Their England*, Cambridge, 1932, pp. 59-62; K. Dockray, 'Why did Fifteenth-Century English Gentry Marry?', in M. Jones, ed., *Gentry and Lesser Nobility in Late Medieval Europe*, Gloucester, 1986, pp. 69-71.

far women of humble rank were confined within their homes prior to churching or how commonly they were allowed the assistance of the sort of monthly nurse (to adopt nineteenth-century terminology for a woman who assisted the mother during the period between delivery and churching) observed in respect of Ellen de Rouclif ('Childhood' [3] depositions of Cecily de Shupton). Female kin and friends would have lent support (and for new mothers no doubt advice) and may have attended at the delivery along with the midwife, though it would seem that parochial clergy also had a duty to visit women in childbed [4b] (and cf. [6]).[29] Mothers normally suckled their own children and for extended periods.[30] Many married women would consequently have passed their years between marriage, and the end of their childbearing period some two decades later, either nursing or pregnant. During this period a wife might be expected to experience some dozen or more deliveries.[31]

Not all couples would have been able to have children.[32] Again we are given almost no insight into their feelings, though one sad case of a couple who kept an empty cradle by their bed [4a] may speak volumes. In canon law an annulment of marriage on the grounds of male impotence was possible, though a woman needed to assert that she desired such an annulment because she wished to be a mother ('Prostitution' [17]). When working with the records of the Church court, however, it is necessary to remember the clerical bias that shapes the material; from a clerical perspective the primary purpose of marriage was procreation and hence a woman wanting to terminate a sexually and emotionally sterile marriage could only claim that she desired children.

Although not an explicit part of the words of the marriage contract before the first Book of Common Prayer, wives were expected to be obedient to their spouses. This is implicit in the legal term for the

29 Biller, 'Childbirth in the Middle Ages', pp. 42-9. Hanawalt's suggestion that the midwife regularly employed two assistants seems to be a confusion of the normal presence of 'gossips' at the delivery: B. A. Hanawalt, *Growing Up in Medieval London: The Experience of Childhood in History*, New York and Oxford, 1993, pp. 42-3.

30 See 'Childhood' above.

31 Margery Kempe gave birth to fourteen children. Not all pregnancies would have gone to term and in practice only a proportion of all children born would have survived childhood; of the seventeen children whose births are noted in ('Childhood' [3]), only eight are definitely known still to be alive at the time of the case and two are said to have died very soon after birth.

32 Modern evidence suggests that some ten per cent of marriages are naturally sterile.

murder of the husband by his wife, viz. petty treason, and it also explains the willingness of the royal courts to exempt from punishment wives who acted in partnership with felonious husbands [23a, b]. It is also implicit in the assumption that husbands would normally be aware of and consent to their wives' business activities [2c]. It is a philosophy that is explicitly articulated by Thomas Nesfeld by way of justification for striking his rebellious wife [16], but it was a philosophy that also extended to the marital bed. In canon law spouses were deemed to owe one another the conjugal debt. A wife could not therefore refuse her husband sexual services, a perspective summed up in John de Walkyngton's reported statement to his alleged wife, 'You are mine. I am yours, as well you know. And I refuse to seek permission from you to do my will with you' ('Widowhood, poverty, and old age' [13] deposition of Maud Katersouth). It follows that medieval society had no concept of marital rape.

As so often, it is the evidence of discord and of marital relations that have broken down that most readily impinges upon the record. We have therefore an optical illusion that abusive and unloving relationships were commonplace. A more careful reading of the sources may suggest a more subtle and nuanced picture. Certainly husbands were permitted to strike their wives in order to 'correct' them. Thomas Nesfeld, as we have just seen, is depicted as a dutiful husband who would strike his wife with his fist for specifically going against his directions; the rebellious wife is constructed in language reminiscent of the description of the Harlot in the book of Proverbs ([16] deposition of John Semer). But the implication is that it was wrong to strike a wife other than to correct disobedience (and hence the depositions of Joan White and Margery Speight consciously exclude all reference to the circumstances of the husband's alleged violence so as to suggest that it lacked provocation) and that whereas a hand was a reasonable instrument of chastisement, weapons certainly were not. Even for a husband to strike his wife with a rod, if used without good cause or excessively, could (we may assume) provoke neighbours to intervene and bring the matter to the notice of the Church courts [15]. On the other hand the suggestion that wives living within a violent or abusive relationship might dissemble [14] for the sake of avoiding scandal (and perhaps worse violence from the husband) or because they can see no way out seems all too plausible.

That some marriages broke down entirely is apparent from the documentary evidence. Husbands who threw out or abandoned their wives were frowned upon and could even be ordered by the Church courts to take back their wives [2c], [10b], [18b], [19d], but canon law recognised that some couples might be permitted to live separately where one of the parties had committed adultery [18d] or the husband had behaved with excessive cruelty to his spouse [16]. We may suspect a double standard here: married men sometimes kept mistresses [20] or used the services of prostitutes, but adultery by a wife was immediate grounds for a man to repudiate her ([18c]; 'Law and custom' [14] deposition of Sir Ralph Amcotes). Such actions for divorce from bed and board are uncommon and courts seem to have been reluctant to grant such separations. The authority of the Church courts, however, did not go unchallenged [18d] and it is patent that some couples separated and even made de facto divorces and remarriages in defiance of the Church's teaching [9a], [10], [19a, b, c]. We may even notice an early example of a folk tradition of divorce by means of a wife sale (the purchaser invariably being the wife's new lover) [18b]. In a few instances couples attempted to obtain actual annulments of established marriages by alleging 'remembered' precontracts [9b], [11]. It would, however, be mistaken to imagine that such abuses of canon law were common or that couples regularly 'discovered' impediments in order to dissolve unhappy marriages. Though impediments of, for example, consanguinity or affinity, were sometimes discovered, couples were as likely to seek retrospective dispensation [12] if such dispensation had not been obtained prior to marriage ('Adolescence' [34a], [35]).

Occasionally discord ended in tragedy. Margery Nesfeld, faced by a violent husband, allegedly claimed that she could murder him in bed at night [16] and court records provide instances of women who did so act ([23c], 'Law and custom' [72b]). The murders of wives by spouses were probably more common [21], but may be disguised in the record as accidents or even suicides. Coroners' rolls contain numbers of examples of women who died, according to the verdict of the jurors, as a result of accidently falling down a well whilst fetching water. As always, however, the verdict is in a sense a fiction (cf. 'Law and custom' [73b]) which may have more or less basis in actuality since many accidents were unwitnessed. We may suspect, therefore, that some of the women discovered drowned in a well were pushed rather than fell.[33] We may be similarly sceptical of some of the suicide verdicts found by the earlier sixteenth century [22]; social taboo ensured that suicide verdicts were hardly ever returned at earlier periods. This is perhaps particularly true of instances where women were said to have cut their own throats given the real difficulty of successfully accomplishing this form of self destruction [22a, b].

## Widowhood, poverty and old age

The logic for treating the themes of widowhood, poverty, and old age together is that in practice they overlap to a very marked degree. Not all women were elderly at the point of being widowed, nor were all widows poor or all poor women widowed. On the other hand many were, and younger widows and more prosperous widows were probably more likely than poorer or older widows to remarry and thus disappear from the population of widows.[34] For many women, moreover, the loss of a spouse meant the simultaneous loss of a breadwinner and of access to material resources. A great deal of nonsense has been written about widowhood as a liberating experience for medieval women as if the circumstances of a privileged few were typical of most.[35] In fact the experience of many widows would have been of increasing age going hand in hand with growing hardship. This is reflected on one level in the tragic tales told by coroners' rolls, on the other by the provision of welfare specifically for women.

The elderly as a group are not well served by the surviving records, but their lack of visibility cannot be explained solely by reference to supposedly low expectations of life in the medieval era. For peasant society manor court rolls indicate some of the mechanisms used to provide the elderly and widows in particular with some degree of economic security. Under common law widows of free tenants had a right to dower of one third of their late husbands' holdings. In practice widows might sometimes have to turn to the law to see that these rights were enforced, although the complexities of customary law and

33 See 'Law and custom' below.

34 Such a pattern has been described with more confidence for early modern Abingdon: B. J. Todd, 'The Remarrying Widow: a Stereotype Reconsidered', in M. Prior, ed., *Women in English Society 1500-1800*, London, 1985, pp. 54-92.

35 Happily there has been a recent flourishing of scholarly literature on the subject of widows that tends to be a little more critical, e.g. L. Mirrer, ed., *Upon My Husband's Death: Widows in the Literature and Histories of Medieval Europe*, Ann Arbor, 1992; C. M. Barron and A. F. Sutton, *Medieval London Widows 1300-1500*, London, 1994. Poor widows remain, however, a neglected topic. The chapter bearing that title in the last named collection is actually based on probate evidence!

the fact that recent widows may not always have been well advised or knowledgeable about the law meant that they were not always successful [1]. That such widows had sometimes remarried by the time of the action [1b] is also indicative that the legal process moved slowly.[36] For villein women customary dower rights were often more generous [5]. Manor court rolls demonstrate that villein widows likewise sometimes had difficulty defending these rights and had in any case to pay both a heriot (death duty) in respect of their late husbands' tenancy [4b] and their own entry fines. Land alienated after the marriage [9b] would moreover be lost from the widow's dower (hence the need to be certain of a wife's consent to such land transactions by the husband). Not all couples chose to rely upon custom. Men may be found surrendering their land in the customary court in order to receive it back jointly (jointure) with their wives, hence giving their widows full and automatic possession of the land on their decease without need to pay heriot [9a].[37] Similar arrangements for jointure are found in respect of freemen [7a].

Some widows remarried, but it is difficult to assess how common this was. By analogy with early modern Abingdon, it may be that widows would have been more inclined to remarry if they had young children to support and also when the wider economy tended to be detrimental to women's employment.[38] Thus we might expect high levels of widow remarriage in the late thirteenth and early fourteenth centuries and again from the later fifteenth century.[39] By the beginning of the sixteenth century, furthermore, widows of artisans might sometimes prefer to marry their apprentice ('Husband and wife' [3]) than be forced by guild and community pressures to give up control of the inherited workshop. Former husbands only occasionally seem to have used their wills to encourage their widows to remain single [7a] and even in such cases the assumption was that the new husband would

36 S. S. Walker, 'Litigation as Personal Quest: Suing for Dower in the Royal Courts, circa 1272-1350', in eadem, *Wife and Widow*, pp. 81-108.

37 R. M. Smith, 'Women's Property Rights Under Customary Law: Some Developments in the Thirteenth and Fourteenth Centuries', *Transactions of the Royal Historical Society*, XXXVI, 1986, pp. 165-94; idem, 'Coping with Uncertainty: Women's Tenure of Customary Land in England c. 1370-1430', in J. I. Kermode, ed., *Enterprise and Individuals in Fifteenth-Century England*, Stroud, 1991, pp. 43-67.

38 Todd, 'The Remarrying Widow', pp. 54-92.

39 My own findings for widow remarriage using testamentary evidence from York between 1389 and 1520 lends some support to this hypothesis: Goldberg, *Women, Work, and Life Cycle*, pp. 266-72.

support her and hence there would be no need to provide more than the minimum customary allowance. We know that lords sometimes put pressure on villein widows to remarry during the former period and matrimonial litigation sometimes shows that gentry widows were likewise pressurised by their families to remarry. The same source would also suggest that widows were customarily permitted a year's mourning, and Cullum has observed that widows taking vows of chastity ('Devotion' [23]) regularly did so within a year of their husbands' deaths.[40] The remarriage of widowers seems, however, to have been much more common than that of widows and there is little to suggest that celibacy or remarriage were options for very many widows, but rather eventualities forced upon them by circumstance.

Widows with under-age children often seem to have been allowed rights of nurture [5] even where the formal guardianship of the child was allowed to another, though outside of feudal society such guardians were often close kin [4c].[41] Widows also took on responsibilities as household heads, could be held answerable in respect of other household members [4a], [7b], and as tenants in manorial society owed suit of court and could act as pledges ('Law and custom' [7a]).[42] Widows thus appear in rentals, which can provide a clue as to their numbers, and in tax returns. These last provide an indirect indicator of the more marginal economic position of widows in so far as the proportion of women (nearly all of whom can be presumed to be widows even if not stated as such) paying tax is invariably small (and smaller than that suggested from rental evidence) and the amounts of tax paid are often below the mean for all tax payers [6]. The Edwardian subsidies, unlike the fifteenths and tenths after 1334, are of particular interest because they may provide some information on chattels, livestock, and crops. Some of the early sixteenth-century subsidies likewise record income from lands, houses, goods, and wages.[43]

40 P. H. Cullum, 'Vowesses and Veiled Widows', paper given at conference on Medieval Women: Work, Spirituality, and Patronage, York, 1990.

41 B. A. Hanawalt, *The Ties that Bound*, pp. 222, 248-9; eadem, *Growing Up in Medieval London*, pp. 92-3. The case of Alice de Rouclif ('Childhood' [3]) was essentially a dispute between her mother and her uncle for control of the child and her marriage. Alice probably remained with her mother following her father's death, but subject to her uncle's guardianship.

42 Bennett, *Women in the Medieval English Countryside*, pp. 153-5. We can sometimes know of widows owing suit of court from the record of essoins or excuses for failure to attend court.

43 E.g. the surviving early sixteenth-century subsidy rolls for Norwich in Norfolk and Norwich Record Office, Case 7, Shelf i.

Although widows often controlled only limited resources, their principal concern would have been for security. Well-to-do women might purchase corrodies (see 'Devotion' below) and for peasant widows, land or even housing [8] could be used to buy security. Elderly peasant couples and widows are found entering into maintenance agreements whereby holdings were surrendered to the lord and immediately regranted to another party on condition that the incoming tenant provided for the original tenant. Such maintenance agreements often specified provision of food, clothing, and even accommodation [8], [10], [11] and can thus provide clues about diet and standards of living. It is noteworthy that the retiring couple or widow were to be housed separately from the incomers even where these were close kin. This is also reflected in poll tax evidence in so far as women who can be identified as widows are frequently found living alone. Often, but by no means always, the incomer was unrelated to the former tenant [10]. It may be that similar arrangements with children or other close kin [11], where dispute was not anticipated, were not always recorded since the purpose of the court roll entry (for which a registration fee would have been charged) was to provide security by way of legal redress should the agreement not be honoured.[44]

Although manor court rolls by their nature are biased towards the landed, not all peasant widows had been married to landholding tenants. They therefore had neither dower land at their disposal, nor land to trade for security in the form of a maintenance agreement. For the landless old age was undoubtedly more precarious, but here it is even harder to identify individuals. The poor are often noted in wills as the beneficiaries of doles of money [14d, e, f, j, k], food, or clothing [14a, c], often, but by no means always at the time of the testator's funeral. Household accounts also indicate that such charity was by no means limited to the deathbed [20]. Women seem to have been especially charitable in their practical support for the poor generally and poor women in particular [14c, f, g, h, i, j].[45] Members of the aristocracy often provided for their poor tenants, though again such provision would not aid those without land. Hospitals and almshouses

44 E. Clark, 'Some Aspects of Social Security in Medieval England', *Journal of Family History*, VII, 1982, pp. 307-20; C. Dyer, *Standards of Living in the Later Middle Ages*, Cambridge, 1989, pp. 153-4; R. M. Smith, 'The Manorial Court and the Elderly Tenant in Medieval England', in idem and M. Pelling, eds., *Life, Death, and the Elderly: Historical Perspectives*, London, 1991, pp. 39-61.

45 P. H. Cullum, '"And Hir Name was Charite": Charitable Giving by and for Women in Late Medieval Yorkshire', in Goldberg, ed., *Woman is a Worthy Wight*, pp. 182-211.

provided for the old and bedridden [14b, c], but probably not in great number. Whereas many hospitals were founded for both men and women, by the middle of the fifteenth century a growing number of such institutions – the civic maisondieu (almshouse) on Ouse Bridge in York is an example [14b] – appeared to have accommodated only women (cf. also [16]).[46] This last is a reflection of the feminisation of poverty in the face of growing economic hardship through the later fifteenth century. Hospitals and almshouses provided primarily for the elderly and the bedridden, though some may also have provided a limited quantity of outdoor relief. (It may be that the larger endowed hospitals discriminated in favour of the 'respectable' poor, but this was not necessarily true of smaller almshouses, some of which provided little more than night shelter to paupers who were expected to beg for alms during the day.)

Food doles are also found tied to obits (anniversaries of the deaths) of wealthy benefactors or provided by the wealthy and the charitable [18]. Poor women might also beg for food in return for odd jobs. The depositions concerning Maud Katersouth from a matrimonial cause of 1355 [13] are in this respect singularly illuminating. She is observed selling cloth as a huckster, fetching water, milling by hand, and, if the depositions designed to undermine her credibility as a witness are to be believed, using flattering words to beg alms, taking extended credit by dishonouring verbal agreements to repay, and accepting bribes to commit perjury. This is a loaded picture, but it uniquely permits us some insight into the life of a poor woman on the very margin of subsistence who must use her wits to survive. Women might also use young children as an aid to solicit alms ([15]; 'Childhood' [8]). The lives of such women cannot have been easy and the coroners' rolls for the lean years at the end of the thirteenth century and beginning of the fourteenth have a depressing litany to tell [17].

## Work in the countryside

For both town and country it is paid employment, which generates records of payments and of disputes over terms of contract, that is documented. Work performed as part of the household or familial

46 P. H. Cullum, '"For Pore People Harberles": What was the Function of the Maisondieu?', in D. J. Clayton, R. G. Davies, and P. McNiven, eds., *Trade, Devotion and Governance: Papers in Later Medieval History*, Stroud, 1994, p. 48.

economy (including child-rearing, cooking, and other 'housework'), and thus without formal payment, is much harder to detect, yet this probably collectively accounted for a far larger share of women's time. It may be useful to assume some correlation between those tasks some women performed for wages and those others performed within the context of the familial economy without wage. Laundry work is a pertinent illustration of this point ([5], [8b, c]; 'Work in the town' [1]). Didactic [1] and literary [2] sources are of particular value here, but need, as always, to be used with circumspection. Fitzherbert's treatise [1] seems especially level-headed, which may explain its popularity, and it reads as if the author indeed consulted women about some of the tasks described. On the other hand the first part of Fitzherbert's discussion of the wife's tasks is strikingly reminiscent of the quoted stanzas of the 'Ballad of a Tyrannical Husband' [2]. It may be that they actually derive from a common genre, although they are directed at audiences of slightly differing social status, the one keeping servants, the other not.

Other work-related activities within peasant society may be noted because they are the cause of dispute or breach of customary law. Villein women, other than as tenants, did not normally owe labour services to the lord, but it appears that they could be required to perform occasional tasks (boon works) during harvest [6c]. Women seem to have had particular responsibility for poultry [1], [2], [6d], [7], [8a, b], [20] and also the dairy [1], [2], [20], [21]. Country women would regularly bring eggs, poultry, milk, butter, and cheese to market to sell [1], [4], (cf. 'Work in the town' [10c, d], [11c]), so much so that the dairy produce market at Nottingham was known as the 'Woman Market'. Women are also presented for taking wood, nuts, or berries ('Law and custom' [7b]), for illegal gleaning (reserved for the poor, primarily poor women [14]), allowing livestock to stray or graze illegally, or for using hand-mills to the detriment of the lord's mill.[47] Two activities, viz. the brewing and sale of ale [1], [2], [3a], [6a], [10], [11], [12a, d, f], [13b], [18b] and, less commonly, the baking of bread [1], [2], [9a], are especially well documented because they were subject to formal price regulation under the Assizes of Ale and of Bread. Lists of persons fined for breach of these assizes are found in the records of the view of frankpledge, a court ancillary to the manor court concerned with a variety of petty offences reported

47 For an invaluable discussion of gleaning see W. O. Ault, *Open-Field Farming in Medieval England*, London, 1972, pp. 29-32.

under a system of self-policing. It is likely that such fines were often levied by way of licensing commercial brewing and baking, though some element of quality control is also present [12d]. Women are conspicuous among those so fined, especially in respect of ale fines, though local recording conventions may obscure the actual involvement of married women either by recording the husband's name (as responsible for the fine, cf. [6d]) or, as Graham has argued, only recording the names of those women whose husbands were not present at the customary court.[48] Women's high profile in the rural brewing industry is further suggested by their regular appearance as maltsters, i.e. manufacturers of barley malt that was the essential ingredient in the brewing of ale [9b].

Manor account rolls and household accounts may include payments for a variety of agricultural and building works, but individuals are seldom named and groups of workers will invariably be described as 'men' unless exclusively composed of women (cf. [21]). Thus women may be found, for example, washing and shearing sheep, weeding, carrying turves, or assisting thatchers.[49] Payments to dairymaids as part of the lord's permanent staff (or *famuli/famule*) may also be noted [20], [21], but for the later fourteenth century and earlier part of the fifteenth we have another important source for waged work in the form of presentments under the Statute of Labourers (1351). Numbers of women's names are recorded in Peace Sessions' rolls for allegedly receiving 'excess' wages (i.e. above the level of 1346), taking work outside the vill when work was available within, or charging excessive prices [16], [17], [18].[50] Most women were presented in respect of seasonal work, viz. reaping or work in autumn, i.e. harvest, when labour would have been particularly stretched and hence women could command good wages [16b, c], [17a], [18c, d]. It may be that in this respect the Statute was only codifying and extending earlier practice

48 H. Graham, "'A Woman's Work...'": Labour and Gender in the Late Medieval Countryside', in Goldberg, ed., *Woman is a Worthy Wight*, pp. 136-44.

49 J. E. T. Rogers made use *inter alia* of this class of record to construct his *A History of Agriculture and Prices in England*, 8 vols., Oxford, 1866-1902. It should be remembered that these and other tasks would be performed by women without payment in the context of the family holding and the familial economy, but these will not enter the record. Equally works performed for the lord as customary, and hence unpaid, labour services will likewise go unrecorded.

50 This source has been used to good effect in S. A. C. Penn, 'Female Wage-Earners in Late Fourteenth-Century England', *Agricultural History Review*, XXXV, 1987, pp. 1-14. See note 74 below.

reflected in village bylaws designed to ensure a sufficient supply of labour at harvest time [9c], [13a]. Women were also presented for taking excess wages for spinning and weaving [17c], [18d]. There is ample evidence that the Statute was resented and periodically resisted even before the Revolt of 1381 [16a, d], [17a], [18e], not least because the Statute abrogated the right of labourers freely to negotiate contracts and its partial enforcement unfairly favoured lords over other smaller employers competing for labour.

Coroners' rolls have also been used by Hanawalt as a source for work since many accidental deaths occurred whilst women were engaged in work-related activities [3], [4], notably drawing water, brewing [3a], and cooking. She has tried to use this source to show that there was a gender division of labour along spatial lines: women's work was largely confined within or near the home, men's out in the fields and forests.[51] This approach confuses the spatial patterns associated with hazardous work activities, i.e. those most likely to result in fatal accident and thus impinge upon the coroners' rolls, for the spatial pattern of all work activities.[52] As has already been seen women regularly worked in the fields, particularly during the hay [8b] and grain harvests [3b], [6c], [9c], [16b], [18d], but also at harvesting pulses [14], hoeing [16d], and winnowing [1], [20] grain. Women also seem to have had control over gardens [1], often used inter alia to grow flax, itself a crop worked by women [1], [2].[53] We may suggest, therefore, a more subtle picture of work patterns, in which seasonal tasks regularly took women out into the fields, but the weekly market and a variety of other activities, be they taking geese to pasture, milking cows, working gardens, or tending livestock, ensured that women were not confined to the hearth and the well.

A more substantial source for women's work in the countryside are the lay poll tax returns for 1379 (imposed on persons over sixteen years) and 1381 (imposed on persons over fifteen years).[54] Relatively few

---

51 Hanawalt, *The Ties that Bound*, p. 145.

52 Goldberg, 'The Public and the Private', pp. 75-89.

53 For crops grown in gardens see C. Dyer, 'Gardens and Orchards in Medieval England', in idem, *Everyday Life in Medieval England*, London, 1994, pp. 116-27.

54 In addition to children, the poor were not liable to the poll tax, but it appears that in practice many more, and especially the unmarried and women, were omitted from the returns. This is particularly true of the 1381 tax. For a fuller discussion see P. J. P. Goldberg, 'Urban Identity and the Poll Taxes of 1377, 1379, and 1380-1', *Economic History Review*, 2nd ser., XLIII, 1990, pp. 194-216.

nominative listings survive for 1377 and those that do fail to record occupations. Although not a requirement in 1381, many returns do record occupations, and in a few instances more freely than in 1379 since this information was not tied to the level of tax. In 1379 a graduated tax imposed higher rates on persons assessed as artisans (and still higher rates on merchants, farmers of manors, the aristocracy etc.) and in some returns such persons, including numbers of women, were specifically identified by occupation. The returns for Asmunderby with Bondgate [22] are perhaps unusual in describing the occupations of a couple of wives separately from those of their husbands, but are otherwise unremarkable. We may presume that most householders not taxed above the minimum rate were husbandmen or labourers. The presence of numbers of carpenters and weavers (and also a couple of tanners) is telling evidence that this was a wood pastoral economy, and this is further suggested by such bynames as Wetherhird, Pynder, and Oxenhird. It is notable that, apart from the franklin whose name has been placed at the head of the list, it is largely the artisans who are associated with servants. A small number of widows, not here specified as such, appear to have been assisted or supported by their adolescent or adult daughters.

## Work in the town

There is a considerable body of medieval antifeminist literature which constructs women as idle, spendthrift, prone to gossip, wayward, and wanton. Some of these vices are alluded to by the Tyrannical Husband ('Work in the countryside' [2]), a fictional persona, by John Semer ('Husband and wife' [16]), a 'real' person drawing upon a clerical antifeminist discourse, and implicitly by the Goodwife, another fictional construct, in order to educate her daughter. That literary culture was so permeated by this essentially clerical discourse (and the exceptions are rare indeed [1]) means that unless we look elsewhere, and specifically to a range of more mundane historical sources, it is hard not to end up believing the fiction. That is not to imply that these other sources are unproblematic or free from ideological constraint, and, as before, the range of unremunerated tasks that were so much a part of many women's lives invariably go unremarked [1]. We can, however, uncover a host of activities in which women were to a greater or lesser degree involved, but because the various sources each have their own biases it is no easy matter to assess the actual levels of participation of women, how this changed over time, or how this was composed in terms of marital and social status.

As in the countryside, women seem to have played a prominent role in the brewing industry. This is reflected, for example, in the language and provision of borough ordinances [4], [5]. Borough court rolls likewise include presentments for brewing and selling against the Assize of Ale [8a], [9g]. It may even be that, outside larger towns and before beer brewed with hops became common from the late fifteenth century, the brewing and, even more markedly (cf. the numbers of tapsters noted in [28]), the retailing of ale was largely a female concern and that men appear in the records primarily because legally responsible for their wives' debts. On the other hand court records demonstrate that women sometimes found themselves in direct competition with male brewers [2], [3]. Borough court records, which include leet or wardmote courts, mayors' courts, mayors' tourns etc., are not confined to records of the Assize of Ale. The involvement of women in a range of other victualling trades, notably fish, bread, poultry, and dairy produce, but also for forestalling (buying up goods before they reached the official market) and regrating (selling in invariably small, non-standard quantities) a range of other foodstuffs [5], [6], [7a, c, d], [8b, c], [9], [10b, c], [11], [13a, b], is apparent from such court records, from Peace Sessions' records, and from civic ordinances. This reflects the particular concern of urban authorities to regulate prices, the functioning of markets, and quality of foodstuffs in order to ensure that the working population was adequately and inexpensively supplied with essential commodities and that civic revenues from market tolls were not eroded. They throw some light on female traders both in respect of debt litigation and for breach of borough ordinances. Analysis of debts, debtors, and creditors can likewise provide some information on the level of female involvement in trade in addition to providing names of women traders.[55]

Women's entry into employment was constrained by their limited access to training, wealth, or citizenship in its widest sense. Few women served apprenticeships, the extended term of recognised training that could act as a stepping stone to guild mastership and enfranchisement, though many would have gained informal training

55 The most useful recent analysis of women and debt is M. Kowaleski, 'Women's Work in a Market Town: Exeter in the Late Fourteenth Century', in B. A. Hanawalt, ed., *Women and Work in Preindustrial Europe*, Bloomington, Ind., 1986, pp. 149-59.

through service. Inheritance customs ensured that women were always at a disadvantage to men and were thus unlikely to inherit substantial set-up capital. Most single women consequently supported themselves, if not in service, in occupations that required little capital outlay, viz. spinning, needlecrafts, petty retailing, laundry work, or general labouring. Young women from more well-to-do backgrounds would normally marry men with their own workshops and would not attempt to establish workshops in their own right whilst still single, hence their occupation would be determined by marriage and not by prior training or calling. Married men were considered in law to be answerable for debt or breach of contract on the part of their wives other than where a married woman traded independently of her husband [15c, d, e]. This provision should have made it easier for such women to trade, but it may have been designed to protect their husbands from such claims and hence undermined wives' credit standing and thus their capacity to trade.

Access to trade in medieval towns was also controlled by borough authorities and, at least from the later fourteenth century (and rather earlier in London), by craft guilds. Only members of the franchise, known as burgesses in boroughs or citizens in communities enjoying the status of cities, were legally entitled to set up shop, employ apprentices, participate in civic elections, and enjoy any other privileges granted to the burgesses or citizens by right of seigneurial or royal charter. (Strictly all other trade was restricted to the market and was liable to the exaction of market tolls.) Originally holders of burgages, i.e. substantial householders, were considered burgesses, but by the later Middle Ages the franchise came to be associated with guild affiliation and could be entered into by right of purchase (redemption), apprenticeship, or inheritance. Women consequently were at a disadvantage under each of these heads, though small numbers of women were admitted in their own right in a number of towns [30].[56] Many more women shared in the privileges of being free as a burgess or citizen by marriage to a freeman [15f] and would appear to have continued to enjoy these rights when widowed even though such women were not separately registered. Such widows (and even daughters of freemen [32]) appear sometimes to have been able

---

56 For an interesting discussion of women and the urban franchise see M. C. Howell, 'Citizenship and Gender: Women's Political Status in Northern Medieval Cities', in M. Erler and M. Kowaleski, eds., *Women and Power in the Middle Ages*, Athens, Geo. and London, 1988, pp. 37-60.

to pass rights of enfranchisement to their new husbands, but only so long as such husbands were thought of suitable social standing [31]. In practice rather more women were licensed to trade by the year as at Canterbury, Hull, or Nottingham [7a], [29], a much cheaper option than enfranchisement by redemption, or were fined for illicitly trading outside the franchise. This last occurs so frequently in towns such as Norwich not operating a licensing system that it effectively constituted such a system [9b, c, d]. Guilds, which were effectively cartels of employers, also came to exercise considerable control over trade.

For urban society the ordinances of craft guilds, often surviving as part of borough rather than guild archives, sometimes make reference to the brothers and sisters of the craft, i.e. guild masters or employers [24b, d], and to women working within the craft, i.e. as employees [25], [27], though often the impersonal use of 'men' may imply both males and females [24d]. Very occasionally women, presumably widows continuing to run workshops, are named as assenting to guild ordinances [24b].[57] The ordinances provide evidence that wives of guild masters, i.e. those who had their own workshops and who might train apprentices, normally assisted their husbands in their craft [24a, c], [25], [27], (cf. 'Adolescence' [24] deposition of John Wyrsdall), and hence would be competent to run workshops in their husbands' absence (cf. 'Adolescence' [23] stanzas 15-19) and to continue to run workshops after their husbands' deaths. The absence of guild provision in respect of widows is actually telling evidence that this last was often the case. This is indeed evident from wills [16a, b, c, f, j, k], poll tax returns (cf. Joan the ironmonger noted in [28]), and court records [10d], [13c], (cf. also [7e]), though the number of widows so trading would always have been comparatively small since most widows would not have survived their husbands by many years and younger widows would often have remarried. Similarly we find from customs' accounts merchants' widows continuing to trade, though rarely for more than a year or two [22], [23]. Guilds rarely made specific ordinances in respect of widows and invariably only when economic recession made prospects for former apprentices wishing to set up shop very difficult

---

57 E.g. the late fourteenth-century ordinances of the York dyers, glovers, and parchment-makers respectively: M. Sellers, ed., *York Memorandum Book*, I, Surtees Society, CXX, 1912, pp. 50, 82, 112. The survival of guild records in borough archives serves to create the impression of greater civic control of guilds than may in fact have been the case. It means also that the socio-religious dimension of these craft guilds is often obscured as borough authorities were interested in recording only those ordinances that related to trade and the regulation of labour.

[26], [27]; by curbing widows' rights to continue trading, established workshops could be made available to (male) former apprentices (cf. [24b]). Restrictions on female employees follow much the same pattern, there being generally little restriction during the later fourteenth and earlier fifteenth centuries and most within the weaving industry from the later fifteenth century [25], [27].

Although the wives of artisans appear regularly to have worked alongside their husbands, they might also supplement the familial income by engaging in other tasks [7d], [9a], [10e], [24c] and a few women appear to have pursued crafts independently of their husbands or, to use contemporary terminology, in their own right as *femme sole* or sole trader [7b], [15d, e, f], ('Law and custom' [35]). As we have already seen many other women made their livelihood or helped support their families by trading in foodstuffs, but considerable numbers did so through a range of retail activities, i.e. as hucksters, tranters, or regrators [5], [7a], [9c], [10a], [12a], [18b], [21], ('Widowhood, poverty, and old age' [13] depositions of Sir Thomas Castleford and William de Warnfeld), as spinsters and kempsters (wool carders) [16g, h], [28], ('Adolescence' [24] deposition of John Wyrsdall), or in service occupations [12a], [14], [15a], [17a], [18a], [19], [20] or other employments for which they would be paid on a piece-rate basis [15a], [17b], [19], [20]. (The Oxford poll tax returns for 1381 [28], like those for Southwark, are unusual in specifically listing numbers of spinsters, kempsters, hucksters, shepsters (dressmakers), and laundresses, though some other returns for 1379 and 1381 allow such women to be tentatively identified from the evidence of bynames.) It would be too simplistic to argue that such women were denied guild organisation on grounds of gender; as employees rather than employers of labour their status was analogous to that of male journeymen or labourers who might be subject to guild discipline, but were permitted no guilds of their own.[58]

---

58 Spinsters, for example, were provided with raw wool by textile entrepreneurs and subsequently paid by the weight for the spun yarn. As the probate evidence suggests, those women who depended upon their craft for a livelihood tended to be poor; borough ordinances attempted to protect spinsters from exploitation by demanding that employers used lawful weights and paid wages in cash, though the repetition of such ordinances suggests that they were widely flouted: Goldberg, *Women, Work, and Life Cycle*, pp. 118-20, 144-5. For a different view on women's role in guilds see M. Kowaleski and J. M. Bennett, 'Crafts, Gilds, and Women in the Middle Ages: Fifty Years after Marian K. Dale', *Signs*, XIV, 1989, pp. 474-88.

# Prostitution

Although it is not difficult to find evidence for prostitution in later medieval England, it tends to be primarily urban, to be concentrated within certain periods, and, with few exceptions, to be quite unlike the evidence that survives for some more southerly regions of Europe.[59] That the evidence is primarily urban is unsurprising. Only places enjoying both significant resident and transient populations could have provided sufficient demand (and sufficient anonymity) for women to be able to make, or at least supplement, their livelihoods through selling their bodies or for this trade to have been of concern to the local authorities. The same is also true of the major fairs during their heyday in the thirteenth century [12]. It does not follow that prostitution was unknown in smaller rural communities (cf. [15], [16]). It is conspicuous that urban governors were most actively concerned to regulate prostitution in the late thirteenth and early fourteenth centuries and again from the later fifteenth century, although London seems also to have been active in the later fourteenth century. The hardening of attitudes in the later fifteenth century is particularly clearly documented and widely observed, as at Leicester [5], York [7], and most strikingly Coventry in 1492 [6]. Otherwise there seems to have been a pragmatic toleration of prostitution as a necessary social evil and civic concern seems to have been directed more at procuresses than prostitutes themselves [10]. The probability is that in times of recession when the supply of labour outstripped the demand for workers, women in particular were marginalised and consequently forced into a variety of illicit activities including prostitution in order to survive.[60] This was true of the latter years of demographic growth that culminated in the Agrarian Crisis of 1315-17 and also of the years of economic recession from the later fifteenth century, a period that coincided with the first stages of demographic recovery. London [3b] may uniquely have experienced difficulties in the decades immediately following the plague due to the failure of the local economy to absorb the massive influx of rural migrants, an

---

59 Cf. L. L. Otis, *Prostitution in Medieval Society: The History of an Urban Institution in the Languedoc*, Chicago, 1985; J. Rossiaud, *Medieval Prostitution*, trans. L. G. Cochrane, Oxford, 1988. Despite their titles, both these are specifically regional studies.

60 M. K. McIntosh, 'Local Change and Community Control in England, 1465-1500', *Huntington Library Quarterly*, XLIX, 1986, pp. 219-42; Goldberg, *Women, Work, and Life Cycle*, p. 155.

experience that may have helped shape contemporary labour legislation and also Langland's *Piers Plowman*.

The third observation, that the English experience was unlike that of southern Europe, is apparent from the absence of evidence for regular brothels or for any coherent policy of regulation outside those towns already noted. Most towns seem instead to have adopted a policy of forbidding prostitution within the walls (cf. [2b], [7a]), but only to have enforced this at best spasmodically. Making ordinances in respect of prostitution was in any case always easier than policing the same [11a]. Prostitutes were not confined to institutionalised brothels, though evidently some women did work within private brothels (cf. [1], [4], [5]). At least before the Black Death it would appear that civic authorities took upon themselves the power to render uninhabitable such premises by removing the doors and windows (cf. [1], [2b]). In practice streetwalking seems often to have been tolerated, though sometimes dress codes were enacted both to distinguish prostitutes from other women and to prevent prostitutes dressing above their station (cf. [2a], [3a], [13b]). The evidence for women soliciting in public places, including taverns [3b] and churchyards [9], is, however, often confined to the tragic circumstances chronicled in coroners' rolls. The same source together with court rolls indicates that women would often go to their client's place of residence, a practice than can only have added to the dangers of the profession (cf. [8], [10]). Some women seem to have worked for or been controlled by a procuress (cf. [10], [11c], [16b]), but implicitly many others were freelance.

Only in a very limited number of instances, viz. the stews of Southwark [3b], [11c] (on the opposite bank of the Thames to the city of London and effectively a suburb of the same) and the ports of Southampton [13] and Sandwich, do we find evidence of regulated brothels.[61] It may be that these communities, as ports with markets in southern Europe, were influenced by Continental customs or alternatively attempted to provide for a transient population of sailors and merchants used to a system of brothels and otherwise a potential source of disorder. The paucity of evidence for such institutions elsewhere, despite the survival of quite extensive records from a

---

61 R. M. Karras, 'The Regulation of Brothels in Later Medieval England', *Signs*, XIV, 1989, pp. 399-426. The ordinances for the Southwark 'stews' are translated in ibid., pp. 427-33, and are edited in J. B. Post, 'A Fifteenth-Century Customary of the Southwark Stews', *Journal of the Society of Archivists*, V, 1977, pp. 423-8. Karras writes in terms of 'brothels' as if analogous to the Languedocian institution.

number of towns, suggests that relatively few women were in any sense tied to brothels and hence to prostitution as their sole livelihood. This is further suggested by evidence from act books, which may sometimes include cases arising from visitations (cf. [15], [16]). Relatively few women are identified as prostitutes and relatively few names recur frequently under presentments for fornication or adultery.[62] Most of the female deponents who were employed as expert witnesses in a case where an annulment of marriage was sought on grounds of the husband's alleged impotence [17] can in fact be identified as prostitutes from act book evidence.[63] Many women, it may be surmised, turned to prostitution on a casual basis when times were hard and drifted back into legitimate employment at other times.

Although much can be gleaned from careful reading, the records are often more informative of élite attitudes than of social practice. It is no accident that some Bristol ordinances of 1344 [2b] refer to prostitutes in the same clause as lepers. Similarly the York ordinance of 1301 [1], made in the context of Edward I's temporary removal of significant parts of the machinery and personnel of government to York, links pigs and prostitutes under the same heading for good reason. In the medieval imagination the pig was associated with lust. Like the harlot of the book of Proverbs, moreover, it was liable to wander freely through the streets. It may be that the frequency with which London records name Italians [11c] and urban records more generally clergy and other religious (cf. [8], [10], [11b], [13a]) as the clients of prostitutes may reflect prejudice against aliens and clergy over whom civic authorities had only limited jurisdiction. (Clergy and religious [14] were, however, undoubtedly significant users of commercial sex, an observation that is further reflected in sexual slander (cf. 'Law and custom' [13a], [14]).) That prostitutes themselves were often outsiders [3b] is likewise a reflection of social prejudices that would have made it harder for women considered to be aliens to find more legitimate forms of employment.[64]

62 Goldberg, *Women, Work, and Life Cycle*, pp. 149–57.

63 Ibid., p. 151. An article that erroneously uses precisely the same evidence, but without reference to the archival source, to argue that the jurors were in fact 'wise matrons' is J. Murray, 'On the Origins and Role of "Wise Women" in Causes for Annulment on the Grounds of Male Impotence', *Journal of Medieval History*, XVI, 1990, pp. 235–49.·

64 Kowaleski, 'Women's Work in a Market Town', p. 154; Post, 'A Fifteenth-Century Customary', p. 418; Goldberg, *Women, Work, and Life Cycle*, p. 152.

# Law and custom

Women are much less conspicuous than men in most legal records. They often appear as victims and the records themselves sometimes suggest women were less likely than men to succeed when bringing litigation.[65] Legal records can, therefore, present a very negative impression of women's lot in late medieval society. This needs some qualification. The business of medieval courts was not a simple mirror of society. A woman's standing before the law, moreover, depended on her legal status, viz. free or servile, her marital status, and the nature of the jurisdiction and the law, viz. customary law, common law, borough law, statute law, or canon law.[66] Customary law, i.e. the law of the customary or manorial courts, and borough law varied from place to place and even over time; the practice in any one place can only be determined from surviving customaries, from ordinances, and from the records of the courts themselves.[67] It is also apparent that the

65 This is what Bennett found for the manor of Brigstock: Bennett, *Women in the Medieval English Countryside*, pp. 28-31, 76-8. Donahue has suggested from an analysis of patterns of litigation in the consistory (Church) court of York that women were not disadvantaged as litigants there: C. Donahue, Jr., 'Female Plaintiffs in Marriage Cases in the Court of York in the Later Middle Ages: What Can We Learn from the Numbers?', in Walker, ed., *Wife and Widow*, pp. 183-213. My own analysis of the same source at least suggests a prejudice against female deponents: Goldberg, *Women, Work, and Life Cycle*, pp. 221-2. Cf. 'Husband and wife' [16] where the testimony of one male deponent and another male character witness is preferred to the testimony of two female witnesses to the same events.

66 This is not an exhaustive list. Further confusion is caused by the multiplicity of sometimes competing jurisdictions and the possibility of a legal action being pursued simultaneously within more than one court. This is apparent in the Rouclif case ('Childhood' [3]) which was conducted in the consistory court according to canon law, but apparently also according to feudal law before the king. For a bibliography of recent writings on women and the law see J. S. Loengard, '"Legal History and the Medieval Englishwoman" Revisited: Some New Directions', in J. T. Rosenthal, *Medieval Women and the Sources of Medieval History*, Athens, Geo. and London, 1990, pp. 210-36.

67 The variety of courts and names of courts found in boroughs permits only the crudest generalisation. Three broad levels of jurisdiction may often be identified. At the lowest level were the leet or ward courts. The business of these seems to have been eroded over the course of the later Middle Ages and they were increasingly concerned only with such matters as the obstructing of ways with dung or with eavesdroppers. Debt, petty misdemeanours, and private plaints tended to fall within the jurisdiction of the sheriff's court. More serious matters relating to trade, law and order, and real estate were the business of the mayor's court. The ways in which women were presented in borough courts for trading offences or breach of the Assizes of Bread and Ale has been noted, but women traders are also noted in relation to debt litigation. Often the sums involved were very small and women appear more frequently as debtors than as creditors, sometimes as a consequence of

procedure of courts also changed over time.[68] Generalisations are thus hazardous, but some observations may be offered.

Medieval law distinguished between the most serious offences, including homicide, arson, rape, robbery, and grand larceny (i.e. theft of goods valued in excess of a shilling [$12d = 5$p]), which were normally classed as felonies, and other lesser offences known generically as trespasses. Felonies were reserved to the royal courts and were punishable by death, hence the frequent reluctance of juries to convict. Royal justice claimed no monopoly, however, in respect of trespass and at the level of servile peasant society trespasses were part of the regular business of the customary or manorial court.

Peasants were born free or servile [3], i.e. villein, serf, bondsman or bondswoman, or neif, though servile peasants could be granted their freedom (manumitted) by their lord [4]. Villeins were legally the chattels of their lord [1], required the lord's licence to leave the manor [3] or to marry, had no access to the royal courts, and owed a variety of services (often commuted to money payments) to the lord [2b]. Villein tenants, i.e. those who held land, owed labour services (fixed by custom, but likewise often commuted) and paid heriot in the form of the best beast (or money in the case of poorer tenants) when they gave up their tenancy (often, but not always at death). Although land legally belonged to the lord, in practice it was heritable and was transmitted according to local custom. Invariably women only inherited in the absence of male heirs [2c], and sisters as heiresses inherited in equal portions [2a]. Only tenants of the lord were formally obliged to attend (i.e. owed suit at) the regular sessions of the court. This effectively meant that of the female population of the medieval manor, only some widows and a few unmarried heiresses owed suit of court or had other labour obligations to the lord. Widows are indeed sometimes recorded as making excuse (essoin) [7a] or being fined (amerced) for failure to attend court. Similarly some few widows are found acting as pledges (guarantors that fines will be paid or persons will be present in court etc.), but most pledges were males.[69]

---

pawning goods for credit [36]: R. H. Hilton, *The English Peasantry in the Later Middle Ages*, Oxford, 1975, pp. 103-4.

68 R. M. Smith, 'Some Thoughts on "Hereditary" and "Proprietary" Rights in Land under Customary Law in Thirteenth and Early Fourteenth Century England', *Law and History Review*, I, 1983, pp. 95-128.

69 Bennett, *Women in the Medieval Countryside*, pp. 25, 152-5, 193-5.

The business of the customary court fell under three broad heads, viz. presentments for transgressions under customary law, land transactions, and 'private' litigation between peasants. From the later thirteenth century presentments for transgressions were regularly made by a jury of (male) villeins, usually substantial tenants, and it is unlikely that they always acted impartially [5a, d], [6], [8], [58b]. The same may be true of juries of inquest appointed in effect to decide between the conflicting claims of parties engaged in litigation [2c], [5g], [9]. These observations may have some bearing upon the way women, and perhaps particularly single women, were treated by the court. Women feature before the customary or manorial court under each of these three heads, though widows, who enjoyed a legal capacity similar to adult men are most conspicuous. Married women, so far as they appear in their own right, are frequently associated with their husbands [2a, c], [8c]. Widows as holders of dower lands may be noticed in disputes relating to the holding [8], and subletting, of land or over their dower rights. Married women and widows, as has been noted before, were regularly presented for breach of the Assizes of Ale and of Bread. A few women were presented for illegal gleaning, presumably because they were not considered sufficiently poor to be allowed to glean licitly (cf. 'Work in the countryside' [14]). Younger women, often identified as daughters or servants, were presented for taking wood [7b] or nuts without permission. Unmarried women are also found in connection with merchet (marriage) or legerwite or leyrwite (fornication) fines ('Adolescence' [39], [42], [43]). These last may be associated with prior presentments before the Church courts.[70]

Women had access to the Church courts regardless of their marital status if of free status and full age. (Under canon law women achieved their majority at twelve, men at fourteen. This is generally younger than customary ages of majority in respect of inheritance, which for women was usually fifteen [28].) They could initiate litigation (known as instance actions) in such matters as marital (cf. 'Childhood' [3]; 'Adolescence' [24], [25], [26]; 'Husband and wife' [11], [16]; 'Widowhood, poverty, and old age' [12]) and testamentary disputes, defamation, and breach of promise [35], all areas over which the

---

70 Cf. Poos and Smith, "'Legal Windows'", pp. 149-50. North has suggested a direct link between legerwite and presentments for fornication. His argument rests on the presumption that women would fine to avoid doing penances for fornication in person, but this is not supported by church court evidence: T. North, 'Legerwite in the Thirteenth and Fourteenth Centuries', *Past and Present*, CXI, 1986, pp. 3-16.

Church had jurisdiction, though only in respect of the two first did it enjoy a monopoly. Debt litigation, for example, could be conducted in borough [36] or customary courts, but equally as an action for breach of promise within the Church courts [35]. Precisely why the latter course was sometimes preferred is unclear. Women appear prominently in defamation cases probably because their reputations, invariably constructed in sexual terms, were so much more vulnerable than those of males to sexual slander [14], [16]. Instance cases were conducted by the interrogation of witnesses of either sex according to series of questions drawn up in advance. Written depositions were compiled from these answers and these sometimes survive.[71] Before the fifteenth century, however, depositions were invariably recorded in Latin, although the actual questioning was conducted in the vernacular. There seems to have been some prejudice against female witnesses and this may have been more marked by the end of our period.[72] The questions posed, moreover, were focused on points pertinent to the law and may illuminate the actual circumstances behind the case only tangentially. This is particularly true of marriage litigation where the court was primarily interested in the words used and whether there were any canonical impediments standing between the parties, although the historian may well be more interested in how and why the action came to court and what it has to say about marriage practice. Verdicts only sometimes survive, but they are never explained. Where only act books survive it is even harder to reconstruct the circumstances behind an action, though some are very much more informative than others.[73]

Women could also be cited before the Church courts at the instigation of the head of the court or Official for a variety of sins, notably fornication, adultery, defamation, using spells (though it should be noted that accusations of witchcraft are hardly found before the end of the fifteenth century) [26], failure to attend church [19d, h, i], or working on Sundays or other festival days. These are known as *ex officio* actions and were the regular business of ruridecanal and other lesser courts. Sometimes these matters would become known as a consequence of an episcopal visitation and certainly the records of such

---

71 The definitive discussion of marriage cases before the Church courts is Helmholz, *Marriage Litigation in Medieval England.*

72 Goldberg, *Women, Work, and Life Cycle*, pp. 221-2.

73 Important studies using act book evidence are Sheehan, 'The Formation and Stability of Marriage', pp. 228-63, and Finch, 'Parental Authority and the Problem of Clandestine Marriage', pp. 189-201.

visitations record such allegations [13b, c, e], [19], [20]. Defendants could confess their guilt or alternatively attempt to purge themselves by bringing a specified number of persons to vouch their innocence [11], [13a, c, e]. In cases of guilt the court could impose a variety of penances [12], [27] and even in more serious cases excommunication. A few presentments for fornication could lead to instance actions if one of the parties alleged that they were in fact married, but this was denied by the other. Where children were born of illicit unions, the court could order the man to pay maintenance for the support of the child in infancy ('Husband and wife' [32c]).

As we have noted before, antifeminist discourse constructed women, if ungoverned, as prone to evil conversation, promiscuity, and other such immoral behaviour (cf. [19e, g], [23b], [26]). The harlot of the book of Proverbs offered one such archetype, the sexually experienced older woman, found in the person of la Vieille in the *Romance of the Rose* or Chaucer's Wife of Bath, another. Both borough and customary courts appear to have regarded women's language as particularly subversive and hence a proper matter for control [21]. Scolding was thus a gendered offence and one for which men are only rarely presented [22]. It may be in response to the stereotype that older women were particularly liable to be so presented [13b], [14]. The frequency with which women were presented in both borough and customary courts for transgressions against trading regulations, for prostitution, and other petty transgressions, especially during the later thirteenth and earlier fourteenth centuries and again from the later fifteenth century (cf. [19h, i], [20], [23b]) probably only served to impress upon the minds of the ruling élite that women, and single women in particular, tended to conform to misogynist stereotypes. This goes some way to explaining the concern at the earlier period to ensure that single women (perhaps more than men who were in any case liable to be incorporated within the self-policing system of the tithing) could only take lodgings if properly vouched for [5c, f], [43a] and by the later period the social pressures on women to marry or enter service so as to be firmly under male authority (cf. 'Prostitution' [6]).

Women, even if free, had only limited access to the royal courts and consequently tend only to appear as plaintiffs in respect of the murder of their husbands or of rape [34b]. On the other hand, women regardless of status were liable to be prosecuted in royal courts for a variety of felonies and, increasingly by the later fourteenth century and with the extension of royal justice into the regions by means of the

Peace Sessions conducted by itinerant justices of the Peace, of trespasses. In borough society by the fifteenth century urban magistrates were also sometimes given powers as justices of the Peace and hence exercised royal justice through the borough courts. If a woman evaded justice she could be waived, equivalent to being outlawed, but technically different because of the legal fiction that women would be subject to men and were not themselves sworn to the peace as members of a tithing [34a], [75], [44], [45]. A fugitive from the law could seek sanctuary at a church and subsequently abjure the realm [33], though certain major sanctuaries such as Durham, Beverley [32], and Westminster seem to have served as havens for criminals and fugitives from justice. If convicted of a felony, the penalty was death by hanging [37b], [42], except in the case of the murder of a husband (and after 1401 heresy) where burning was prescribed, though juries were often reluctant to convict if they considered the penalty did not fit the crime. Occasionally convicted women were able to appeal to the king for pardon [44], [45], [75]. A pregnant woman could not be put to death until she was delivered of her baby [31] (cf. 'Devotion' [26]) and a married woman who had assisted her husband to commit a felony would be spared because her duty to her husband was considered to have excused her actions ('Husband and wife' [23a, b]). Prison was not primarily used for the punishment of offenders, but rather to hold prisoners awaiting trial [30], [31] or, in the case of pregnant women who had already been condemned, until they had given birth [33]. Conditions for women prisoners were probably particularly grim at least before it became customary in the fifteenth century to provide them with separate accommodation from male prisoners [29].

Women appear in Peace Sessions' rolls primarily in respect of presentments for various kinds of assault including homicide (a felony) and battery (a trespass), theft (including petty larceny, a felony), and, after 1359 when justices of the Peace took over the work of justices of Labourers, violation of the Statute of Labourers (1351) in respect of wages, prices, and terms of employment.[74] Women are found as the perpetrators of theft of various kinds [37], [39a, e, f], [42], [44], but are more likely than men to be associated with the theft of food and poultry [38], [39b, d, g], [43a], [45] or cloth and clothing [39c], [41]. Women were also presented for receiving stolen goods [37] and giving shelter to criminals [46], including their own spouses or other close kin [47], [48]. Women most frequently occur as the alleged victims rather than as the perpetrators of assaults, though sometimes women assaulted other women [52b, c, d], [53c, e], [54], [55], [58b, c]. The circumstances behind such assaults are, however, unrecorded and the extent of the injuries inflicted may often be exaggerated. Some assaults were committed in the course of theft (muggings in modern parlance) [50], [51], others as a consequence of disputes [58a], [59], but a number may have been sexually motivated (cf. [52d], [53d], [56b], [64a]); medieval law did not distinguish sexual assault as a separate category of trespass and women who had been raped (or perhaps the community) may sometimes have preferred that assault charges be brought since women may not have wanted to publicise that they were rape victims and male jurors appear not to have been prepared to convict rapists.

Medieval law failed to make a clear distinction between rape and abduction, though we observe some differences in the cases presented.[75] Abduction, unlike rape, was essentially a crime against a husband [61] or guardian [60] rather than the woman herself; it treated the woman as property, but the woman herself may often have gone willingly with her 'abductor' to be with a lover or to escape unsatisfactory domestic circumstances. Rape was supposedly a crime against the woman, but until at least the earlier fourteenth century it seems that only the rape of a virgin was normally entertained by the courts [68], [69]. Rape was thus at that date essentially regarded as a property crime, i.e. the theft of virginity, a wrong that could even be made good by marriage [69b], rather than a violation of a woman's body. Despite the provisions of statute law, moreover, rape was not always treated as a felony before the earlier fourteenth century and rape cases can occasionally be found in the customary court treated as trespasses.[76] By the later fourteenth century presentments for alleged rapes against

74 See 'Work in the countryside' above. The numbers of women presented for breach of the Statute of Labourers varies markedly from roll to roll. It has been suggested that this may represent a greater willingness on the part of some jurors to present women in order to enforce wage differentials, but it may simply reflect differing levels of female participation in paid employment within differing agrarian economies. Numbers of women were presented for going outside their vill to take work at higher wages. Some evidence for patterns of mobility may be derived where the name of the place of work is recorded as well as that of the home vill. Penn, 'Female Wage-Earners', pp. 1-14.

75 For an excellent brief introduction to this thorny issue see P. C. Maddern, *Violence and Social Order: East Anglia 1422-1442*, Oxford, 1992, pp. 100-3.

76 J. B. Post, 'Ravishment of Women and the Statutes of Westminster', in J. H. Baker, ed., *Legal Records and the Historian*, London, 1978, pp. 150-64. The only monograph on the subject, viz. J. M. Carter, *Rape in Medieval England*, Lanham, Md., 1985, is not entirely satisfactory.

married women are found [63a], [65b] and the language of the record comes to include terms such as 'he lay with her against her will' [62], [63b], [65a] and 'he violated her body' [63a, c], but there was no concept of rape within marriage. Sometimes a related series of presentments suggest some kind of feud in which rape constituted a particularly humiliating form of assault [64b], but otherwise the motive was probably sexual. The evidence does not normally allow us to see how far rape or the fear of rape was a common experience for women [65]. Victims could be distressingly young [63b], but it is probable that few women reported the crime; the failure of medieval juries to convict even alleged serial rapists [65b] or rapist murderers [65a] probably meant that few women would have had any confidence in the law and rape victims may have been socially stigmatised. The judicial system, moreover, created many obstacles in terms of the procedure demanded [69a] and many cases were abandoned before a verdict was reached. The pressure put on one rape victim to withdraw her charge even after securing a guilty verdict [69b] appears particularly significant and raises the question of whether women initiated actions to restore their honour rather than necessarily to secure a conviction. It is unsurprising that in this context some victims preferred extra-judicial means in order to punish their attackers [66].

Women appear both as victims and as perpetrators of homicide, sometimes with their husbands [71a], sometimes against their husbands (petty treason) ([72b]; 'Husband and wife' [23c]), and sometimes at the hands of their husbands [73a]. Again the frequently bald judicial record allows little insight into circumstances or motives, although crimes of passion and family feuds are sometimes apparent [71b], [72a]. Alleged homicides, as also accidental or suspicious deaths, were supposed by law to be reported first to the coroner. Litigation in the royal courts would then follow if the coroner's jury upheld a homicide verdict. This process appears to have given the local community a degree of initiative in terms of whether to report suspicious deaths to the coroner in the first instance (cf. [74]) or in the verdict reached by the jurors who were drawn from the more substantial men of the community. It might have been in the community's interest to shield its own members from suspicion by claiming that a homicide had been committed by an unknown outsider, by a (perhaps fictitiously) named outsider who had run off, or even a mentally ill outsider [73b]. Alternatively a possible homicide could be constructed as an accidental death. The only circumstances that

distinguish the murder of Agnes Dryvere by her husband [73a] from
the accidental deaths of numbers of other women found down wells is
that she survived long enough to tell her story. We may suspect that
some suicide verdicts, rare before the earlier sixteenth century,
likewise sometimes disguise actual homicides ([76]; 'Husband and
wife' [23]; 'Widowhood, poverty, and old age' [19]). Equally it is
probable that before the sixteenth century actual suicides were often
presented as accidents or were simply not reported to the coroner.

## Recreation

Recreation, like so much of the mundane and everyday, is singularly
hard to reconstruct. It is occasionally glimpsed from deposition
evidence, but more usually from literary rather than archival sources.
Many sports, such as football, tennis, or wrestling, seem to have been
young men's activities, though women may have looked on. The
fictional Goodwife, for example, specifically advised her daughter
against going to wrestling matches and to the sport of shooting at
cock (in which a cockerel appears to have been used as an archery
target: 'Adolescence' [23] stanza 12), a sure indication that young
women attended such events. It would, however, be too easy to
conclude from the relative paucity of evidence that women had, like the
also fictional wife of the 'Tyrannical Husband' ('Work in the countryside' [2]) no time for recreation. Though it is quite possible that adult
women generally had less free time than their brothers or husbands,
this is not to say that they had no recreations. Indeed conversation as
a recreational activity was not incompatible with work, as for example
spinning, washing clothes, using the communal oven, or brewing. I
have not so far found hard evidence of groups of women spinning
whilst engaging in conversation such as has been observed in early
modern Canterbury and in Continental Europe, but I do not doubt
that such practice was normal earlier, especially once the spinning
wheel came to displace the more portable distaff, perhaps from the
later fourteenth century. Female dyers' employees are observed in
conversation whilst washing cloth in the River Ouse in York from a
defamation suit within the consistory court.[77]

77 P. Clark and J. Clark, 'The Social Economy of the Canterbury Suburbs: The
   Evidence of the Census of 1563', in A. Detsicas and N. Yates, eds., *Studies in Modern
   Kentish History*, Kent Archaeological Society, 1983, p. 80; BIHR, CP.F.61.

Women's conversation was all too readily understood by contemporaries as, at best, worthless 'jangling', at worst, subversive 'scolding'.
(The pejorative term 'gossip' is post-medieval in this sense, though it
was used to mean a woman's friend.) This alerts us to the distorting
lens of misogyny that we must try to compensate for when reading the
sources, and clerical/literary sources in particular.[78] Within a system
of binary polarities (Eve and Mary, the Good Wife and the Harlot
etc.), silence was a virtue in women – Mary spoke but four times in her
life, but most women fell well short of this ideal and therefore needed
to be bridled.[79] Women's conversation was, moreover, a threat to the
good (i.e. patriarchal) order of society (cf. 'Husband and wife' [2]; 'Law
and custom' [21]) for had not Eve led Adam astray by her conversation? Similarly the woman who, like the Harlot of the book of
Proverbs, desired to be outside the shelter of her home (cf. 'Adolescence' [23] stanza 10; 'Husband and wife' [16]) was regarded as
morally lax. To participate in public activities at which men were also
present was to compound this prejudice, hence the Goodwife's
strictures to her daughter. To dress too fashionably or to use artifice
to enhance one's appearance (cf. [8], [9], [10]) was likewise liable to
be constructed as sinful because it was against nature [9], perverted
the divinely sanctioned order of society as reflected in dress code [10],
was a cause of pride in the woman [7], [8], [9], and a cause of lust
in men.[80]

To move away from these loaded constructions, it is possible to detect
the existence of female friendship networks which also served as a
source for information (cf. 'Childhood' [3] deposition of Eufemia, wife
of John; 'Adolescence' [23] stanza 10). This is reflected in women's
wills which are often characterised by numbers of small bequests to
women, both kin and non-kin (cf. 'Devotion' [14c]). It is possible that
these networks were strengthened through common guild member-

---

78 Bennett has recently tried to argue that misogyny played a significant role in
   'popular' culture, but unfortunately the sources she cites, viz. Langland, Lydgate,
   and Skelton, are exclusively élite and reflect only a learned clerical, antifeminist
   discourse: J. M. Bennett, 'Misogyny, Popular Culture, and Women's Work', *History
   Workshop Journal*, XXXI, 1991, pp. 166-88.

79 To cite another exemplar, Noah in the Wakefield pageant from the Corpus Christi
   cycle there, when provoked by his wife's protestations, advises the men in the
   audience to chastise their wive's tongues 'whilst they are young'.

80 For a discussion of some of these attitudes see P. J. P. Goldberg, 'Women', in R.
   Horrox, ed., *Fifteenth Century Attitudes*, Cambridge, 1994, pp. 112-31. For an edition
   of some of the texts that reflect these concepts see A. Blamires, ed., *Woman Defamed
   and Woman Defended: An Anthology of Medieval Texts*, Oxford, 1992.

ship ('Devotion' [22]) or by social drinking ([11]; 'Adolescence' [23]
stanzas 10-11). Pilgrimages might similarly have served in part a
recreational function allowing people of both sexes to socialise
('Devotion' [17]) and is likely that a certain amount of conversation
went on in church, though the Pauline injunction against women
speaking in church means that it was women's conversation that was
censured.[81] The parish church also validated certain recreational
activities. Thus we find from churchwardens' accounts groups of
(young?) women dancing to raise funds for lights [1] or other fittings
within the parish church [3a]. Hocktide celebrations might also be
incorporated into the process of fund-raising [5].[82] Women were also
active in organising church ales, for which they would brew and sell
ale to raise funds [3b], [4].[83] Parish guilds might also enact plays to
tell the story of their patron saint and in some larger towns guilds
produced pageants for the feast of Corpus Christi. Though there is
no consensus among scholars that women would have been involved
in these, and certainly by the early modern era professional actors
who were exclusively male were regularly employed, the banns (or
announcement) of the now lost Chester Assumption play [2] suggest
that women did participate.[84]

Other seasonal recreations are only occasionally observed from
churchwardens' accounts, perhaps because they were not always felt
appropriately Christian. Summer games are sometimes noted, but the
fullest account of celebrations involving the young unmarried men and
women of the village for which a king and queen, seneschal, and
knights were elected the previous Sunday is found in a matrimonial
cause of 1450 (cf. [7]).[85] Hocktide celebrations whereby women held
men and men held women hostage for forfeits on successive days were,
it has been claimed, a new (youth?) craze of the beginning of the

---

81 Tutivillus, the devil who recorded the words of women who conversed in church,
   is sometimes found depicted in sculpture and also in contemporary religious drama.

82 For Hocktide see below.

83 J. M. Bennett, 'Conviviality and Charity in Medieval and Early Modern England',
   *Past and Present*, CXXXIV, 1992, pp. 19-41, especially p. 40.

84 The conventional view is still that female roles were played by male actors, but the
   only substantial evidence to support this does not predate the latter part of the
   fifteenth century and relates to the employment of semi-professional actors. That
   women as guild members, i.e. the wives or widows of master artisans, may have
   been involved in truly amateur guild productions that I would suggest were more
   normal in the later fourteenth or earlier fifteenth centuries.

85 At Wistow in the East Riding of Yorkshire: BIHR, CP.F.246.

fifteenth century, initially frowned upon by civic authorities [6]. Only subsequently did it acquire sufficient respectability to be used for parish fund-raising.[86] The lighting of bonfires on the eve of St Peter (28 June) [1] was no doubt an extension of Midsummer festivities usually associated with the eve of St John (24 June), but evidently it provided an opportunity for girls to take part in the celebrations. It may be that this and other such occasions also witnessed dancing by women (the term 'gathering' [1], [5] is hardly informative). The singing game described by Iona and Peter Opie, moreover, had its roots in the carole or dance accompanied by song of the medieval era.[87] Clearly some of these occasions of merrymaking and socialising could have provided opportunities for courtship (cf. 'Work in the countryside' [5]).[88]

# Devotion

There is an element of caprice and artificiality in trying to divide the lives of medieval women under particular heads. This is especially true of the label 'devotion'. The culture of later medieval England was a Christian culture and Christian ideology permeated every aspect of life. The laity had obligations to attend parochial worship and pay tithes for the support of clergy on a regular basis. The doctrine that souls might be purged of their sins in the fires of Purgatory for hundreds of years placed continuing obligations of prayer on the living and ensured that lands and properties were tied to the support of chantry priests. Saints might be called upon for aid in sickness, in childbirth, in peril, or to watch over their devotees. The calendar of the Church dictated which were days of labour, which days were holy. It determined on which days people should abstain from meat (cf. [26]) or from eggs, butter, and other dairy products. It decreed when people might be wed and whom they were permitted to wed, when they might have sexual relations and in what manner. It taught that contraception and abortion were sinful. The social hierarchy was held to be divinely ordained and wives were to submit themselves to their husbands (cf. 'Husband and wife' [16]). In short, the Church and its teachings touched almost every facet of people's lives, helped uphold the

86 R. Hutton, *The Rise and Fall of Merry England: The Ritual Year 1400-1700*, Oxford, 1994, pp. 59-60.

87 I. and P. Opie, *The Singing Game*, Oxford, 1985, pp. 5-21.

88 See 'Adolescence' above.

institutions of government, the law, and the social hierarchy, and played a significant role in the shaping of gender identities.

Pauline teaching ensured that women's role in orthodox religion was unequal to that of males. Women were denied entry into holy orders and, with the sole exception of baptism that might be administered in an emergency by the midwife, were debarred from administering any of the sacraments of the Church. To conclude that women would have felt alienated by orthodox catholicism or the extremes of clerical misogyny found in the writings of some of the early church fathers and still circulating in the later Middle Ages, or that they would consequently have found the apparently more egalitarian teachings of Lollardy [26] particularly attractive is to misconstrue the evidence. There were no doubt women (and men) for whom the obligations of the faith were just that. The surviving sources (and current historiography) tends to privilege especially pious women and to neglect those many who may only have gone through the motions. On the other hand there was plenty of room for devotion. Women could lead fulfilling lives as active Christians without feeling in any way alienated from the Church or inadequate as females. The different roles that women might play, as nuns, anchoresses, hospital sisters, vowesses, guild sisters, or simply as parishioners are discussed below. I shall conclude finally with a brief discussion of the one major native heretical movement of the later Middle Ages, namely Lollardy.

Nuns tended to be drawn from the lower ranks of aristocratic society, though the daughters of men of noble rank and of merchants, other more substantial townsfolk, and even perhaps the upper echelons of peasant society are also found.[89] To some extent this can be determined from the evidence of family names in the clerical poll tax returns [7], but it may also be apparent from will bequests to individual nuns who were kin to the testator. There is indeed a sense in which nunneries served primarily as places where the daughters of gentry for whom adequate dowries could not be found might be provided, and they in return offered spiritual service for their kin and forebears. (Chaucer's fictional prioress is clearly of this mould and has herself helped shape modern perceptions.) This may explain the apparent lack of spiritual verve and over-concern with purely worldly matters that emerges from our most substantial source for individual

89 M. Oliva, 'Aristocracy or Meritocracy? Office-holding Patterns in Late Medieval English Nunneries', in W. J. Sheils and D. Wood, eds., *Women in the Church*, Studies in Church History, XXVII, 1990, pp. 197-208.

nunneries, viz. visitation returns and injunctions recorded in bishops' registers (cf. [2], [3], [5a]). Such records focus on what was deemed unsatisfactory about the state of the house, such as the failure to observe appropriate sobriety of dress [2a], excessive contact with outsiders [2b], dissensions within the community [3b, d], even the practice of sleeping two to a bed [3b]. They thus present a one-sided view of convent life and should be balanced against the evidence for a deeper spirituality found for example at Syon Abbey.[90]

The visitation material offers clear evidence for the erosion of the communal life and even the development of separate households (familie), after the fashion of gentry households, within nunneries. At Elstow Abbey [2a], for example, the bishop at his visitation in 1421-2 was concerned to ensure that the nuns normally sleep together in the common dormitory and attend all the canonical offices. He further directed that the abbess change her chaplains (nuns who acted as her personal aids) yearly and invite to her table (implicitly only) those nuns in need of extra nourishment so as to prevent the abbess forming her own favoured clique from amongst the community. At Godstow Abbey some dozen years later [2b] he directed that there be three households each comprising six to eight nuns in addition to that of the abbess, though the language used implies that this was an attempt to rationalise a greater number of smaller households found at visitation. He further forbade the practice of drinks after compline. Similar trends are apparent from the depositions of the nuns of Burnham Abbey at visitation in 1521 [3b]. Interestingly the development of separate households impinged upon the architectural arrangements and hence the archaeological record.[91]

Inevitably the practice of sending girls to become nuns before they were adult [5c] meant that some nuns lacked a real vocation and were liable to go astray [5b]. Evidence of nuns having unauthorised contacts with lay men [2b] and even affairs with outsiders [3a], [6], monastic servants [4], or priests [3c], [4] are not hard to find, but again they probably give a distorted view of convent life. A more general cause for concern were the limited financial resources of many nunneries [5d]. This may have shrunk as a consequence of the fall in rental income in the decades after the Black Death and the continual

---

90 A. M. Hutchison, 'Devotional Reading in the Monastery and in the Late Medieval Household', in M. G. Sargent, De Cella in Seculum: Religious and Secular Life and Devotion in Late Medieval England, Cambridge, 1989, pp. 215-27.

91 R. Gilchrist, Gender and Material Culture: The Archaeology of Religious Women, London, 1993, p. 123.

cost of maintaining old buildings in an era of rising labour costs, although contemporaries tended to blame problems largely on poor financial management (cf. [2a], [3b], [4]). The sale of corrodies [2a], whereby lay women would buy board and lodging in old age in return for a lump sum payment, was a particular source of concern since the actual costs of such provision were rarely covered by the initial outlay. Nunneries were probably also hampered, at least by the late Middle Ages, by their lack of access to Latin [1] – French, and increasingly English being the common vernaculars of nuns – and their need always to act through male intermediaries. The refusal, for example, of the bailiff of Godstow to talk to the nuns [2b] must have made for problems. For a few nunneries, as at Marrick Priory in the North Riding of Yorkshire, account rolls are extant and these can provide a more specific insight into the convent economy.[92]

Although it would be entirely mistaken to imagine that Chaucer's prioress, Dame Eglantyne, was representative of convent life, equally it is apparent that nunneries failed to meet the spiritual needs of all. Some nuns wished a solitary enclosure as an anchoress [8b], [10], although anchorholds were certainly not filled exclusively by former nuns.[93] Anchorholds were invariably located adjoining or as an actual part of the fabric of a church, monastic or parochial. Gilchrist suggests that anchorholds for women tended to be located by the nave or western parts of the church.[94] The anchorhold would have a squint or small window giving view of the high altar and the elevation of the host at mass and a shuttered opening for confessional purposes. Many anchoresses were associated with (often poorer) urban parishes [8a] and appear to have served as spiritual counsellors to the lay community. Margery Kempe, to cite the best known example, consulted the anchoress Julian of Norwich, author of the *Revelations of Divine Love*, but lay patronage is perhaps reflected more generally in the evidence of alms and bequests to anchoresses [8b], [9]. Anchoresses sometimes had servants, no doubt to minister to the material needs of their mistresses, and they too are sometimes remembered in wills.

92 E.g. J. H. Tillotson, *Marrick Priory: A Nunnery in Late Medieval Yorkshire*, Borthwick Papers, LXXV, York, 1989. The most substantial discussion of nunneries remains E. Power, *Medieval English Nunneries c. 1275 to 1535*, Cambridge, 1922. Children resident in nunneries are discussed above under 'Childhood'. Lay women residents are considered below.

93 For a discussion of anchoresses see A. K. Warren, *Anchorites and their Patrons in Medieval England*, Berkeley and London, 1985.

94 Gilchrist, *Gender and Material Culture*, pp. 178-9.

Many of the greater hospitals of medieval England were religious houses staffed by canons and sisters who lived communally following the rule of St Augustine [7d]. The actual nursing care of the bedridden seems to have been left to the sisters [11] who might be assisted by lay sisters or female employees [12]. A few hospitals also provided for (unmarried) expectant mothers and, as at St Katherine's Lincoln [7d] or St Leonard's York, orphaned children.[95] This last had separate accommodation under the charge of a sister for the orphans and kept a cow to provide milk. Smaller hospitals, almshouses, or maisonsdieu tended not to be so institutional, but were probably often staffed by one or more female nurses.

Hospital work can be seen as a quintessential, but not necessarily particularly popular manifestation of female piety. To gain a more representative insight into lay piety current research has made much of probate evidence (wills) [13], [14], [18], [21] and, most recently, churchwardens' accounts [19], [20], although few scholars have used these sources to ask questions specifically about female piety.[96] Indeed, much work on female piety has made use of specific texts, particularly visionary writings, and has focused primarily upon women of high status. On the other hand it needs to be observed that neither wills nor churchwardens' accounts can throw much light on the beliefs and practices of women from the lower echelons of society. Female will makers, for example, were primarily the wives and, more often, the widows of substantial peasants, urban artisans, merchants, or aristocracy.[97] Wills by non-aristocratic testators are moreover comparatively rare before the later fourteenth century and churchwardens' accounts are likewise very uncommon before about the middle of the fifteenth century. In the absence of many alternative sources, it follows that the study of female lay piety in later medieval England must be full of lacunae.

Wills are highly formal documents. Often they were made near (and

---

95 R. M. Clay, *The Medieval Hospitals of England*, London, 1909, pp. 25-6, 126-77; P. H. Cullum, *Hospitals and Charity in Medieval England*, Manchester, forthcoming. It will be seen from [7d] and [7e] that the clerical poll tax returns for 1381 fail to note the hospital sisters returned in 1377.

96 Extensive use of churchwardens' accounts is, for example, made in E. Duffy, *The Stripping of the Altars: Traditional Religion in England c. 1400–c. 1580*, New Haven and London, 1992.

97 For an excellent discussion of the reasons for a decline in the proportion of wills left by married women over the course of the later Middle Ages see R. H. Helmholz, 'Married Women's Wills in Later Medieval England', in Walker, ed., *Wife and Widow*, pp. 165-82.

always in anticipation of) death and are consequently focused on the needs of death, hence the proper concern for burial, funeral doles [13a], the provision of prayers and masses [13a], [14a, c], and other works of piety. The relation of such death-bed piety to life-time practices and priorities is difficult to establish, though certain clues may be derived from a reading of wills of both men and women. Women's wills reflect a greater interest in practical charity as an extension of their household responsibilities and, by implication, something women may have done whilst living. This is most strikingly demonstrated by the number of bequests of fuel for the poor in winter [21e] found in women's wills, but also by very personal provision for the poor ([21a, b]; 'Widowhood, poverty, and old age' [12] deposition of Roger Marschall, [14c, f, h, i]).[98] Manor court records likewise demonstrate that peasant women would sometimes leave land for charitable purposes [15]. Devotion to particular saints is also reflected in bequests to images [14a], lights [14a, b, c], or particular guilds [14a]. That this is an extension of life-time piety is reflected in a like concern to maintain images [19a] and lights [19d] found in churchwardens' accounts and also guild ordinances [22].[99] A few women specifically requested burial in front of, or left their rings or prayer beads to be placed on the image of, a particular saint. How far certain saints, for example St Anne [14c] or St Sitha (Zita) [18a], the patroness of housewives and servants, were more popular with women than with men has yet to be properly explored.[100]

In addition to providing for images and the maintenance of lights within their parish churches, women would often provide in money or

98 P. H. Cullum, "'And Hir Name was Charite'": Charitable Giving by and for Women in Late Medieval Yorkshire', in Goldberg, ed., *Woman is a Worthy Wight*, pp. 196-7.

99 Guilds also performed pageants of saints' lives etc. in which women might be involved (cf. 'Recreation' [2]). By the later fifteenth century we can also observe the emergence of subgroups, e.g. young men, maidens [19d], wives [21d], within the parish which are akin to guilds: Duffy, *The Stripping of the Altars*, pp. 147-8. Churchwardens' accounts throw light on seating arrangements within parish churches once pews became common during the later fifteenth century [19e, f, g], [20b]. As Aston has observed, these suggest that women were given priority when provision was still limited, but there is nothing here to suggest a general sexual segregation during worship: M. Aston, 'Segregation in Church', in Sheils and Wood, eds., *Women in the Church*, p. 264.

100 Cf. K. Ashley and P. Sheingorn, eds., *Interpreting Cultural Symbols: Saint Anne in Late Medieval Society*, Athens, Geo. and London, 1990; S. Sutcliffe, 'The Cult of St Sitha in England: an Introduction', *Nottingham Medieval Studies*, XXXVII, 1993, pp. 83-9.

in kind for the purchase of vestments ([14a], [19a]; 'Recreation' [3b]), making of altar cloths [14c], [20a], communion towels [14b], [19c], or for items of plate etc. ([14c], [19b]; 'Widowhood, poverty, and old age' [14g]).[101] Bequests were also regularly made to parochial clergy [13b], [14b], friaries [13a], and, less commonly, monasteries [13a], guilds [14a], and hospitals and almshouses (cf. [21a]; 'Widowhood, poverty, and old age' [14c, i]). Clearly there is little to suggest, at least in the light of the present limited stage of research, that such forms of piety were especially feminine. The same is true of (religious) guilds [22], which performed functions as burial clubs, mutual aid societies, devotional collectivities, and social clubs, or pilgrimage in which both males and females participated [17], [18].[102] It may be, however, that the use of primers (books of hours) [16] or of devotional writings [21c] was to a degree gendered.[103] To pursue the argument further, it is possible that particular attention to one's devotions was seen primarily as a feminine responsibility or virtue (cf. [16]; 'Adolescence' [23] especially stanzas 2-4). Certainly the widow Agnes Grantham is constructed as a woman of particular piety in a matrimonial cause of 1411, charitable to her poor neighbours and punctilious in her devotions at the parish church ('Widowhood, poverty, and old age' [12] depositions of Roger Marschall and Agnes Kyrkeby). Dutton has indeed argued recently that for married women and widows to present themselves as pious was an effective way of securing their (sexual) reputations.[104]

Women may also have used their faith as a way of creating a space within their lives over which they had some control, whether that space was   physical, identified by a devotional picture or image (cf.

---

101 Communion towels were used at the annual parish communion when they were held under the communicants in order to catch any crumbs of the holy wafer that might be dropped. As has been seen before, women played an active role as fund-raisers within the parish ('Recreation' [3], [4], [5]).

102 For a few individual guilds accounts, deeds, and membership lists variously survive. These last are particularly valuable in determining the nature of the guild, the extent of its appeal, and the class of women that were among its members. Numbers of guilds, however, were probably too poor and too transitory to have left any record, especially for areas where few or no medieval wills survive.

103 An analysis of women's devotional reading is contained in Anne Dutton's forthcoming University of York doctoral thesis. A rather unsatisfactory, but much reprinted essay on a related theme is S. G. Bell, 'Medieval Women Book Owners: Arbiters of Lay Piety and Ambassadors of Culture', *Signs*, VII, 1982, pp. 742-68.

104 A. M. Dutton, 'Harley 4012: Devout English Noblewomen and Clerical Authority', paper given at Seventh York Manuscripts Conference, 1994.

[21b]), or created in their imaginations.[105] A text such as *The Abbey of the Holy Ghost*, which in its original French version was addressed specifically at women, used the analogy of a nunnery to allow the reader/hearer who was unable to enter a religious order to create the same in their imagination.[106] Similarly a small number of women, almost invariably widows of aristocratic or mercantile rank, opted for a chaste life, following the various offices of the day, but without retreating from the world. By taking a vow before their bishop (or his deputy) they became known as vowesses ([23]; 'Widowhood, poverty, and old age' [12] deposition of Agnes Kyrkeby).[107] Other women chose to retire to nunneries, but without taking vows [2b]. Devotional practice was thus not confined within church, nor necessarily to women of good family, for even poor women could afford a ceramic image or devotional print and even the busiest of housewives could find a moment to escape into the realms of the conscience. On the other hand visitation and church court evidence reveals that some women failed to honour their obligations as members of a Christian society to abstain from work on the Sunday and to attend parish church [24], [25]. The same source will show up women using charms to help women find marriage partners or effect cures.[108] This is enough to suggest the existence of subcultures that had different understandings of Christianity, were not fully Christianised, or challenged the dominant (Christian) morality as the morality of their social superiors.

One group that in a very conscious way challenged the authority of the late medieval Church were the Lollards.[109] This group emerged initially as a consequence of proselytising by Oxford followers of John Wyclif in the late fourteenth century, but following the Statute *De*

---

105 A. Cheifetz, '"Spiritual Mansions": Female Space and the Privatisation of Piety in Late Medieval England', unpublished University of York M.A. dissertation, 1992. For a less focused and more geographically confusing essay see D. M. Webb, 'Woman and Home: the Domestic Setting of Late Medieval Spirituality', in Sheils and Wood, eds., *Women in the Church*, pp. 159-73.

106 Translated in R. N. Swanson, *Catholic England: Faith, Religion and Observance Before the Reformation*, Manchester, 1993, pp. 96-104.

107 Cullum, 'Vowesses and Veiled Widows'.

108 E.g. J. Raine, ed., *Depositions and other Ecclesiastical Proceedings from the Courts of Durham*, Surtees Society, XXI, 1845, pp. 29, 33.

109 There is a growing literature on the subject of Lollardy, much of which is based on trial material. An important recent study that attempts to reconstruct Lollardy from less hostile evidence is A. Hudson, *The Premature Reformation: Wycliffite Texts and Lollard History*, Oxford, 1988.

*Heretico Comburendo* (1401), which allowed for the burning of lapsed heretics, and Oldcastle's rebellion (1414) the movement, if it may be so-called, went underground and became rooted primarily in a small number of communities scattered across the south-east, the Thames Valley, and the West Country. Periodically Lollard groups, who normally coexisted amicably enough with their orthodox neighbours, came to the attention of the local bishop. From the resulting trial material it is possible to learn something of the sect, its beliefs, and its practices. It had become remote from the academic theology of Wyclif himself and found instead a following among substantial peasants, artisans, and some merchants, precisely those groups who through their own initiative were able to benefit from the changing economic order following the Black Death. It was also among these groups that literacy through the medium of English was beginning to take a hold. As a newly literate sect, Lollards had an obsessive veneration for the written word and laid particular emphasis on the texts, including their translation of the Bible, that circulated among Lollard activists. Just such a text is referred to in Joan Clyfland's deposition in respect of the Lollard Margery Baxter, a Norwich carpenter's wife [26].

Lollards used their texts to justify a rejection of many aspects of orthodox teaching, particularly in relation to the sacraments and the powers of a separate order of clergy. Because Lollardy tended to be propagated through the family – from wife to husband, husband to wife, parents to children, employers to servants – and because Lollards, by rejecting the separate order of the priesthood, argued that there was no bar to women administering the sacraments, the conventional view has been that Lollardy was particularly attractive to women.[110] (Much the same argument has been made in relation to Catharism.) Certainly it is possible to find examples of Lollard women enthusiasts such as Margery Baxter, but the premise that Lollardy was attractive to women because it was more egalatarian than orthodox catholicism seems flawed. Lollardy, notwithstanding its rejection of the clerical hierarchy, does not seem to have challenged the patriarchal order of society. Indeed it appears to have laid stress on the obligations of wives to husbands and servants to masters that would have been so

---

110 See M. Aston, 'Lollard Women Priests?', *Journal of Ecclesiastical History*, XXXI, 1980, pp. 441-61; M. C. Cross, '"Great Reasoners in Scripture": The Activities of Women Lollards 1380-1530', in D. Baker, ed., *Medieval Women, Studies in Church History*, Subsidia I, 1978, pp. 359-80. For a rare dissenting voice see S. McSheffrey, 'Women and Lollardy: a Reassessment', *Canadian Journal of History*, XXVI, 1991, pp. 199-223.

pertinent within the context of the workshop or the family farm.[111]
Women's involvement in Lollardy as part of the household, moreover,
may not have been substantially different from that of orthodox wives,
daughters, and servants. We know, for example, about Lollard reading
groups [26] because the possession and use of heretical texts was
taken as evidence of actual heresy and thus features in trial material.
The perhaps parallel use of devotional literature by orthodox (men
and) women is so much harder to detect because our evidence is limited
to bequests of books and the evidence of surviving manuscripts.[112]

Lollardy is invariably constructed in terms of a somewhat puritanical
rejection of orthodox beliefs and practices as Joan Clyfland's testimony
in respect of Margery Baxter shows. In this respect her testimony is
as much evidence of orthodox practice as of Lollard belief. For
example, Margery's rejection of images or even churches follows
Joan's explanation of her custom of saying five Paternosters and the
Ave whilst kneeling before the cross upon entering the church.
Margery's rejection of pilgrimage and, even more vehement, of images
represent attacks on practices held dear by many orthodox believers.
Indeed it was men and women from precisely the same social milieu as
Margery who provided monies to erect, maintain, and burn lights
before such images. Margery's rejection of transubstantiation was
likewise a direct assault upon popular eucharistic devotion, implied, for
example, in the provision of altar cloths and communion towels, upon
the feast of Corpus Christi, marked by guild pageants and processions,
and upon provision for funerary masses and obits, indeed the whole
institution of Purgatory.


It will be apparent from the foregoing discussion that for many aspects
of the lives of women below the level of the aristocracy during the
English later Middle Ages archival material does exist. So long as we
are aware of the purpose behind the construction of these sources, that
they are invariably written by men about women, that they frequently
reflect the concerns and prejudices of male élites, and that they are
often constructed according to bureaucratic conventions and formulaic
language, then they have much to tell us. On the other hand, however

111 Much the same argument has been made of Reformed ideology: L. Roper, *The Holy
Household: Women and Morals in Reformation Augsburg*, Oxford, 1989.

112. For example the vernacular devotional poem 'The Prick of Conscience' exists in
over a hundred surviving manuscripts and was the subject of a window in the
parish church of All Saints in North Street, York.

closely we interrogate these sources, they will often yield ambiguous answers. The social status, marital status, and ages of women noted in records is often unstated or at least uncertain. Married women, we may suspect, are often hidden behind the names of their husbands. The circumstances behind an action for assault or for debt, the reasons why a contract of marriage came about or was challenged, or why one woman used defamatory words against another must remain matters for speculation. Similarly it is a matter of interpretation how we relate those activities that enter the record to the generality of activities involving women. On the one hand, the relationship of disputed marriage cases to the great majority of marriages, which, because not subject to litigation, go unrecorded, is problematic. On the other hand, manor court rolls may tell us much about women who brewed or who entered into sexual relations outside of wedlock, but little about how the majority of peasant women passed their lives. But despite the multiplicity of records, the thoughts, feelings, fears, and emotions of ordinary women regularly remain obscure. Deposition evidence can provide rare glimpses, but otherwise we must rely upon a common sense of humanity, that mothers tended to love their children, that teenagers tended to rebel against their parents, that marriages were not necessarily devoid of affection, even love, that fear of violence and of sexual violence was a commonplace, or that most women chose to find strategies to survive within the contemporary social order rather than to challenge it.

# I: Childhood

## 1. 'The English Trotula'

British Library MS. Sloane 2463. Language: English. Date: early fifteenth century. Translated from B. Rowland, *Medieval Woman's Guide to Health*, Kent, Ohio, 1981.

[a] Therefore you shall understand that women have less heat in their bodies than men have and more moistness for default of heat that should dry their moistness and their humours, but nevertheless [they have] bleeding to make their bodies clean and whole from sickness. And they have such purgations from the time of twelve winters' age until the age of fifty winters. But nevertheless some women have it longer, such as they that are of high complexion and nourished with both hot meats and with hot drinks and live in much leisure. And they have this purgation once in every month unless they are women that are with child or else women that are of dry complexion and work a great deal. For women, after they are with child until they are delivered, they do not have this purgation at all for the child in the womb is nourished with the blood that they should be purged of.

[b] Also the root of iris put up into the womb or fumigated from below with iris makes her lose her child, for iris roots are hot and dry and have the virtue to open, to heat, to consume, and to waste. For when the woman is weak and the child is unable to come out, then it is better that the child is killed than the mother of child dies as well.

[c] ... and if she desires to conceive a male child, they [the man and the woman] must take the womb and the genitalia of a hare, dry them in the aforesaid manner, powder them, and drink the powder of them with wine. And if the woman desires a female child, let her dry the testicles of a hare and at the end of her period make a powder of them and drink them when going to bed, and then make love with her mate. Another medicine for a woman that is unable to conceive: take the testicles and the liver of a pig that is delivered of a single sow and make a powder of them and give the woman it to drink with when she goes to bed with her husband and she shall conceive as witnesses Trotula.

## 2. Will of Robert Lascelles of 'Brakenburgh'

Language: English. Date: 1508. Translated from J. Raine, ed., *Testamenta Eboracensia*, IV, Surtees Society, LIII, 1869.

Also, one small girdle harnessed with silver and gilt, which is an heirloom, called Our Lady's girdle, for sick women with child, I will that it be delivered to my son Roger, to remain as an heirloom.

## 3. Church court, York.

Language: Latin. This case is rich in information about childbirth, baptism, and the role of godparents, churching, wetnursing, and the way in which women were able to locate past events comparatively precisely by reference to their own experience of childbirth. The deposition of Anabilla Pynder refers to the use of a writing, perhaps a prayer, used as a charm in childbirth. The use of wetnurses is largely undocumented below the level of the lesser aristocracy, the social rank of the Rouclif family at the centre of this case. Alice de Rouclif's alleged words as reported in the deposition of Anabilla, wife of Stephen Wasteleyne, ring true and may represent a unique record of the speech of a girl of eleven or twelve years. The depositions are written on a number of separate membranes which were originally stitched together to form a long roll. The precise order of the depositions is now difficult to reconstruct as only some of the depositions appear to be dated and the apparent order of the enrolled material is not chronological. Translated from BIHR, CP.E.89. The guardian of Alice, daughter of Gervase de Rouclif c. John Marrays.

[The following five deponents were examined 1 November 1365.]

Agnes, called Gervaus Woman[1] of Rawcliffe, aged 24 years...

Concerning Alice's age, she says that come her birthday, which will be in the following Lent, that is to say a fortnight before Easter, Alice will be thirteen, and she knows this from being told by Gervase de Rouclif, Alice's father, whose servant this witness was for two years before his death...

Ellen de Rouclif, widow of Elias de Rouclif...

... she says that she knows well that, come Saturday before the first Sunday in Passiontide next, Alice will be thirteen years and not before. She knows this, as she says, by the fact that this witness gave birth to a daughter, Katherine by name, on the eve of the feast of the Purification of the Blessed Mary[2] thirteen years ago next, and on the

1 I.e. Gervase (de Rouclif's) woman or servant.

2 14 August.

Saturday before the first Sunday in Passiontide following the feast of
the Purification Ellen, then wife of Gervase de Rouclif, gave birth to
the Alice in question. She was not then present at the birth, as she says,
but she saw Ellen, Alice's mother, pregnant with her shortly before...

Richard Bernard...

[Gives evidence respecting the contract of marriage similar to that
contained in Ellen de Rouclif's deposition, p. 63 below.]

Beatrix de Morland of York...

... she says that she heard well it said that the said parties contracted
marriage together and, as she says, Alice did this freely and willingly
without either force or fear brought to bear by anyone involved in this
contract. The contract was made, as this witness says, a year ago so
she believes and, as she says, Alice was a full eleven years at the time
of the contract, and on Saturday before the first Sunday in Passiontide
following this contract Alice completed twelve years of age. She
remembers this, as she says, because this witness was at that time the
wife of John de Midford, now deceased, who was killed in Bootham on
the Sunday after the feast of Corpus Christi[3] following Alice's birth,
and she further remembers about Alice's birth because on the feast of
the Purification of the Blessed Virgin before Alice's birth and John's
death this witness gave birth to a daughter who is now dead, and on
Saturday before the first Sunday in Passiontide, about which she
deposed above, and following this witness' delivery, of which she
deposed above, Alice was born. She says she remembers Alice's birth
for the reasons just mentioned and especially by reason that Alice's
mother did not give birth to any more children from the time that
Alice was born. She says that Ellen, Alice's mother, and Gervase, her
father, invariably stabled their horses at this witness' hostelry for the
length of their stay whenever they came to the city of York and they
were lodged with her. She says further that she certainly heard say
that after the contract she was obedient to John as to her husband
because she lay with him in one bed alone and naked together and she
would be obedient still if she were able... She knows not to depose
otherwise on the said articles as she says. She would rather that John
Marrays should succeed in the cause, as she says, than Alice because
she believes that John has right. Public voice and report circulated and
circulates still on the aforesaid matters after the manner of her

---

3 I.e. two weeks after Pentecost.

deposition in the village of Rawcliffe and its neighbourhood. She has goods to the value of twenty shillings.

Margery, the wife of John Gregson of Clifton otherwise called Bell, having in goods, allowing for monies owing, scarcely five shillings...

Asked concerning Alice's age, she says that on the Saturday before the first Sunday in Passiontide last she reached twelve years of age, and she remembers this because, as she says, when Ellen, Alice's mother, was pregnant with Alice, this witness gave birth to her most recent child on the morrow of St Luke[4] before Alice's birth which, if he were alive now would be twelve years and approaching thirteen years of age. She says that there circulates common report and rumour that Alice is of this age. Asked how she knows that Ellen was pregnant with Alice at the time of this witness' delivery as she deposed above, she says by that when Alice was born it was discussed among her friends and neighbours that Gervase's wife had given birth to a daughter that was Alice, and she does not know otherwise as she says. She does not care which party gains victory in the present cause as she says.

[The following nine deponents were examined 12 November 1365.]

Anabilla, wife of Stephen Wasteleyne, blood sister of the John in question...

Concerning the first and second articles she says that they contain the truth and this she knows by confession of the parties in dispute and by the account of others and common report circulating about them and that three weeks before Christmas last John took Alice to stay with this witness and about a week before they contracted marriage together. Alice stayed with this witness from that time until the feast of St James following and one night, viz. the night of Saturday before Christmas last, the said John and Alice lay together in one bed in a room in this witness' house in Kennythorpe alone and naked together from bedtime until dawn the next day. Asked how she knew this, she said by that Alice told this witness and likewise told one Joan, the witness' daughter. She says that about a fortnight later, as this witness recalls, Alice said to this witness, 'Dame, I have a secret to tell you if you will hear it'. Then, at the witness' request, she said, 'Dame, I should like the marriage between your brother and me to be solemnised and I ask you that you persuade him to do this, saying that after her own mother she trusted most in this witness... I am old enough and mature

4 19 October.

enough to be his wife, but not his mistress' – in English 'leman'. This witness then asked, 'Do you want to plead these matters before him when he comes?', to which Alice said, 'Yes, certainly, and more besides when he comes.' Afterwards in the following Lent in this witness' orchard at Kennythorpe, the said John, Alice, and this witness alone being present, Alice said the same words that she had previously spoken to this witness adding, 'Sir, I do not wish further to lie with you in bed before marriage is solemnised between us, for I am mature enough to be a true wife and not a mistress' – in English 'leman'. John replied to her saying, 'You will not speak like that any more. You know the agreement between your mother and other of your friends and me that I will espouse you at a future date and I will stand by the agreement because I do not want to lose a hundred marks or a hundred pounds' (this witness was unable to depose for certain which of these sums he named, but she says that Alice kept on repeating unreasonably this reply). She says that Alice was twelve years or more last Easter. This she learned from the account of others and does not otherwise know, but says that the whole time she was with this witness she was an adolescent and from her physical appearance it appears that she were fourteen years. She says that Alice received a knife from John of John's gift and before Easter last a blue cloth for a tunic, coat, and hood. After receiving this cloth, Alice said to this witness, 'Dame, I know that I will not have more cloths of my master before I have the veil for my marriage.' She was displeased that John came from London and did not bring ?silks and feminine ornaments for Alice's head. She says that John gave Alice a kerchief and other little gifts before Alice came to stay with this witness...

Alice de Rolleston, daughter of Anabilla, her fellow witness, aged 14 years and more...

[Makes similar deposition to that of her mother.]

Stephen Wasteleyne...

[Knows about marriage by hearsay only.]

He says that at or about the feast of St Andrew,[5] by John's arrangement Alice boarded with this witness and his wife and stayed with them until the feast of the translation of St Thomas,[6] around which feast she was taken and carried away by force of arms. Often within that time he heard Alice acknowledge the contract of marriage and she was

5 30 November.

6 7 July.

displeased because John put off carrying forward and completing the solemnisation of the marriage...

Margaret de Rouclif, Alice's aunt ... aged 60 years and more...

... concerning Alice's age she says that she will be thirteen years come Saturday before the first Sunday in Passiontide next and not before. She gives as the reason for her knowing the fact that Gervase, Alice's father and this witness' blood brother, died at Michaelmas four years ago and Alice was then aged nine years and over by the time from her birthday to the Saturday of that time of year immediately following, and that on the day after Alice's birth this witness came to her brother's house to see Alice lying in her cradle, and by counting the years from that time she knows Alice's age...

Dom William Marrays, abbot of St Mary's, York, admitted, sworn, and asked on the aforesaid articles, says on the first and second articles that they contained the truth as he heard well from those who were present at this contract, but this witness was not present, as he says, at this contract. Asked about the third article he says that it contains the truth by reason of her physical appearance, as anyone examining her can clearly see, and by relation of others who associate with Alice and who have had sufficient knowledge of her age. Asked on the fourth article, he says that after the contract of marriage John and Alice ratified this contract of marriage and spousals and lay together alone and naked. This he knows from the relation of both parties, viz. John and Alice, and from a certain Joan de Rolleston, who was at that time Alice's companion in bed and lay in the same room with them, that Alice was present on the night immediately following the feast of St James the Apostle[7] last and John then knew Alice carnally, as Alice told this witness after Easter last in the fields of Grimston and elsewhere, and Joan also told this witness that she saw John and Alice lying together in the same bed and heard a noise from them like they were making love together, and how two or three times Alice silently complained at the force on account of John's labour as if she had been hurt then as a result of this labour...

Alice de Beleby, wife of Richard de Warwyk, godmother to the Alice in question, and asked, with the consent of the party producing her, solely about Alice's age, she says that according to the knowledge of this witness it was at least twelve years ago before the Saturday before

7 25 July.

the first Sunday in Passiontide last, according to what he dares say on oath before God. Alice was baptised that Saturday and was born that day or the Friday before, and she knows no other reason to offer for her knowing other than that she has thought it out thus in her heart, and according to what this witness has calculated from her memory, so she remembers that the year in which Alice was born fell in the third or fourth year at most after the great pestilence,[8] and that this witness has a son of the Carmelite order who was made a brother in the order in the year before Alice's birth, and fourteen years or more have gone by from the year he was made a friar. She says further that at the time her son was made a friar, William la Zouche of happy memory was archbishop of York and she believes, as she says, that Alice was born in the time of Archbishop William...

Ellen, widow of Gervase de Rouclif, mother of Alice...

The witness says that she was present one Friday, as she remembers, a fortnight before last Christmas in the evening in Richard Bernard's room within the precinct at St Mary's Abbey where and when John Marrays and Alice in question contracted marriage together after the said Richard's direction. First John, instructed by Richard, said to Alice, 'Here I take you Alice to my wife to have and to hold until the end of my life and to this I plight you my troth.' Alice immediately stepped forward replying to John, 'Here I take you John to my husband to have and to hold until the end of my life and to this I plight you my troth,' and they released hands and kissed one another. At the time the couple contracted there were present this witness, the said Richard, Master Adam de Thornton, notary public, John Fische, and Robert de Rouclif. Also, she says that she knows from the relation of John Marrays and Anabilla, his sister, the wife of Stephen Wascelyne that John and Alice lay together for a night in one bed alone and naked together and that John knew Alice carnally, but she does not know, as she says, what time of year that night was. She says that Alice received various little presents from John as though from her husband, that is to say a furred robe with 'Wildeware', two kerchiefs, three tunics, and a cloak. After the contract of marriage was concluded she often saw John and Alice embrace each other and kiss as man and wife... Asked what Alice's age was, she says that come Saturday before the first Sunday in Passiontide next she will be at least thirteen years, which she well knows, as she says, because the late Gervase de Rouclif, Alice's father and this witness' husband, went the way of all flesh on

8 I.e. the Black Death which struck this region in the autumn of 1349.

Michaelmas day four years ago and at that time Alice was a full eight years of age and more by as much as is the time from that Saturday to Michaelmas, and by this she says that, counting those eight years and the years following after the death of Gervase de Rouclif, Alice will be a full thirteen years of age come the first Sunday in Passiontide next. She says further that Alice received little gifts from John after she had reached adolescence, as she deposed above, to fix in the mind the aforesaid marriage and spousals...

Cecily de Shupton...

... this witness, as she says, was present at her birth and, going on from year to year from that time, concerning Alice's age she calculated that come Saturday before the first Sunday in Passiontide she will be a full thirteen years... Alice was maintained by John and stayed with John's sister until after the feast of the apostles Peter and Paul[9] last when she was taken and abducted from the company of John's sister by Sir Brian de Rouclif...

Emmot Norice[10] of Hoby...

Concerning Alice's age, she says that on Saturday before the first Sunday in Passiontide next Alice will be thirteen years of age. This witness knows this, as she says, by the fact that the witness herself gave birth to a son born a week after the Michaelmas before that Saturday. Her son died, as she says, the Friday before that Saturday and this witness was then hired so that she should be nurse to Alice, and so she was, as she says, for the following three years, excepting a fortnight only, Alice's nurse...

[The following four deponents were examined 18 November 1365.]

Alice Sharpe of Rawcliffe, widow, a tenant of Sir Brian de Rouclif, knight, having goods to the value of forty shillings...

[Concerning Alice's birth, remembers] ... because it was one Simon de Folifayt who revived a child, that is to say the daughter of one Maud de Herthill who was born on St Bartholomew's day...

Alice, wife of William de Tange, of Rawcliffe, tenant of Sir Brian de Rouclif having goods to the value of one mark...

[Concerning Alice's birth]... Asked how she knows, she says by that this witness gave birth to a son at Rawcliffe on the Wednesday before

9 29 June.

10 I.e. Emmot the nurse.

the feast of the Purification of the Blessed Virgin Mary twelve years ago, and on the Saturday before the first Sunday in Passiontide immediately following that Wednesday, Alice was born...

Agnes Quysteler of Rawcliffe, wife of Robert Quysteler of the same, having little in goods ... says that she had lived in the village of Rawcliffe for about ten years...

[Only knew about date of Alice's birth from neighbours.]

Robert Thewed of Rawcliffe, tenant of Sir Brian, neither affine nor blood relative of Alice...

[Concerning Alice's birth] ... this he knows and remembers, as he says, because this witness has a son aged eleven years come next Lent and because he was present at the churching of Alice's mother and was friend enough of Alice's father that he knew about almost all his doings and he told him at Alice's birth when she was born and of the time of his wife's churching, and he even invited him to his feast on the occasion of the aforesaid churching. In the Lent following his son was born...

[The following two deponents were examined 27 November 1365.]

Margery, wife of Robert Thewed, of Rawcliffe, tenant of Sir Brian de Rouclif, knight...

[Concerning Alice's birth]... Asked how she knows this, she says because at the time this witness was a servant in Sir Brian's garden at Rawcliffe and likewise one William de Tange who had a son on Wednesday before the feast of the Purification of the Blessed Virgin Mary eleven years ago born of his wife still living whom Gervase de Rouclif, Alice's father, raised from the holy font, and on the Saturday before the following Sunday, about which he deposed above, Alice was born in her father's house at Rawcliffe...

Margaret de Folifayt...

[Concerning Alice's birth] ... remembers this because one Maud de Thornhill [sic] gave birth on the morrow of St Bartholomew before the time of Alice's birth by Simon de Folifayt, the brother of this witness, which child still survives and lives with this witness and was twelve years of age on the morrow of the feast of St Bartholomew last...

Alice, wife of Adam Porter, living at Clifton...

[Concerning Alice's birth]... Asked how she knows, she says by that this witness was then living at Skelton, which is a mile distant from the village of Rawcliffe where Alice was born, and she heard well it said by the neighbours of Rawcliffe and by Ellen Grigge who was present at Alice's birth and by the wife of William de Tange and others who knew well the time of Alice's birth and also from the report of Henry Vaux who served Alice's father when Alice's mother was pregnant with her... She has goods to the value of five marks and holds land of Sir Brian in the fields of the village of Clifton. She was asked by Thomas de Midelton to come as a witness to give testimony in the present cause. She does not care which party gains victory in the present cause as she says.

Beatrix, wife of John Milner, of Clifton, whose goods are worth nine marks...

[Concerning Alice's birth]... She remembers this because at the time of her birth this witness was living in Rawcliffe, and at the Pentecost following this witness moved to live in Clifton and has lived there from that time forward and lives there at present. She remembers well that it is still not yet a full twelve years from that time, nor will it be before the feast of Pentecost next, and she says that she knows otherwise by the telling of Ellen Grigge who was present at Alice's birth, Henry Vaux who served Alice's father at the time her mother was pregnant with her, and other neighbours of Rawcliffe who knew Alice's age well...

Agnes the Ald, living in Clifton, is not a tenant of Sir Brian de Rouclif, having goods to the value of twenty-two shillings as she says...

[Concerning Alice's birth] ... knows, as she says, because exactly a fortnight before the day of Alice's birth this witness gave birth to a son at Rawcliffe, now dead, who had he lived would not have completed twelve years of age before next Lent...

Eufemia, wife of John the son of Elias de Rouclif, tenant of Alice, formerly daughter of Gervase de Rouclif, having goods in common with her husband to value of five marks or more...

[Concerning Alice's birth] ... she does not know to depose other than what she learned from the relation of women...

[The following three deponents were examined 28 November 1365.]

William de Tange of Rawcliffe, tenant of Sir Brian de Rouclif, having goods to the value of one mark...

[Concerning Alice's birth]... Asked how he knows, he says because Alice, the witness' wife, gave birth to a son at Rawcliffe on the Wednesday after the feast of the Purification of the Blessed Virgin Mary twelve years ago next, and on Saturday before the first Sunday in Passiontide following that Wednesday Alice was born... The witness was then and is still is a neighbour near the house in which Alice was born and, by the age of his own son, he remembers well Alice's age and because Gervase, Alice's father, was his son's godfather...

Thomas Broun of Rawcliffe...

[Concerning Alice's birth] ... he says that at the time of the death of Gervase, Alice's father, he heard Ellen, Alice's mother, say that Alice, her daughter, was a full seven years of age and approaching the eighth year of her age...

Henry Vaux of Rawcliffe, born there, tenant of Sir Brian de Rouclif, knight, having goods to the value of five marks...

[Concerning Alice's birth]... Asked how he knows, he says by that this witness came from St James[11] a fortnight before the feast of the nativity of St John the Baptist[12] twelve years ago, and on that feast day this witness came to serve Gervase de Rouclif, Alice's father, and stayed with Gervase in his service from the feast of the nativity of St John until the following Martinmas, and Ellen, Alice's mother, was pregnant with Alice and on Saturday before the first Sunday in Passiontide following that Martinmas Alice was born...

[The following two deponents were examined 6 December 1365.]

Agnes de Fritheby, living in Bootham, York...

[Deposes that Alice will be thirteen come the Saturday before the first Sunday in Passiontide.]

Asked how she knows and remembers this after the passage of so much time, she says by that she was present at the churching of Alice's mother after her birth and by that this witness gave birth to a daughter, still living, on the eve of St Lawrence[13] following Alice's birth who is now twelve years of age and come the vigil of St Lawrence next will be thirteen years of age...

11 This reference is unexplained, but presumably implies a return from pilgrimage to Santiago de Compostella.

12 I.e. 10 June.

13 9 August.

Isold, wife of William de Kirkeby, living in Bootham, York...

[Deposes that Alice will be thirteen come the Saturday before the first Sunday in Passiontide.]

Asked how she remembers after the passage of so much time, she says by that this witness gave birth to a son a fortnight after Michaelmas fourteen years ago and on the Saturday before the first Sunday in Passiontide a whole year later Alice was born. On the Sunday the day after she was born she was baptised and this same witness says that she was present at the time of her baptism and carried to the church in which she was baptised the towel and ewer with which the godfather and godmothers washed their hands...

John Fische, uterine brother of the Alice in question, aged 26 years, sworn and examined on the previously mentioned articles. He says that he was present one night, viz. before dinner time before last Christmas, that is a year ago or a little more, in Richard Bernard's room within the precinct of St Mary's Abbey where and when the John and Alice in question contracted marriage together using this form of words, viz. John taking Alice first by the right hand and speaking to her thus, 'Here I take you Alice to my wife to have and to hold and to this I plight you my troth,' and Alice immediately replying to him, 'And I take you John to my husband to have and to hold until the end of my life and to this I plight you my troth,' and, releasing hands, they kissed one another. There were then present both the parties contracting, Sir Adam de Thornton,[14] Richard Bernard, Robert de Rouclif, Ellen, his mother, and this witness and others. He says that Alice contracted marriage willingly and with a cheerful countenance, compelled neither by force nor by fear...

[Deposes that Alice aged eight when her father died at Michaelmas four years ago.]

He says that he was present in the house of Stephen Wasteleyne at Kennythorpe for a day and a night around Pentecost last (he is unable to remember the actual day as he says) where and when this witness and Alice lay alone in the one room for the entire night. Jesting, this witness asked Alice, his sister, whether she would prefer to be married to John or to remain single, and he says upon his oath that Alice replied to this witness intimating that she would much rather be married to the said John than to remain thus single...

14 Here styled 'dominus', but elsewhere 'magister'.

Master Adam de Thornton, clerk, by apostolic authority notary public...

[Deposes concerning the contract of marriage as in previous deposition.]

Robert de Rouclif, blood brother of the Alice in question, says that he was present in Richard Bernard's room when the John and Alice in question contracted marriage together by words of present consent of their free will without either force or fear placed on either party. Concerning Alice's age he says that come the Saturday before the first Sunday in Passiontide next she will be a full thirteen years, and this he knows from being told by Alice's mother and her nurse.

Robert de Normanby...

... Alice was for half a year or more completely supported at the charge and expense of John, and he placed Alice at board with Anabilla, wife of Stephen Wasteleyne, and John's sister, at Kennythorpe, and John had common access to Alice as to his wife...

Adam Porter, gatekeeper of St Mary's Abbey...

... after the contract of marriage this witness and William Potell took Alice at John Marrays' instruction to Stephen Wasteleyne's home at Kennythorpe...

William Pottell sworn and examined on the previously mentioned articles. Asked about the first and second articles, he says that they contain the truth and this he knows because he stood at the doorway of Richard Bernard's room within the precinct of St Mary's Abbey at the time when John and Alice contracted marriage together, as is set out in the first article, but, as he says, he did not hear the words. Asked concerning the third article, he says that it contains the truth, and this he knows from being told by Alice's mother, Thomas Smyth of Clifton, her godfather, and Alice de Beleby, her godmother, and he knows not to depose otherwise on this article as he says. Asked about the fourth article, he says that it contains the truth. Asked how he knows, he says by the fact that this witness often carried at John's behest clothes, kerchiefs, and other necessaries to Alice as John's wife at Kennythorpe. Alice was often asked by this same witness why John Marrays, her husband, absented himself so much from her, and she sent him her greetings as her master. Asked concerning the fifth article, he says that it contains the truth and this he knows because Alice never denied it during the whole of the aforesaid time.[15] Asked in respect of the sixth article, he says that it contains the truth and he knows this because this witness made the bed in which John and Alice lay together at Kennythorpe alone and naked together in a certain room. He says that he asked Alice whether she was happy with John as her master. She replied to him that she was well satisfied to have him for a husband, and then this witness said to Alice, 'May you grow up sufficiently that he is able to do ?with you as is fitting', and she said to him in reply, 'I am quite adequate to be his wife, but not his whore'...

Isabel de Rouclif, wife of John de Grandesby of Tollerton having goods in common to the value of more than ten marks...

[Deposes that Alice will be thirteen come Saturday before the first Sunday in Passiontide.]

Asked, she says she knows this by that this witness, immediately after Ellen, Alice's mother, gave birth to Alice and before Ellen's churching in respect of Alice, came to serve Ellen and Gervase, her husband, who was whilst he lived the uncle of this witness, as she says, and by that this witness was married on Sunday in the feast of Holy Trinity nine years ago next, and Alice was at that time in her fifth year of age...

Katherine, wife of Robert de Rouclif...

... she says that she often asked Alice if she was happy to have John as her husband as much before the contract of marriage made between them as after, and especially on the day when Alice was sent by John to John Marrays' sister at Kennythorpe because on the day that she went Alice stayed in this witness' house in Bootham from the hour of matins to high noon, and Alice always replied that she was happy to have John as her husband. The witness then asked Alice is she was quite willing to go to Kennythorpe away from her mother and she replied yes, that she wanted, as she said, to go wherever John wished her to go, and she says upon her oath that she was never able to examine why Alice was, from the time she first saw John, always so well disposed to have him as her husband, as she says. Concerning Alice's age she says that come Saturday before the first Sunday in Passiontide next she will be thirteen years of age, and she remembers this as she says because at the time when Ellen, Alice's mother, was pregnant with her, this witness was pregant with a daughter to which she gave birth on the Thursday before Lent twelve years ago...

15 The article alleges that Alice contracted marriage of her free will and in the presence of witnesses.

Isabel de Strensall, living in Jubbergate, York...

[Deposes that she did not know Alice's witnesses, but knows and upholds standing of John Marrays' witnesses, except Margery de Rouclif, Emma Norice, Margery Gregson, Alice de Frithby, and Isold, wife of William de Kirkeby.]

Item, she says about the second article of the replications that it contains the truth because this witness remembers well the time of the birth of John, the son of Gervase and Ellen because she was present, as she says, at the churching of Ellen after the birth of John and at the feast held for that reason at Martinmas fourteen years ago. Asked how she remembers after the passage of so much time she says by that at the time of the churching she was pregnant, but she does not know whether with a boy or a girl, nor at what time of year she gave birth to the child, and by that after the churching she lived in Bootham for two years and afterwards she moved to live within the city and has lived there for twelve years...

Agnes, wife of Robert de Richmond, of St Marygate, aged 29 years...

[Deposes that she knows John Marrays' witnesses except Alice de Boleby, Emma Norice, Alice de Frithby. Witnesses surpass Alice's witnesses 'in wealth, eminence, and renown'. Deposes that John de Rouclif would have been fourteen last Martinmas.]

... she does not know on what day between Michaelmas and Martinmas John was born, nor who were John's godfathers or godmother, nor who were present at his birth. Asked how she remembered after the passage of so much time, she says by that at the time of Ellen's churching in respect of John, her son, this witness was in service with Robert de Rouclif and saw that Ellen came to York on St Martin's day and went away from York after her churching to Rawcliffe...

Agnes del Polles, wife of Ralph de Hesyngwald, aged 26 years...

[Deposes that she knew all John's witnesses except three and all were more trustworthy than Alice's.]

[John de Roucliff] ... was born, as this witness says, three weeks before Martinmas fourteen years ago and on that feast day Ellen was churched. This witness saw her on that day when she came to be churched and when she returned after she had been churched because at that time she was living in St Marygate, and she remembers after the passage of this time because the following Christmas this witness came to serve Robert de Rouclif and stayed with him for four years, but she was not present at John's birth, nor does she know who was at his birth, nor who were the godfathers or godmother of John, who from the time of his birth lived until a fortnight after the subsequent Easter, and in Lent following John's death Alice was born... This witness has nothing by way of goods, as she says, save a ?boy and a wheel with a pair of cards.[16]

Margery de Rouclif...

[Deposes that of Alice's witnesses knows only William de Tange, Alice, his wife, and Henry Vaux. Knows all John's witnesses.]

... was present for three weeks before Martinmas fourteen years ago in the house of Gervase de Rouclif, the witness' brother whilst he lived, when John, son of Gervase and Ellen, his wife, was born, but she does not remember which day. Asked who were then present, she says that she cannot remember, and she says that Margery, the widow of John de Rouclif was John's godmother as she recalls and John de Thornton godfather, and she cannot remember the name of the other godfather at present. Item, she says she was present at Ellen's churching and at the feast held for that reason on St Martin's day following John's birth...

Cecily de Shupton...

[Of Alice's witnesses deposes that she knows only Robert Thewed, Margaret de Folifayt, and William de Tange. Does not know if they are trustworthy or not. Knows all but two of John's witnesses.]

Asked about the second article of the replications, she says that for a month before Martinmas fourteen years ago last (she does not know what day, as she says, but remembers well that it was a month, as she says) she was present in the house of Gervase de Rouclif then husband of Ellen when Ellen gave birth to her son John, about whom mention is made in this article, and was likewise present with Ellen on the following St Martin's day when Ellen was churched in respect of this delivery. She says that John de Melsa and John de Thornton were John's godfathers and Margery, the widow of John de Rouclif was John's godmother...

[The following three deponents were examined 28–29 January 1366.]

Ellen, wife of Thomas Taliour, of Skelton, previously admitted, sworn, and examined in the present cause on behalf of the Alice in question, and now appearing afresh examined on the present enrolled articles.

16 The Latin 'puerum' in abbreviated form seems clear enough. Cards are instruments for carding wool, a process prior to spinning.

Asked about the first article, she says she knows not to depose on that. Asked about the second article, she says that it contains the truth and she says the same of the third and following article. Asked how she knows this, she says because in autumn thirteen years ago and afterwards until the following Martinmas this witness was servant to William de Huntyngton, now dead, and on the vigil of St James the previous autumn gave birth to a son still living, and three weeks before the feast of St Mary following Ellen, the widow of Gervase de Rouclif, gave birth to her son John, who is noticed in the present articles. Asked if she was present at John's birth, she says not, but she says that Ellen was churched in respect of her delivery on St Martin's day, which she described previously, and William de Huntyngton was present at the feast held by Gervase after the churching because Gervase and William were great friends. That same Martinmas this witness left William's service and then Emma de Huntyngton, William's wife, wished to hire this witness that she should be John's nurse and this witness responded that she loved her son just as much as Ellen loved hers and consequently she did not want to allow her own son to die on account of Ellen's son and so she refused to be John's nurse. She says further that in Lent following John's birth, this witness came to live in Rawcliffe and stayed there for the following three years. At the time she came to live in Rawcliffe she saw and recognised in his cradle John, who lived, as she remembers, until the following Pentecost or a little after when he died. She knows well that Alice de Rouclif, who is now in question, was born after the time of John's birth by a year and more by as much as is the time of year from when John was born until the Saturday before the first Sunday in Passiontide following. Alice was born on the Saturday and this witness was present at her birth, and on the day of Alice's birth this witness came to serve Gervase as a nurse to Alice and was her nurse for the following three weeks and not longer because she was prevented by illness such that she was unable thereafter to be nurse to Alice nor to feed her, nevertheless, as she says, she stayed in service with Gervase from that time for a whole year and more, that is to say until Pentecost a whole year later...

Maud de Herthill of Rawcliffe, of free condition as she says, previously admitted, sworn, and examined in the present cause on behalf of Alice de Rouclif, and now sworn afresh, examined, and asked on the aforesaid articles. Asked about the first article, she says that it contains the truth and this she knows because many of the witnesses named in this article are of the consanguinity or affinity of Ellen de Rouclif who makes herself as much a party in the present cause and is as concerned as is stated in this article. Asked about the second, third, and fourth articles, she says that they contain the truth and this she knows because marriage was contracted and solemnised between Gervase and Ellen around Michaelmas sixteen years ago and this witness was in service with Ellen for half a year from that time. When this was over she left and remained outside her service for a year and a half, which past she returned to Ellen's service at Martinmas, and from that Martinmas she stayed with her through the time she was pregnant with John, and at the time when she gave birth to him she herself was present. John was born, as she says, one Friday three weeks and two days before Martinmas day thirteen years ago, and this witness held him in her arms immediately after his birth whilst his mother Ellen was taken to and made ready for bed. In the following autumn this witness gave birth at Rawcliffe to a daughter, still living, who is twelve years of age coming up thirteen years, and at the time of this witness' delivery Ellen was pregnant with Alice, who was born on Saturday before the first Sunday in Passiontide following this witness' delivery, and this she knows well because she was present in the village of Rawcliffe at the time of Alice's birth and saw her in her cradle...

Anabilla Pynder of Rawcliffe, of free condition, sworn and examined on the aforesaid articles. She was not examined on the first article by consent of the party. Asked about the second, third, and fourth, she says that they contain the truth because Ellen, after marriage was contracted between Gervase and herself, conceived in different years and gave birth to two children by him, the first a boy child, who was called John and was born, as this witness says, at Rawcliffe three weeks before Martinmas thirteen years ago, whom this witness saw and recognised in his cradle, and she was present, as she says, in the village of Rawcliffe when he was born, and at that time this witness was pregnant and close to giving birth to a son of whom she was delivered on the Tuesday following Martinmas. From these things and also because on Monday, the day after Martinmas, which that year fell on a Sunday, Ellen, who was churched after the birth of her son that St Martin's day, sent this witness some writing which was said to be good for pregnant women, she remembers about the birth of John, the son of Gervase and Ellen. She further says that for a year after John's birth and more by the length of time from John's birth until a fortnight before Easter following, that is Saturday before the first Sunday in

Passiontide, Ellen gave birth to her daughter Alice, who is being discussed at present, and she was present, as she says, and living in the said village of Rawcliffe at the time the said Alice was born and saw her in her cradle and knew her from that time up until the present day...

[The following deponent was examined in the church of St Wilfrid, York, 29 January 1366.]

Lady Margery de Rouclif, aged 70 years as she says, sworn and examined on the aforesaid articles. Asked about the first article, she says that she believes that the persons named in that article are supporters of John Marrays and desire victory on John's behalf such that he can have Alice, against whom the cause is directed, for his wife. Asked about the second, third, and fourth articles, she says that they contain the truth because, as she says, one Friday three weeks and two days before Martinmas, which feast day then fell upon a Sunday, thirteen years ago Ellen, wife of Gervase de Rouclif, there being an established marriage between Gervase and Ellen, gave birth to a son who was called John and on Saturday, the day after the Friday, John was baptised in the abbey of St Mary's, York and this witness was his godmother, and John de Melsa and John de Thornton were his godfathers, and was present at his baptism. Asked how she remembers after the passage of so much time, she says because on the one hand William Fairfax, who married this witness' daughter, had that year a son born of his wife who was called John before he was baptised because his imminent death was feared, and on the other hand she remembers by the dates of writings and indentures by which she demised certain of her lands at farm, and otherwise by the births of other children at Rawcliffe who were born a short time before and after the birth of John of women neighbours of the village of Rawcliffe where this witness was then living. Asked whether she knows how to depose concerning the time of Alice's birth, she says that she does not clearly remember this at present, but she knows well that she has not yet completed twelve years of her age as she heard from the account of many who knew well the time and date of Alice's birth. Asked about the fifth article, she says she heard well it said that Ellen de Rouclif, being in the presence of Lord de Percy, who now is, and of many knights and esquires, confessed and acknowledged just as is stated in the present article...[17]

[The following two deponents were examined at 'Houton', 3 February 1366.]

17 I.e. that Ellen de Rouclif had acknowledged within two months of the present action that Alice was not yet twelve.

John de Melsay, sworn and examined on the aforesaid articles, says that Ellen, the widow of Gervase de Rouclif, there being an established marriage between Gervase and Ellen, gave birth to two children at different times and years. The first, a son, was born three weeks before Martinmas thirteen years ago and this witness, as he says, was at that time living at Shipton and was godfather to the son and called him his own name John, and he says that John de Thornton of York was John's other godfather and Lady Margery de Rouclif his godmother. Asked how he remembers after the passage of so much time, he says because he has lived and had his home at 'Houton' for twelve years come a fortnight after Michaelmas next, and if his godson John had lived at that time he would have been two years of age less three weeks, and so he says that if John were alive now he should not have completed fourteen years of his age since the time of year when he was born, that is to say three weeks before the feast of Martinmas.

Lettice, wife of John de Melsay...

[Deposes concerning marriage of Agnes and Gervase and birth of their two children as before] ... she remembers after the said lapse of time, as she says, because at that Martinmas when Ellen was churched after the birth of John, this witness was very ill and was living then at Shipton with her husband, and then, the following year having gone by, in the second year after the birth of John, Gervase's son, this witness conceived by her husband and gave birth in that second year, that is to say on the feast of the Nativity of the Blessed Virgin Mary, to a son who is still living, about the time of his birthday a full eleven years of age and no more as she says upon oath, and she also remembers after the passage of time because within six weeks of the birth of this witness' son, she and her husband moved with their family to live and make their home at 'Houton' where they now live. She says that this was a fortnight after Michaelmas eleven years ago last, and she says that she remembers otherwise because this witness' father died when she was so pregnant with her child that she was unable to strive to attend her father's burial, and thus she says that John son of Gervase, if he had lived, would have completed thirteen years of his age last Michaelmas and no more...

[The following deponent was examined 3 February 1366.]

Ellen, widow of Gervase de Rouclif, Alice's carnal mother...

[Deposes that she gave birth to John de Rouclif between Michaelmas and Martinmas fourteen years before.]

Asked how she remembered after the passage of so much time, she says by that two years before that Michaelmas this witness was joined in marriage to Gervase, and the marriage between them was solemnised at the church of Alne one Friday before Michaelmas, and at the Martinmas about which it is noted above she was churched in respect of John in the church of St Olave...

[Following four deponents questioned on an exception of John Marrays, 2 March 1366.]

Adam Gaynes, living in St Marygate in the suburbs of York...

[Deposes that he knew Alice's witnesses for ten years. All are poor. He knew John's witnesses for twenty years. They are wealthier than Alice's witnesses.]

John Barbour...

[Deposes that he does not know Alice's witnesses, but knows several of John's witnesses for six years.]

William de Kirkeby ?Breuster...

[Deposes that he knew Alice, daughter of Gervase, Robert Thewed, Alice, wife of Adam Porter, Beatrix, wife of John Milner, William de Tange, and Henry Vaux for seven years, but 'never heard any good of them'. Knew John's witnesses were more influential than Alice's.]

John de Alne, aged 18 years...

[Knew Alice's witnesses for six years] ... each and all are tenants of Sir Brian de Rouclif, and he says that Maud de Herthill is of ill repute and low standing and perjured in that she swore on the book that Gervase de Rouclif did not know her carnally in adultery and she swore falsely as subsequently she confessed that she had committed adultery with Gervase, and he had heard it said that Ellen, the wife of Thomas Taliour committed adultery with John [ ... ] of Skelton, and that the witnesses are for the most part poor people having little in goods, and he says that they are perjured in this present cause ... and Alice Shap is a servant in Sir Brian's garden...

[John's witnesses surpass Alice's in wealth] ... except that Beatrix de Morland and Margery, wife of John Gregson do not surpass Alice's witnesses in wealth or influence... He says that there is greater trust in John's witnesses than in Alice's...

[Following deponents examined on an exception of Alice Rouclif.]

Ellen Taliour, wife of Thomas Taliour of Skelton, sworn, examined both about the articles and the interrogatories present attached. Asked about the first she says she is unable to depose. Asked about the second article, she says that it contains the truth, and this she knows because she was present in a basement room of the main home of Gervase de Rouclif in the village of Rawcliffe on Saturday before the first Sunday in Passiontide eleven years ago after dawn and before sunrise of that day together with a certain ?old woman living in Rawcliffe, now senile because of old age, Alice's mother, and no others, where and when Alice was born. She remembers her birth in that this witness had a son feeding, and at that time aged one and a half, and she was hired by Alice's mother to give milk and feed Alice, and this witness carried Alice to the church of St Olave that same Saturday, where she then received the sacrament of baptism, and, after she had been thus baptised, carried Alice back to Rawcliffe to the home of her father, and she fed her until Sunday in the octave of the Easter following when this witness began to be feverish and was unable to feed Alice thereafter. Nevertheless she served Alice's parents for a whole year following and until Pentecost the year following that first Sunday...

[Deposes that witness was married when Alice was a year old.]

Maud de Herthill, living in 'Slaykston', having goods to the value of twenty shillings as she says and servant to Master Robert de Slaykston, sworn and examined on the previously mentioned articles. She says that on the first article she does not know how to depose. Asked on the second article, she says that she knows well that Alice had not yet completed twelve years of her age, nor will complete until a fortnight before next Easter, and this she knows, as she says, because she gave birth to a daughter still living on the morrow of St Bartholomew[18] twelve years ago, and Alice was born the Saturday before the first Sunday in Passiontide at Rawcliffe where this witness was then living... She said that she was asked to proffer her testimony by Sir Brian de Rouclif, but was not instructed.

Joan Symkyn Woman of Rawcliffe, having almost nothing in goods save her clothing for body and bed, and a small brass pot, tenant of Sir Brian de Rouclif...

... she was present when Maud, her immediate fellow witness, gave birth to a daughter still living who was twelve years of age last feast of St Bartholomew...

18 25 August

Anabilla Pynder, living with her mother at Rawcliffe...

[Concerning Alice's birth less than twelve years before] ... she remembers because Alice's mother wanted to hire this witness that she should be nurse to Alice and she refused this because she had a son of her own feeding, who was then a year old and more by as long as it is from the Martinmas before Alice's birth until the time of her birth, and it seemed to her that her son was too young to be taken off milk...

[The following three deponents were examined 27–28 March 1366.]

Thomas de Bulmer of York, potter, sworn, examined, and diligently questioned about the exception and the present attached interrogatories, says that he does not know any of the witnesses written in the exception other than Ellen, the mother of Alice de Rouclif, who is a supporter of John Marrays and against Alice in this cause, and he knows this because he heard many in the city of London say that Ellen was there and told our lord the king and his council many evils concerning Sir Brian de Rouclif, mover of the said cause, and there obtained royal letters sealed under his private seal directed to the said Brian, but he does not know what was contained in these letters, as this witness says. Afterwards on the day of his deposition this witness talked with Ellen, and at that time Sir Brian said, indicating the said Ellen, 'Look, here is that lady. She knows whether she promotes and prosecutes the cause against her daughter or not.' To him Ellen replied, 'I wish to support my daughter.' The witness says that he heard many say that Ellen promoted the said cause and desires victory on behalf of John. Concerning the matters contained in the said exception he does not know to depose otherwise...

William de Lynton, sworn and examined on the aforesaid articles, says that he does not know any of the witnesses named in the exception apart from Ellen de Rouclif, and he says that he believes that she promotes the present cause on behalf of John against Alice de Rouclif and she strives rather for victory in the said cause on behalf of John against Alice, than against, because, just as he heard it said, she is a promoter of the said cause and prosecutes it just as it were her own cause. Otherwise on this exception he does not know to depose as he says.

William Sampson, goldsmith, York, sworn and examined on the aforesaid articles, says that he knows Margery de Rouclif, who is Alice de Rouclif's aunt, and Cecily de Shupton, who is a friend of Ellen de Rouclif, and Ellen herself, Alice's mother. He does not know the other sses named in the said exception. He says that Margaret [sic], y, and Ellen are promoters of the present cause on behalf of John Marrays and against Alice, and especially Ellen who just lately pursued the present business in the presence of the lord king in his council and took away royal letters to the parties to have justice and also proceeded before Lord de Percy before Christmas last in order to have his help to gain restitution of her daughter Alice, and that she provided witnesses to come and give testimony in this cause and thus she promoted this cause as he deposed above. Also, he says that they strove and she strove, each of them, for victory on behalf of John, but whether justly or unjustly this witness does not know as he says. He says that on the 27th day of the present month of March this witness heard Sir Brian de Rouclif say in the presence of this witness and his fellow witnesses and the said Ellen, 'Now you are able to see whether this lady is the promoter of this cause or not,' to whom Ellen said in reply, 'I wish to help get back my daughter'. He is not instructed or informed, as he says, and he wishes that justice should be done between the said parties.

[Following four deponents questioned on the replications of Alice de Rouclif, 27–28 February 1366.]

John de Hornyngton of York, sworn, examined, and asked on the replication for Alice's party against John Marrays...

... says he has known Margaret de Folyfayt and Margery, the wife of Robert Thewed for twenty years and Joan Symkyn Woman, Alice Sharp, Alice, wife of William de Tange, Robert Thewed, William de Tange, and Henry Vaux, witnesses named in the present replication, for eight years, and for the whole of that time they were reputed persons of good standing and worthy of trust... [Deposes that they were more trustworthy than witnesses for John Marrays]

John de Killom of Clifton...

[Knew all the witnesses named for sixteen years. All are of sufficient wealth.]

John called Bawines, living in York, butcher...

[Knew all the witnesses for ten years.]

Thomas Broun of Rawcliffe, of free condition living at Rawcliffe and so living for the past ten years...

[Knew all the witnesses for ten years.]

## 4. Accounts of parish priest, Hornsea.

Language: Latin. Date: 1482-3. Translated from P. Heath, *Medieval Clerical Accounts*, Borthwick Papers, XXVI, York, 1964.

Following the feast of St Mark in the aforesaid year...

Item, for the purification of William Hall's wife, 1½d.

Item, on the wedding day of William Roos' servant, 4d.

Item, for the purification of William Pellow's wife, 1½d.

Item, on the day of the purification of John Watson's wife, 1½d.

...

Item, for the purification of six different women, 9d.

...

Item, on the day of burial of William Cadby's wife, 6d.

...

Item, for the purification of Thomas Wheytley's [wife], 1½d.

Item, for the purification of Henry Schomaker's wife, 1½d.

Item, for the purification of John Maior's wife, 1½d.

Item, for the purification of six different women, 8d.

Item, from the Thomas Wood's wife on Easter Day, 8d.

## 5. Household accounts.

Language: English. Date: 1521-2. Translated from W. H. Stevenson, ed., *Report of the Manuscripts of Lord Middleton*, Historical Manuscripts Commission, LXVI, 1911.

Also, for your reward to Mr. Digby's nurse when you christened his child the last day of August [1521], 12d.

...

Also, paid to a nun of Nun Eaton the 28th day of August [1522] for boarding of John German's children of Cossington, 10s.

## 6. Coroners' rolls, Bedfordshire.

Language: Latin. Translation by Hunisett in R. F. Hunnisett, ed., *Bedfordshire Coroners' Rolls*, Bedfordshire Historical Record Society, XLI, 1961.

[a] [1276] About prime ... while William Sagar of Sutton was at the

plough, his wife Emma took a bundle of straw inside the courtyard of his house in Sutton in order to go and heat an oven. She came to a part of the courtyard near their dwelling house and near a well to the north of the house and by misadventure fell into the well and drowned. Maud, daughter of Ellis Batte of Sutton was sitting in William's house keeping watch over Emma's child Rose, who was lying in a cradle. She heard the noise ... went outside, found Emma drowned, and continously raised the hue and cry...

[b] [1274] About prime ... Joan, a poor child of five, went through Riseley to beg for bread. She came to a bridge called 'Fordebrugge' and, as she tried to cross it, fell into the water and drowned by misadventure. Her mother, Alice, daughter of Bicke first found her...

[c] [1270] ... Emma, daughter of Richard Toky of Southill went to 'Houleden' in Southill to gather wood. Walter Garglof of Stanford came carrying a bow and a small sheaf of arrows. He seized Emma and tried to throw her to the ground and deflower her, but she immediately shouted and her father came. Walter shot an arrow at him, striking him on the right side of the forehead and mortally wounding him. He shot him again with an arrow under the right side and so into the stomach. Seman of Southill came and asked why he wanted to kill Richard. Walter immediately shot an arrow at him and struck him in the back so that his life was despaired of. Walter then fled. Later Emma, wife to Richard came and found her husband wounded to the point of death and shouted. Neighbours came and carried him to his home. He had the rites of the Church, made his will, and died at twilight...

[d] [1269] ... thieves came to a house in Roxton in which there were two girls, Margaret and Alice, daughters of Ralph Boverton. They broke the wall, entered, and robbed and carried off all the goods of the house. Then they went to the next house in which were staying Maud del Forde and Alice Pressade, both of Roxton. They broke the west wall, entered, and, finding Maud in bed, struck her above the left ear so that her brain spilled out and she died instantly. They struck Alice on the top of her head with, it seems, a Danish axe so that she lay without speaking and died the same night. They then carried away all the goods of the house...

## 7. Coroners' rolls, London.

Language: Latin. Date: 1340. An abridged translation by Sharpe from R. R. Sharpe, ed., *Calendar of Coroners Rolls of the City of London A.D. 1300–1378*, London, 1913.

Tuesday before the feast of St George the same year, information given to the aforesaid coroner and sheriffs that Mary, daughter of Agnes de Billingesgate, aged nine years, lay dead of a death other than her rightful death under the wharf of Thomas de Porkele in the parish of All Hallows the Less in the ward of Dowgate. Thereupon they proceeded there and having summoned the good men of that ward and the ward of Langbourn where the said Mary lived with her mother, they diligently enquired how it happened. The jurors ... say that on the preceding Sunday after the hour of vespers, the aforesaid Mary filled an earthen pot with water on the aforesaid wharf, the Thames being in flood, when she fell into the water and was drowned.

## 8. Mayor's court, London.

Language: Latin. Date: 1373. Translation by Riley from H. T. Riley, ed., *Memorials of London and London Life*, London, 1868.

On Monday the feast of St Benedict the Abbot in the 47th year etc., Alice de Salesbury, a beggar, was sentenced to the pillory ordained for women called the 'thewe' by judgement of the mayor and aldermen to stand there for one hour in the day, because on the previous Sunday she had taken one Margaret, daughter of John Oxwyke, grocer, in the Ropery in London, and had carried her away and stripped her of her clothes, so she might not be recognised by her family, so that she might go begging with the same Alice...

## 9. Court of Common Pleas.

Language: Latin. Translated from M. S. Arnold, ed., *Select Cases of Trespass from the King's Courts 1307–1399*, I, Selden Society, C, 1985.

[a] [1380] ... And regarding the beating and wounding of the aforesaid Joan, he [Adam] says that some while ago he married one Cecily, mother to the aforesaid Joan, and that at the time of celebrating the espousals between them the same Joan was of tender age, and for fifteen years and more she lived with Adam and Cecily as their servant and under their nurture. And during that time, that is in the time of the lord Edward, lately king of England, grandfather of the present

lord king, because the same Joan was disobedient and daily behaved badly towards the same Cecily her mother, and further negligently and of her own will wasted and completely lost three quarters of the same Adam's malt in brewing, the same Cecily wanted to chastise the same Joan by reason of nurture and for the aforesaid cause. The same Joan did not permit this and took her aforesaid mother and wife of Adam by the right thumb with her teeth and so strongly compressed that thumb between her teeth by biting almost to the middle that the same Cecily thought herself to be dying there and lost consciousness, and rousing herself from this raised on high the hue and cry to which the same Adam came immediately and, seeing his aforesaid wife in such mortal danger and the same Joan not ceasing to so wound her, immediately snatched Joan from her aforesaid mother, and in rescue of his aforesaid wife and so as to chastise her whilst being thus snatched away, and at the particular request of the aforesaid Cecily her mother under whose and Adam's nurture the same Joan was at that time, he struck her with a rod that he had in his hand...

[b] [1381] ... And regarding the beating etc. he [John Raven, chaplain] says that the aforesaid Isold is his blood relative and that at the time when the aforesaid trespass is supposed to have been done, the same Isold was of tender age living in the company of that John, and by reason that the same Isold desired to spend her time among boys and company improper to her rank and not to conform with honest behaviour, the same John reproved the same Isold by way of chastisement and instruction and to draw her away from such company, and chastised her at various times with small rods...

[c] [1389] ... And with regard to the taking and abducting of the same Joan, not recognising that Joan was ever the servant of the aforesaid Katherine [Swayn], they [John Hunt and others] say that at the time when the aforesaid trespass is supposed to have been done they found the same Joan, being at that time four years of age, in the aforesaid vill wandering without any kind of protection, because of which for the sake of charity they took the same Joan so as to nurture her and find her necessary sustenance for the love of God. They seek judgement, therefore, whether the aforesaid Katherine ought to maintain her aforesaid action [for abduction of a servant] against them in this party by her aforesaid brief etc.

And the aforesaid Katherine, not recognising that the aforesaid Joan at the time when the aforesaid trespass was supposed to have been done was of such tender age as is before alleged, says that at that time the same Joan was Katherine's servant and was in the same Katherine's service and not wandering as the aforesaid John Hunt, John Asshewelle, William, and Richard have alleged above...

... the aforesaid Katherine does not deny that at the time the aforesaid trespass is supposed to have been done Joan did not in fact exceed the age of four years, which they are prepared to verify if etc., in which case the same Joan cannot be considered at such an age anyone's servant by contract or in any other way according to the law of the land...

## 10. Petition to the lord chancellor.

Language: French. Date: 1420-2. Translation by Baildon from W. P. Baildon, ed., *Select Cases in Chancery AD 1364 to 1471*, Selden Society, X, 1896.

William Burton, servant to Master Robert Burton, clerk, one of your chaplains, most humbly beseeches and grievously complains of Lewis Gryville of the county of Oxford, that whereas one Robert Archer, late of Winchester, merchant, with the assent and abatement of the said Lewis, did, on the Tuesday before the feast of the Ascension of our Lord in the eighth year of the reign of our sovereign lord the present king, ravish [i.e. abduct] one Alice Wodeloke, daughter and heir apparent of Parnell, the wife of the said suppliant, the same daughter being of the age of seven years, and being found at Collingburn in the county of Wiltshire, in the guardianship of one John Santon [to whom she was] committed by the said suppliant, and brought her thence to the house of the said Lewis at Drayton in the county of Oxford. And the said Lewis still detains the same Alice wrongfully and against law, right, and good conscience, and against the will of the said suppliant, and will not deliver the said Alice to the said suppliant unless he will make fine with the said Lewis for 40 marks and release by his writing to the said Robert all the debt which the said Robert owes the same suppliant... May it please your most gracious lordship to consider this matter and thereupon to ordain that the said suppliant may have restitution of the said Alice, as law and conscience demand, with their damages in this behalf, for God and as a work of charity.

## 11. Papal register.

Language: Latin. Date: 1364. Abridged translation from *Calendar of Papal Registers*, IV, London, 1902.

To the bishop of Lichfield. Mandate to summon those concerned, and make order touching the case of Isabel de Scarsbrok, of the diocese of York, who in her tenth year was espoused to Henry Molineux, and was carried off without knowledge thereof, by John de Yorke, citizen of York, more desirous of patrimony than of matrimony, and was terrified into a clandestine contract of marriage. Afterwards, being freed from the said John by her relations, she remained with them until she became of marriageable age, and, keeping to her first espousals, publicly married Henry. John then, falsely asserting that she was contracted to him first, brought an action against her as his lawful wife, before the official of York, and so treated her advocates and proctors that no one dared to defend her, nor did dare to appear in person before the archbishop, being in fear of John, who, with a multitude of armed men, lay in wait for her.

## 12. Will of John Broune, founder, York.

Language: English. Date: 1493. Translated from BIHR, Prob. Reg. 5 fo. 425.

Also I leave my daughter Susan to Robert Preston with her portion and I leave to Janet his wife for to be a good mother to her, 6s 8d.

# II: Adolescence

## Servanthood

*See also 'Childhood' [3] depositions of Agnes de Polles, Cecily de Shupton, Ellen Taliour, and Maud de Herthill; 'Husband and wife' [1], [11] deposition of William Coke; 'Widowhood, poverty, and old age' [12] depositions of Agnes Kyrkeby, Thomas Catton; 'Work in the countryside' [18], [22]; 'Work in the town' [15f], [28]; 'Law and custom' [35] deposition of Joan Scharp, [64b], [65a]; 'Devotion' [26].*

### 1. Italian Relation.

Language: Italian. Date: ?1497. Translation by Sneyd in C. A. Sneyd, ed., *A Relation ... of the Island of England ... about the Year 1500*, Camden Society, XXXVII, 1847.

The want of affection in the English is strongly manifested towards their children, for after having kept them at home until they arrive at the age of seven or nine years at the utmost, they put them out, both males and females, to hard service in the houses of other people, binding them generally for another seven or nine years. And these are called apprentices, and during that time they perform all the most menial offices, and few are born who are exempted from this fate, for everyone, however rich he may be, sends away his children into the houses of others, whilst he, in return, receives those of strangers into his own. And on inquiring their reason for this severity, they answered that they did it in order that their children might learn better manners. But I, for my part, believe that they do it because they like to enjoy all their comforts themselves, and that they are better served by strangers than they would be by their own children. Besides which the English being great epicures, and very avaricious by nature, indulge in the most delicate fare themselves and give their households the coarsest bread, and beer, and cold meat baked on Sunday for the week, which, however, they allow them in great abundance. That if they had their own children at home, they would be obliged to give them the same food they made use of for themselves. That if the English sent their children away from home to learn virtue and good manners, and took them back again when their apprenticeship was over, they might, perhaps, be excused. But they never return, for the girls are settled by their patrons, and the boys make the best marriages they can and, assisted by their patrons, not by their fathers, they also open a house and strive diligently by this means to make some fortune for themselves...

### 2. Coroners' rolls, Sussex.

Language: Latin. Date: 1522. It is very rare to find girls in service under twelve years of age, though the very poor may have had greater incentive to send their children into service early. It may also be that orphaned children were sometimes sent into service at an early age. Cf. 'Childhood' [9]. Translation by Hunnisett in R. F. Hunnisett, ed., *Sussex Coroners' Inquests 1485-1558*, Sussex Record Society, LXXIV, 1985.

On 3 March Lucy, aged 12, servant of John Love of Battle and daughter of a vagrant stranger, fell into a pit full of water in a yard within the inn called the Chequer, formerly called the George in Battle and was drowned by misadventure.

### 3. Will of Agnes de Kyrketon of York.

Language: Latin. Date: 1408. Servants of the same name were often distinguished by the epithets 'little' and 'big'. The reference here to years of discretion suggest that Margaret was under twelve years of age. Translated from YML, D/C Reg. 1 fo. 151.

Also I leave to little Margaret my maidservant for her sustenance, ten silver marks if she lives to years of discretion...

### 4. Will of Thomas Parys, carpenter, of York.

Language: Latin. Date: 1408. Most servants appear to have served for a year at a time and, at least in respect of older servants, made verbal contracts directly with their employers (see 'Husband and wife' [11]). This example is unusual and may represent a contract originally made on behalf of a youngster. Translated from BIHR, Prob. Reg. 3 fo. 282v.

Also I leave to Alice my servant if she will serve my wife for me to the end of the term made between me and her mother for five years, 2s.

### 5. 'The Serving Maid's Holiday'.

Language: English. Date: mid fifteenth century. Translated from R. H. Robbins, ed., *Secular Lyrics of the XIVth and XVth Centuries*, Oxford, 1955.

All this day I have tried,
I have not wound spindle or reel;
To great bliss I am brought
    on this high holiday.

I cannot weave nor wind nor spin,
For joy that it is a holiday.

All unswept is our floor,
And our fire is unlit,
Our rushes are still uncut,
    on this high holiday.

I cannot weave nor wind nor spin,
For joy that it is a holiday.

I must go and bring herbs in;
Thread my kerchief under my chin;
Dear Jack, lend me a pin
    to thread me this holiday.[1]

I cannot weave nor wind nor spin,
For joy that it is a holiday.

Now it draws near to noon
And all my chores are undone;
I must clean my shoes a little
    to make them soft on this holiday.

I cannot weave nor wind nor spin,
For joy that it is a holiday.

I must milk in this pail;
I should have ?cooked [or ?lined] this whole dish,
The dough is still under my nails
    as I knead on this holiday.

I cannot weave nor wind nor spin,
For joy that it is a holiday.

Jack will entice me on my way,
Desire to enjoy himself with me;

---

1 This is, of course, a *double entendre*. The reference to herbs may likewise be an oblique reference to contraception.

I am not even afraid of my dame
    on a good holiday.

I cannot weave nor wind nor spin,
For joy that it is a holiday.

...

## 6. Fair court, St Ives

Language: Latin. Date: 1316. Translated from C. Gross, ed., *Select Cases Concerning the Law Merchant*, I, Selden Society, XXIII, 1908.

Agnes Litelfayr was attached to answer Isold Clerevaus in a plea of debt, and whereof she complains that the same Agnes detains from her unjustly and does not pay ten shillings of silver which she owes her, unjustly because when the aforesaid Isold and Agnes were in the town of Lynn the first day of Lent in the eighth year of the reign of King Edward and agreed among themselves that the aforesaid Isold be in the aforesaid Agnes' service from that day to the same day the following year, that is a whole year, taking ten shillings of silver from the same Agnes for her service, but she paid her nothing of the said ten shillings of silver within this term and owed them to her and still unjustly owes them to her damage, 2s, and hence she brings suit. The aforesaid Agnes [is] actually present etc. and denies that she owes the said ten shillings of silver, nor even a penny, from the said Isold as she charges her, and she asks that it be inquired, and likewise the opposing party. And the inquest comes and says that the aforesaid Agnes owes the same Isold the said ten shillings. It was judged therefore etc. that the said Isold recover the said ten shillings against her together with damages assessed at six pence, which she gave to the clerk, and the aforesaid Agnes is in mercy, 6d, for the unjust detention, Nicholas Lambert, pledge.

## 7. Manor court rolls, Tottenham (Pembrokes).

Language: Latin. Date: 1394. Translation by Oram in R. Oram, trans., *Court Rolls of the Manors of Bruces, Dawbeneys, Pembrokes (Tottenham) 1 Richard II to 1 Henry IV (1377-1399)*, Manor of Tottenham Series, II, London, 1961.

Robert Sampson complains of Adam Sown in a plea of trespass, and therein complains that the said Adam unjustly entered his tenement and eloigned Alice his servant to his own service, to his damage 20s.

## 8. Peace session rolls, Lincolnshire.

Language: Latin. Translated from R. Sillem, ed., *Records of some Sessions of the Peace in Lincolnshire 1360-1375*, Lincoln Record Society, XXX, 1937.

[a] [1375] Also they say that John Nuttyng junior, John Nuttyng, Robert son of Roger ... [and eight other named men] by force of arms came to Sutterton on Thursday before Pentecost in the 41st year of the reign of King Edward III and entered the home of Hugh Fiskemere and assaulted the same Hugh, beat, and ill treated him, broke his door, and took and led away his servant Margaret, daughter of Roger son of Hugh de Fiskemere ... [place name lost from record] and held her there against the peace for the eight days following so that Hugh lost her service.

[b] [1373] Also they present that Felicity, daughter of John Dammeson of West Keal, in the service of William Davy in East Keal, lately constrained by the order and direction of the constable of the vill as is the custom to remain from Martinmas in the 47th year [of Edward III] for the whole year following, left this service before the end of the aforesaid term without reasonable cause and licence of William Day.

## 9. Petition to the lord chancellor.

Language: French. Date: 1389. Translation in Baildon, ed., *Select Cases in Chancery*.

... whereas the said constables were required by one John Godfrey and Stephen Catfield of the same hundred to arrest Maud, formerly servant of Simon Bukmonggere and Cecily, the daughter of John Spenser of the same hundred, who were at large out of their services, not having lands or tenements, nor other chattels by which they could live, there came William Hacoun, William Sekdele, and John Deneys of the county of Suffolk and others with them of their covin and assent, and seized the aforesaid servants Maud and Cecily in the county of Norfolk, being in the possession of the said constables by way of arrest, and brought them into the county of Suffolk, contrary to the statute [of Labourers] and against the will of the constables...

## 10. Peace sessions, Lincolnshire.

Language: Latin. Date: 1387. Translated from E. G. Kimball, ed., *Records of some Sessions of the Peace in Lincolnshire 1381-1396*, II, Lincoln Record Society, LVI, 1962.

Also that Joan Shepherd of Claxby, formerly servant to John de Northorp of Sausthorpe on Monday after the feast of St John the Baptist in the tenth year of the reign of King Richard II broke the house of the said John and left the service of John against the peace of the lord king.

Also that Alice de Sodilton, servant of Alan de Wadmyln of Hameringham on Monday after Martinmas in the ninth year of the reign of King Richard II broke the said Alan's house and left Alan's service against the peace of the lord king.

## 11. Church court, York.

Language: Latin. Date: 1363. Right hand margin is damaged. No depositions survive. Translated from BIHR, CP.E.241P. Master John de Rissheton c. Isabel, servant of Thomas de Queldale.

... the same Isabel the whole [?time] around the said feast of St Martin in the winter last was and still is ready to serve the same Master [John de Rissheton] as mentioned. In no way whatsoever was it the case or is it the case that Isabel served or serves at present the same John because at the said feast of St Martin and at all times thereafter she had been and was compelled by dreadful threats that could and should befall, both seizure, imprisonment, torture of her body, and reasonable fear, to remain steadfast as a woman in the service of the said Thomas de Queldale and to serve the same Thomas and not Master John. The aforesaid Master John and Thomas had the same Isabel taken and, by the bailiffs of the city of York or by their authority, physically imprisoned for the length of a whole month and more immediately following the aforesaid feast [of St Martin] in the city of York, and they held her in the custody of prison as a recluse [...] until the suit or dispute between the said John and Thomas arising from Isabel's service had been considered by the same bailiffs and finally ended by judicial deception [sic], that is which of them the said Isabel should serve. The aforesaid Isabel by judicial precept and definitive sentence of the said bailiffs, judges in this party appropriate in this Statute, duly and correctly delivered and published according to the laws and customs of the realm of England, which Isabel dared not and dares not resist nor [...] contravene, was and is delivered to the aforesaid Thomas de Queldale [ ?by ] the same bailiffs and bound to serve the same [Thomas] for the said time until the feast of Martinmas next. Master John [...] sought all his losses and damages from Isabel due to the loss of the same Isabel's service before the said bailiffs if he were in any way able by sentence of the judges and assessment of the said bailiffs and their secular court. He [?for] his part was and is fully satisfied before the present action was moved. The said Master John recognised all these matters in the presence of the party of the said Isabel and of other trustworthy persons of his free will and certain knowledge. These things are public knowledge and plain in the city of York and neighbouring parts and concerning these the public voice and report has circulated and circulates still. For this reason he seeks as proctor ... to show by right the said Isabel, his client, and he in her name, to be judicially absolved from the petition and disturbance of the said Master John in this party and discharged absolutely in peace...

### 12. Manor court, Halesowen.

Language: Latin. Translated from R. A. Wilson, ed., *Court Rolls of the Manor of Hales*, III, Worcester Historical Society, 1933.

[a] [1276] Thomas son of Richard of Oldbury and others from the same vill present that William de Chiselhurst and Amice Bude, servants of William Yedrich, quarrelled together and William de Chiselhurst struck her and she raised the hue. William Yedrich as a consequence guaranteed to make amercement on behalf of his [male] servant and it was judged that he may hold back the wages of his said servants.

[b] [1277] It was ordered that, because Agnes the maidservant of Thomas took away against the peace of the Abbot the said Thomas' draught animals which had been impounded at the Abbot's house in Oldbury where J. le Per used to live, she should be summoned to the next court to answer for the damage they had done to the said lord Abbot through William de Welbec, warrener, whence the said William raised the hue on the said Alice.

### 13. Bristol cordwainers' ordinances.

Language: French. Date: 1408. Translated from F. B. Bickley, ed., *The Little Red Book of Bristol*, II, Bristol, 1900.

... And in so far as it is said that the wives of masters of the aforesaid craft have secretly given and promised certain favours and gifts to their servants over and above their contract whereby the said masters have been greatly harmed...

### 14. Will of Joan Buckland, widow, of Edgcott (d. 1462).

Language: English. Date: 1450. Translated from A. Clark, ed., *Lincoln Diocese Documents, 1450-1544,* Early English Text Society, original ser. CXLIX, 1914.

...

All my other gowns and kirtles, that they be given to my women servants dwelling with me at my departure.

...

Also to the woman that is by me at my departing, 100*s*, one silver bowl, two spoons, and one gown furred with mink.

...

### 15. Will of William Nunhouse, fishmonger, of York.

Language: Latin. Date: 1444. Translated from BIHR, Prob. Reg. 2 fo. 97.

Also I leave my servant Margaret a Prussian chest, a brass pot of my wife's choosing, a coverlet, and a blanket with a pair of sheets so that the aforesaid Margaret does not leave or depart from my wife Joan's service during the term of her hire and contract made between me and her. Also I leave Cecily my servant 2*s*. Also I leave Agnes my servant 12*d*.

### 16. Court of Common Pleas.

Language: Latin. Date: 1373. Translated from Arnold, ed., *Select Cases of Trespass.*

... And the aforesaid William [atte Hall] and Joan [his wife] come in their own persons and deny force and wrong when etc. And they say that on the aforesaid day and year and before, the same Denise [the wife of John Bray] was single and in the service of the same William and Joan, and retained under this condition, viz. that she well and faithfully serve the same William and Joan in the office of maidservant for a year, and if it happened within that time that the same Denise were wickedly or seriously at fault in anything or disobeyed the orders of the aforesaid William and Joan, that it would be quite proper then for William and Joan to chastise the same Denise with a slap or some other slight blow. And they say that the same Denise thus in the service of the said William and Joan went at night from the home of the aforesaid William and Joan without their permission or agreement, regardless of her service aforesaid. For this the same Joan reproached the aforesaid Denise such that, heated words having arisen between them, the aforesaid Denise said that the aforesaid Joan, then her

mistress, had lied, upon which the same Joan struck the said Denise on
the jaw with the hand by way of chastisement...

## 17. Borough court, Nottingham.

Language: Latin. Date: 1404. Translated from W. H. Stevenson, ed., *Records
of the Borough of Nottingham*, II, Nottingham, 1883.

Joan Potter of Nottingham through her guardian Geoffrey Baker
complains of John Lorymer in a plea of trespass in that he, here at
Nottingham, on Sunday after the feast of the conception of the Blessed
Mary last, assaulted the said Joan, beat her there, wounded and ill
treated her, and did other injuries to her to the serious damage of this
plaintiff, 100s, wherefore etc. He comes and defends etc., and he says
that Joan is and was the servant of John Lorymer, and the said Joan
gave him a contrary reply, and consequently this John Lorymer took
an 'elenwand' and struck her on the head and elsewhere as is just. And
the aforesaid Joan, through the said Geoffrey and John Braydsale, her
attornies, seeks judgement in respect of his answer, and John likewise,
and so judgement is respited until the next court...

## 18. Manor court rolls, Tottenham (Dawbeneys).

Language: Latin. Date: 1393. Translation in Oram, trans., *Court Rolls of the
Manors of Bruces, Dawbeneys, Pembrokes (Tottenham)*, II.

Maud (2d) the wife of Henry Forner has assaulted Juliana her maid
against the peace. And Juliana has raised the hue against the said
Maud justly. Therefore she is in mercy. By pledge the said Henry.

## 19. Borough memoranda, Southampton.

Language: Latin. Date: 1482. Translated from R. C. Anderson, ed., *The Assize
of Bread Book 1477-1517*, Southampton Record Society, XXXIII, 1923.

Memorandum that Nicholas de Prese of Southampton, cordwainer,
and [   ] his wife for certain offences of promoting illicit sex between
a captain of a Venetian galley and a servant girl staying with the said
Nicholas and [   ] his wife in which offences they colluded...

## 20. Visitations, archdeaconry of Buckingham.

Language: Latin. Date: 1505. Translated from E. M. Elvey, ed., *The Courts of
the Archdeaconry of Buckingham 1483-1523*, Buckinghamshire Record Society,
XIX, 1975.

The churchwardens of Borstall informed the office that one Robert Browne and his wife of the same parish promote illicit sex, viz. they make one Katherine Bronyng their servant lie in the bed where one John their son is wont to have recourse making her pregnant. This same Katherine humbly performed public penitence, but the aforesaid Robert still remains unpunished.

### 21. Wills, diocese of York.

Language: Latin.

[a] Will of Agnes Hylyarde, widow, of Beverley. Date: 1497. Translated from BIHR, Prob. Reg. 5 fo. 491.

To the poor of the almshouse in Wood Lane, viz. Cecily there, formerly my mother's servant, 12d, and to two other women there, 8d.

[b] Will of Joan Smyth of York. Date: 1440. Translated from BIHR, Prob. Reg. 2 fo. 672.

In the name of God, amen. The twentieth day of the month of April in the year of the Lord 1440, I Joan Smyth of York, lately servant to Sir Thomas Skynner of York, chaplain, of sound mind and remembrance, make my will in this manner. Firstly...

[c] Will of Emmota Page of York. Date: 1390. Translated from BIHR, Prob. Reg. 1 fo. 9.

In the name of God, amen. The first day of the month of June in the year of the Lord one thousand three hundred and ninety, I Emmota Page, servant of Katherine Lakensnyder of York, being of good remembrance, make and ordain my will in this manner. Firstly...

### 22.   Churchwardens' accounts, St Mary at Hill, London.

Language: English. Date: 1505-6. Translated from H. Littlehales, ed., The Medieval Records of a London City Church, Early English Text Society, original ser. CXXV, CXXVIII, 1904-5.

Received of Mistress Halhede for [the burial of] her maid in Pardon churchyard, 2s.

# Instruction

 'How the Goodwife Taught her Daughter'.

Language: English. Date: early fifteenth century. This text was evidently designed primarily for an urban audience. Adolescent girls living at home with their mothers would have little need of such a text. Since, however, many teenage girls, particularly after the Black Death and particularly within town society, would leave their natal homes to go into service, it is likely that one use of this text would have been to instruct female servants, possibly by way of reading practice. It consciously draws upon a cosy and perhaps nostalgic image of the mother teaching her daughter, but behind the 'Goodwife' is no doubt a male, and perhaps clerical author. Translated from T. F. Mustanoja, ed., *The Good Wife Taught Her Daughter*, Helsinki, 1948, pp. 197–203, an edition of a later version of a text that dates originally to at least the middle of the fourteenth century, but which remained in circulation until at least the end of the fifteenth century. This version is contained in MS. Lambeth Palace 853 which also contains a parallel, but unrelated didactic text 'How the Wise Man Taught his Son'. This version is also printed in Furnivall, ed., *The Babees Book*, Early English Text Society, original ser. XXXII, 1868.

> The Goodwife taught her daughter
> Very many times and often
> A truly good woman to be,
> And said, Daughter to me dear,
> Some good you must learn,
> If ever you would thrive.
>
> Daughter, if you want to be a wife, look wisely that you work;
> Look willingly, and in good life you love God and Holy Church.
> Go to church when you may, see you spare for no rain,
> For you fare the best every day when you have seen God.[2]
> He must need well thrive
> Who lives well all his life,
> My dear child.
>
> Gladly give your tithes and your offerings both.
> The poor and the bedridden, see that you hate not.
> Give of your own goods, and be not too hard,
> For seldom is that house poor where God is steward.
> Well he turns out
> That loves the poor,
> My dear child.

2 I.e. in the form of the host elevated at mass.

When you sit in the church, your prayers you shall offer.
Make you no chattering to friend or to relation.
Laugh you to scorn neither old folk nor young,
But be of fair bearing and of good toungue.
  Through your fair bearing
  Your honour will increase,
   My dear child.

If any man pays court to you, and would marry you,
Look that you scorn him not, whoever he is,
But show it to your family and hide you it not.
Sit not by him, nor stand; there sin might be done,
  For a slander raised ill
  Is evil for to still,
   My dear child.

The man that shall wed you before God with a ring,
Love you him and honour most of earthly things.
Meekly you him answer, and not as a shrew,
And so may you calm his mood, and be his dear darling.
  A fair word and a meek
  Does wrath still,
   My dear child.

Fair of speech you shall be, glad, and of mild mood,
True in word and in deed, and in conscience good.
Keep you from sin, from villainy, and from blame,
And look that you conduct yourself so that men speak no ill of you,
  For he that in good life runs,
  Very often happiness he wins,
   My dear child.

Be of becoming appearance, wise, and other good manner,
Change not your countenance for anything that you may hear.
Act not like a giddy girl for anything that may happen.
Laugh you not too loud, nor yawn too wide,
  But laugh you softly and mild,
  And be not of cheer too wild,
   My dear child.

And when you walk in the street, don't go too fast,
Brandish not your head, nor your shoulders shrug.

Have you not too many words, to swear be you not too inclined,
For all such behaviour comes to an evil end.
       For he that gets himself an evil name,
       It is to him foul fame,
              My dear child.

Go you not into town as if you were a flighty person
From one house to another in search of vain amusement;
And go not to the market your burrel to sell,[3]
And then to the tavern to destroy your reputation.
       For they that haunt taverns,
       Their prosperity they bring down,
              My dear child.

And if you be in a place where good ale is aloft,
Whether that you serve thereof, or that you sit quietly,
Moderately take you thereof that no blame befalls you,
For if you are often drunk, it reduces you to shame.
       For those that be often drunk,
       Prosperity is taken away from them,
              My dear child.

Go not to wrestlings, nor to shooting at cock,[4]
As if you were a strumpet or a wanton woman.
Stay at home daughter, and love your work much,
And so you shall, my dear child, soon grow rich.
       It is evermore a merry thing,
       A man to be served of his own thing,
              My dear child.

Acquaint yourself not with each man that goes along the street;
If any man speak to you, swiftly you him greet.
Let him go by the way; do not stand by him,
That he by any villainy your heart might tempt.
       For not all men are true
       That know how to proffer fair words,
              My dear child.

3 Burrel was a coarse cloth. Women may often have traded in such inexpensive fabric, cf. Maud Katersouth ('Widowhood, poverty, and old age' [13]), but it may be that such women were perceived as being of a lower social standing than the Goodwife or her daughter.

4 The sport of shooting at cock, in which a cockerel is used as an archery target, is illustrated, for example, in the Queen Mary's Psalter.

Also that you accept no gifts for any covetousness,
Unless you know very well why, else you forsake him soon,
For with gifts men may women overcome,
Though they were as true as steel or stone.
          Bound forsooth is she
          That takes gifts of any man,
                    My dear child.

And wisely govern your house and your servants;
Be you not too bitter nor too kind with them,
But look well what most needs to be done,
And set your servants thereto both quickly and soon.
          For ready when needed
          Is a task already done,
                    My dear child.

And if your husband is from home, let not your servants go idle,
But look well who does much or little,
And he that well does, pay him well his reward,
And he that does otherwise, treat him as a base person.
          A task already done
          Will another speed,
                    My dear child.

And if your need is great, and your time scarce,
Then go yourself thereto and work a housewife's part.
Then will they all do the better that about you stand.
The work is the sooner done that has many hands.
          For many hands and folk
          Make a heavy task light.
          According to your good service
          Your name shall rise in esteem,
                    My dear child.

And whatever your servants do, about them busy yourself,
And as much as you are able, be at that one purpose,
And if you find any fault, do it soon amend,
So that they have time and space, and themselves may defend.
          To compel a task to be done when there is no time,
          Is but tyranny without temperance or grace,
                    My dear child.

And see that everything is well when they leave their work,
And take the keys into your care, see that they are not forgotten;
And beware to whom you show trust, and spare for no cunning,
For much harm has befallen those that are not wise.
    But, daughter, see that you are wise, and do as I teach you,
      And trust no one more than yourself for any fair words,
        My dear child.

And give your servants their wages at the end of their term
Whether they continue to reside or they go away.
Do well by them of the goods that you have in your management,
And they shall speak well of you, both the young and the old.
    Your good name is to your family
      Great joy and gladness,
        My dear child.

And if your neighbour's wife has on rich attire,
Don't as a consequence mock or scorn, nor burn as fire,
But thank God of heaven for that which he has given you,
And so you shall, my daughter, a good life lead.
    He manages with ease
      That thanks God often and occasionally,
        My dear child.

Housewifely you shall be on the work day:
Pride, rest, and idleness, make prodigality.
And when the holiday is come, well shall you be
The holy day in worship, and God will love you.
    Have in mind, to God is worship,
      For much pride comes of the evil day,
        My dear child.

When you are a wife, a neighbour for to be,
Love then well your neighbours, as God has commanded you.
You are bound so for to do,
And to do unto them as you would be done to.
    If any discord happens night or day,
      Make it no worse, mend it if you can,
        My dear child.

And if you shall be a rich wife, be then not too hard,
But welcome pleasantly your neighbours that come to you

With food, drink, and honest cheer, such as you may offer to them,
To each person according to their status, and help the poor who
  need.
    And also, whatever may come to pass,
    Please well your neighbours that live beside you,
      My dear child.

Daughter, look that you beware, whatsoever happen to you,
Make not your husband poor with spending nor with pride.
A man must spend as he is able that has but modest goods,
For according to the wren's veins, one must let her blood.[5]
    His prosperity waxes thin
    That spends before he earns,
      My dear child.

Borrow not too eagerly, and take not your wages first,
For the more need it makes, and the greater distress.
Do not make yourself appear rich with other men's goods,
But, therefore, spend never more than a farthing.
    For though you borrow quickly,
    It must come home again at last,
      My dear child.

And if your children be disobedient, and will not be respectful,
If any of them misbehave, neither curse them nor storm,
But take a sharp rod, and beat them in a line,
Until they cry mercy, and be confessed of their guilt.
    A dear child needs instruction,
    And ever the dearer, the more,
      My dear child.

And look to your daughters that none of them is lost.
From the very moment that they are of you born,
Busy you, and quickly collect towards their marriage,
And give them to espousing as soon as they are of age.
    Maidens are fair and lovable,
    But of their love very unstable,
      My dear child.

Now I have taught you, daughter, as my mother did me.
Think about this night and day, and see that you don't forget it.

5 The proverb concerning bleeding a wren's veins is equivalent to the current
proverb 'cut your cloth according to your means'.

Have moderation and humility, as I have taught you,
And whatever man shall wed you, then he is not deceived.
    Better were a child unborn
    Than untutored of wise instruction,
        My dear child.

Now wealth and prosperity may you have, my sweet child,
Of all our forefathers that ever were or are,
Of all patriarchs and prophets that ever lived,
Their blessings may you have, and well may you thrive.
    For well is the child
    That with sin will not be defiled,
        My dear child.

The blessing of God may you have, and of his mother bright,
Of all angels and of all archangels, and of every holy person,
And that you may have grace to make your way in righteousness
To the bliss of heaven, where sits God Almighty.
    Amen.

## Courtship and marriage

### 24. Church court, York.

Language: Latin. Translated from BIHR, CP.E.159. Margery Spuret c. Thomas de Hornby. Beatrix de Gillyng c. Thomas de Hornby.

[Following three depositions dated 30 January 1394.]

Isabel Spuret of York, mother of Margery, the party calling witnesses, 40 years of age and more, of free status and good standing as she says, admitted and diligently examined. About the first article she says that it contains the truth and this she knows because she was present in the house of Roger del Grene in Castlegate, York five years ago around the feast of the nativity of the Blessed Virgin Mary in the autumn when the said Thomas said to the said Margery, taking her by the hand, 'Are you willing to allow me to look for a wife wherever I will?' and she replied, 'I am willing'. The said Thomas immediately said, 'I want to have you for my wife' and she replied, 'And I want to have you for my husband'. Present were this witness, Juliana del Grene, her fellow witness, and the contracting parties. Asked about sexual intercourse, she says that he knew her carnally afterwards. Questioned on the second article, she says that she heard, acknowledged, and recognised this contract in the other's presence. Asked about the third article, she says that it contains the truth and this she knows because many talk about this contract, nor is she bribed or suborned etc.

Juliana del Grene of York, aged 30 years and more, of free condition and of good standing, a blood relation of the said Margery in the third degree of consanguinity as she says...

[Deposes concerning contract in her own home as before.]

Katherine, wife of James Sadler of York, aged 20 years and more, of free condition and of good repute, a blood relative of neither party other than that the said Thomas raised a child of the said Katherine from the holy font, so she says, admitted, sworn, and diligently examined. On the first article she says she does not know to depose concerning the contract of marriage between them. Asked about sexual intercourse, she says that he knew her carnally as she learned. Asked about the second article, she says that she heard the woman acknowledge this contract in the said Thomas' presence, but never Thomas himself. Questioned on the third article, she says that there was common report about this contract of marriage four years ago.

[Following two depositions dated 23–24 February 1394.]

Thomas Hornby, senior of York, saddler, aged 40 years and more, of free status and of good standing, a blood relative of Thomas Hornby, junior in the second degree of consanguinity in the transverse line as he says, admitted, sworn, and diligently examined. On the first and second articles he says he knows not to depose. Asked about the third article, he says that Isabel Spuret is the natural mother of the said Margery, but knows not to depose concerning the blood relationship between Juliana and Margery Spuret, and he knows well that Margery's mother strove for her advancement. Asked if Thomas surpassed the said Margery in wealth, renown, authority, esteem, or employment, concerning which matters the article was drawn up, he said that he well knew that he surpassed her in occupation because the craft he follows, that is the saddler's craft, he knows and understands well and he is trustworthy and of good repute, and he believes that the mother of the said Margery strives unduly for a marriage between her daughter and the said Thomas. Asked concerning the fourth article, he says that he believes that it contains the truth because the said Margery was wont to leave York each autumn for a month to reap the harvest for payment. She stayed with this witness up until the time with which the article is concerned and that autumn with which the article is concerned she left York about the feast of the Blessed Virgin

Mary to reap as stated before, but for what length of time she was away he knows not to depose...

Walter de Mellerby of York, saddler, 30 years of age and more, of free status and good standing, a blood relative or affine of neither party as he says, admitted, sworn, and diligently examined. Concerning the first and second articles he says that they contain the truth as he believes, otherwise he knows not to depose. Questioned on the third article, he says that he knows well that Isabel Spuret is the mother of the said Margery, but whether Juliana is a blood relative of the said Margery he knows not to depose. Also, asked, he says that Thomas does not surpass the said Margery in wealth, renown, authority, esteem, or employment as he knew that just as Thomas is able to gain his livelihood from his craft so also can the same Margery from her service. Asked about the fourth article, he says that it contains the truth and he knows this because the said Margery was at the time with which the article is concerned the servant of Thomas Hornby, senior and she made an agreement with her master that he would allow her to absent herself for a month each autumn and the same Margery in the autumn about which the article is concerned for a fortnight before the feast of the nativity of the Blessed Mary about which the article is concerned and on that feast and for a fortnight immediately following was absent outside the city of York. He knows this because this witness carried a jug with water from the River Ouse to his master's house for the whole of the aforesaid time, which duty the said Margery was wont to do when she was present in the city of York. Also, asked about the fifth article, he says that he knows not to depose. Also, questioned on the sixth article, he says that it contains the truth as he deposed above. He is neither bribed or suborned to depose.

[Following two depositions dated 16 March 1394.]

John de Akom of York, saddler, aged 20 years and more, of free status and good repute, a blood relative or affine of neither party as he says, admitted, sworn, and diligently examined on a certain exception given by Thomas' party against the recalled witnesses produced for Margery Spuret's party. He says that on the Saturday before the Sunday, about which was related in the aforesaid exception this witness, Thomas Gasegill, John Crayk, and the aforesaid Thomas Hornby went by mutual agreement in the afternoon of that Saturday from the city of York towards the village of Crayke to view the chattels which the said John Crayk's father left John in his last will. They passed the whole of that Saturday night in the village of Sutton and in the morning of the following Sunday they crossed to the aforesaid village of Crayke and there heard mass and eat, and after breakfast they crossed to the wood and there saw the chattels, which have been spoken of before. They returned to the village of Crayke and stayed a little while and afterwards returned towards York. When they came to Haxby three miles from the city of York it was night so that when they came to the city of York it was almost the tenth striking of the bell commonly called 'Clokke' and they sat in this witness' house for about an hour and drank. Afterwards his three companions left and this witness remained in his home. Also, asked, he says that the village of Crayke is about ten miles distant from York. Also, asked, he says that the said Thomas Hornby was away from the city of York and the home of Roger del Grene in York the whole time the whole of the Sunday in question counting from the middle of the night to the middle of the night other than for two hours as he deposed above. Also, asked, he says that justice should be done to each party.

Thomas Gasegill of York, saddler, aged 24 years and more, of free status and good standing...

[Deposes concerning journey to Crayke. Returned to York at night.]

[Following two depositions dated 18 March 1393–4.]

John Wyrsdall of York, barber, aged 30 years and more, of free status and good repute, a blood relative of the said Margery in the third degree of consanguinity as he says, admitted, sworn, and diligently examined. On the first article he says that it contains the truth and this he knows because he never heard or knew the said women witnesses reproved or attainted on any false crime or perjury and he knew the said Isabel for twenty-six years and more and the said Juliana for fifteen years and more. Also, asked among whom the said witnesses were reputed of good standing, he says among all people. Also, questioned on the second article, he says that it contains the truth and this he knows by what he has deposed above and he has never heard or known to the contrary for sure. Also, asked about the third article, he says that it contains the truth and this he knows because Isabel is an honest widow and lives honourably by the lawful and respectable labour of her own hands and Juliana is a wife and lives by the labour of her husband and of her own hands and for so long as he knew them they were considered and reputed trustworthy women. Also, questioned on the fourth article, he says that it contains the truth and this he knows because he knew the said women witnesses to be wealthy and honourable and he

knew the said Thomas to be a known pauper and burdened by debt and
he knew the said women witnesses about whom the article is con-cerned
to be honest and truthful and that they promoted the marriage as he
believes only in accordance with the truth. Also, asked, he says that the
said women have goods to the value of ten pounds as he believes. Also,
asked what kind of goods these are, he said that they were silver and
household utensils. Also, he says that they practise the craft called
'Kemstercraft'[6] and by this they live and obtain their sustenance and
the said Juliana also follows the craft of the saddler with her husband.
Also, asked, he says that the said Margery has goods to the value of
forty shillings and the said Thomas does not surpass her, as he
understands, in wealth, renown, authority or esteem and this he knows
by what he deposed above and that the said Margery is by descent well
born. Also, questioned about the fifth article, he says that it contains
the truth as he knows that the second Sunday after the nativity of the
Blessed Virgin Mary five years ago towards night the witnesses, about
whom the article relates, came to this witness' house and told him how
the said Thomas contracted marriage with the said Margery on that
Sunday shortly after midday in the house of Roger Grene of York, they
being present and cognisant. He knows not otherwise to depose on
this article other than from the account of those witnesses...

Robert Polayn, tapiter of York, aged 20 years and more, of free status
and good standing...

[Deposes that he knew Isabel eight years and Juliana twenty or more
years, otherwise similar to previous deposition.]

... Isabel and Juliana surpass the said Thomas in goods to the value of
twelve marks and he says that the said Isabel and Juliana never unduly
promoted marriage between the said Thomas and Margery as he
believes...

[Following three depositions dated 20 March 1394.]

John Wyrsedall...

... on the Sunday in question towards night he saw the said Thomas
present in the city of York in a place called 'Stalage' in the parish of St
Michael next Ouse Bridge. The said Margery's mother asked this
witness and Richard Wyresdall, his fellow witness, to come to the
above place at the above time to see how much they liked the said
Thomas as a person and, when he saw the said Thomas, it seemed to

6 I.e. carding wool.

this witness that the said Thomas was quite young to take a wife. Nevertheless this witness said that if this contract of marriage turned out suitable and pleasing to the said Margery and her friends, he wished to give them a horn decorated with silver worth twenty shillings. Cecily, the wife of this witness was present there with this witness and others, but as to the contract of marriage made between the aforesaid parties he knows not to depose other than by the account of those witnesses who were present there. As to the said Thomas' absence at the village of Crayke on the aforesaid Sunday, he says knows not to depose whether he was in the village of Crayke on the aforesaid Sunday, but he says that he could have been in Crayke at dawn of that Sunday and have come to the city of York by two o'clock in the afternoon of that Sunday...

Richard Wyresdall of York, aged 40 years and more, of free status and good standing, a blood relative of Margery in the third degree of consanguinity, admitted, sworn, and examined on a certain replication etc., says that it contains the truth and this he knows because he was present in the city of York that Sunday, about which there is mention, in the house of John Wyresdall, his fellow witness. After vespers he went with John and his wife towards Castlegate, York to talk with Isabel Spuret, Margery, and the aforesaid Thomas about the contract of marriage and when they came to a certain place called 'Stalage' they met there Isabel, Margery, and the aforesaid Thomas, and the said John Wyresdall's wife pointed out the said Thomas Hornby to them and the said John Wyresdall said that if this marriage pleased him, he would give them a horn ornamented with silver. Whether said Thomas was in the village of Crayke that Sunday he knows not to depose...

Margaret Esyngwald of York, aged 40 years and more, of free condition and good standing...

... she says that on the said Sunday in question she heard vespers in the church of the Blessed Virgin Mary in Castlegate, York and, vespers over, she came to Roger del Grene's house, in which Juliana del Grene was then lying sick and this witness had care of the same Juliana, and she found in the said house the said Thomas, Margery, the sick Juliana, and Ellen, the sister of the said Margery and she saw them eating and drinking there and she spoke with them...

[Following three depositions dated 19 February 1394.]

Thomas Menston, goldsmith, of York, aged 30 years and more, of free status and good repute, an affine of the said Beatrix [de Gilling] because he took to wife her sister, admitted, sworn, and diligently examined on the first article, says that it contains the truth and this he knows because he was present in his own room on the Wednesday immediately following the feast of St Katherine the virgin last when the said Beatrix and Thomas contracted marriage together in this manner, the man saying, 'I wish to have you to my wife and to this I plight you my troth', the woman replying, 'I wish to have you to my husband and to this I plight you my troth'... Asked who was present at the time of this contract, he says that Sir Thomas Hawden, a monk of Selby, this witness' wife, and no others were present at this contract.

Alice Menston, wife of the aforesaid Thomas, aged 30 years and more, of free status and good standing, sister of the said Beatrix, admitted, sworn, and diligently examined on the first article, says that it contains the truth and this she knows because she was present...

[As before.]

John Raghton of York, servant of the said Thomas Menston, his fellow witness...

[As before.]

[Report in parish of St Martin, Coney Street and other York parishes.]

[Following two depositions dated 23 July 1394.]

Joan Acok of Haxby, aged 60 years and more, of free condition...

[Evidence concerning journey to Crayke.]

William Helperby of Haxby, aged 24 years, of free status and good standing...

[Following four depositions dated 29 July 1394.]

John Wright, alias Banke of Crayke, aged 25 years...

William Fayrpoynt, wright, of Crayke, aged 40 years...

John Lambard of Crayke, aged 40 years...

Adam Mouthayte of Crayke, aged 40 years and more...

[Following two depositions dated 2 August 1394.]

John de Acom, saddler, 30 years [sic]...

Thomas Gasgyll of York, saddler, aged 26 years...

## 25. Church court, York.

Language: Latin. Translated from BIHR, CP.F.127. Margaret Barker, living with John Marshall, tailor c. John Waryngton, servant of John Bown, cordwainer.

[Following two depositions dated 21 May 1417.]

John Gamesby of the parish of St Helen, Stonegate, York, aged 40 years of free condition and related neither by blood or marriage nor ties of service to either party, as he says, called, sworn as witness, and diligently examined in respect of the present annexed articles. Asked about the first and second articles read out to him, he said that at the time and in the week that the assize and delivery was held at York castle of his certain knowledge, the which assizes were, as far as he can now recall, in the first week of Lent last, that is the Monday of that week as far as he can recall, after the lunch hour about six o'clock in the early evening, candles were brought in the home of John Bown, cordwainer of York. In the presence of this witness, the said John Bown, his wife, and their servant named, he believed, Agnes, John Waryngton and Margaret Barker proferred words of marriage in the following manner: the said John Waryngton took the said Margaret by the right hand and spoke first thus, 'I take you Margaret here as my wedded wife for better or worse, etc., and to this I plight my troth.' The said Margaret replying at once to John said, 'I take you John here as my wedded husband for better or worse, etc., and to this I plight my troth.' These words were exchanged according to the instruction and prior recital of the aforesaid John Bown. Asked if the said John was compelled by fear or threats to contract with the said Margaret as described, he said that on the Sunday immediately before the said Monday John Bown, master to the said John Waryngton, in John's absence, told this witness how the same John Waryngton, his servant, had known carnally a woman, his aforesaid servant, in his aforesaid home. He said that he had made John swear on a book that he would not so misbehave again with any female servant of his in his aforesaid home. Despite this promise he had again found the said John Waryngton alone with the said Margaret in a suspicious place, that is in an upper room in his aforesaid home where hay lies. He believed that John had known Margaret carnally in that place. For this reason John Bown asked this witness for advice, what best he should do with the said John Waryngton, and if it were better to have John put in the prison known as the Kydcot in York. This witness then advised the said John Bown that he should think carefully about such an action, and that he should first talk with John Waryngton and see if he was willing to have Margaret for his wife. On that said Monday night, therefore, as before related, the said John Waryngton appeared before this witness, the said John Bown, and his wife in their aforesaid home, Margaret also being there present. The said John, his master, asked him if he had had sex with the said Margaret, and if he had promised to marry her. John Waryngton then said that he had not known her carnally nor had he promised that he would marry her. The said Margaret then said the contrary was true, namely that the said John had promised to marry her. Then the same John said to Margaret and his said master that he had spoken to Margaret in the following manner: that the said John, his master, was able to make it so and be sufficiently good and generous to him that he would be willing to make Margaret a wife and do honour to her so far as he was able. Immediately after this the said John Bown repeated to John the transgressions committed by the said John Waryngton within his dwellinghouse as before related and how he was able for that reason to have John Waryngton substantially burdened and punished according to the common law. He said that if he was then willing to have and to take the said Margaret as his wife, then he would have done the major part of the amends for the aforesaid transgressions. Then John Bown, his master, asked John Waryngton if he would have the said Margaret for his wife. John stood for a short time without replying, then he said to his master, 'You are able to be so good and so generous towards me and can show me favour such that you can make me more willing to betroth and have her to my wife.' Then the said John, his master, said to John, 'You will take her by the hand and you will say as I say to you.' Then the said John Waryngton said, 'By my faith, if my father and other of my friends[7] were present here now, I would neither betroth her nor take her to be my wife.' Afterwards, as this witness says, the said John Waryngton, because he feared that his master would hand him over and have him committed to prison for his transgressions done within the dwellinghouse of his master as before related, for this reason and for no other cause as he firmly believes in his conscience to be true, the said John Waryngton spoke the words and contracted marriage as before related. He can say no more about these articles as he says. Asked concerning the last article, he says that he has nothing to add to what he has already said. He is neither guided, directed, corrupted nor instructed, but seeks only that there be justice done between the parties involved in this cause as he says on oath.

7 I.e. family.

Margaret Bown aged 30 years and more, of free condition and related neither by blood nor marriage to any party, save that John Waryngton, whom this cause concerns, is the servant of John Bown, husband to this witness, as she says, was called and sworn as witness and diligently examined in respect of the present annexed articles. Asked about the first and second articles that were read to her, she said that one Monday after dinner, which precise hour she could not remember, after the feast of the Purification of the Blessed Virgin Mary last, though she could not remember how much time or how many weeks after that festival, in the home of this witness and of her aforesaid husband, being in the parish of St Martin in Coney Street, York, the aforesaid John Waryngton and Margaret Barker exchanged words of matrimony and contracted together in the following manner: taking the said Margaret by the right hand at the instance of the said John Bown, his master, John spoke first thus, 'I take you Margaret here as my wife to have and to hold in bed and in board for better or worse, and to this I plight my troth.' Margaret immediately replying to John said, 'I take you John here as my husband and to this I plight my troth.' So they were handfast in the presence and hearing of this witness, her said husband, John Gamesby, her fellow witness, the said parties, and no others. Asked how the said parties came to this contract and whether the said John was compelled or moved by fear to contract with the said Margaret as related, she said that on the aforesaid day at the aforesaid hour, John Bown, the master of the said John Waryngton, had caused John to be called and to come from his workshop into his house and the hall of his aforesaid house. His master then said to John before this witness, the said John Gamesby, and the said Margaret, 'You said yesterday when I told you the transgressions you had committed in my house and within my dwelling that to make amends you wished to do as I pleased and to place yourself at my will, and thus you have placed yourself to act according to my will. It is my will, therefore, that you here and now take and betroth before us Margaret Barker as your wife.' John Waryngton stood for a short time without replying, then he said at last, 'I have friends, who, were they here, I should not marry nor betroth Margaret as my wife on this occasion or at this time.' After a lengthy exchange of words between John and his said master, the master then said to him, 'Tell me, are you willing to have Margaret to your wife?' John then said to his master, 'You can make it so that you can make me more willing to have her to my wife.' John at length at the direction of his master thus took Margaret by the hand and contracted marriage with her against his will as before related. This witness, as she says, firmly believes in her conscience this to be true. She is prepared to swear this on the book though she should die now, as she says questioned on her oath, since she knows well that the said John Waryngton feared that if he had not then contracted marriage in the aforesaid manner to Margaret at the mandate of his said master, that his master would have had him imprisoned and otherwise punished according to the common law. This appeared clear to the said John Waryngton on account of certain transgressions committed by John within the dwellinghouse of his said master according to the allegation of his master who said that the said John had known his women servants carnally in his aforesaid house, and that he had found John and Margaret alone together in a suspect place the Sunday immediately before the said Monday, namely in a room where hay lay being in a remote part of his aforesaid dwellinghouse. If John Waryngton had known Margaret carnally after the said contract this witness knows not as she says, since it did not seem to this witness, as she says, that John was well disposed towards Margaret in that for about seven days after the said contract John said to this witness that his master had done ill towards him in making him betroth Margaret as his wife and contract marriage to her, and that he firmly believed that this marriage could not stand or be, since he was never of a mind to have her to his wife. She is unable to depose further on these articles, as she says, except that questioned on the last article she says that what she deposed above has long been and still is the common report and rumour in the aforesaid parish of St Martin. She is neither guided, directed, nor corrupted, and desires only that there be justice in this cause as she says.

[This last deposition is badly damaged.]

John Bown of the parish of St Martin in Coney Street, York, aged 30 years ... the master of the John Waryngton in question...

Questioned on the first and second articles read out to him, he says that in his home in the aforesaid parish of St Martin one Sunday within the time of Lent last, in the week before the middle week of the aforesaid Lent he now recalls, this witness went into a room where hay lay...

[Found John and Margaret alone together and suspected that they had had carnal intercourse together because of where he found them and because John had known another of his servants. He threatened John with force if he did not marry Margaret. Also told Richard Newland, the parish constable, and consulted John Gamesby. Swore 'upon all the books in the world' that John knew and feared what would happen if he did not marry Margaret.]

## 26. Church court, York.

Language: Latin. Translated from CP.F.104. Agnes Brignall of St Michael le Belfrey, York c. John Herford, alias Smyth of St Olave, York.

[The following depositions are dated 17 October 1432.]

Isabel Henryson of Bootham in the suburbs of York, aged 30 years and more, of free status and good standing, the natural and blood sister of Agnes Brignall...

Asked on the first and second articles put to her separately, she says that between eleven and twelve on Wednesday before Palm Sunday last, this witness was personally present in the hall of the said Agnes' home in Bootham together with Katherine Burton, her fellow witness, and the aforesaid Agnes and John Herford, the parties in this action, and none other, where and when the said John took and held the said Agnes by the right hand and spoke to her first in this manner, 'Here I take you Agnes to my wedded wife and to this I plight you my troth'. The same Agnes, replying without hesitation said likewise in this manner, 'Here I take you John to my wedded husband and to this I plight you my troth', and they then released their hands and kissed one another. Asked additionally, she says that at the time of saying the said words the said John, Agnes, and Katherine sat on the principal bench of the said house and this witness stood among them...

[Witness went on to describe colour of their clothes and that the group eat fish together at dinner time.]

And she says that the said day was bright clear considering the time of year. And asked further, she says that she believes for sure that John often knew Agnes carnally after the aforementioned words since this same witness often after that Wednesday found John and Agnes lying naked together in Agnes' bed. She also heard Agnes often say and swear by her faith that he knew her thus carnally...

Katherine Burton of Bootham in the suburbs of York aged 30 years and more...

[Deposes concerning contract as before.]

... she says that according to Agnes' telling, the same John often knew her carnally after that day. And she further says that this witness was personally present on various nights after the contract in Agnes Brignall's home and saw John undress and get into Agnes' bed saying he wished to spend the night there...

[The following deposition dated 18 October 1432 is slightly damaged.]

John Jameson, servant of John Burns of Bootham, York, smith, aged 24 years...

... immediately after sunset on Monday in Pentecost week last, Agnes Brignall, about whom the cause is concerned, asked this witness, who was standing at the doorway of his master's house, if he would go with her to John Herford's room [?to hear] the words spoken and said between them. This witness, as he says, then said that he was quite willing just as in fact, as he says, he [?went] with the same [ Agnes ?and ] came to John's room in a lane called New Lane in a street called St Marygate in the suburbs of the city of York. At Agnes' request he knocked on the door of the same room telling John, who was in the room, that he wished [?to speak] with him, and he says that immediately after, when John had opened the door, this witness and the said Agnes entered the room [...] that immediately after this entry and between the hours of nine and ten after the dinner hour of the said Monday, Agnes [...] to rehearse and explain to John Herford in the presence of this witness and no others how the same John had and held the same Agnes [ ?for some ] time in a fornicatory embrace. She asked John whether he was willing there and then to give her a formal answer [?whether] to take her as a wife or not. John replied to Agnes, as he says, and said it was not his intention [?to have] any other woman than Agnes for his wife. He then asked her had he not before that time made to her the security [?of an oath] on the matter in the presence of witnesses. She then said to him that these witnesses were merely women, therefore [?she asked him] whether he was willing to contract marriage with her in the presence of this witness. John said he would willingly do that and he then took Agnes by the right hand and, in the presence [ of this witness ] and no others, said to her first in this manner, 'Here I take you Agnes to be my wedded wife and to this I plight you my troth.' Agnes replied to John without hesitation and said in this manner, 'Here I take you John to my wedded husband and to this I plight you my troth'. They then let go their hands and kissed one another. Asked further, he says that John, in a leather doublet, Agnes in a blue gown, and this witness also in a blue garment, sat on John's bed at the time of saying the said words of matrimony. Asked, he says that he believes for sure that John often knew Agnes carnally after the said Monday, both because he says that immediately after the said contract, made as described, John put on his outer garment and went with this witness and the said Agnes to Agnes' home in Bootham and said that he wished to spend the night there with the same Agnes, and because he heard Agnes say and relate afterwards that he stayed and lay there the whole night with Agnes...

[The following depositions are dated 5 December 1432.]

Alexander Butler of Pontefract aged 40 years and more...

[Testimony of Isabel and Katherine is perjured as John Herford went with Robert Herford, a monk of St Mary's, York to Pontefract during the time of the alleged contract of marriage so that his employer could buy a horse at the fair there.]

Robert Beche of Pontefract, aged 30 years and more...

William Candy, alias Hostiler of Pontefract, aged 24 years...

William Moreton of Stamford Bridge, aged 30 years and more...

[Went with Ralph Fedirstane, bailiff of Catton, to sell horse in Pontefract on the Saturday and saw John Herford there.]

William Crake of Pocklington, aged 40 years and more...

Thomas Midelham of St Mary's Abbey, York aged 50 years and more... This witness and said John were and are servants within the said abbey...

And he says, asked further, that for the space of sixteen years past this witness had notice of Agnes Brignall, about whom this cause is concerned, and Isabel Henryson her sister, about whom the article is concerned, and for the whole of that time, as he says, Isabel was and still is a household member and well known to be living with the said Agnes her sister. Asked further, he says that he often heard it said by several men and women, residents of the city of York and its suburbs, that John Willerdby of York, a married man, held the same Isabel for many years in the embrace of adultery and procreated three or four children by her. Asked further, he says that Katherine Burton, about whom the article is concerned, was and is still of ill repute and low standing in that according to common talk of others one Sir John Webster, vicar choral of the cathedral church of York, and several other chaplains and married and unmarried men knew her carnally in the embrace of adultery and fornication...

[Deposes that John was in Pontefract at time of the alleged contract.]

William Fox of the parish of St Olave in the suburbs of York, barber, aged 30 years and more...

[Deposes concerning report of affair between John Willerdby and Isabel Henryson.]

### 27. Act book, Dean and Chapter, York.

Language: Latin. Translated from YML, M2(1)f.

[a] [1363] William Trumpour fornicated with Joan de Gyldesum: both appear on 6 July the aforesaid year. She confessed the article and abjured the sin on penalty of six whippings. She has three whippings for her confession. The woman said that the man betrothed her and promised to marry her as his wife. The man denied this on oath and immediately after promised on oath that if he should henceforth know her carnally, he would thereafter have her and hold her as his wife. The woman likewise promised that if hereafter she should allow him to know her carnally, she would have him as her husband.

[b] [1381] Thomas Tavel, parchmentmaker, fornicated recidivously with Ibbot Leche: both appear before the penultimate of March in the year of Our Lord 1381 to purge themselves six-handed. The woman appeared on that day. She confessed the article and abjured the sin on penalty of standing with a candle in the manner of a penitent at the font of St John del Pyke for twelve Sundays, and she has six days for her confession.

The same Thomas fornicated with Ellen de Eskryk, servant of Thomas Parcheminner. They both appear on 29 March. He denies the article and has Saturday or Monday next to purge himself six-handed. Asked, he claims a contract of marriage between them before witnesses. 4 April the said Thomas and Ellen appear. They confess the article. They abjure the sin on penalty of going in the manner of a penitent in front of the procession of the church of York for six Sundays and six whippings around the church...

[c] Deposition of Alice, wife of Adam de Baumburght. Date: 1381.

... On Monday night before the feast of the Ascension last she came to a certain high room located inside the dwellinghouse of the said witness where she found, as she says, Robert and Agnes lying alone together in one bed. The witness asked Robert, 'What are you doing here,

Robert?' To this Robert replied, 'I'm here already'. The witness said to him, 'Take Agnes by the hand in order to betroth her'. Robert said to the witness, 'I beg you wait until the morning'. The witness said to him in reply, 'By God, no. You'll do it now'. Then Robert took Agnes by the hand and said, 'I will take you as my wife'. The witness said to him, 'You will speak in this manner: I take you Agnes to my wife and to this I plight you my troth', and Robert, thus instructed by the witness, took Agnes by the right hand and contracted with her using the words just recited, viz. 'Here I take you etc.'. Asked how Agnes replied to Robert, she said that Agnes replied to him that she considered herself satisfied. She did not depose further save that she went away and left them alone...

[d] [1399] John Esyngwald fornication with one Elizabeth Snawe. They appeared in court as husband and wife 15 February. The man contracted with her speaking these words, 'I take you Elizabeth to my wife and to this I plight you my troth'. The woman replied, 'I take you to my husband and to this I plight you my troth'. The man swore touching the holy gospels that he would solemnise this contract made between them when all obstacles had been withdrawn before the feast of St Mark the Evangelist next.

## 28. Church court, deanery of Droitwich.

Language: Latin. Date: 1300. Translated from F. S. Pearson, ed., 'Records of a ruridecanal court of 1300' in S. G. Hamilton, ed., *Collectanea*, Worcestershire Historical Society, 1912.

[a] Peter de la Holyok fornicated with Isabel Ketel. The man appears, confesses, and is whipped in the usual manner. The man went away. The woman is ill.

[b] Richard the servant of Henry de Wrodenhal fornicated recidivously with Isabel the daughter of Sontassa. Both are commanded to purge themselves six-handed. The man is not purged. The woman purges herself.

[c] Walter Peperwyt fornicated recidivously a third time with Agnes de Malverne. It is pending before the bishop.

[d] John the son of Nicholas the clerk fornicated recidivously with Julia Redes. Both appear, confess, and are whipped once in the usual way through the market. The woman is pregnant.

## 29. Church court, archdeaconry of Buckingham.

Language: Latin. Translated from Elvey, ed., *The Courts of the Archdeaconry of Buckingham.*

[a] [1491] John Godyng and Agnes his wife for illicit sex between Thomas Godyng their son and another woman. They appeared and deny the article. They were ordered to purge themselves four-handed shortly. Afterwards they purged themselves and are dismissed.

[b] [1520] ... John Blakhed alias Oveyate of Leighton Buzzard appeared and said that he had contracted marriage with one Alice Jakeman of Wing. This same Alice, here present in the court, denied such a marriage. Because the said John Blakhed lacked sufficient and lawful proofs of the marriage, the judge on John's petition took the oath of Alice Jakeman, who swore a corporal oath that she had never agreed to such a contract of marriage other than on condition that he was able to have and gain the particular agreement and approval of the said Alice's father, and so the judge left each party to their own consciences.

## 30. Church court, Lincoln.

Language: Latin. Translated from M. Bowker, ed., *An Episcopal Court Book for the Diocese of Lincoln 1514-1520*, Lincoln Record Society, LXI, 1967.

[a] [1517] ... John Uncle of Bolingbroke confessed that he had known carnally Alice Richardson and Joan Barowe, sisters by the same father, and had begotten and procreated several children by each of them and consequently he submitted himself for correction by the reverend father.

[b] [1517] ... Alice Ridyng, unmarried, the daughter of John Ridyng of Eton in the diocese of Lincoln appeared in person and confessed that she conceived a boy child by one Thomas Denys, then chaplain to Master Geoffrey Wren, and gave birth to him at her father's home at Eton one Sunday last month and immediately after giving birth, that is within four hours of the birth, killed the child by putting her hand in the baby's mouth and so suffocated him. After she had killed the child she buried it in a dung heap in her father's orchard. At the time of the delivery she had no midwife and nobody was ever told as such that she was pregnant, but some women of Windsor and Eton had suspected and said that she was pregnant, but Alice always denied this saying that something else was wrong with her belly. On the Tuesday after the delivery of the child, however, the women and honest wives

of Windsor and Eton took her and inspected her belly and her breasts by which they knew for certain that she had given birth. She then confessed everything to them and showed them the place where she had put the dead child. She said further that neither her father nor her mother ever knew that she was pregnant since she always denied it until she was taken by the wives as described. Examined further she said by virtue of the oath she had taken on the gospels that she had never been known carnally by anyone other than the said Thomas and that nobody else urged or agreed to the child's death. She also said that the child had been conceived on the feast of the Purification of the Blessed Virgin Mary last at the time of high mass in the house of Master Geoffrey Wren at Spytell where Master Geoffrey was then infirmarer.

[c] [1519] ... John Asteley [rector of Shepshed] confessed that he had made Agnes Walles, unmarried, pregnant and that she had given birth to a girl child at Hauxley before Christmas. He had supported the child there from his tithes. He also confessed that he had made pregnant Margaret Swynerton, unmarried, and had had three children by her. Margaret is now dead. He also had another child by one Joan Chadwyk, now married, then single. Joan lives at Dunstable. John does not know where Agnes lives now. Because of he confessed these things ... the vicar general ordered that from henceforth no other woman should serve in his home and that he should live continently.

[d] [1520] Agnes Plumrige of Fingerst, the wife of John Plumrige, appeared and confessed that she had been known and made pregnant by her husband before their marriage. The bishop ordered her to go round her neighbours on the feast of the Purification of Mary openly carrying a candle costing four pence.

31. Visitations, diocese of Lincoln.

Language: Latin. Translated from A. Hamilton Thomson, ed., *Visitations in the Diocese of Lincoln 1517-1531*, I, Lincoln Record Society, XXXIII, 1940.

[a] [1518] Alconbury... Edward Kyng has in his house a woman who is the object of suspicion. Henry Man and Christopher Walton's wife are suspected of adultery.

[b] [1518] St Ives. Agnes Haward, wife of John Haward was made pregnant before the solemnisation of the marriage between herself and her husband by John Wiks of Ramsey.

[c] [1518] Bringhurst. Sir Robert Worthington made pregnant his servant Alice. The same vicar previously begot two children by one Elizabeth his servant to his great shame. The mother gave birth in his vicarage.

[d] [1518] Ashby-de-la-Zouche... One Amy Barton of the same, unmarried, became pregnant there.

[e] [1519] Amersham... John Denton keeps company with Alice Fulmer and has done so for the past year, and he is said to have betrothed her last year, but does not want to have it solemnised.

[f] [1519] Surfleet... A baby boy was turned away at the door of Thomas Leeke, but his mother claimed that Thomas Leeke was the father of this baby. Thomas, however, denied this and so the baby was taken away to different places, ill treated, and died.

[g] [1519] Baumber... They say also that one Robert Burwhite betrothed one Alice, formerly a servant with Richard Sawcoen of the same parish, and she lives suspectly in the same Richard's house. They refuse to solemnise marriage at the church door.

[h] [1519] Grainthorpe. Thomas Dam slandered Isabel Gremmesby so that William Pennyngton will not have her for his wife.

[i] [1519] Sutton in the Marsh... Sir John Wymark, lately chaplain there, made Margaret Haburgh pregnant and ... [record damaged] she gave birth [to a baby]. The same Sir John threw the baby in the sea and so killed it. She now lives in Kesteven.

[j] [1519] Walesby... Isabel, the servant of Master Wichecote is pregnant and, it is believed, by the same Master Whichecote.

[k] [1519] Owmby. George Turvey made Joan Hudson pregnant whilst his servant... The said Joan still lives in the said George's home with him.

[l] [1519] Waddingham St Peter's. The rector has a certain old woman in his house together with two young cousins... These women of the said rector are, however, said to be of quite sound repute and honest living.

## 32. Visitations, diocese of Lincoln.

Language: Latin. Date: 1530. Translated from A. Hamilton Thomson, ed., *Visitations in the Diocese of Lincoln 1517-1531*, II, Lincoln Record Society, XXXV, 1944.

[a] On the same day and in the same place [i.e. 23 May, 1530 in Dunstable Priory] Joan Bodyngton appeared and alleged in an oral statement that she had contracted marriage with one Hugh Bodyngton then present and that they had lived together for the space of three years and that she had begot two children by him. The said Hugh admits the aforesaid. The bishop then asked him if he had any reason to put forward why he should not be made to receive her as his wife and treat her with marital affection, and he said he had various reasons. The bishop then directed him to appear on Wednesday, that is the 22nd day of the month of June in the hospital church of St John, Northampton.

[b] Harpenden. John Hunt lives incontinently with Joan Willys his servant... Afterwards they appeared at the priory of St Giles and confessed that they had contracted marriage together.

Also that we charge you that you gave the said woman advice and persuaded her to take and drink certain drinks to destroy the child that she is with.[8] The bishop instructed him to appear the next day at the priory of St Giles and he confessed that he had known her carnally. The bishop directed them that on a Sunday that the vicar general would assign they were to do public penance in a penitential manner before the cross at Harpenden and that they should have their marriage solemnised as soon as they conveniently could. He ruled that under pain of excommunication they should not live incontinently until their marriage was solemnised.

[c] Gaddesden. Thomas Clarke confesses that he had known Agnes Dryvar carnally around Michaelmas and made her pregnant, but he denies that he had contracted marriage with her. The bishop ordered that as soon as he were able he see that the child was supported. The bishop directed the said Agnes to go before the procession on the next Sunday after the [feast of] the Purification in a penitential manner bearing a burning candle in her hand and give the candle into the priest's hand at the time of the offertory.

8 This follows immediately from the previous entry and represents a charge made by the bishop to John Hunt in respect of Joan Willys. The second part of this sentence is in English, but the remainder of the text is Latin.

[d] [St Peter-le-Bailey, Oxford] Widow [*uxor*] Colls receives pregnant women in her home in which they are cared for. Widow [*uxor*] Gybscott is a common defamer of her neighbours.

[e] [Stokenchurch] Joan Schower it is reported was made pregnant by one William Hewes. Midwives examined her to see whether she was or not and having examined her they concluded that she was not pregnant. The aforesaid Joan, however, told the midwives that she had been known carnally by the said William and had become pregnant, but she took a potion by which means she obtained an abortion. She previously had two children for which offence she had not yet been punished at all.

### 33. Visitations, archdeaconry of Buckingham.

Language: Latin. Translated from Elvey, ed., *The Courts of the Archdeaconry of Buckingham.*

[a] [1489] Parish of Langley. Alice [  ] servant with Edmund Nasshenden because she lately gave birth to a child and does not know who the father is. She went away.

[b] [1489] Great Missenden... Richard Egleton because he made pregnant a woman servant of his father. He is let off and dismissed.

[c] [1494] Brill. Joan Baron publicly defamed of the sin of fornication done, it is said, with one [  ] Trussell. She appeared and denied the article and purged herself with Elizabeth Forster, Elina Godynton, Alice Fuller, and Alice Pym. A proclamation was made etc. and because no opposer lawfully appeared, the judge admitted her to her purgation and restored her to her good standing and she was dismissed.

[d] [1497] Newton Blossomville. Alice Mortyn gave birth to a child in the house of the rector there, but the father of the child is not known and, it is said, immediately after the birth the said Alice hid the child in the bog where the child died for want.

### 34. Bishop's register, Salisbury.

Language: Latin. Calendared translation by Horn in J. M. Horn, ed., *The Register of Robert Hallum, Bishop of Salisbury 1407-17*, Canterbury and York Society, LXXII, 1982.

[a] Notorial instrument confirming the dispensation granted by Anthony de Pireto M.Th., minister general of the friars minor, nuncio of Pope John XXIII in England, to Thomas Hulle of Britford and Emmota Randolf of the diocese of Salisbury ... permitting them to marry although they are related in the third and fourth degrees of consanguinity...

[b] [Acta contained in register. Date: 1408]
...

On this day William Sawser and his sister Alice appeared before the bishop, having been summoned to appear by William Broun, chaplain, and together with the defendant, William Roper, they swore on the gospels to speak the truth. Then, when William Roper was asked whether Agnes was his wife, or whether he had lawfully contracted marriage with her, he replied yes. Also whether he was known as her consort, he replied yes. Asked whether he was known as consort to Alice Sawser, he replied yes. Asked whether he had made a pre-contract with her before his marriage with Agnes, he replied no. Asked why he formerly went through a divorce from Agnes, whether he consented willingly to this or not, he replied that it had never been his will, but he had done it through fear, at the advice of certain people. Alice Sawser, asked whether William Roper had contracted marriage with her and was her husband, replied yes. Asked in what words he contracted marriage with her, she replied, 'I William take you as my wife, on account of the scandal which you have endured, being pregnant by me', and she had said, 'I take you as my husband'. Asked who had been present, she said three people, of whom two had died...

[At a later hearing] ... there appeared the said parties and with them John Netterlanus, who had been summoned by the rector of St John, Devizes, mandatory, to give evidence in the case. He swore in the legal way to speak the truth, and said that he had known William Roper for about twenty years. He said he was not present when William contracted marriage with Agnes, although he had been present at the solemnisation because he was then in William's service, and Agnes had been continually in William's house for two years. He was not present at the alleged pre-contract between William and Alice, although once in Lent when William could not for conscience's sake have carnal relations with Alice, he heard him say, 'Do not worry, Alice. I will always love you and never send you away,' however he did not promise this with an oath...

### 35. Papal letter.

Language: Latin. Date: 1391. Calendared translation in *Calendar of Papal Registers*, IV.

To the bishop of Lichfield. Mandate, at the petition also of King Richard, to absolve, a salutary penance being imposed, William de Hypsconys, donsel, and Maud Swyninton, alias Pesal, damsel, from the sentence of excommunication which they have incurred by marrying in a certain private chapel, and without banns, knowing that they were related on both sides in the third degree of kindred. They are to be separated for a time, and are then to be dispensed to remarry, past and future offspring being declared legitimate. Whichever of the two survive the other shall remain perpetually unwed.

### 36. Court of King's Bench.

Language: Latin. Date: 1316. Translated from Arnold, ed., *Select Cases of Trespass*.

... He says in fact that the aforesaid Isabel, whom the aforesaid William [de Cornwall] claims to be his wife, on the aforesaid day and year about which he complains was the same Semeine's wife solemnly joined in marriage to this Semeine, which same Isabel was single at the time of agreeing the contract of marriage between herself and Semeine and in the days and years previous living in Great Yarmouth and was thought of as single. After she and the same Semeine mutually consented to contract marriage between them, banns of marriage were therefore solemnly published in the parish church of the town of Great Yarmouth, which publication neither the aforesaid William nor anyone else reclaimed or challenged. The same Semeine after an interval of time thus publicly and solemnly married her at the aforesaid church door and he had and held her as his lawful wife by reason of the aforesaid marriage for a year and more until the aforesaid William came to these parts and moved a cause against Semeine and Isabel in order to pronounce a divorce[9] between them by reason of a precontract of marriage which he alleged he, William, had made with the aforesaid Isabel, which same cause William prosecuted to the extent that a divorce was pronounced between them for that reason etc. He seeks judgement, therefore, whether an action by the same William against Semeine by this kind of writ [for abduction] is proper in this case etc.

9 I.e. an annulment.

And William says that the aforesaid Isabel on the aforesaid day and year was his wife staying in his company until the aforesaid Semeine abducted her with his goods...[10]

### 37. Wills, diocese of York.

Language: Latin.

[a] Will of Thomas Neleson, merchant, York. Date: 1478. Translated from BIHR, Prob. Reg. 5 fo. 212v.

Also I give and leave for the marriage of poor maidens through my executors below written well and faithfully to be distributed where greater need shall be, £20.

[b] Will of Emma, wife of Henry Preston, merchant, York. Date: 1401. Translated from BIHR, Prob. Reg. 3 fo. 60v.

Also I leave to Alice Stede if she will stay and remain an honest virgin and of good repute until she shall have a husband, that then she shall have five marks to her marriage, but in the event that ignorantly or heedlessly she shall commit fornication or adultery, that she shall have only two marks and 6s 8d...

### 38. Coroners' rolls, Bedfordshire.

Language: Latin. Date: 1270. Translation in Hunnisett, ed., *Bedfordshire Coroners' Rolls.*

Late in the night ... Simon and Richard, sons of Hugh the Fisher of Radwell, came from the house of Alice, Hugh's daughter, towards that of their father in Ashwell. They wished to cross the courtyard of Robert Ball of Radwell, in which Simon, son of Agnes of Rawell, and Juliana, daughter of Walter the Fisher of Radwell, were lying under a haystack. Simon immediately got up and struck Simon the Fisher on the top of his head to the brain, apparently with an axe, so that he instantly died. Richard on seeing this raised the hue and fled. Simon the felon fled and Juliana with him...

---

10 The Latin is 'rapuit', which might be rendered as 'raped', or more affectedly as 'ravished', but there is no hint here that rape in its modern sense is implied. Unfortunately the contemporary record does not always allow such distinctions, blurred as they are in medieval legal thought, to be made.

### 39. Manor court, Halesowen.

Language: Latin. Translated from Wilson, ed., *Court Rolls of the Manor of Hales*.

[a] [1281] Amercement 6*d.* Juliana Bele le Peyneresse amerced for leyrwite. Pledge.

[b] [1300] Juliana the daughter of Richard of Illey gives to the lord twenty-two pence for a marriage licence. She pays at once and consequently does not find pledges.

[c] [1301] Leyrwite. Agnes the daughter of Juliana de Hulle has been violated by the carter of Blakeley.[11] Therefore she will make amends to the lord.

12*d.* Agnes the daughter of John Oniot gives the lord 12*d* for a leyrwite fine. Thomas de la Grete and Henry Oniet pledges.

Distraint. Maud de Edwineshull, a deflowered bondwoman, for leyrwite.

[d] [1301] Maud de Edwineshull made fine of 16*d* with the lord for leyrwite. Thomas Esquier pledge.

[e] [1293] Clement the son of Alexander of Kenelmstowe gives to the lord half a mark to have a licence to marry Emma the daughter of Thomas le Chauner who is the heiress of Maud de Fulfen and to hold her tenement as other customary tenants hold. He found pledges for the aforesaid fine, for the upkeep of the holding, and for the service to be performed for it, viz. Thomas le Esquier and Richard de Edwineshull. The aforesaid Emma came into court and made the aforesaid Clement her attorney. Seisin. Fealty. The same Clement received seisin of the aforesaid holding and did fealty to the lord.

### 40. Manor court, Littleport.

Language: Latin. Date: 1319. Translated from F. W. Maitland and W. P. Baildon, eds., *The Court Baron*, Selden Society, IV, 1891.

It is found by inquest that John de Elm unjustly detains 6*d* of his daughter's dowry from Henry Shepherd.

---

11 'Violated' probably indicates simple fornication and consequent loss of virginity rather than sexual assault.

## 41. Manor court rolls, Tottenham (Bruces).

Language: Latin. Date: 1389. Translation in R. Oram, trans., *Court Rolls of the Manors of Bruces, Dawbeneys, Pembrokes (Tottenham)*, II.

William Bussh surrendered into the lord's hands a messuage with a garden and two acres of land lying in his field called 'Homefeld' on the north part with reservation to the said William of the moiety of the grange on the west part. And the lord thereof grants seisin to the aforesaid William and Katherine Newman whom he takes as wife, to hold to them and the heirs of the aforesaid William by the verge at the will of the lord without prejudice etc. doing services etc. They give to the lord of fine to have entry 3s 4d and do fealty.

## 42. Manor court, Ingoldmells.

Language: Latin. Translation by Massingberd in W. O. Massingberd, trans., *Court Rolls of the Manor of Ingoldmells in the County of Lincolnshire*, London, 1902.

[a] [1303] From Ellen Turs for licence to marry within the manor with five acres of bond land 10s, William Abald pledge.

[b] [1387] Joan Brok, a freewoman holding by villein tenure, has licence to marry William Osmound, and gives to the lord for licence, 40d.

[c] [1401] Christiana Polayn, a bondwoman of the lord, has licence to marry without the lordship etc. Merchet, 6s 8d.

[d] [1404] The presenters present that Agnes, daughter of William Kemp, a bondwoman of the lord, has been seduced etc., also that Beatrice, daughter of Alan Godard, a bondwoman of the lord has been seduced by John Ward, chaplain, therefore etc... Mercy, 3s.

[e] [1411] Also that Ellen, daughter of Robert Godard, a bond-woman of the lord, was seduced by John de Candilesby, chaplain, and the said John gives to the lord for the aforesaid seduction by the pledge of John Ward, vicar of the church of Mumby ... [and two others]. Leyrwyte, 6s 8d.

[f] [1492] Also that Beatrice Bodik, a bondwoman of the lord, has been deflowered by Henry Thory, therefore she is in mercy, and nevertheless it is ordered to levy [   ] from the said Beatrice for leyrwite.

## 43. Manor court, Wellington.

Language: Latin. Translation by Humphreys in A. L. Humphreys, trans., *Materials for the History of the Town and Parish of Wellington in the County of Somerset*, London, 1910.

[a] [1277] Sibyl, who was the wife of John in the Alre, gives to the lord £6 13s 4d that she be able to marry herself within the manor whenever she pleases, one part to be paid at the Purification of the Blessed Mary and the other part at Easter, by the pledge of Walter de Whiteheie, Reginald Hurchel, William de Forde. And it is granted by the steward and by the assent of the aforesaid Sibyl, that, because Walter de Whitheie shall pay the aforesaid fine, when the aforesaid Sibyl shall have married herself, the same Walter shall be able to hold the aforesaid tenement until he shall have levied the aforesaid ten marks.

[b] [1342] Thomas atte Mere (2d) and William atte Mere (2d) in mercy because they did not have Joan atte Mere, the lord's bondwoman, to make a fine because she married herself outside the manor without licence. And let her be distrained to be at the next to make [fine] etc.

[c] [1383] Katherine, daughter of John Tylyhey gives a fine of 20s for licence to marry and dwell where she pleases within the lordship of the lord or without so that henceforth she may not be molested or challenged because of villeinage for ever, by pledge of John Tylyhey.

[d] [1464] And, as many times, the whole homage with the next blood is ordered to inquire against the next [court] to whom the two daughters of Richard Buckewell, the lord's villein by blood, are married without licence at Exeter, and also it is ordered to inquire concerning the names both of the men and of the women against the next [court] under pain of 40d.

# III: Husband and wife

*See also 'Adolescence' [24] deposition of John Wyrsdall; 'Widowhood, poverty, and old age' [13] deposition of Maud Katersouth.*

## 1. Poll tax, Carlisle.

Language: Latin. Date: 1377. Translated from J. L. Kirby and A. D. Kirby, 'The poll-tax of 1377 for Carlisle', *Transactions of the Cumberland and Westmorland Antiquarian and Archaeological Society*, new ser. LVIII, 1959, p. 116.

...

William de Karlton, senior, and his wife
his daughter
William his servant

William Sadiller and his wife

John de Skaleby and his wife

Robert de Strayte and his wife
Thomas his servant

John Julson and his wife

widow Sundirland[1]

Adam Emson and his wife

William Carnfox and his wife
Henry his servant

Thomas Carnfox

Mariota de Esyngwald

John Gayte and his wife
Thomas his servant

Richard de Carruthires and his wife

John de Lyland and his wife

Margaret Allerdale
Agnes de Burgh

John de Kyrkby and his wife

1 *Uxor* Sundirland.

Henry ⎫
Isabel ⎬ his servants

Adam Idwyne

Margaret Launder

Mariota Mawer
Alice with her in the house

William Pan

John de Boelton and his wife

Emma de Hardgill

Joan Jestour

Christinana Ra

Alan de Blenerhayset and his wife
Margaret de Layburne
James
Joky [sic] ⎬ his servants
Margaret ⎭

John Post and his wife
Mounce

William Dobson and his wife
Christiana his servant

Isabel Waferer

William Waite

Gilbert Pepis and his wife

...


## 2. Borough ordinances.

Translated from M. Bateson, ed., *Borough Customs*, I, Selden Society, XVIII (1904).

[a] Salford. Language: Latin. Date: c. 1230.

Also, anyone can plead for his wife and his family and anyone's wife can pay rent to the reeve doing what ought to be done, and follow a plea on behalf of her husband if by chance he were away.

[b] Ipswich. Language: French. Date: 1291.

Also, the use is that a married woman be brought to justice by the bailiffs of the said town to answer before them in a plea of trespass punishable by imprisonment or the cucking-stool according to the law and usage of the same town, she may be judged as if she were sole without a husband, that is in respect of her personal trespass, unless the trespass concerns a free tenement.

And further it is the use that the husband answers in the court of the said town to any plaint of debt that his wife owed before their marriage and for debt which she may have incurred after their marriage just as he would for his own debt. But if the wife becomes a pledge for debt, the husband is not bound to answer for that.

[c] Norwich. Language: Latin. Date: c. 1340.

Concerning a plea of debt to be recovered from a man which his wife took from a burgess of the town.

Also, in a case where someone's wife has taken goods of her neighbour, a citizen of this city, on loan, without pledge or with pledge, without the knowledge of her husband, the husband should answer for the goods borrowed by his wife in his absence so long as the husband and wife get along well together, that is that the husband's wife is living with her husband or living apart with his consent and good will at the time goods were taken, and that there be common knowledge of the said wife's good conduct, and that she does not by her own temerity deceitfully or wickedly turn away from her husband without an evil or harsh ejection by her husband through that husband's wickedness, and not through the dishonourable faults of the wife, and that she does not turn away from him to create trouble, in which case, if these things can be shown to be true, the husband is not bound to restore the goods thus taken. And such creditors should beware that without the husband's consent they lend to any women thus wickedly separating themselves only at their own risk.

[d] Lincoln. Language: English with headings in Latin. Date: 1481.

Concerning trespass done by a married woman.

And if a plea of trespass be made against a man and his wife for trespass done by the wife alone, she shall be arrested and a day given for the husband to appear. And if he make default she shall be put to answer and have her plea as a sole woman. And if she be attainted, she shall be condemned and committed to prison until she has come to terms with the plaintiff.

A married woman shall recover her damages.

And if a plea of trespass be made by the husband and the wife for trespass or battery done to the wife, she shall be received to plead for herself and her husband and recover her damages against the defendant if her husband is not in court.

### 3. An account of England by an Italian visitor.

Language: Italian. Date: 1497. Translation by Malfatti in C. H. Williams, ed., *English Historical Documents*, V, London, 1967.

They have several harsh laws and customs, one of which, still in force today, we would consider the most severe of all. This lays down that, at death, a man must leave all his property to his wife, completely excluding the children, for whom they show no affection, lavishing all their love on their wives. And consequently since wives have the same dislikes for their children, they choose in the end a husband from among the servants and ignore the children. This custom, apart from being contrary to nature, may also be objected to as impious and profane. There are also other habits in this style, very different from our own customs, but from what I have said it can easily be guessed what they are.

### 4. Church court, diocese of Lincoln.

Language: Latin. Date: 1518-19. Translated from Hamilton Thomson, ed., *Visitations in the Diocese of Lincoln*, I.

[a] South Leigh... John Phipes and Alice his wife are suspected of idolatry. They have a cradle near their bed every night and it is used as if there were an infant in it.

[b] Haseley... The same rector will not visit any woman lying in childbed nor other sick persons.

### 5. 'Le Court de Baron', a guide for the conduct of the customary court.

Language: Latin. Date: mid to later thirteenth century. Translated from Maitland and Baildon, eds. *The Court Baron*.

Sir, my wife was confined a whole month and could only eat and drink what she fancied, and, because of the craving she had to eat a perch, she sent me to the edge of the fish pond to take a single perch.

### 6. Church court, diocese of Lincoln.

Language: Latin. Date: 1530. Translated from Hamilton Thomson, ed., *Visitations in the Diocese of Lincoln*, II.

[Dunstable] ... Sir Thomas Pett, friar of the Order of Preachers ...
denies the fifth article, but says that there is a collect in the book; if a
priest says the collect for a woman being with child and in labour, she
shall speed the better. He then takes money for his mass, and thus he
tells married women.[2]

## 7. Borough court, London.

Language: Latin. Date: 1379. Translation in Riley, ed., *Memorials of London*.

Alice, wife of Robert Godrich, was attached to make answer to
William Walworth [alderman and sometime mayor of London, and
notably at the time of the Peasants' Revolt] in a plea of contempt and
trespass as to which, by Ralph Strode, his attorney, he made plaint that
the said Alice on the 27th day of June in the second year of the king
then reigning [1378], maliciously plotting how to aggrieve and
scandalise the same William, came to his house in the parish of St
Michael, Crooked Lane, in London and there and elsewhere within the
city of London did uncouthly raise the hue and cry on the said William
as though against a thief, and without cause, calling him a false man
and charging him that he had unjustly disinherited her of £20 value
of land yearly and that he, by his mastery unjustly detained the
aforesaid Robert, her husband, in prison for that reason, to the great
scandal of the offices which the said William had formerly held in the
aforesaid city, and to his own damage of £100. As to which, he asked
that the same Alice, for the reason before alleged, might be chastised
that such scolds and female liars might be fearful to slander reputable
men wihout cause in the future. By reason of which plaint, the same
Alice on the 12th day of July in the third year [1379] was brought
here and asked as to the aforesaid matters. Asked if she would have a
counsel to aid her and speak on her behalf, she, refusing all counsel,
said of her own accord that she was no way guilty of the aforesaid
matter and put herself upon the country as to the same etc.
And the jurors ... declared upon their oath the said Alice to be guilty
... to the damage of the said William of £40 etc. And by common
assent of the mayor and aldermen, according to the custom of the city
of London in suchlike cases, it was pronounced that the said Alice ...
should have the punishment of the pillory, called the 'thewe', provided
for such women, to stand upon the same for one hour in the day with
a whetstone hung round her neck for that time, and that the same
William should recover against the said Robert and Alice £40 as his

2 'The wiffes'.

damages assessed by the court etc. And thereupon the said William came here, begging and entreating the mayor and aldermen that the punishment of the pillory might be remitted to the same Alice, upon which, at his request such punishment of the pillory was remitted. And as to the sum of money so adjudged to the said William, he asked thereof might be put in respite during the good behaviour of the said Alice and that she might be released from prison, and accordingly, at such request, she was released etc.

## 8. Coroners' rolls, Bedfordshire.

Language: Latin. Date: 1271. Translation from Hunnisett, ed., *Bedforshire Coroners' Rolls.*

... Lady Christine de Fornival's servant, Alexander le Gardiner of Potton was digging under the walls of an old dovecote in the garden in Lady Christine's courtyard in Sutton to demolish them. As he dug the wall, by misadventure, fell upon him and broke his head so that he died there at once. His wife Alice came with his breakfast, looked for him, saw his surcoat and cap and the spade with which he dug and so found him dead...

## 9. Visitations, archdeaconry of Buckingham.

Language: Latin. Translated from Elvey, ed., *The Courts of the Archdeaconry of Buckingham.*

[a] [1489] Dorney, parish of Burnham... Richard Bisshop because he keeps Alice Marchall as his wife when in fact she is not since the woman has another husband living. The lord bishop of Lincoln has the cause and so it is dismissed from this court.

[b] [1492] Wycombe. 12th day of the month of May in the above written year of the Lord [1492] Christine Forster alias Swayn, the pretended wife of John Swayn, was ordered to show that the same John had another wife living at the time when they contracted, and that he had cohabited with the same Joan, and also that marriage had been solemnised between them at the feast of the purification of the Blessed Virgin Mary sixteen years ago.

Roger Bramston, John Blakkepoll, Robert Michell, William Alyn, and Thomas Hamonde were produced as witnesses.

## 10. Church court, diocese of Lincoln.

Language: Latin. Date: 1518. Translated from Bowker, ed., *An Episcopal Court Book for the Diocese of Lincoln.*

[a] John Faringdon of Bedford appeared in person and swore on the holy gospels to reply faithfully to the articles ... as follows:

Of the first, that John lived in Bedford in the diocese of Lincoln and for that reason was subject to the jurisdiction of the reverend father, he acknowledges. Asked where John and Joan, now living with him as his wife, were married at the church door, he replied that marriage was solemnised between them at the church of St Margaret Pattens in the city of London. Asked what time of day and year, he said one Monday around the feast of St Hilary four or five years ago, but he cannot say more precisely... Asked where he was living at the time of this contract, he said that he was living in the parish of Garlickhithe in the city of London... Asked further if he had previously contracted and solemnised marriage with any other woman, he said that before this he had contracted and solemnised marriage with one Elizabeth Hall in the town of Bedford and had lived with her for several years and had had four children by her as he believes. Elizabeth then left him and committed manifest adultery. Some time later he received her back again to himself and his home. Elizabeth then said to him openly that she was not John's wife, but that, before they had been joined in marriage, she had contracted marriage with one Coverdale of Bedford, dyer. On hearing this, John Faringdon told Elizabeth that he would not keep another man's wife in his house and he wished to send her to a nunnery near St Albans, so Elizabeth left him. Then John Faringdon contracted marriage with Joan Faringdon.

[b] William by God's grace bishop of Lincoln sitting in judgement in the chapel at the Old Temple, London, ordered Thomas Halys of Henley on Thames in the diocese of Lincoln and Agnes his wife, who were appearing in person there before him and who for some time previously had separated from bed and board contrary to the rules of canon law, that they should forthwith live together as man and wife, that Thomas should treat Agnes in a proper way as his wife, and that Agnes should obey Thomas as her husband. He further ordered Thomas to remove one Margaret Fuller his servant from his service, his home, and his society, and henceforth provide and employ to help him respectable servants of good standing and honest behaviour. He also directed Thomas to pay the expenses incurred by Agnes.

## 11. Church court, York.

Language: Latin. The evidence of a precontract is used here to petition for the annulment of an established marriage, but since evidence is also brought that the 'husband' of the first contract had not been seen for three years the effect was to attempt to procure a divorce. Translated from BIHR, CP.E.155. John de Thetilthorp c. Joan, daughter of Peter atte Enges.

[The following two depositions were made 28 February 1374.]

William Coke, living in the parish of St Clement without the walls, York, 50 years of age and more, of free condition as he says, neither affine, servant, nor household member of either party in question in the present cause, admitted as witness, sworn, examined, and asked on the first concerning acquaintance of the parties. He says that he knew Richard, son of Thomas Carter for fourteen years and Joan, daughter of Peter atte Enges of Patrington for thirteen years and more by as much as the time from Pentecost week, but he did not know John Thetilthorpe so he says. Asked how he knew them, he says that the said Richard was a servant of Philip Fyscher, a neighbour of this witness, and he found the same Joan on Wednesday in Pentecost week thirteen years ago in her home at Clementhorpe in the parish of St Clement without the walls, York sitting with her family, which same Joan he took to serve him for six shillings the year. Questioned concerning the second article, he says that one day, he knows not which, about a week before the feast of the nativity of St John the Baptist thirteen years ago in the house of Philip Fyscher, after breakfast and before the hour of vespers of that day, the aforesaid Richard and Joan contracted matrimony together in these words, 'Here I take you Joan to my wife for fairer, for laither,[3] for better, for worse until the end of my life and to this I plight you my troth'. And the woman subsequently said and replied, 'Here I take you Richard to my husband for fairer, for laither, for better, for worse until the end of my life and to this I plight you my troth'. Asked who was present when this contract was made, he says that there were then present Philip Fyscher, John Watterson, and this witness, but he does not remember whether there were any more or not. Asked whether they contracted sitting or standing, he says that he does not remember, nor the clothes of the parties contracting. Asked how he knew, he says that he was present and heard the aforesaid words. Asked, he says he knows nothing of the said contract made between the aforesaid John and Joan,

---

3 Uglier. Unsurprisingly this formulation was dropped by the time of the first Book of Common Prayer.

nor the time of the said contract. Questioned on the penultimate article, he says that he knows not to depose otherwise in this cause than he deposed above. Asked on the last article, he says that public voice and report circulated and was circulating on the aforesaid matters in the parish of Clementhorpe without the walls, York among known persons and neighbours...

Philip Fyscher, living in Clementhorpe without the walls, York, aged 60 years and more, of free status...

And on the first concerning knowledge of the persons, he says that he knew Richard, son of Thomas Carter of Nun Monkton for eighteen years and more and Joan, daughter of Peter atte Enges of Patrington for fourteen years and more, but by how much he knows not to depose. He did not know John de Thetilthorpe so this witness says. Asked how he knew, he says that the said Richard was a servant of this witness for two years and afterwards went away from him and served with Stephen Walker for half a year as this witness believes.

[Deposes concerning marriage contracted between Richard and Joan. Notes that Agnes, wife of William Coke was a witness.]

Asked whether they contracted the aforesaid marriage sitting or standing, he says that each was sitting on this witness' bench, but in what clothes the said persons contracting were dressed at the time, he does not remember...

[Did not know of intercourse between Richard and Joan or of contract between John and Joan.]

[The following two depositions were made 24 March 1374.]

Adam Roger of Ketleby, living in Ketleby from birth, in the parish of Althorpe, diocese of Lincoln, 26 years of age, of free status so he says, neither a relative, affine, household member, nor servant of any party in the present cause other than that he took John de Thetilthorp's sister to wife, admitted as a witness, sworn, and examined. And on the first concerning knowledge of the persons, viz. John de Thetilthorp and Joan, daughter of Peter atte Enges of Patrington about whom the present cause relates, he says that he knew the said John de Thetilthorp for twenty years and Joan, daughter of Peter atte Enges of Patrington from the feast of St Hugh five years ago and more by the time from the feast of St Hugh last to the present day. Asked how he knew, he says that that much time had elapsed since the said John and Joan were espoused together, but he did not know her previously as he says. Asked about the first article, he says that at the feast of St Hugh five years ago in the parish church of Althorpe banns were read and the marriage solemnised at the church door between the aforesaid John and Joan. Asked how he knew, he says that he was present, saw, and heard and gave the said Joan by the hand into the hands of one Sir Roger Nalson, parish chaplain of Althorpe, at the door of the same parish church of Althorpe as is the custom in those parts. Asked by whom the said marriage at the church door was solemnised, he says by the aforesaid Sir Roger Nalson of Hampcotes, at that time the parish chaplain there. Asked about the hour, he says that almost immediately after prime of that day, that is on aforesaid feast of St Hugh...

Thomas Nade, living in the parish of Althorpe from the time of the first pestilence,[4] aged 45 years and more, of servile status as he says, neither affine, relative, household member, nor servant of any of the parties in the present cause, admitted, sworn, and examined. And on the first concerning knowledge of the persons, viz. John de Thetilthorp and Joan, daughter of Peter atte Enges of Patrington, he says that he knew John de Thetilthorp for twenty-four years and more. Asked how he knew, he says that he has lived for almost the whole of that time in Althorpe and in the neighbouring parish and often worked and spoke with him. He knew the aforesaid Joan a little before the feast of St Hugh five years ago and more, but by how long he knows not depose for certain...

[Deposes concerning contract and solemnisation of marriage as before.]

Asked on the second and penultimate articles, he says that he knows not to depose for sure other than he heard from others who said that one Richard, son of Thomas Carter of Nun Monkton and Joan, daughter of Peter atte Enges of Patrington contracted words of matrimony or spousals together, and this Joan often acknowledged to this witness at Ketleby...

[The following deposition was made 17 June 1374.]

John, son of Thomas Carter of Nun Monkton, aged 40 years, of free condition, brother of Richard Carter, about whom the present cause relates, admitted as a witness, sworn, and examined. He says that on Sunday in the feast of St Bartholomew the Apostle three years ago, the said Richard and this witness talked together at Nun Monkton in the house of Alan, son of Philip de Cade and elsewhere in the village, and the following day the said Richard departed from this witness. Afterwards he did not appear, nor had he certain intimation or was he able to know

4 I.e. the Black Death.

for sure whether the said Richard is alive or not. He says, however, that he heard the said Richard say that he espoused Joan, daughter of Peter atte Enges of Patrington, and he does not know to depose further as he says.

## 12. Papal letter.

Language: Latin. Date: 1391. Translation in *Calendar of Papal Registers*, IV.

To the bishop of Hereford. Mandate to grant dispensation to William Parys and Sibyl Leton so that they may remain in the marriage contracted by them in ignorance that they were related in the third degree of affinity, declaring their past and future offspring legitimate.

## 13. Manor court rolls, Halesowen.

Language: Latin. Date: 1276. Translated from Wilson, ed., *Court Rolls of the Manor of Hales.*

William le Teining granted in full court half his entire holding to William le Archer together with his own daughter Juliana and the entire holding after his and his wife's deaths on condition that they support him so long as they stay together. If they are not able to stay together, they will have half, not counting the capital house, and live on their own. He gives 12s to the lord.

## 14. *Fasciculus Morum.*

Language: Latin. Date: ?early fourteenth century. Translated from S. Wenzel, ed., *Fasciculus Morum: A Fourteenth-Century Preacher's Manual,* Philadelphia and London, 1989.

... as a wife wrongly treated by her husband suffers patiently lest her husband loses face by censure, and if, to his shame, by chance a lesion appears without from beatings, she carefully pretends otherwise, claiming she had incurred some other misfortune.

## 15. Church court, Droitwich.

Language: Latin. Date: 1300. Translated from Pearson, ed., 'Records of a ruridecanal court of 1300'.

Thomas Louchard ill treated his wife with a rod. The man appears, confesses, and is whipped in the usual manner once through the market. He went away.

## 16. Church court, York.

Language: Latin. The plaintiff is here seeking judicial separation (divorce *a mensa et a thoro*) from her husband on the grounds of cruelty. Although she is able to produce two witnesses to the same event, it appears that the court preferred the testimony of the one male witness supported by a further character witness. Translated from BIHR, CP.E.221. Margery, wife of Thomas Nesfeld c. Thomas Nesfeld.

[Following two depositions are dated 13 January 1396.]

Joan White of York, aged 25 years and more...

... this witness was present together with Margery Speight, her fellow witness, and John Semer, servant of Thomas Nesfeld of York in the same Thomas' house in the parish of Bishophill, York, on the Saturday before the feast of St Bartholomew four years ago next within the darkness of night where and when she saw the said Thomas throw Margery, his wife to the ground with a club and beat her severely with the same and afterwards he drew his baslard and gravely wounded her in the arm and broke the bone of that arm, commonly called 'le Spelbon' and he would then have killed her that night if he had not been prevented by this witness, the said Margery, her fellow witness, and John Semer, then servant of the same Thomas. Afterwards for a week or two, as this witness believes, when the same Margery, wife of the same Thomas, was somewhat healed and restored, she went away from Thomas, her husband because she dared not stay longer with him for fear of death...

Margery Speight of the parish of Kilderwick, aged 18 years and more...

[Deposition substantially the same as Joan White's.]

[Following two depositions are dated 21 January 1396.]

John Semer of the parish of Ouseburn, aged 20 years, of free condition, a blood relative, servant, or affine of neither party...

Examined on the first article, he says that it contains the truth and this he says he knows because one day in autumn, which day he does not remember, four years ago the said Margery left her home in the parish of Bishophill and went to a house, the which this witness does not remember, in the city of York without and contrary to the said Thomas, her husband's mandate and precept, and stayed there from noon of that day until the darkness of night. When she returned to the house shared by the said Thomas and the said Margery his wife, Thomas asked why she had left her home against his will and precept.

She replied that she wished to go where she would against the will of the same Thomas her husband, and then Thomas, seeing Margery's rebellion, struck her with his fist in order to chastise her. Asked how he knows that the aforesaid Margery went from her aforesaid shared home against the will and precept of the said Thomas, he says that this same witness was at that time servant to Thomas and was present in the aforesaid house when Thomas, the husband told Margery that she should not leave the house and was present in the house also when Margery returned and when Thomas slapped her on the face for the aforesaid matters. Asked who were then present with him, he says that he does not remember. This witness further says that he was present one day, the which he does not remember, around the feast of the nativity of St John the Baptist four years ago in the aforesaid house when he heard the said Margery swear and say to Thomas her husband that she could kill him in bed at night if she wanted, which same Thomas, roused by anger, wanted to strike her with his fist. She immediately fled outside the door into the highway crying, wailing, weeping, and publicly exclaiming that Thomas, her husband, wanted to kill her. Item, asked who were then present, he says this same witness, the said Thomas, and Margery, and none other to his knowledge. He further says that he never saw or heard that the said Thomas was harsh or cruel towards Margery his wife unless provoked by the fault and wrong of the same Margery, his wife, as he relates that he knew the said Thomas for the past six years and stayed with him all that time until last Martinmas and never heard to the contrary...

Richard Hanley of York, aged 60 years and more...

... he says that he knew the said Thomas for the past twenty years and never saw or heard that he beat the said Margery, his wife or used any cruelty against her, but he was from the time of this witness' observation and is still humble, mild, merciful, and kindly towards the same Margery...

[The court rejected Margery's petition for divorce *a mensa et a thoro*.]

## 17. Bishop's register, Salisbury.

Language: Latin. Date: 1410. Calendared translation in Horn, ed., *The Register of Robert Hallum.*

Commission to the abbot of Sherborne to hear before Whitsun the complaint of Alice Amisell of Sherborne, in the abbot's jurisdiction, daughter of William Amisell, against Stephen Carlell alias Scryveyn, her husband, who, she alleges, has committed adultery with Joan, wife of John Iveyn, tailor of Sherborne. The abbot is to certify the bishop before Trinity Sunday. Potterne, 8th April 1410.

## 18. Church court, archdeaconry of Buckingham.

Language: Latin. Translated from Elvey, ed., The Courts of the Archdeaconry of Buckingham.

[a] [1485] Hartwell. Agnes Chardesley is accused with Edmund Bampton on the sin of adultery. She appeared and denies the article. She appeared with Marion Hikkes, Christine Hare, Alice Smewyn, and Alice Cowper and lawfully purged herself and is dismissed.

[b] [1486] Chesham. Thomas Godyng sold his wife and holds another. He appeared and confesses that he has a wife living and is ordered to abstain from that woman entirely.

[c] ... Roger Calaber on account of the adultery and drunkeness by Elizabeth his wife. He sought a divorce in respect of bed and board. He had a day to prove the said adultery and drunkeness etc. On 28th day of July the year of the lord 1496 in the parish church of Beaconsfield before master Nicholas Treble, the official of the lord archdeacon of Buckingham for the tribunal sitting to carry out the law, the same Roger appeared with William Clerk and Alexander Heron. They were admitted and sworn and a day was assigned for the sentence to be heard shortly. This next day, viz. 7th day of the month of October the year of the Lord 1496, having arrived, the aforesaid Roger Calaber and Elizabeth his wife appeared in person in the parish church of Beaconsfield before master Nicholas Treble, the official of the lord archdeacon of Buckingham sitting for the tribunal. This same Roger alleged adultery committed, as he said, by the said Elizabeth his wife. Because sufficient proof for Roger Calaber's present petition was had in this regard, the judge divorced and separated them in respect of bed and board instructing each and both of them to keep continent and live chastely under penalty of the law...

[d] On which day [6 February 1520] John Cutte of Drayton and Margaret his wife appeared reported for having for a long time lived apart and that the aforesaid Margaret will not abide with her husband. The judge ordered them to live together without delay and that each should live with the other in future under pain of excommunication. But the woman expressly denied the judge's order, therefore the judge

sitting in judgement on the day and in the place directed that excommunication be put in writing against Margaret. Afterwards the aforesaid parties agreed and Margaret promised to live with her husband on condition that her husband treat her in future well, decently, and favourably. The parties made their pledge to the judge in the aforesaid manner and were dismissed.

### 19. Church court, diocese of Lincoln.

Language: Latin. Date: 1518-19. Translated from Hamilton Thomson, ed., *Visitations in the Diocese of Lincoln*, I.

[a] Ellington... James Moyses and his wife do not live together as man and wife.

[b] Tingewick. Agnes Bevre does not live with John Bevre her husband.

[c] Warboys. Agnes Chipney, the wife of William Chipney said still to be living, is now married to John Angell.

[d] Epworth. James Post drove out his wife and defamed her.

### 20. Will of John Goddysbruk, merchant, York.

Language: Latin. Date: 1407. Translated from BIHR, Prob. Reg. 3 fo. 276.

Also I leave to Emmot with whom I had a daughter, 20*s*, and that it be sent to her secretly.

### 21. Coroners' rolls, Bedfordshire.

Language: Latin. Date: 1273. Translation from Hunnisett, ed., *Bedfordshire Coroners' Rolls.*

At night ... Raymond le Tailur and his daughter Eve killed his wife Emma, Eve's step-mother, cutting her throat and shins, and buried her in a dung-pit outside Raymond's house in St Macute in Eastcotts. She remained buried for a fortnight before being discovered...

### 22. Coroners' rolls, Sussex.

Language: Latin. Translation in Hunnisett, ed., Sussex Coroners' Inquests.

[a] [1506] Between 5 and 6 a.m. on 7 June Joan Sebeche, late of [    ] in Sussex, housewife, went out her house into the garden and with a

knife called 'a redyng cut'[5] which she held in her right hand voluntarily cut her throat from right to left.

[b] [1508] About 9 p.m. on 4 September Joan, late the wife of Stephen a Myll of Chiddingly, feloniously cut her throat in her husband's house at Chiddingly with a knife worth 1*d*, which she held in her right hand, and immediately died.

[c] [1526] Between nine and ten o'clock before midnight on 23 February Margery, late the wife of Richard Avys, voluntarily and alone placed herself on a piece of wood in her husband's kitchen in Groombridge in Loxfield hundred with a halter about her neck and hanged herself without anyone's aid or advice.

## 23. Trailbaston, Wiltshire.

Language: Latin. Translation by Pugh in R. B. Pugh, trans., *Wiltshire Gaol Delivery and Trailbaston Trials 1275-1306*, Wiltshire Record Society, XXXIII, 1978.

[a] [1276] Selkley and Swanborough. Edith de Helmerton, taken at Henton with Robert [Boket] her husband for stealing sheep at Alton Priors, for which theft Robert was hanged in Selkley hundred, she being pregnant was sent to Salisbury gaol and there kept until her parturition, says she was Robert's wife. The jury of twelve of Selkley and Swanborough hundreds sufficiently declare that she was his espoused wife. So one quit.

[b] [1277] Westbury. William de la Pleystowe and William Balle and Isabel his wife, taken and imprisoned for slaying John Brond, Iseult his wife, and Christine his daughter, and Nicholas Cunduyt, taken and imprisoned for sheep stolen in Westbury hundred, plead not guilty. The twelve of that hundred say that William de Pleystowe and Nicholas are not guilty, and that the others are guilty, but that Isabel acted on her husband's orders. So three quit and one hanged. Chattels, 2*s*, whereon the tithingman is answerable.

[c] [1305] Joan who was the wife of Richard de Langleton (quit) for procuring unknown men to slay Richard her husband at Coulston.

---

5 Hunnisett suggests either a reeding knife or a knife for splitting known as a redding.

# IV: Widowhood, poverty, and old age

## 1. Eyre rolls, Oxford.

Language: Latin. Date: 1285. Translated from J. E. Thorold Rogers, ed., *Oxford City Documents*, Oxford Historical Society, XVIII, 1891.

[a] Claremunda, who was the wife of Henry Whirll, claims against Thomas Feteplace a third of a messuage with appurtenances in North Osney by Oxford as dower etc. of the endowment of the aforesaid Henry, formerly her husband etc., and Thomas comes and says that the aforesaid Claremunda ought not thus to have her dower because he says that the aforesaid Henry, formerly the husband of that Claremunda, was never in possession of the aforesaid tenement as of fee so that he was thereby able to endow her, and in respect of this he puts himself on the country, and Claremunda likewise, therefore let there be a jury about this...

[b] Alice, who was the wife of William Attemontes, claims against Walter de Witteney and John Attemontes the third part of a messuage with appurtenances in Oxford as dower etc., and Walter and John come and say that the aforesaid Alice after the death of the aforesaid William, formerly her husband, held the aforesaid messuage in the name of her free bench and was thereby in possession for forty days and more, and they say that the custom of the town of Oxford is such that when a woman after the death of her husband resides in a tenement in the name of free bench for forty days or more and afterwards she married someone, that she is ever after prevented from claiming an action for her dower in respect of that tenement. They also say that because the aforesaid Alice held the aforesaid messuage in the name of free bench as is said previously, she is excluded from her action seeking dower in respect of the aforesaid tenement, and they seek judgement. Alice says that she never had anything in the aforesaid messuage in the name of free bench other than by name of caring for one Robert, the son and heir of the aforesaid William formerly her husband, and because it is thus she places herself on the country, and John and Walter likewise, therefore let there be a jury about this... The jurors say on their oath that the custom of the town is such that when a woman resides in a tenement which was her

husband's for forty days in the name of her free bench and afterwards takes a husband, then she ought not in way to have dower in respect of that tenement, and they say that the aforesaid Alice resided in the aforesaid tenement after her husband's death for forty days by claiming her free bench in the same, therefore it is judged that the aforesaid Walter and John [go] thence without a day, and Alice [is] in mercy.

## 2. Halmote court, Durham.

Language: Latin. Date: 1364. Translated from *Durham Halmote Rolls*, I, Surtees Society, LXXXII, 1882.

Jarrow: Of Agnes who was the wife of Agnes [sic, for Adam] Gedde for merchet, 2s.

...

John Simson came to court and took a cottage and 12 acres of land, which Agnes the widow of Adam Gedde formerly held and which was taken into the lord's hand because the said Agnes went away from the said land without permission and lives in the county of Northumberland, to have and to hold for the term of his life rendering an annual farm and doing [service]. Fine 7s.

## 3. Visitation, diocese of Lincoln.

Language: Latin. Date: 1519. Translated from Hamilton Thomson, ed., *Visitations in the Diocese of Lincoln*, I.

Wrawby... Katherine Vintyner, widow, is pregnant, but by whom is not known.

## 4. Manor court, Halesowen.

Language: Latin. Translated from Wilson, ed., *Court Rolls of the Manor of Hales*.

[a] [1300] Christine Adam of Illey, who found pledges for bringing her son Robert and her servant Henry to this court, came, but did not produce them and therefore puts herself at mercy.

[b] [1276] William de la Penne is distrained to bring Joan his wife to answer the charge that she unjustly and against the liberty holds back and concealed half a sow which ought to be of the lord's portion and did not present her best beast, which she ought to have given for her late husband's heriot, but that she concealed to the abbot's loss, viz. 20s.

[c] [1279] William the son of J. Steinulf gives to the lord abbot a silver mark as relief for his land and he has seisin in full court. William his uncle received seisin of half his land for the term of six years on condition that he find the boy six measures of hard corn, a quarter of oats, clothes, shoes, and all necessities for the said term, and the said boy will be in the custody of his mother. William his uncle is to do suit of court three times a year until the end of the aforesaid term.

5. Manor court rolls, Tottenham (Bruces).

Language: Latin. Date: 1395. Translation in Oram, trans., *Court Rolls of the Manors of Bruces, Dawbeneys, Pembrokes (Tottenham)*, II.

To this court has come Alice, late wife of Thomas Ederych and receives of the lord the tenure of five acres and three roods of land to hold to herself until the legal age of John, the youngest son of the aforesaid Thomas, who, according to the custom of the manor, will inherit the land in bondage, and the aforesaid Alice is to keep the said John, who is now six years of age, in food and clothing well and competently until his legal age, and she gives to the lord of fine for entry 2s and does fealty, and she finds pledges John Malton and Thomas Fynch. And after the full age of the said heir, if she shall have kept herself sole and in good repute without husband, then she shall have the said tenement and lands for her whole life, and if she shall not, then it is to be taken into the lord's hands according to the custom of the manor.

6. Lay subsidy returns, 1297.

Language: Latin. Translated from A. T. Gaydon, ed., *The Taxation of 1297*, Bedfordshire Historical Record Society, XXXIX, 1959.

[a] [Bedford]

Sibil de Steventon: 5 ewes, 5s; 2 quarters drage, 5s; brass pots, 2s; a chamber, 2s. Total 14s. Ninth 18¾d.

Agnes Courtepi: 1 cow, 5s; lead and wooden vessels, 3s; brass pots, 2s. Total 10s. Ninth 13½d.

Alice de Stachenden: 5 pigs, 6s 8d; 6 ewes, 6s; 3 quarters malt, 10s; lead and wooden vessels, 2s 10d; brass pots, 2s. Total 27s 6d. Ninth 3s ¾d.

Felicity Lanvaly: 4 pigs, 4s; 2 quarters malt, 6s; 2 quarters oats, 3s; lead and wooden vessels, 4s; brass pots, 3s; a chamber, 3s; hay and forage,

3s; wood, 2s. Total 28s. Ninth 3s 1½d.

Agnes Haliday: 3 quarters drage, 7s 6d; 2 quarters oats, 3s; lead and
wooden vessels, 4s; brass pots, 2s. Total 19s 6d. Ninth 2s 2d.

Widow of John de la More: 1 cow, 5s; 2 quarters malt, 6s; lead and
wooden vessels, 3s; brass pots, 2s; a chamber, 2s. Total 9s 6d. Ninth
12¾d.

[note: total of 98 persons assessed; total of ninth £14 1s 1d.]

[b] [Shillington]

Ellen de Chubbell: 1 affer, 2s; 1 cow, 5s; 1 quarter 2 bushels wheat, 4s
2d; 1 quarter drage, 2s 6d. Total 13s 4d. Ninth 16½d.

Maud de Wodemanend: 1 affer, 3s; 1 bullock, 5s; 1 cow, 5s; 1 young
bullock, 18d; 1½ quarters wheat, 5s; 1 quarter drage, 2s 6d; 1 quarter
beans, 3s. Total 25s. Ninth 2s 9½d.

Edith the widow: 1 affer, 2s; 1 cow, 5s; 1 quarter wheat, 3s 4d; 1 quarter
drage, 2s 6d; 1 quarter oats, 18d. Total 14s 4d. Ninth 19¼d.

[note: total of 33 persons assessed; total of ninth £3 2s 11½d.]

## 7. Wills, diocese of Lincoln.

Language: English. Translated from Clark, ed., *Lincoln Diocese Documents*.

[a] Codicil to will of Richard Welby of Moulton. Date: 1465.

... Also, I will that, if my wife can find sufficient surety to my
executors that she shall never have a husband after my decease, that
then she be my chief executrix, but otherwise not to be, nor to have
any more than her jointure and one half of my household goods...

[b] Will of Robert Hardy of Lyddington. Date: 1517.

... Also I will that Joan my wife have the profit and the governance of
the house and lands for the term of her life, and if any of my children
be obstinate and cause trouble towards their mother against my will,
he that so troubles is to have nothing other than at his mother's will...
The residue of my goods not bequeathed, I give to the disposition of
my wife whom I make my sole executrix to dispose for me as is most
expedient for the health of my soul...

### 8. Manor court, Littleport.

Language: Latin. Date: 1321. Translated from Maitland and Baildon, eds., *The Court Baron.*

Elizabeth la Lange surrenders into the lord's hand part of a cottage containing 20 feet. Nicholas Ixseninge came and took the said portion to have and to hold according to the custom of the manor. The said Nicholas shall give Elizabeth 12*d* a year for her whole life and he gives the lord 12*d* for having entry.

### 9. Manor court, Tottenham (Bruces).

Language: Latin. Translation in Oram, trans., *Court Rolls of the Manors of Bruces, Dawbeneys, Pembrokes (Tottenham),* II.

[a] [1380] Richard Reve who held of the lord a messuage and eighteen and a half acres of land and one acre and three roods of meadow with appurtenances, in good and sound memory being sick in body caused to be surrendered into the lord's hands, in the presence of William Ede the lord's reeve, according to the custom of the manor the aforesaid land and tenements with appurtenances to the use of Alice his wife and their heirs if the same Alice should outlive him, and the said Richard has died meanwhile and upon his death the lord thereof grants seisin to the said Alice to hold to her and her heirs by the verge without prejudice etc. doing services etc. She gives to the lord of fine for having entry etc. and does fealty etc.

[b] [1386] John Fuller and Christine his wife surrendered into the lord's hands one and a half roods of meadow in 'Thornerershote' next to the meadow of William Drake, parcel of the tenement of the aforesaid Christine, to the use of the said William Drake and Maud his wife to hold to them and their heirs by the verge without prejudice etc. doing services etc. They give to the lord to have entry 2s and do fealty etc. And the aforesaid Christine is examined and says that she does this freely and without compulsion etc.

### 10. Manor court, Wellington.

Language: Latin. Date: 1382. Translation in Humphreys, trans., *Materials for the History of the Town and Parish of Wellington.*

William Horeknoll renders into the lord's hand one messuage and one fardel of land of ancient hearth with the associated overlond to the use of Richard Smyth, and the heriot of the same William is part of the fine written below by agreement. And hereupon the said Richard and Edith his wife come and give to the lord of a fine 40s for having entry etc. The tenant is to render yearly to Christine Horeknoll during her life one quarter of wheat, five busshels of rye, half a busshel of green peas, and half a busshel of pilcorn at the four terms of the year, and 16d and one pair of shoes at the feast of the nativity of St John the Baptist with the crop of half an acre of meadow, pasture for one cow, and half an acre for sowing, and she shall have a house upon the said tenement for her dwelling, and one pig going upon the said tenement at her own cost.

## 11. Manor court, Horsham St Faith (Norfolk).

Language: Latin. Date: 1312. Translated from E. Clark, 'The quest for security in medieval England' in M. M. Sheehan, ed., *Aging and the Aged in Medieval Europe*, Toronto, 1990, pp. 189-200.

Hubert at the Gate releases back into the lord's hand from himself and his heirs a messuage with six acres and three roods of land of a tenement to the use of William Heryng and Beatrix, daughter of the aforesaid Hubert, and the heirs lawfully procreated by them. And if it happens that Beatrix, daughter of the aforesaid Hubert, dies without issue lawfully procreated of herself and the aforesaid William, then the aforesaid William may marry another having gained the lord's will. And if they shall have a lawfully procreated heir, then they shall have and hold the aforesaid tenements to themselves and their heirs as aforesaid. And if it happens that the aforesaid William shall die without an heir lawfully procreated by himself and the aforesaid Beatrix, and the said Beatrix outlives the same William, then the aforesaid Beatrix may take another husband according to the will of the lord. And if they shall have an heir lawfully procreated of themselves, then they shall have and hold the aforesaid tenements with their appurtenances to themselves and their heirs as aforesaid. And if all the aforesaid shall die without an heir lawfully procreated by them as is said before, then all the aforesaid tenements together with all their appurtenances shall remain to Roger, son of the aforesaid Hubert, and his heirs for ever. And the aforesaid William and Beatrix promise for themselves and their heirs to find all necessaries according to their ability as in food and clothing, maintenance, houses etc for the aforesaid Hubert and Emma his wife for the whole of their lives. And the aforesaid William and Beatrix promise for themselves and their heirs and recognise that they owe the aforesaid Roger, son of the aforesaid Hubert, and Margaret his wife for the whole of their lives one quarter and a half of barley, paying both of them or whichever one of them shall survive at the feast of All Saints following the deaths of the aforesaid Hubert and Emma his wife. And if it happens that the aforesaid Hubert shall die before Emma his wife or else Emma before Hubert, then they recognise that they owe the aforesaid Roger and Margaret his wife or whichever one of them shall survive six busshels of barley to be paid as aforesaid etc. And the aforesaid William and Beatrix shall give to the lord two marks for fine for having entry and seisin in the aforesaid tenements...

### 12. Church court, York.

Language: Latin. Translated from BIHR, CP.F.36. John Dale c. Agnes Grantham and John Thornton.

[The substance of Agnes Grantham's defence of John Dale's suit for enforcement of a contract of marriage between them survives in a lengthy series of thirty-two articles. These allege that Agnes was ambushed whilst on her way to have dinner with the master of St Leonard's at Acomb Grange, abducted and subsequently raped by John Dale after being forced to exchange words of marriage with him. John Dale's articles allege that this version of events was untrue and that Agnes continued to live in her own home rather than, as she alleged, move to William Pountfret's house out of fear of further attack.]

[Following three deponents examined 14 March, 1411.]

Roger Marschall, alias Tayliour of the parish of St Michael le Belfrey, York, aged 50 years, of free status...

Examined on the first article, he says that he knew Alice Rayner, William Pountfret, and the others named in this article well, with the exception only of Richard Clay, Sir William Wystow [priest], and John Newton, from contact and discussion had with them, some for sixteen years, some for seven, and others for two years...

[Deposes that these witnesses do not favour John Thornton or Agnes Grantham contrary to justice and that Agnes moved from her home in the parish of St Michael le Belfrey at night on the feast of St Margaret to William Pountfret, draper's house in parish of All Saints, Pavement, but continued to return home.]

... because she had various goods which without a long time could not be moved [ ?swiftly ] suddenly, her household at the same Agnes' charge, malt that she had there in the making and not yet complete in great quantity, both for brewing ale and selling, and for the most part remaining there until shortly before Martinmas last...

[Agnes never spent the night there, but moved]

... because she feared that John, about whom this present cause is concerned, had access and entrance through the grammar school situated next to her at the house she then lived in and should thus any time by force and armed might seize and abduct her unwilling and protesting from the city of York to places more agreeable to him...

... the said Agnes often at various times between the feast of St Margaret and Martinmas last came and had access to the house in which she lived in the aforesaid parish of St Michael le Belfrey to see her household, which she kept there, and her chattels, so that nothing unpleasant or detrimental should occur or be suffered, and also to give alms to the poor by bringing them wood, fuel, and other necessaries just as she was often wont to do in the year of habit to the observation and knowledge of this witness...

[Deposes that John and Agnes both of good standing, but did not know if Agnes was the wealthier through rental income in York and elsewhere.]

Agnes Kyrkeby of the parish of All Saints on the Pavement, York, aged 20 years...

... she says that upto last Martinmas and for the two years immediately before this witness was a waged servant of William Pountfret, of whom there is mention in the article, and the said Agnes lived in person in the home of the same William Pountfret, to this same witness' sight and knowledge, and had residence and eat and drank from the feast of St Margaret last until the said Martinmas and even afterwards upto the present day save that meanwhile the same Agnes had periodic access to the house she had lived in previously in the parish of St Michael le Belfrey, York to see her household and goods left by her there and to arrange for them that they might be moved more quickly to the said parish of All Saints, more pleasing to her, where she had her breakfast and a bed and was disposed to stay and have her abode at the dwelling house of the aforesaid William Pountfret. She always returned without having stayed long so that this witness served the same Agnes on separate days and nights for the most part from the feast of St Margaret until the aforesaid Martinmas in the said house of William Pountfret with food and drink and by carrying with her own hands a lighted, burning candle. Agnes for the most part kept her bed and slept with a certain devout woman, Dame Christiana by name, a blood relative of the said William Pountfret who, by taking the mantle and ring, entered a vow of chastity, having a room and living within the dwelling house of the said William Pountfret. Frequently she went over to the bed with her, often covering her naked in bed with sheets, as at times in like manner other women and servants of the same house often did in the sight and knowledge of this witness as she says. The aforesaid Agnes was a parishioner of the said church of All Saints from the feast of St Margaret until the aforesaid Martinmas and continuously afterwards. She was a parishioner there for all communions of the said parish commonly held and named, and this she knows by what she deposed above, and also because she very often saw the same Agnes on weekdays and holidays in the said church of All Saints, as a parishioner of the same, to be present at divine services, listen devoutly to them, make oblations at masses celebrated, and receive holy water and blessed bread from the hand of the parish priest. Lately also, when brought down by serious illness and being at the point of death, she was confessed in the dwelling house of William Pountfret by the aforesaid parish priest and would then have received the consecrated Host from the same if the said illness had not proved worrying, particularly because she was unable to hold down for long any foods or liquids taken by her, but by reason of this illness quickly expelled them by vomiting...

[Deposes that Agnes visited old home, formerly belonging to her late husband, Hugh Grantham] ... so that neither the said goods nor household should suffer loss or harm in any way and also to perform other pious works of charity and almsgiving...

Isabel Nesswyk of the parish of All Saints on the Pavement, York, aged 20 years...

... she says that she was a servant and member of household of William Pountfret ... from Martinmas last year to the present day...

[Provides substantially similar evidence. Notes that Agnes' old home was in Petergate.]

[Following two deponents were examined 13 March 1411 and deposed in like manner.]

William Smyth, of the parish of St Michael le Belfrey, York aged 50 years...

Isabel Smyth, wife of William Smyth, of the parish of St Michael le Belfrey, York aged 50 years...

[The following three deponents were examined 20 November 1410.]

Thomas Catton, of the parish of St Michael le Belfrey, York aged 50 years and more...

... he often saw, so this witness says, the said Agnes' servants take away and carry ale to the master of St Leonard's Hospital, York for the use of the aforesaid William Feryby and his household...

John Eberston, of the parish of St Michael le Belfrey, York aged 40 years...

[Deposes that Agnes' servant, Alice, came to this witness to report the attack on her mistress.]

Richard Ulskelf, walker, of the parish of St Margaret, York aged 40 years...

[Deposes that Agnes told him of the attack in her home in the parish of St Michael le Belfrey.]

[The following deponents testify to a contract of marriage between Agnes and John Thornton.]

Alice Rayner of the parish of St Michael le Belfrey, York, aged 25 years and more ... servant and household member of Agnes Grantham...

... she says that on the vigil or in the night of St Margaret last now gone by after the vespers' hour, the aforesaid John and Agnes contracted marriage together by words of present consent in a certain arbour within the garden of John Laxton of the aforesaid parish of St Michael le Belfrey... This witness, William Pountfret, John Laxton, Richard Walker, and Agnes, the wife of the said John Laxton were present and heard this contract...

William Pountefret, draper, of the parish of All Saints on the Pavement, York, aged 60 years...

Richard Ulskelf...

John Laxton, of the parish of St Michael le Belfrey, York aged 40 years...

Agnes, wife of John Laxton ... aged 40 years and more...

### 13. Church court, York.

Language: Latin. Translated from BIHR, CP.E.82. Maud de Bradelay c. John de Walkyngton.

[Following three depositions are dated 28 February 1355.]

Maud Katersouth, admitted as a witness, sworn, and examined on the article...

... she knew Maud for eighteen years and more and John for last two years and more. Asked if she had ever heard any words of matrimony proferred between John and Maud, she says because she was present on the Tuesday after the feast of St Mary Magdalene last in the house of the said Maud in a street called North Street, York where and when she saw and heard said John and Maud talking together in the aforesaid house. Asked what were the words then spoken between them at that time, she says that she heard the said John, being then in bed in the said house, say to the said Maud, 'Come to bed!' This the same Maud absolutely refused to do. John then said to her, 'You are mine. I am yours, as well you know. And I refuse to seek permission from you to do my will with you.' She then said to John, 'I for sure will never get into bed with you unless you give me your faith – in English "plyth me yi trouth" – that you will take me to your wife.' The said John then said to Maud, 'See, here is my faith that I want to have you to my wife and that I will take you to my wife and that I have not thought otherwise from the time that we first spoke together about this matter,' and she then replied, 'See, here is my faith that I want to have you to my husband, and now you can do your will with me.' After these words she got into the bed in which John was then lying and lay with him until morning. Asked at what hour of the day she heard these words, she says about the ringing of the curfew bells on Pavement, York. Asked about intercourse between them, she says that she believes that he knew her carnally afterwards and that he was subsequently accused of this before the rural dean, York and that he was convicted of this and corrected before him, and she likewise. Asked about the rumour, she says that there is common report and discussion among all the neighbours of North Street, York on the aforesaid matters on which she deposed.

Robert, son of the said Maud...

... knew Maud for past two years and John de Walkyngton from the Tuesday after the feast of St Mary Magdalene last...

[Deposition substantially the same as before.]

John de Staynlay...

[Deposes that he knew parties for two years and more, but only knew of contract by hearsay.]

[Following two depositions are dated 15 April 1355.]

Maud Katerforth [otherwise Katersouth] ... says that Robert her son was aged 14 years coming up 15 years at the time he was examined in Maud de Bradley's matrimonial cause...

... she heard him [John de Walkyngton] get into bed and saw him lying in bed with her at dawn of the following day, alone and naked together, and get up from the same bed, and she believes that they lay together in bed the whole night with it in mind to have intercourse together.

Robert, son of the same Maud Katerforth, asked by reason of his youth what age he was at the time of his examination made in the aforesaid cause, says 15 years and more as he heard his father, who is living still, swear and stoutly assert...

... he believes that they had intercourse and thus [i.e. naked] he saw them get out of bed at dawn the next day and he says that he heard that night from that place the sound of them making love.

[Following three depositions are dated 16 June 1355.]

William de Warnefeld...

He says that he was never present in any place where and when Maud, about whom there is notice in the article, pledged herself by her faith to pay Sir Thomas de Castleford, chaplain any sum of money, but he was present one day, the which he does not remember, around Michaelmas last in the street of Skeldergate, York in the house of William de Swanlond where and when he heard and saw the said Maud receive from the said Sir Thomas a day, then to come and now past, to pay him four shillings, so he believes, for a broadcloth fourteen ells in length sold by her, and on the said day she did not pay the said money as she had promised. After the said day had gone by, this witness, at the request of the said Sir Thomas, asked why she had not paid the said money as she promised, but he did not attach her because William de Swanlond asked and received on her behalf another day to pay, but this witness believes, as he says, that no part of the said money has yet been paid. He knows not to depose further on the said article, as he says, because he does not know Robert, son of the said Maud, about whom there is notice in the article.

Sir Thomas de Castelford...

... around the feast of Pentecost a year ago this witness gave the aforesaid Maud a broadcloth to sell and afterwards, about the following Christmas, this witness found the said Maud in the street of Skeldergate, York at William de Swanlond's porch and asked her for the silver that she had received for the said broadcloth. She said, 'For sure I don't have the silver, but wait for me a little while and as soon as I am able to have the silver, I will pay you half,' and then William de Swanlond asked the same Sir Thomas whether he would be willing to give the said Maud a day to pay. The same Sir Thomas, at the said William's request, gave her a day, then to come and now past, on which day the said Maud came and paid six pence and asked him not to think ill of the fact that she had not paid what she had promised, that she was unable to obtain more at that time, but as soon as she was able to obtain some more money, she would willingly pay him it until the whole amount was paid. Asked what the sum was, he said 4s 3d. Asked whether the said Maud pledged herself by her faith to pay the said money on the said day, he says that he does not know for certain, but he believes that she said thus, 'Here is my faith that I will pay you on the said day the said sum if I am able to obtain it in any way in the meantime'. Asked whether Robert, son of the said Maud was at the time of his reception and examination entangled in the crime of theft or was held or reputed a thief among the neighbours of Micklegate and North Street, York, he says that not by reason of anything that he ever knew or heard. He knows not to depose further on the said articles as he says.

Adam Taillour...

[Hearsay evidence concerning Maud's debt.]

[The following three depositions appear not to be dated.]

Robert de Harwod of York, aged 20 years as he says...

... he knew the man and the woman [John and Maud] from the feast of Pentecost last, but not before and was a neighbour of them for the whole of the aforesaid time, so he says, and is still. Asked if he ever heard of any marriage made or contracted between John de Walkington and Maud de Bradley of York, the parties in question, the witness says that before the time the present action was moved concerning the matrimonial cause between the same John and Maud, he never heard tell of marriage between them, but only of concubinage so he says. Asked whether and for how long he knew Maud Katersouth and Robert, her son, witnesses called for the party of the said Maud against the aforesaid John de Walkington in the aforesaid matrimonial cause, he says that he knew each for about the past two years. Asked whether they were for the aforesaid time and are still considered and reputed poor, worthless, needy, and base persons ... he says that the aforesaid Maud is a poor little woman and needy, having nothing by which she is able to live and not able to work for her livelihood, but daily obtains her food and likewise takes her necessities around her neighbours' houses with flattering words. Asked about the reputation and standing of the same, he says that she is of little standing and of such repute that ... no faith is derived from her words among her neighbours nor do her words have any weight among them. Asked, he says that Robert, the aforesaid Maud's son is poor and needy, of little repute that many times he knew and heard him commit perjury in the street of North Street when playing among his friends or when showing he was displeased with them. He believes that he is willing for a small consideration to commit perjury and bear false testimony if commissioned and put up to this. Asked about the said Robert's age, he says that he knows for certain that he is fourteen years of age and more...

... he says that last Sunday he was present in the house of Alice de Thorlthorp when he heard it said that the said Robert acknowledged that he and his mother had been bribed by the said Maud de Bradley to bear testimony in this cause. Asked if he heard tell that he had received anything for bearing this testimony in this cause other than he ought licitly, he says that he did not hear it said other than that he took payment for bearing his testimony...

... he says that one Wednesday three weeks ago as he now recalls, that is in the evening and almost in the darkness of the night, this witness was present in his own home in the street of North Street where he lives where and when he heard contentious words and banging at the doorway of John de Walkington and as soon as the said witness heard he looked out into the king's highway through a window and saw the aforesaid John de Stanlay coming from the said John de Walkington's house saying he was ready to fight the said John de Walkington with his fist alone, and the next day he saw John de Walkington's hand wounded and the doorway of his house broken and it was said, as much by the said John de Walkington as by his neighbours, that the said John de Stanlay had done this wrong ... and that for three weeks immediately following they were continuously enemies. Asked if he were his capital enemy for the whole of the time following and that he wished to kill him or instill the fear of death, he says that on this he knows not to depose other than he has deposed above, but he believes that he wished rather to bring about harm rather than good towards him for the whole of the aforesaid time...

Robert de Popilton, aged 20 years...

... says that he knew the said John de W[alkington] and Maud de Bradeley, the parties in question, for sixteen years and more. Asked if he knew or heard say that Maud Katersouth, Robert, her son, and and John de Stanlay were witnesses ... of this he knows not to depose as he says. Asked concerning acquaintance with the aforesaid persons of Maud Katersouth and Robert, her son, he says that he knew them for about the past four years. He says that Maud Katersouth is a poor and needy woman and has nothing in goods, but for a little bread or a draught of ale she will fetch water for the use of her neighbours and mill in their homes and work as one poor little woman is able, and thus she lives and is supported among her neighbours. Asked about the standing and reputation of the said Maud ... he says that she is thus [i.e. untrustworthy and of low repute] reputed among her neighbours and that for a small consideration she will conceal the truth and speak untruth. Asked if he ever knew or heard that the said Maud was bribed to speak faleshood and to have kept silent the truth, he says not, but he had frequently heard it said that she wished to do so... Asked about the standing and repute of Robert, son of the said Maud, he says that he is silly and untrustworthy and does not care what he says or what he speaks, so he says...

... he says that he heard from others it said that Robert acknowledged many times that he and his mother had received payment for their testimony in the aforesaid matrimonial cause from the party of Maud de Bradley, although he never heard the said Robert say thus, nor does he remember the names of those who heard Robert so speak...

... asked how long a time he knew John de Stanlay ... he says he knew him for the past ten years ... he says that he heard it said that John de Stanlay broke John de Walkington's doorway and wounded him in the hand...

Peter Webster, aged 20 years so he says...

... he says that he knew John de Walkington and Maud de Bradley for the past two years. Asked whether he ever heard say that Maud de Katersouth and Robert, her son were witnesses ... he says that he did not hear before the Saturday before the feast of St Gregory last... Asked how long a time he knew Maud Katersouth and Robert, her son, he says he knew them for the past two years... He says that he often heard it said that the said Maud and Robert were perjured and five weeks ago he was present in the house of Ellen, called Webster, of North Street where and when he heard the aforesaid Maud Katersouth swear by her faith that she would pay the said Ellen the money that she owed her for ale within a certain time that is now past, within the which time she did not pay the said money, heedlessly breaking her oath. The said Robert, so he says, is willing to commit perjury for a halfpennyworth of ale or a ?crust. Asked how he knows this, he says that he was often present when the aforesaid Robert frequently committed perjury playing the game called 'Croysers'...

... he believes that the said Robert has completed fourteen years of his age. Asked, he says that he was present in the home of John de Walkington ... on Friday before the feast of St Gregory last in the presence of the said John de Walkington, Thomas de Beverley and his wife, and Robert, the servant of the said John de Walkington, where and when he heard the aforesaid Robert knowingly and freely acknowledge that he and his mother had been bribed by the said Maud de Bradley to proffer testimony in the aforesaid matrimonial cause and he was compelled by his aforesaid mother to come and undergo examination in the aforesaid matrimonial cause...

... about three weeks ago the same witness stood at the doorway of John de Hoperton, his master, almost in the darkness of the night, when he saw John de Stanlay ... give insult to John de Walkington standing within his own home and break the doorway of his house with his foot and wound the said John's hand with a knife...

[Following two depositions are dated 1 July 1355.]

John de Hoperton...

... he says that Robert and Maud Katersouth, witnesses called for the party of Maud de Bradley in the said appealed cause, were the whole time of their reception and examination in the same cause and are still, and each of them was and is still of good standing, trustworthy, and held and considered of spotless repute in the parish of the church of All Saints in North Street, York and in neighbouring parts. Asked how he knows this, he says that from the time of the last mortality [i.e. the Black Death] right up to the present day he knew the aforesaid Robert and Maud well and for the whole of that time he well knew that they were held and reputed trustworthy people by all their neighbours and others who had acquaintance with them.

William Hare...

... he says that he knew Robert and Maud, about whom there is notice in the aforesaid exception, well for the past four years and more and for the whole of that time he well knows and knew that the said Robert and Maud were held and reputed in the streets of Micklegate and North Street, York and neighbouring places trustworthy folk of good character and spotless repute...

### 14. Wills, diocese of York.

[a] Will of Thomas Bracebrigg, merchant, York. Language: Latin. Date: 1436. Translated from BIHR, Prob. Reg. 3 fo. 489.

And I leave 10s to buy and give 20 pairs of shoes for poor women immediately after my death according to the good discretion of my executors.

[b] Will of William Skynner, vintner, York. Language: Latin. Date: 1474. The term 'maisondieu', i.e. God's house, is the normal northern regional term for a small hospital or almshouse. Translated from BIHR, Prob. Reg. 4 fo. 214v.

And I leave to the poor women in the maisondieu on Ouse Bridge, 3s 4d.

[c] Will of Joan Cotyngham, widow, York, Latin 1459. Translated from YML, D/C Reg. 1 fo. 290v.

Also I leave to Joan Day a poor little woman staying in a certain maisondieu my russet gown lined with buckskin and a chemise of linen cloth.

[d] Will of Roger de Burton, mercer, York. Language: Latin. Date: 1393. Translated from BIHR, Prob. Reg. 1 fo. 55v.

Also I leave to be divided and distributed among the poor and widows continuously lying in their beds in York who are unable to go out to seek for themselves the necessities of life, 40s sterling.

[e] Will of Richard Wartere, merchant, York. Language: Latin. Date: 1458. Translated from BIHR, Prob. Reg. 4 fo. 115v.

Also I leave to each poor woman or widow having a child or children within the aforesaid parish of St Saviour, 12d. Also I leave to every other poor person living within the same parish, 4d.

[f] Will of Avice, wife of William Pontefract, draper, York. Language: Latin. Date: 1404. Translated from BIHR, Prob. Reg. 3 fo. 111.

Also to a certain poor woman living in the cemetery of my parish church aforesaid, 4d.

[g] Will of Marion, wife of John Marton, tanner, York. Language: Latin. Date: 1441. Translated from BIHR, Prob. Reg. 2 fo. 27v.

Also I leave to the said church a bench to be set among poor widows and others at the burial mass of their husbands and of other poor people as is the custom there.

[h] Will of Katherine Radclyff, merchant's widow, York. Language: Latin. Date: 1458. Peat turves were a common source of fuel, particularly at a period when wood was becoming increasingly scarce, and hence expensive, and coal was only mined in limited quantities and in a small number of localities. (See [i] below.) Translated from BIHR, Prob. Reg. 2 fo. 375.

Also I leave for the purchase of a boatload of turves to be distributed to the poor in the city of York in the next wintertime following my death, 40s.

[i] Will of Agnes Broune, Scarborough. Language: Latin. Date: 1400. As a coastal town and port, Scarborough would have access to coal imported from Newcastle. Translated from BIHR, Reg. 16 fo. 172v.

And to render annually six quarters of sea coal to the poor in the house that I have built at the bottom of the garden of the capital messuage...

[j] Will of Emma, wife of William Paynot, Easingwold. Language: Latin. Date: 1346. Translated from BIHR, Reg. 10 fo. 305.

Also to every widow of Easingwold, 3d, total by estimation, 10s 9d.

[k] Will of William de Huntyngton, apothecary, York. Language: Latin. Date: 1362. Translated from YML, D/C Reg. 1 fo. 37v.

Also I leave to the poor clerks and widows singing psalms and watching around my body, 6s 8d.

[1] Will of Nicholas Blakburn, merchant, senior, York. Language: English. Date: 1432. Translated from BIHR, Prob. Reg. 2 fo. 605.

Also I will that Margery my wife, out of what I have notified her of in my testament, has the means to find herself a gentlewoman's livelihood for herself whilst she lives, a priest, and a servant.

[m] Will of Richard Torald, esquier, York. Language: Latin. Date: 1439. Translated from BIHR, Prob. Reg. 3 fo. 583.

And I leave to Agnes Mirfeld, sister to my wife, 20 marks, but under this condition, that the aforesaid Agnes stay with Elizabeth my wife so long as the same Elizabeth wants the aforesaid Agnes.

### 15. *Fasciculus Morum.*

Language: Latin. Date: ?early fourteenth century. Cf. Childhood [8]. Translated from Wenzel, ed., *Fasciculus Morum.*

Poor little beggar women, however, carry to the doors of the rich children whom they make to cry so that they may receive alms more readily.

### 16. Papal letter.

Language: Latin. Date: 1391. Calendared translation from *Calendar of Papal Registers,* IV.

Relaxation, at the petition of Francis, bishop of Palestrina, vice-chancellor of the holy Roman Church, of five years and five forty day periods of enjoined penance to penitents who on the feasts of the Nativity, Annunciation, Purification, and Assumption of the Blessed Virgin, the Resurrection of the Lord, and three days immediately following it (on which three days a great concourse of people takes place) and during the octaves of the said Nativity and Assumption, visit and give alms for the sustentation and conservation of the church of the Augustinian monastery of St Mary Bishopsgate, without the walls, London, the chapels and altars situated therein and those in the solemn hospital of the Blessed Virgin founded within the said monastery, in which hospital very many poor widows and orphans are continually sustained.

### 17. Coroners' rolls, Bedfordshire.

Language: Latin. Translation in Hunnisett, ed., *Bedfordshire Coroners' Rolls.*

[a] [1273] Towards vespers ... Joan Fine of Milton Bryant came to Houghton Regis carrying Henry, aged two, in her arms and went from door to door seeking hospitality. They came to Richard Red's house, where they were given shelter in a barn. They sat down there and Henry went out of its doors, fell into a ditch, and drowned by misadventure. Joan Flye [sic, presumably for Fine] first found him...

[b] [1270] Towards vespers ... Lucy Pofot, formerly the wife of Thomas of Houghton came from the tavern in the house of John of Cranfield of Aspley Guise in Aspley Guise and went to her house. A lewd stranger came and asked for entertainment and Lucy entertained him. At dawn the next day Andrew, son of Simon of Houghton Regis, servant, came to draw water at a well called 'Swetewell', came to Lucy's house, saw her dead with five wounds to the heart apparently made with a knife...

[c] [January 1274] ... Emma of Hatch came from Beeston, where she had been begging for bread from door to door, and towards vespers she returned towards Beeston to seek lodging. She came to a piece of cultivated land called 'Pokebrokforlong' in Northill, was overcome by cold, and died by misadventure...

[d] [1273] ... Beatrice Bone, a poor woman, went from door to door in Turvey begging for food. She came to Alice Mordant's house in 'Arneburwey', fell down because she was weak and infirm and died there by misadventure between prime and tierce...

## 18. Coroners' rolls, Oxford.

Language: Latin. Date: 1300. The holding of a coroner's inquest on what was in effect an aborted foetus is very unusual, but see 'Law and custom' [34b]. Deaths of both adult females and males due to crushing in similar circumstances are also found in London coroners' records for the hungry years of the early fourteenth century. Translated from Thorold Rogers, *Oxford City Documents.*

Inquest was made before the coroner of the lord king for the town of Oxford on Saturday in the feast of St George in the 28th year of the reign of King Edward son of King Henry concerning the death of Roger, the son of Emma de Hereford, who was found dead in the parish of St Thomas the Martyr on the previous Friday by the oath of Henry Jolif etc., who say on their oath that they do not know of anyone culpable of the aforesaid Roger's death, but they say that Emma, the mother of the said Roger, was at a food dole at the house of Sir Boniface, Archdeacon of Buckingham, in the town of Oxford that year, and there was a great number of poor at that dole, and Emma was knocked down amongst them and trampled so that the said Roger met his death on the following Friday in his mother's womb.

### 19. Coroners' rolls, Sussex.

Language: Latin. Date: 1524. Translation in Hunnisett, ed., *Sussex Coroners' Inquests.*

About 11 p.m. on 6 May Margaret Owtered, widow, without anyone's aid or advice, hanged herself with her own chemise which she fixed onto an iron support for a window of her house in East Grinstead. She had goods and chattels worth 40s...

### 20. Accounts for household of Robert Waterton of Methley.

Language: Latin. Date: 1416-7. Translated from C. M. Woolgar, ed., *Household Accounts from Medieval England,* Records of Social and Economic History, new ser. XVII-XVIII, 1992-3.

And paid to a certain woman of Altoft in alms, 4*d.*

...

And paid to a certain woman of Altoft in alms on the master's instruction, 3*d.*

And paid to a certain woman of Felby in alms on the master's instruction, 4*d.*

# V: Work in the countryside

## 1. Anthony Fitzherbert, *The Boke of Husbandry.*

Language: English. Date: 1523. Translated from Williams, ed., *English Historical Documents*, V.

What tasks a wife should do in general.

... And when you are up and ready, then first sweep the house, set the table, and put everything in your house in good order. Milk your cows, suckle your calves, strain your milk, get your children up and dress them, and provide for your husband's breakfast, dinner, supper, and for your children and servants, and take your place with them. Send corn and malt to the mill so that you can bake and brew whenever there is need. Measure it for the mill and from the mill, and see that you have your measure again, less the toll, otherwise either the miller acts dishonestly with you or else your corn is not as dry as it should be. You must make butter and cheese whenever you are able, feed your pigs both morning and evening, and give your poultry their food in the morning. When the appropriate time of year comes around, you must assess how your hens, ducks, and geese lay, and collect their eggs, and when they get broody, put them such that no beasts, pigs, or other vermin may harm them. You should know that all web-footed fowls will sit for a month and all claw-footed will only sit for three weeks except a peahen and large fowls such as cranes, bustards, and the like. When they have hatched their chicks, see that they are well protected from kites, crows, polecats, and other vermin. At the beginning of March, or a little before, it is time for a wife to make her garden and to get as many good seeds and herbs as she can, and especially those that be good for the pot and to eat. As often as shall be necessary, it must be weeded, otherwise weeds will choke the herbs. March is also the time to sow flax and hemp, the reason being that I have heard old housewives say that March coarse flax is better than April flax, but I do not need to show how it should be sown, weeded, pulled, rippled, watered, washed, dried, beaten, bruised in the brake, tawed, heckled, spun, wound, wrapped, and woven for they are knowledgeable enough. From this they can make sheets, broadcloths, towels, shirts, smocks, and other such necessaries, and therefore let your distaff always be ready for a pastime so that you are not idle. Although there is no question that a woman can make an honest living by spinning with the distaff, it meets a need and should be practised. When the flax pods have been stripped off, they must be sifted from the weeds and made dry in the sun in order to get the seeds out. One kind of linseed, however, called locked seed, will not open in the sun and therefore, when they are dry, they must be thoroughly bruised and broken – wives know how – and then winnowed and kept dry until the appropriate season returns. Your female hemp must be pulled from the male hemp, for it does not bear seed, and you must treat it the same way as you did with the flax. The male hemp bears seed, and beware the birds do not eat it, as it grows. The hemp from it is not so good as the female hemp, but it will still serve well. It may sometimes happen that you have so many things to do that you do not clearly know where it is best to begin. If so, consider what job would be the greatest loss if it were not done and how long it would take to do. Then think what is the greatest loss and start there. But in case the job that is of greatest loss takes a long time to do, and you could do three or four jobs in the same time, then consider carefully, if all these jobs were added together, which of them would be the greatest loss. If all these jobs together be of greater loss and may be done in as short a time as the other, then do your many jobs first.

It is appropriate for a husband to have sheep of his own for many reasons. If so, let his wife have part of the wool to make her husband and herself some clothes. At the very least, let her have the locks of the sheep, either to make clothes or blankets and coverlets, or both. If she has no wool of her own, she may take wool to spin from clothiers and by that means she may have a suitable livelihood and sufficient time to do other tasks. It is a wife's occupation to winnow all kinds of grain, to make malt, to wash and wring, to make hay, reap corn, and in time of need to help her husband fill the muck-wain or dung cart, drive the plough, load hay, corn, and such other, and to go or ride to the market, sell butter, cheese milk, eggs, chickens, capons, hens, pigs, geese, and all types of grain, and also to buy all the sorts of things necessary for the household, and to make a true reckoning and account to her husband of what she has spent. If the husband goes to the market to buy or sell, as they often do, he is then to show his wife in the same way, for if one of them should practise to deceive the other, he deceives himself and he is unlikely to prosper, and therefore they must be honest to one another...

## 2. 'Ballad of a Tyrannical Husband'.

Language: English. Date: ?later fifteenth century. Translated from T. Wright and J. O. Halliwell, eds., *Reliquae Antiquae*, 2 vols., London, 1841. This is an old edition of an apparently corrupt, late version of the text. The verses are ostensibly intended to be publicly narrated by a man in defence of women to a mixed audience. This interesting text is very much in need of a modern scholarly edition.

...

The goodman and his lad to the plough are gone,
The goodwife had much to do, and servant had she none,
Many small children to look after beside herself alone,
She did more than she could inside her own house.

Home came the goodman early in the day
To see that everything was according to his wishes.
'Dame,' he said, 'is our dinner ready?' 'Sir,' she said, 'no.
How would you have me do more that I can?'

Then he began to chide and said, 'Damn you!
I wish you would go all day to plough with me,
To walk in the clods that are wet and boggy,
Then you would know what it is to be a ploughman.'

Then the goodwife swore, and thus she said,
'I have more to do than I am able to do.
If you were to follow me for a whole day,
You would be weary of your part, I dare bet my head.'

'Blast! In the devil's name!' said the goodman,
'What have you to do, but sit here at home?
You go to your neighbour's house, one after the other,
And sit there chattering with Jack and with Jane.'

Then said the goodwife, 'May you rot!
I have more to do, if everything were known;
When I lie in my bed, my sleep is but small,
Yet early in the morning you will call me to get up.

'When I lie all night awake with our child,
I rise up in the morning and find our house chaotic.
Then I milk our cows and turn them out in the field,
While you sleep quite soundly, Christ protect me!

'Then I make butter later on in the day.
Afterwards I make cheese – these you consider a joke -
Then our children will weep and they must get up,
Yet you will criticise me if any of our produce isn't there.

'When I have done this, yet there comes even more:
I give our chickens food or else they will be lean;
Our hens, our capons, and our ducks all together,
Yet I tend to our gosling that go on the green.

'I bake, I brew, it will not otherwise be well,
I beat and swingle flax, so help me God,
I heckle the tow, I warm up and cool down [or I winnow and
      ruddle [sheep]],
I tease wool and card it and spin it on the wheel.

'Dame,' said the goodman, 'the devil have your bones!
You do not need to bake or brew more than once a fortnight.
I see no good that you do within this big house,
But always you excuse yourself with grunts and groans.'

'Either I make a piece of linen and woollen cloth once a year,
In order to clothe ourselves and our children in together,
Or else we should go to the market and buy it very dear;
I am as busy as I may every year.

'When I have done this, I look at the sun,
I prepare food for our beasts before you come home,
And food for ourselves before it is noon,
Yet I don't get a fair word when I have done

'So I look to our welfare both outdoors and inside'
So that nothing great or small is lacking...


### 3. Coroners' rolls, Bedfordshire.

Language: Latin. Date: 1270. Translation in Hunnisett, ed., *Bedfordshire Coroners' Rolls.*

[a] ... Amice daughter of Robert Belamy of Staploe and Sibyl Bon-chevaler were carrying a tub full of grout between them in Lady Juliana de Beauchamp's brewhouse in the hamlet of Staploe in Eaton Socon, intending to empty it into a boiling leaden vat, when Amice slipped and fell into the vat and the tub upon her. Sibyl immediately

jumped towards her, dragged her from the vat, and shouted. The household came and found her scalded almost to death. A chaplain came and Amice had the rites of the Church and died by misadventure the next day about prime...

b] About midday ... Amice, daughter of William le Lorimer of Bedford went into 'Wilputtesburne' in Cardington field by Cardington wood to gather corn. Thunder and lightning came on and she was struck and fell and died instantly. Maud, daughter of Nicholas de Augul first found her...

## 4. Coroners' rolls, Sussex.

Language: Latin. Date: 1524. Translation in Hunnisett, ed., *Sussex Coroners' Inquests.*

About 10 a.m. on 21 May, when a cart belonging to John Brownyng, late of Barlavington, yeoman, came and stood quietly in a hidden place in Shopton Lane in the king's highway in the tithing of Sutton, Margaret late the wife of Ralph Derbye of Bury, labourer, came from Bury on a grey mare belonging to her husband. Wishing to hurry on her business to Petworth market, she put caution to one side and forced the mare to pass by the near wheel of the cart where an embankment about four feet high had been erected, upon which the mare raised its front hoofs so that on account of the mare's violence and insecurity Margaret was thrown from its back and fell to the ground on her neck, receiving a large wound on the neck of which she immediately died; and so the mare murdered her. It is deodand and worth no more than 5s. It remains with Ralph for the king's use.

## 5. Visitation of Huntingdon Priory.

Language: Latin. Date: 1422. Translated from A. Hamilton Thomson, ed., *Visitations of Religious Houses in the Diocese of Lincoln*, I, Lincoln Record Society, VII, 1914.

Also that the women who wash clothes have no access to the claustral precinct in order to take in or return clothes to be washed, but when these washerwomen come, let them wait at the priory's outer gate and let the clothes to be washed be brought out to them and, when washed, be taken back by some secular person and under no circumstances by the canons.

## 6. Manor court, Halesowen.

Language: Latin. Translated from Wilson, ed., *Court Rolls of the Manor of Hales.*

[a] [1278] The tasters beyond the Stour say that Felicity the weaver sold against the Assize at the house of her brother, William the smith.

[b] [1299] The vill of Ridgeacre say for the postponed verdict [in the case] between Roger Fokerham and Joan de la Grene that the aforesaid Joan and her family unjustly mowed grass on the bound between them and took more than she ought to do. Accordingly it is judged that the aforesaid Joan is in mercy and Roger should receive damages from her.

[c] [1300] Day in autumn. The daughter of William de Wylinghurst, two daughters of Nicholas le Yonge, two daughters of Thomas Colling, and the daughter of Dygan to work two days for the lord in autumn, each of them one day at the wheat.

[d] [1302] Amercement for chickens. Richard the son of Malle put himself at mercy for his wife's wrongdoing.

Amercement for chickens. Maud Hychcok puts herself at mercy for a like transgression.

## 7. Peace sessions, Bedfordshire.

Language: Latin. Date: 1358. Translated from E. G. Kimball, ed., *Sessions of the Peace for Bedfordshire 1355-1359, 1363-1364*, Bedfordshire Historical Record Society, XLVIII, 1969.

They say further that the same William [le Rook] in the twenty-sixth year of the present king made himself a purveyor of the lord king without warrant taking geese, capons, and a cock of Katherine Boweles, John le Taillour, Maud de Kempston, and others...

## 8. Household accounts.

Language: Latin. Translated from Woolgar, ed., *Household Accounts from Medieval England.*

[a] Diet account of Edmund Mortimer on journey to Scotland. Date: 1378.

For a woman hired to find poultry on several occasions, 14*d*.

[b] Household and receiver's account for Sir William Mountford. Date: 1433-4.

Also, for twenty chickens purchased from Margery Clerke, 20*d.*

...

Also, paid to various women making hay, 20*s* 3d.

...

Also, paid to Margery Barbur for making wax for Purification and for Easter, 7*d.*

Also, paid to Agnes Walron for washing, 18*d.*

[c] Cash account for household of Isabel, Lady Morley. Date: 1363-4.

And paid to Alice Chyrche, the lady's washerwoman, for her stipend this year, 6*s* 8*d.*

### 9. Manor court, Littleport.

Language: Latin. Translated from Maitland and Baildon, eds., *The Court Baron.*

[a] [1324] Elisota Jordan was deficient in the weight of a halfpenny whole-wheat loaf by 5*s* 2*d.* Let her have judgement etc. Afterwards she made fine of 6*d* by pledge of Thomas Tame.

[b] [1325] William Hewen and Margaret his wife were attached to answer Robert le Carter in a plea of covenant. He complains that he gave Margaret ten quarters of barley to make into malt for his own use, but that the malt was found to be unsatisfactory, to the said Robert's loss and against the contract...

[c] [1326] And that Mabel Beucosyn absented herself in the autumn and would reap neither the lord's corn nor her neighbours' for her wages, but went from the vill against the ordinance of the bylaw.

### 10. Halmote court, Durham.

Language: Latin. Date: 1364. Translated from *Durham Halmote Rolls.*

Southwick: It is ordered that Hugh Raynoldson and his wife should not hold a brewhouse on any land other than the lord's land under penalty of losing the land they hold of the lord.

Shiels: The brewsters of Shiels are instructed not to sell a gallon of ale for more than 1½*d.*

Coupon: Of Agnes Postell and Alice de Bellasyis because they refused to sell by the gallon, pottle, and quart when asked for ale as was found by the tasters, of each 6*d.*

## 11. Manor court, West Halton, Lincolnshire.

Language: Latin. Date: 1315. This case may be suggestive of a degree of competition between male and female brewers. Translated from R. H. Helmholz, ed., *Select Cases on Defamation to 1600*, Selden Society, CI, 1985.

Cecily Öde was summoned to answer William the clerk concerning a plea that on Friday before the feast of Pentecost last she called him false etc. and says that the said William's ale was not sound etc. whereby the said William lost the sale of the aforesaid ale etc. to the said William's loss, 40d, and thence he produces suit etc. And the said Cecily comes and says that she is not guilty thereof and this she seeks that this be inquired. The inquest says that she is guilty. Therefore it is judged that the said William shall recover damages of four pence as is taxed by the inquest. And the said Cecily [is] in mercy. John the clerk, pledge.

## 12. Manor court, Tottenham.

Language: Latin. Translation in Oram, trans., *Court Rolls of the Manors of Bruces, Dawbeneys, Pembrokes (Tottenham)*, II.

[a] [Bruces, 1380] And that the wife (3*d*) of John Godhewe, the wife (3*d*) of Thomas Duke, the wife (3*d*) of Gilbert Page, are regrators of ale, therefore etc. And that the same regratrices (3*d*) are in rebellion in not permitting the aletaster to do his office, therefore etc.

[b] [Pembrokes, 1383] John Hood complains against Maud Taillour (2*d*), pledge for prosecution John Brodelane, and says that the said Maud entered with her pigs and destroyed his corn within his close, viz. beans and peas to the damage of the same John 3*s* 4*d*, and the said Maud says she is not guilty and seeks view of law three-handed against the next court, and afterwards they have leave to make concord, therefore the said Alice is in mercy, pledge Geoffrey Hecpole.

[c] [Pembrokes, 1392] Isabel de ?Crave, by attorney the beadle, complains of Robert Lemman in a plea of debt that he owes her 4½*d* for horse bread and ale bought of her to the damage 12*d*, and the said Robert admits it, therefore in mercy (2*d*) by the pledge of William Godewyne.

[d] [Pembrokes, 1393] Also they present that Christiana Bakere (12*d*) has sold one gallon of unpleasant, second-rate ale and outside the statute of the Assize, therefore in mercy.

[e] [Pembrokes, 1397] Also they present that Joan Walsyngham (*2d*), Alice Petyt (*2d*), Isabel Sadelere (*2d*), Mariota Goodestre (*2d*), have cut the grass in the meadow and the lord's and tenants' field, therefore in mercy.

[f] [Pembrokes, 1398] The wife of John atte Belle brews and is not mandated by the ale-tasters, therefore in mercy.

## 13. Manor court rolls, Ingoldmells.

Language: Latin. Translation in Massingberd, trans., *Court Rolls of the Manor of Ingoldmells.*

[a] [1387] The inquisition of the free [tenants] presents that Alan Souter, Maud Souter, William Ingraine, and Thomas de Tointon went out of the lordship of this manor last autumn to take excessive salaries, therefore each is in mercy (*7s 10d*).

[b] [1419] The aletasters present that the wife of Robert Herryson refused to sell her ale to be tasted by the same etc., and it is not willing to expose the sign called alestake, therefore etc. Mercy, *2d.*

## 14. Village ordinances, Wymeswold.

Language: English. Date: early fifteenth century. Translated from Stevenson, ed., *Report of the Manuscripts of Lord Middleton.*

... all manner of men that have any peas in the field when shelling time comes, let [them] shell in their own lands[1] and not in other men's. And other men or women that have no peas of their own growing, let them gather them twice in the week on Wednesday and on Friday, reasonably going in the land furrows and gathering with their hands and with no sickles, once before noon and no more. For if any man or woman other that has any peas and goes into any other [person's land], for each time [to] pay a penny to the church and lose their pods, and they that have none and do other than the aforesaid [ordinance provides], with sickle or without, shall lose the vessel they gather them in and the pods and a penny to the church.

...

Also, no man or woman that works harvest work [is to] carry home no sheaves of no man, for if it may be known, for each sheaf that they bear home [they] shall pay a penny to the church.

1 I.e. strips.

Also, no man or woman [is to] glean no manner of corn that is able to work for their living... No other gleaners that may not work [is to] glean in no kind of way among no sheaves, for if they do they shall lose the corn and a penny to the church for each load.

### 15. Household accounts.

Language: Latin. Translated from Stevenson, ed., *Report of the Manuscripts of Lord Middleton.*

[1521] Also, the Thursday, the 27th day of June, for your reward to 2 women that washed lead ore as you went to St Ann's [Well], 2d.

Also, to [the] women that gathered lead ore, 1d.

Also, for your reward the Friday, the 30th day of June [sic] to a woman that brought a bottle of wine from Lenton, 1d.

...

[1522] Also, for a maid that brought rushes, 1d.

...

[1526] Also, paid to Robert James' wife and Slade's wife for their costs that watched with a prisoner that was hanged at Basset Cross, 3s 10d.

...

[1527] Also paid the same time to Key's wife for a week making candles, 4d.

### 16. Peace sessions, Lincolnshire.

Language: Latin. Translated from Sillem, ed., *Records of some Sessions of the Peace in Lincolnshire.*

[a] [1360] Also they say that when Thomas Leuelaunce, lately a justice of the Statute of Labourers, and a constable of Manton attached Denise, the wife of Thomas Crake and assigned her according to the Statute to work for Sir Philip Nevyle, who was the employer of Denise's labour, the aforesaid Thomas Crake came by force of arms and broke the attachment and took and withdrew her from the service of the said Sir Philip...

[b] [1373] And that Alice, the servant of William de Scampton of North Carlton, who was assigned and charged by the constable of the vill of North Carlton to serve the abbot of Barlings in reaping his grain in the autumn in the 47th year [of Edward III], left the vill to take a higher wage and refused to serve the abbot in contempt of the king etc.

[c] [1373] Also they present that John, son of Sibilla de Swallowe on Tuesday after the feast of the Assumption of the Blessed Virgin Mary in the 47th year [of Edward III] came into the territory of Croxby and took and led Alice Treu of Croxby away from there to Swallow giving her for the entire autumn fourpence a day and board which Alice took from John against the form of the Ordinance...

[d] [1374] Also they present that Agnes, wife of the aforesaid Thomas [the shepherd of the vicar of Langton], who keeps two maidservants, was instructed by John de Malteby of Langton on Tuesday after the feast of St Barnabas the Apostle in the 48th year [of Edward III] to stay with the aforesaid John Malteby at hoeing time to hoe his grain according to the form of the Ordinance of Labourers. Agnes, however, refused to do this and neither allowed her maid-servants to be judicially compelled nor to work at the aforesaid task...

[e] [1374] Also they say that Alice Milner of Heckington staying there this summer was admitted by officers of the lord king to serve Henry Asty in the autumn, but in the first week of Lent in the 47th year of the reign of the present king [Edward III] the same Alice withdrew herself and went from the vill to Sleaford and Burton against the Statute.

17. Peace sessions, Lincolnshire.

Language: Latin. Translated from Kimball, ed., *Records of some Sessions of the Peace in Lincolnshire.*

[a] [1383] Also they say that Emma Dagge and others are common labourers and refuse to swear before the constable to take by the day during autumn wages according to the ordinance of the Statute...

[b] [1387] Also they say that John Cotu' of Snarford asked Maud, daughter of Richard Nevyll of Snarford, a vagrant, to serve him as a spinster at Snardford from Easter ... until the same feast a year following. The said Maud entered the said John's service, but at the instigation of John Schipman of Lincoln, skinner, Maud left John de Cotu's service inside the aforesaid term contrary to the Statute and entered the said John Shipman's service.

[c] [1388] Also that one Cecily de Malberthorp, linen weaver took this year from William Warn of Mablethorpe for weaving 15 ells of linen cloth three farthings an ell and a gratuity worth 5d and would not take less for an ell, hence an excess of 5s.

## 18. Peace sessions, Yorkshire.

Language: Latin. Translated from B. A. Putnam, ed., *Yorkshire Sessions of the Peace, 1361-1364*, Yorkshire Archaeological Society Record Ser., C, 1939.

[a] [1361] And that John Storthwayt bought two quarters of barley by heaped measure from Josiana de Pokelyngton.

...

And that Isabel in le Wylughes bought barley of Cecily Petregate by heaped measure etc.

[b] [1363] And that Alice the wife of Robert Aunger brews and sells contrary to the statute, viz. by unsealed measure.

...

And that Agnes the chaplain's servant, brewster, sells using measures not sealed, but false.

[c] [1361] And that Beatrix de Bedford, weaver, took contrary to the Statute and refused to serve her neighbours.

...

And that Alice Tincler and John Freman went away from the aforesaid vill of Escrick in order to gain a higher salary in the autumn.

[d] [1363] The jurors present ... that Alice servant of Margaret de Cayton will not serve other than by the day and has gone outside the vill.

...

And that Matillis, the daughter of Agnes de Stakeston will not serve other than by the day and goes outside the vill.

...

And that Agnes atte Milne, reaper, went outside the vill in the autumn taking 4d [a day] and board.

...

And that Margaret Kemster, Dyota atte Westend, Isabel Aungers, Alice Scoy, Agnes Smert, Beatrix Siliben, Joan wife of Richard Bigg, Beatrix Curtays, Matillis wife of William Hert, Katherine wife of Thomas Castell, Agnes Wyles, Joan de Wharrum, Joan Schephird, Beatrix de Ruston, Elen Ketewell, Joan de Hundemanby, Matillis Walker, Joan wife of Walter atte Westend, Elizabeth Aungers, reapers, take by the day more than they were wont, viz. each of them 3d a day with board.

And that Margaret Peperwhyte and Margaret de Carlel, spinsters, take more that they were wont, viz. 1d with board.

...

And that Margaret Pochet, spinster and reaper, takes by the day contrary to the statute, viz. 2*d* with board.

...

And that Margaret Iollan went outside the vill last autumn to reap various grains in different places, taking 4*d* a day and board.

And that Agnes, servant of Adam de Boulton, labourer, takes from the aforesaid Adam a halfpenny a day and a meal and refuses to serve by the usual terms against etc..

...

... they presented that Alice wife of Peter Chauntrell went out of the vill of Pocklington in the autumn as far as Tibthorpe and there took by the day 4*d* and board for reaping.

...

And that Matillis Swan and Alice de Skerne, weavers, each of them took 1*d* an ell where they used to take only 2*d* for 5 ells.

...

And that Isabel Clerk of Stillingfleet wife of John Skinner of Stillingfleet took at Moreby on Monday after the feast of St Laurence ... 6*d* a day and this for the whole autumn.

...

[1364] And that Alice Milner, Joan Fox, Matillis Badd, Matillis Swan, Matillis de Rottese, Alice de Skyren, Matillis atte Cotes, spinsters, take each of them for spinning a stone of wool 18*d* where they were wont to take 12*d*, against etc.

[e] [1363] Also they say that Simon the smith and Joan his wife refused to swear before the constables to abide by the statute of labourers according...

### 19. Will of Ellen, wife of David Holgrafe, Bothall.

Language: Latin. Date: 1403. Translated from BIHR, Prob. Reg. 3 fo. 102.

Also I give and leave to the three women serving me in my illness, viz. the wife of Peter Forster, the wife of John Slikborn, and Ellen de Benton, to each of them a cow.

### 20. *Seneschaucy.*

Language: French. Date: c. 1276. Translation by Oschinsky in D. Oschinsky, ed., *Walter of Henley and other Treatises*, Oxford, 1971.

The dairymaid ought to be loyal, of good repute and clean; she ought to know her work and what relates to it. She ought not allow under-dairymaids or anyone else to take or carry away milk, butter, or cream whereby the cheese will be less and the dairy will lose...

The dairymaid ought to help to winnow the corn whenever she can; she ought to keep geese and hens and answer for the yield...

## 21. The Husbandry.

Language: French. Date: end of thirteenth century. Translation in Oschinsky, ed., *Walter of Henley and other Treatises.*

And the dairymaid ought to winnow all the corn, and half of her pay shall be for paying the woman who will help her.

And the dairymaid ought to look after all the small stock which are kept on the the manor such as sucking pigs, peacocks and their issue, geese and their issue, capons, cocks, and hens and their issue in chickens and eggs.

...

If there is a manor in which there is no dairy then it is always advisable to have a woman there for much less money than a man would take, to take care of the small stock and of all that is kept on the manor and answer for all the issues there just as the dairymaid would do... And she ought to be responsible for half of the winnowing of the corn just as the dairymaid would be.

...

The dairy woman ought to make cheese from Michaelmas until Christmas, but from this time it is more profitable for the lord to sell the milk than to make cheese or butter, because one can sell one gallon of milk for a higher price than one can sell three in summer or any other season.

...

And you ought to know that five men can easily reap and bind two acres of any kind of corn in a day... And in places where four men take each 1½*d* a day and the fifth, because he is the binder, 2d, one ought to give 4d per acre... But you should engage the reapers as a team, that is to say five men or women, whichever you wish, and whom you term 'men', make one team...

## 22. Poll tax, Claro Wapentake, West Riding of Yorkshire.

Language: Latin. Date: 1379. Translated from 'Rolls of the Collectors in the West Riding of the Lay-Subsidy (Poll Tax) 2 Richard II', *Yorkshire Archaeological Journal*, VII (1882), p. 30.

Asmunderby with Bondgate.

| | |
|---|---:|
| John de Morpath and his wife, franklin | 40*d.* |
| William, his servant | 4*d.* |
| Eleanor, his servant | 4*d.* |
| William Hegh and his wife, spicer | 12*d.* |
| Richard, his servant | 4*d.* |
| Thomas Wright, carpenter | 6*d.* |
| Robert Scayff and his wife | 12*d.* |
| Robert, his son | 4*d.* |
| Joan, his daughter | 4*d.* |
| Henry Smith and his wife | 12*d.* |
| John, his servant | 4*d.* |
| Alice, his servant | 4*d.* |
| Thomas Wright and his wife | 12*d.* |
| Agnes Webster | 4*d.* |
| Nicholas Hamund, shoemaker, and his wife, mason | 6*d.* |
| William Brame, tanner, and his wife, smith | 12*d.* |
| Hawis Milner | 4*d.* |
| Alice her daughter | 4*d.* |
| Richard Milner and his wife | 4*d.* |
| John de Whityngton and his wife, spicer | 12*d.* |
| John, his son | 4*d.* |
| William, his son | 4*d.* |
| Alice, his daughter... | 4*d.* |
| John Webster, weaver | 6*d.* |
| Alice de Baxby | 4*d.* |
| Thomas Pogg, slater, and his wife | 6*d.* |
| Robert, his servant | 4*d.* |
| John Inchefer | 4*d.* |
| Thomas de Colton and his wife | 4*d.* |
| William de Kirkeby and his wife | 4*d.* |
| Avice Walker | 4*d.* |
| William Wynpeny | 4*d.* |
| John Smith, smith | 6*d.* |
| Robert Goderik | 4*d.* |
| Thomas Henrison, carpenter | 6*d.* |

| | |
|---|---|
| John Hors, weaver, and his wife | 6*d.* |
| John Edeson | 4*d.* |
| Margaret Lenas | 4*d.* |
| Elizabeth de Snayth, weaver | 6*d.* |
| Cecily, her daughter | 4*d.* |
| Elizabeth del Chambre, her blood relative | 4*d.* |
| Robert, her servant | 4*d.* |
| John de Hetton, tanner | 6*d.* |
| Anot, his servant | 4*d.* |
| Henry, his servant | 4*d.* |
| Adam Hyne and his wife | 4*d.* |
| Adam Tournour and his wife, cooper | 6*d.* |
| Roger Swalowe, weaver, and his wife | 6*d.* |
| Juliana, his servant | 4*d.* |
| Robert Pyper and his wife | 4*d.* |
| Robert de Worsall, carpenter | 6*d.* |
| Elizot Walker | 4*d.* |
| Alice, her daughter | 4*d.* |
| Alice, her servant | 4*d.* |
| Henry Haybergh, carpenter | 6*d.* |
| Avice Hunter | 4*d.* |
| Alice, her daughter | 4*d.* |
| Joan, her daughter | 4*d.* |
| John Wethirhird | 4*d.* |
| John Carter and his wife | 4*d.* |
| Thomas de Eyrom and his wife | 4*d.* |
| Thomas Ormud and his wife | 4*d.* |
| William Pynder | 4*d.* |
| Alice, his daughter | 4*d.* |
| William Farnham, servant | 4*d.* |
| Seril Pynder | 4*d.* |
| Joan, her daughter | 4*d.* |
| Maud Choune | 4*d.* |
| Walter Carter, servant | 4*d.* |
| Robert Gryme and his wife | 12*d.* |
| Walter Carter and his wife | 4*d.* |
| Richard Oxenhird and his wife | 4*d.* |
| Thomas de Hede and his wife | 4*d.* |
| John Colstane and his wife | 4*d.* |
| Richard, his son | 4*d.* |

# VI: Work in the town

*See also 'Childhood' [3] deposition of Beatrix de Morland; 'Adolescence'
[24] depositions of John Wyrsdall and Margaret Esyngwald; 'Widowhood,
poverty, and old age' [12] deposition of Roger Marschall, [13] depositions
of Sir Thomas de Castleford and William de Warnefeld; 'Law and custom'
[35].*

### 1. 'Women are worthy'.

Language: English. Date: earlier sixteenth century. Translated from R. T.
Davies, ed., *Medieval English Lyrics*, London, 1963.

> I am as swift as any roe
> To praise women where'er I go.

To dispraise women it is a shame,
For a woman was your dame:
Our Blessed Lady bears the name
Of all women where'er they go.

A woman is a worthy thing:
They do the wash and do the wring;
'Lullay, lullay,' she does you sing,
And yet she has but care and woe.

A woman is a worthy wight:
She serves a man both day and night;
Thereto she puts all her might,
And yet she has but care and woe.

### 2. Court of King's Bench.

Language: Latin. Date: 1386. Translated from Arnold, ed., *Select Cases of
Trespass.*

... And with regard breaking house etc. the aforesaid Richard
[Gryndere] says that he is the beadle of Billingsgate ward, in which
ward the aforesaid house is located, and that the custom of the city of
London is and for all time has been such that if any man conceals

himself in the house of any woman or any woman in the house of any man in order illicitly to sleep together there and suspicion arises thence and rumour comes to the beadle's ears, it is that beadle's duty to enter that house and search every part of that house and expel from that house all persons found concealed there. And because report and rumour came to that beadle that the aforesaid Joan [Garton] kept in her house aforesaid a certain married man hidden for the purpose of illicitly sleeping with the same Joan, the same Richard, beadle of the aforesaid ward, entered that house and for that reason had the house searched according to the force and effect of the aforesaid custom...

And the aforesaid Joan says that she does know such a custom to be used in the aforesaid city. She says in fact that the aforesaid John [atte More] is a brewer and often sells ale in bulk and also at retail in a tavern, and the same Joan often bought ale from the same John to sell by retail, and because the same Joan refused to buy ale from John and bought ale that suited her better from other brewers, and because the same Joan sold much ale near that John's tavern and refused to buy from the same John all the ale that she thus sold, the same John, moved for that reason by anger against the same Joan, urged the aforesaid Richard to break and enter her aforesaid house in contempt of the same Joan in order to make the aforesaid Joan go away from that ward...

### 3. Church court, diocese of Canterbury.

Language: Latin. Date: 1413. Translated from Helmholz, ed., *Select Cases on Defamation.*

John Sanden of the parish of Whitstable, the diocese of Canterbury, and living there for 16 years, 40 years of age and more, of free condition as he says, being sworn etc. Asked first on the petition proferred in place of the libel during the proceedings on behalf of Christine Colmere's party against Simon Daniell of the parish of Seasalter in a defamation cause presented for the same Christine's party, this witness says that the article proferred in place of the libel contains the truth in that and by that on the feast of St John the Baptist in the year of the Lord 1413 this witness was talking with the said Simon in a street called Dog Lane near a cross standing there and, among other things, the aforesaid Simon said to this witness that many people were afraid to drink of the said Christine's ale because she was seriously infected and struck by the disease of leprosy. This witness then said, 'what you are saying is not true because I spoke with the aforesaid Christine a little while ago and she was then well and unblemished in appearance just as she always was without disfigurement of leprosy.' ...

## 4. Borough ordinances.

Translated from Bateson, *Borough Customs*, I.

[a] Bury. Language: French. Date: 1327.

And if a brewster can acquit herself single handed that she has in no way sold contrary to the Assize, she shall be quit.

[b] Torksey. Language: Latin. Date: c. 1345.

The brewsters ... shall be asked whether or not they brew and sell ale outside the house against the Assize. If they say not, they shall have a day at the next court to make their law three-handed with women neighbours on either side or with others.

## 5. Borough ordinances, York.

Language: Latin. Date: 1301. Translation by Prestwich in M. Prestwich, *York Civic Ordinances*, 1301, Borthwick Papers, XLIX, York, 1976.

[a] Brewers and alewives.

Ale shall be brewed from good grain and malt. If it is sweet, well brewed and blended, and put in tuns, two gallons shall sell for a penny. When it is well prepared and put in casks, a gallon of the best shall cost 1d, and a gallon of the second quality ¾d. If a brewer or alewife sells ale contrary to the assize, by false measure, the measure shall be burned. For the first and second offences they shall be heavily fined, and for the third shall go to the tumbrel... This ordinance is not to prevent men in the city from brewing their own ale, provided they do not put it on sale in taverns contrary to the assize. If the price of grain goes up or down, the assize is to be set accordingly.

Regrators.

Concerning regrators who buy badly-baked bread, and short-weight bread, and mix good and bad ale together, thus selling bread and ale contrary to the assize, it is ordained that no regrator shall sell any merchandise for more than the tradesman who produced it. Anyone so convicted shall be punished exactly like the tradesman. Regrators shall not place bread together with oil, butter, fat and other contaminating goods in their windows for sale, as they used to do, but bread shall be placed by itself, cheese by itself, and all kinds of goods separately, so that they do not affect each other, but are properly, honestly and individually set out for sale. If butter and fat are found together in a regrator's window for sale, they shall be forfeit, and the finder shall have them, by view of the bailiffs of the city or any of those appointed to keep these ordinances.

...

Forestallers.

It is ordained that no forestaller shall go out of the city by land or water to buy meat, fish or other merchandise being brought to the city, nor shall anyone sell the merchandise of others. Anyone convicted is to go to the pillory, from the hour of Prime to midday for the first offence. For the second, they are to be dragged on a hurdle from the church of St Michael at the bridge over the Ouse, through the middle of the main street to the great church of St Peter. For the third offence, they shall be imprisoned for forty days, and then be exiled from the city.

...

Cooks.

No cook shall buy fresh meat which has been on sale for more than a day in summer, nor shall he use meat or fish that is not good, sound, and healthy. Roast chicken or chicken in bread is not to be sold for more than 2d, roast goose for more than 4d, other food is to sold at reasonable prices. His business is to be conducted by view and ordinance of the keepers of the ordinances. Anyone convicted of selling bad or unhealthy meat, or badly-cooked food, or of putting other than good, sound meat in bread is to be judged as is set out above for forestallers.

...

Hostelers and landlords.

It is agreed that hostelers who take in strangers, and those who rent out houses, rooms, stalls or other accommodation, shall not take more than ½d for stabling a horse for a night. If the guest has no horse, the hosteller shall be content with 1d a night for his bed and a room, but this is not to apply to boys and other poor people who cannot pay...

[b] [names of trangressors against the 1301 ordinances]

Bakers of black bread.

William de Steingate
Robert de Gotherungate
Robert the parchmentmaker
...

Alice de Popelton
[seven further male names]
Agnes Crokhowe

Cooks.

[nineteen male names]
Maud de Blakeburn
William de Butercramb
...

Maud de Miton
Maud de Barton
[twelve further male names]

Brewers.

Walter de Bebyri
Agnes le Cordewaner
William de Brunneby
Thomas de Tollerton
Agnes Dodeman
Gilkyn de Craban
John de Dureme
[nine further male names]
Mariota Fraunceys
[six further male names]
The wife of Robert Takel
The wife of Nicholas the
    saucemaker
Mariota Aunsel
William de Oseneye
John de Castro
The wife of William the mason
[eight further male names]
Alice le Somenour

Malkyn Aunger
Alice de Cawod
Adam de Denton
John de Lincoln
Henry the tailor
Ellen Lyngetayl
Richard de Bilburgh
Magota de London
Christine de Skerreby
The wife of William de la Launde
The wife of Thomas de Hodleston
The wife of Thomas de
    Burghbrigge
The wife of Walter de Storreby
The wife of Robert de Mek
The wife of Robert de Lyndeseye
[twelve further male names]
Juliana de Knottingley
[three further male names]

Poulterers.

[ten male names]
Anne, wife of Gregory
Alice de Spuxton
[twelve further male names]
Margery, wife of Robert le Soure

Letice le Cornemanger
[eight further male names]
Juliana, widow of Astun
John son of Gilbert
Gilbert de Tockeworth

Forestallers of fishmongers.

[four male names]                    Alice de Colton
Emma Foeward                         Nalle the carter
Helot her associate                  Gilbert Sotheron

Regrators.

Agnes Grym                           John Kyng
Nelle de Berdsay                     William de Mildeby
Emma del Albay                       Isabel Busker
Alice Godwyn                         Juliana de Graystock
Alice de Acaster                     Isabel de Fyndelen
Cecily Halfmark                      Margaret Crane
Agnes le Lorimer                     Serlo le Bultir
Agnes le Spurier                     Richard de Coppegrave
Agnes le Hoton                       Juliana, wife of Adam
Hawise Cundy                         Walter de Marton
Alice Mundy                          Agnes le Doway
Juliana de Honington                 [four further male names]

Hostelers.

[six male names]                     [eleven further male names]
Juliana del Wyk                      Alice de Coppegrave
Ellen de Dumfres                     Henry the clerk
Isold Johun                          Agnes Skayl
[four further male names]            Adam the mason
Alice le Breuster                    Margaret de Lonsdale
Henry Calfhird                       [six further male names]
Mariota Fraunceys[1]                 Alice Fader
William de London                    [two further male names]
Alice staying[2] in William Fader's house


6. Peace sessions, Lincolnshire.

Language: Latin. Date: 1375. Translated from Sillem, ed., *Records of some Sessions of the Peace in Lincolnshire*.

[a] Item they present that Agnes, wife to William Sadelere of Louth is a common forestaller of both salt and fresh fish at Louth and

---

1 Also noted as a brewer.

2 Prestwich prints 'Maners', but this is presumably a mistranscription of the Latin 'manens' = staying.

elsewhere in the 48th and 49th years [of Edward III] by meeting fish
before it could come to market and, having bought it by forestalling,
sold it by retail and made an excessive profit of 10s against the form
of the Ordinance etc.

[b] The twelve jurors ... present that Nicholas Belman of Boston,
Stephen Croune of the same, Alice de Lundon of the same, Roger de
Lofft of the same, John Gonnesill of the same, Sokyn, wife of Simon
Candeler of the same, Alice Drope of the same, and John Brayder of the
same are common forestallers of fish...

## 7. Chamberlains' accounts, York.

Language: Latin. Translated from R. B. Dobson, ed., *York City Chamberlains'
Account Rolls 1396-1500*, Surtees Society, CXCII, 1980.

[a] [1445-6] And from Joan Bell, huckster for a licence granted to her
to sell by retail until the feast of the Purification, 20*d.*

[b] [1453-4] And of Robert Horman, tailor in order that his wife shall
follow the trade of the cardmakers by herself and whichever of her
servants, 3*s* 4*d.*

[c] [1475-6] Of the wife of John Sharpe, breadseller for defective
weight in a farthing loaf, 20*d.*

[d] [1499-1500] And received of the wife of Thomas Milner in
Micklegate, saddler for bread defective in weight etc., 4*d.*

[e] [1486-7] Margaret Burton (13*s* 4*d*) barker [tanner] for a transgression in her craft.

## 8. Fair court, St Ives.

Language: Latin. Translated from Gross, ed., *Select Cases Concerning the Law
Merchant.*

[a] [1300] ... The brewsters selling ale in boats and carrying
measures into court, Henry de Holebrok and many others of the
bishop's [of Ely] household then present:

Agnes Hervy of Ely, having a boat, brought a gallon, a pottle, and a
quart. [The quart] was sealed and was found false. It was broken by
judgement in full court.

[b] [1302] From Margaret de Rydon, baxter[3] for a wastel-bread of Alice de Northampton, regratress,[4] deficient [in weight] forty pence, and for a default of thirty pence [in weight] in a wastel-bread of Alice de Fenton [regratress], 6d.

[c] [1316] Sarah Poke and Alice, her maidservant and mainpast,[5] were arrested to answer John le Redeknave in a plea of trespass, whereby he complains that when the same John [was] in the vill of St Ives by the bridge, the said Alice came there and charged him that he stole a cheese of the said Sarah which the said Alice had for sale to John's damage and disparagement etc. And the aforesaid Sarah, [then] present, denied [the charge] etc. and says that she is not bound to answer for her mainpast and therefore she put herself on the decision of the court. She says for her own part that she is in no way guilty and asks that inquest be made etc. And a day is given to the parties on the following Wednesday etc. And the jurors say that the aforesaid Sarah and Alice made trespass against the aforesaid John, the said trespass [being] as he complains, to his injury, twelve pence, which they shall pay. And for the trespass etc., 3d, pledge Robert Wlne [Olney].

### 9. Leet court, Norwich.

Language: Latin. Translated from W. Hudson, ed., *Leet Jurisdiction in the City of Norwich during the XIIIth and XIVth Centuries*, Selden Society, V, 1892.

[a] [1287-8] They also say that Milicent de Melton, the wife of Henry the carpenter of 'Sucling' secretly buys grain before it comes to market, by which etc., and she is accustomed so to do.

[b] [1312-13] Concerning Rose, daughter of William Gerberge of 'Chategrave' because she buys grain and sells ale as if a citizen, but she is not of the liberty (12d).

[c] [1374-5] Katherine Skynner is likewise a common huckster and is not a citizen (6d, forgiven).

[d] [1374-5] Alice Wigmaker likewise buys and sells and is not a citizen (2s).

Agnes Bookbynder likewise is not a citizen.

---

3 Female baker.

4 I.e. in the possession of Alice for sale.

5 I.e. dependent.

[e] [1287-8] They say that Agnes Gossibe living in Pottergate buys wholesale and sells retail.

[f] [1287-8] They also say that Margaret Isak bought whelks and other merchandise such that the market was deprived.

[g] [1295-6] Concerning Margaret de Brundale because she sells ale with an earthenware pot which is not of the assize of the lord king.

## 10. Borough court rolls, London.

Language: Latin. Calendared translation by Thomas in A. H. Thomas, ed., *Calendar of the Early Mayor's Court Rolls*, Cambridge, 1924.

[a] [1305] Robert le Brokettour and Maud his wife were attached to answer Thomas Dogget in a complaint that whereas the plaintiff handed to Maud a cloth of woollen yarn worth 12s 6d that she might sell it for that price, she sold the cloth and retained the money, and afterwards she and her husband went to the plaintiff's house and by false suggestion made to Alice, the latter's wife, demanded and carried away half a cloth of woollen yarn worth half a mark. The defendants admitted the debt of 12s 6d, which they were ordered to pay within the fortnight,[6] but regarding the half cloth, they said that they took it away to sell by the plaintiff's direction, and demanded a jury. Afterwards the jury of the district round the church of St Margaret atte Patines ... said that Maud took the half cloth by fraud. Judgement that Thomas recover the half mark from Robert and Maud. And Maud was to deliver to the sheriff by Richard de Croftone until etc.

[b] [1306] Because Isabel, wife of Nicholas de Tenete, bought hens and capons coming towards the City, a jury of the district of Bridge was summoned to say whether she was a common forestaller of victuals for the profit of her husband. The jury ... said she went to meet poultry at Southwark and bought it before it could come to the City. She was committed to prison and was mainprised by Robert de Rye, John le Chapeler, Stephen le Taverner, and William le Chapeler. Afterwards she paid 40d fine to Richard Poterel, chamberlain.

[c] [1306] Reginald de Thunderle, Sheriff of London, was summoned to answer Richard Priour, Osbert the poulterer, John de Bumpstede, Richard le Wilde, Golding the poulterer, Margaret the buttermonger, John de Alegate, Alice de Dunstaple, John de Wautham, Alice de

6 Strictly the quinzaine or period of fifteen days.

Haliwelle, and Felicity, daughter of Hugh Elyng, poulterers, in a plea of trespass wherein they complained that he took from them 51 pigeons, 7 hens, 6 capons, 8 pullets, and two and a half hundred eggs and 5 cheeses. The defendant said that he took the above goods lawfully as forfeitures to the sheriff because the plaintiffs were common forestallers who forestalled poultry both in the lodgings of poulterers and by meeting foreigners[7] coming to the City. Afterwards a jury of Cornhill gave a verdict for the defendant. Judgement was given that the plaintiffs be committed to prison until etc. and that the poultry be forfeited to the sheriff.

[d] [1306] Maud Fattyng was summoned to answer Warin Page, her apprentice, for unjust dismissal. She pleaded that the plaintiff beat her, her daughter, and her household, despised his food, tore his linen clothes, and lent to others against her will the money which she had entrusted to him to trade with to the sum of 69s 4d, and also she had paid 13s for him for a maiming done by him on Alice Martyn, and consequently she had dismissed him until he should pay the above debts. The plaintiff denied these charges and demanded a jury. Afterwards a jury ... said that the plaintiff did not beat the defendant, despise his food, or tear his clothes. A day was given to hear judgement. Afterwards the parties made agreement by permission of the court on the terms that Maud relinquish all actions against the plaintiff, for which the plaintiff pay her 102s 8d. Maud was in mercy, which was condoned for 2s 8d, which she paid to Richard Poterel the chamberlain.

[e] [1306] Stephen the barber of London was attached to answer Robert the barber of Gracechurch and Maud his wife in a plea of trespass, wherein they complained that Stephen came to their house with a woman and asked to see the solar and to drink there, and when Maud heard them making a noise she went up to the solar and found Stephen pulling up his breeches, and he struck her on the head with a quart pot and kicked her, to her damage £20. The defendant pleaded that he only went to drink and buy wine, and that the plaintiff assaulted him first. Afterwards the jury of Gracechurch ... found for the plaintiff with damages 10 marks. Judgement was given for that amount, and the defendant go to prison.

[following day]

Robert the barber of Gracechurch and Maud his wife were summoned to answer Stephen the barber in a plea of trespass, wherein he

7 I.e. non citizens.

complained that when he went to Robert's house to drink, Maud and
her maidservant assaulted him, and tore out his eye while he was in the
custody of Thomas Juvenal the bailiff. A jury of the district ... found
for the defendants. Judgement accordingly.

## 11. Borough court records, Nottingham.

Language: Latin. Translated from W. H. Stevenson, ed., *Records of the Borough
of Nottingham*, I, Nottingham, 1882.

[a] [1395] Also they say that all the female poulterers of Nottingham
sell garlic, flour, salt, tallow candles, butter, cheeses, and suchlike
things too dearly against the statute, and that each of them makes
candles without putting a wick in them to the deception of the people,
and is a common forestaller of such victuals aforesaid coming to be
sold in the town of Nottingham, standing at street openings where
such victuals come to be sold etc.

[b] [1395] Also they say that Isabel de Belton, Alice Anker, Anne
Hukkester, Maud Okkebrok, Alan Culchi's wife, Katherine, the wife of
Richard Byrford, mason, Ibot, the wife John Albayne, Margaret
Glover, Maud Skynner, Isabel, the wife of John Hakkenay, Robert
Ostiler, and Henry de Hykkeling are common forestallers of geese,
capons, hens, poultry, doves, and such victuals before the due hour etc.

[c] [1396] ... also they present that Maud Okkebrok and John
Fitheler's wife are common forestallers of all cheeses, butter, and
suchlike victuals coming to the town etc., and they sell candles without
a wick against the assize etc.

[d] [1396] Also they say that Joan Taverner, John Wyrhall's wife, Joan
Payn, Katherine Fischer, Robert Hayward's wife, Magot[8] Berbour,
Christiana Dey, and Gilbert de Lammeley sold five herrings prepared
in stock for a penny in the Saturday Market and in the Daily Market
when they ought to sell six herrings prepared in stock for a penny
according to the proclamation of Sir Walter de Clopton, justice of the
King's Bench and clerk of the market of the lord king, and of the mayor
of the aforesaid town, to the great prejudice of the whole country and
of the aforesaid town etc. coming there etc.

---

8 A diminutive form of Margaret, just as Emmot is a diminutive or pet form of Emma.

## 12. Guild ordinances, Bristol.

Language: French. Translated from Bickley, ed., *The Little Red Book of Bristol*, II.

[a] Ordinances of the fullers, 1346.

Also that no tranter, huckster, or any other person of the town receive oiled wool or woollen yarn to buy, sell, or pledge on pain of losing that which is found in their possession. And if any such yarn be brought for sale by whoever it belongs to or by the woman porter [porteresse], that it be brought on a Friday and not on any other day.

...

Also if any porteress be found who carries oiled wool or woollen yarn on other days then Friday to sell or to put in windows to sell, then the first time the goods be taken and likewise the second time, and if it is found the third time, then the good be again taken and the said porteress forswear her office for ever.

[b] Latin heading, ?1346.

Note concerning tapsters.

It is ordained and agreed that every brewer and brewster who has ale for sale keeps their ale to sell in a public place and not in solars, chambers, or other secret places, and that the sign of that ale be at the door of the house where the ale will be sold all the time the said ale is for sale...

## 13. Borough court, London.

Language: Latin. Translation in Riley, ed., Memorials of London.

[a] [1310] On the Monday before the feast of St Hilary in the third year of the reign of Edward, son of King Edward, the bread of Sarah Foting, Christine Terrice, Godiva Foting, Maud de Bolingtone, Christine Princhet, Isabel Sperling, Alice Pegges, Joan de Caunte-brigge, and Isabel Pouveste, bakeresses of Stratford [le Bow], was taken by Roger le Paumer, sheriff of London, and weighed before the mayor and aldermen, and it was found that the halfpenny loaf weighed less than it ought by eight shillings.[9] But seeing that the bread was cold, and ought not to have been weighed in such state by the custom of the City, it was agreed that it should not be forfeited this time. But in order that such an offence as this might not go unpunished, it was judged in respect of the bread so taken that three halfpenny loaves should in all cases be sold for a penny, but that the aforesaid bakeresses

9 I.e. the weight of silver pence to the value of 8s.

should this time have their penny.

[b] [1372] On Saturday next after the feast of St Giles the Abbot in the 46th year of the reign of King Edward the Third etc., Margery Hore, fishwife, was brought here before the mayor and aldermen with certain fish called soles, stinking, rotten, and unwholesome for the use of man, which she had exposed for sale at the Stocks[10] on the aforesaid day in deceit of the common people and against the ordinance published thereon, and to the scandal of the City etc. Which Margaret, being questioned thereupon, did not deny the same, etc. Therefore it was judged that she should have the punishment of the pillory ordained for women called the 'thewe' for her aforesaid fraud and deceit, and that the said fish should there be burnt etc., and the cause of her punishment be proclaimed there.

[c] [1374] On Monday next after the feast of St Valentine in the 48th year etc., Henry Clerke, John Dyke, William Tanner, and Thomas Lucy, tapicers [tapestry workers] and masters of the craft of the tapicers in London, caused to be brought here a 'coster'[11] of tapestry wrought upon the loom after the manner of Arras work and made of false work by Katherine Duchewoman in her house at Finch Lane, being four yards in length and seven quarters in breadth, seeing that she had made it of linen thread beneath, but covered with wool above, in deceit of the people and against the ordinance of the aforesaid craft, and they asked that the 'coster' might be declared to be false and for that reason burnt... Therefore, after due examination thereof by the aforesaid masters and other reputable men of the same craft, by assent of the mayor, recorder, and certain of the aldermen, it was ordered that the said 'coster' should be burnt... And be it known that it was agreed by assent of the masters and other reputable men of that craft that the execution of the aforesaid judgement should not be done on this occasion for certain reasons etc.

## 14. Letter patent.

Language: Latin. Date: 1352. Calendared translation in  *Calendar of Patent Rolls, 1350–54*, London, 1907.

Grant to Agnes Pore, late nurse of the king's daughter, Margaret de Wyndesore, in lieu of a grant to her for life of ten marks yearly at the

10 A market.
11 Rectangular piece used as a wall hanging.

Exchequer by letters patent surrendered, of ten marks yearly from Michaelmas next out of the farm of the alien priory of Hamble during the war with France. If the war end in her lifetime, she shall then take the said sum at the Exchequer according to the form of the previous letters patent.

## 15. Borough ordinances.

Translated from Bateson, *Borough Customs*, I.

[a] Northampton. Language: Latin. Date: c. 1190.

If anyone has a weaver or nurse and they shall withdraw themselves out of anger or ill will and escape from their contract and consequently a plea arises, the bailiffs shall immediately attach that plea and thence do justice from day to day.

[b] London. Language: Latin. Date: 1419.

And where women are impleaded in such cases [of debt] and wage their law, they may make their law with men or women as they wish.

[c] London. Language: French. Date: 1419.

Also, an action of account is maintainable by custom against a sole woman and against children below age if they are traders or if they keep open shops for craft or the sale of goods, and actions for debt in the same way for matters pertaining to their craft or their trade.

[d] Lincoln. Language: English with heading in Latin. Date: 1481.

A married woman can be impleaded without her husband.

And if any woman that has a husband follow any craft within the city in which her husband is not involved, she shall be charged as a sole woman in respect of such matters as pertain to her craft. And if a plea is made against such a woman, she shall answer and plead as a sole woman, and make her law, and take other advantage in court by plea or otherwise for her discharge. And if she be condemned, she shall be committed to prison until she comes to terms with the plaintiff. And no goods or chattels that belong to her husband shall be attached or charged for her.

[e] Hastings. Language: English. Date: 1461-83.

How a woman that is married may be impleaded in court by plea.

If a woman who is married be impleaded in court for debt, or breach of covenant, or for withholding of goods, if she is reputed or taken to be a trader, she may answer in her husband's absence.

[f] London. Language: French. Date: 1419.

And married women who follow certain crafts in the city by themselves without their husbands may take women as their apprentices to serve them and to learn their crafts, and these apprentices shall be bound by their indentures of apprenticeship to the husband and his wife to learn the wife's craft.

## 16. Wills, diocese of York.

Language: Latin.

[a] Will of John Walton, weaver, York. Date: 1455. Translated from BIHR, Prob. Reg. 2 fo. 312.

Also I leave to the same Margaret my wife my best woollen loom with those things that pertain to it.

[b] Will of John Rodes, fishmonger, York. Date: 1457. Translated from BIHR, Prob. Reg. 2 fo. 357A.

Also I leave my wife Margaret from my part, assigned to me after appraisal has been made, £10 sterling, one cogship, and my terms in the house on the staith by the salt hole under Ouse Bridge.

[c] Will of Emmot Pannall, widow, York. Date: 1458. Translated from BIHR, Prob. Reg. 2 fos. 363v-4.

Also I leave Richard Thorpp my servant every single tool of my workshop relating the saddler's craft and 26s 8d in money from selling, discharging, and releasing my goods.

[d] Will of Margaret Crosseby, seamstress, York. Date: 1432. Translated from BIHR, Prob. Reg. 2 fo. 603.

In the name of God, amen. The fourteenth day of the month of March in the year of the Lord one thousand four hundred and thirty-one, I Margaret Crosseby of York, seamstress, of sound mind and remembrance, make and ordain my will in this manner. Firstly...

[e] Will of Adam Hecche, armourer, York. Date: 1404. Translated from BIHR, Prob. Reg. 3 fo. 102v.

Also I leave my son John all my tools relating to my craft of furbisher

... Also I give and leave to my daughter Agnes one of the better brass pots and all the tools of my craft pertaining to mailwork.[12]

[f] Will of Thomas Wod, York. Date: 1484. Translated from BIHR, Prob. Reg. 5 fo. 235v.

Also I leave to Margaret my wife my terms in my fulling mill if she keeps herself sole after my death, if not then I will that my son William shall have them.

[g] Will of William Shipley, draper, York. Date: 1435. Translated from BIHR, Prob. Reg. 3 fo. 437.

Also to each poor woman who was wont to work and spin for me, 6d.

[h] Will of William Crosseby, dyer, York. Date: 1466. Translated from BIHR, Prob. Reg. 4 fo. 70.

And I leave 20s to be divided by my executors for the poor women of custom working and travailing in carding and spinning my wool.

[i] Will of Alan de Hamerton, merchant, York. Date: 1406. Translated from BIHR, Prob. Reg. 3 fo. 244.

And I remit to Beatrix Sleford of Hull 50s which she owes me for brewing vessels bought from me.

[j] Will of William Gilliott, bower, York. Date: 1438. Translated from BIHR, Prob. Reg. 3 fo. 539.

Also I give and leave to the aforesaid Robert my apprentice two buck skins. And to the same 3s 4d on condition that he stays and remains with my wife to sell, and other things pertainining to my craft.

[k] Will of John Nonhouse, weaver, York. Date: 1440. Translated from BIHR, Prob. Reg. 3 fo. 596.

And I leave to my son Robert my best loom with all manner of tools in the house pertaining to my work. And I leave to William Whitwell one other loom with two combs always provided that Isabel my wife has the said two looms with all the tools pertaining to them whilst sole...

---

12 A furbisher finishes weapons. Mailwork presumably refers to the manufacture of chainmail. The participation of women in the small metals' trades is comparatively common and it may be that the manufacture of chain mail regularly drew upon female labour.

## 17. Household accounts.

Language: Latin. Translated from Woolgar, ed., *Household Accounts from Medieval England.*

[a] Diet account of the household of John Hales, Bishop of Coventry and Lichfield. Date: 1461.

And paid to Joan Boteler of Heywood for washing three 'dozens' from the lord's chamber and nine 'dozens' belonging to the lord's pantry and scullery, 2s.

...

Item, given to a woman for cleaning the buttery at Lichfield and the vessels there, 4d.

...

Item, given to a woman for carrying various necessaries from town to the castle, 1d.

[b] Accounts for household of Robert Waterton of Methley. Date: 1416-17.

And paid to Hugh Praune's wife for making 140lbs of Paris candles this year, 4d.

## 18. Churchwardens' accounts, St Ewen's, Bristol.

Language: Latin. Translated from B. R. Masters and E. Ralph, eds., *The Church Book of St. Ewen's, Bristol 1454-1584*, Publications of the Bristol and Gloucestershire Archaeological Society, Record Section VI, 1967.

[a] [1489-90] ... paid for washing of the vestments and other ornaments of the church to William Clerk's wife for all this year, 16d.

[b] [1492] Item to Isabel Wyne for 1,000 lath nails, board nails, and hatch nails, 1s 1½d.

## 19. Churchwardens' accounts, St Mary at Hill,

London. Language: English. Date: 1510-11. Translated from Littlehales, ed., *The Medieval Records of a London City Church.*

Paid for 28 ells of linen cloth for 4 surplices, for every surplice 8 ells, 6½d the ell. Total, 15s 2d.

Paid to Margaret Sutton for making them, 4s.

...

Paid to Alice Smale for washing of the church linen for a whole year, 3s 4d.

Paid additionally to her for washing of Mr Sutton's corporases and for apparelling of his albs, 4d.

## 20. Churchwardens' accounts, Andover.

Language: English. Translated from J. F. Williams, ed., *The Early Church-wardens' Accounts of Hampshire*, London, 1913.

[1471] Unto Agnes Maynsak for washing the church vestments, 3s 6d.

. . .

[1472] To Agnes Maynsak for an amice cloth and the making [of the same], 5d.

. . .

To Clyfford for mending a surplice, 4d.

To his wife for washing our ornaments, 4d.

. . .

[1472-3] To Joan Broghten for washing the ornaments of the church, 1s 6d.

To the same for mending the albs and surplices, 1s.

## 21. Aulnage accounts, York.

Language: Latin. Translation by Lister in J. Lister, ed., *The Early Yorkshire Woollen Trade*, Yorkshire Archaeological Society record ser., LXIV, 1924.

[a] The 8th day of the same month [October, 1394]

| | |
|---|---|
| Of John de Somerby ½ a red cloth | 2d |
| William Fouleford ½ a 'plunket'[13] cloth | 2d |
| Beatrice Warde ½ a 'meld' cloth | 2d |
| Agnes de Wellom ½ a 'meld' cloth | 2d |
| Joan de Dryghous 5 ells of 'plunket' | 1d |
| Joan de Burton 6 ells of white | 1d |

| | |
|---|---|
| Sum: Cloths | 2 and 11 ells |
| Subsidy | 10d |
| Aulnage | 1½d |

. . .

13 Coarse woollen.

The 26th day of the same month

| | |
|---|---|
| Of John Taillour ½ a russet cloth and 7 ells of white | 3*d* |
| Alice de Langton ½ a russet | 2*d* |
| Joan de Brereton 7 ells of 'meld' and 7 ells of white | 2*d* |
| Alice Sporear 7 ells of 'meld' | 1*d* |
| Joan Hukester 7 ells of white | 1*d* |
| Alice de Otryngton ½ of blue cloth | 2*d* |
| Agnes de Wellom 6 ells of green | 1*d* |
| John de Raghton 4 blue cloths | 16*d* |
| William Redhode 1½ russet cloths | 6*d* |

|  |  |
|---|---|
| Sum: Cloths | 8½ and 2 ells |
| Subsidy | 2*s* 10*d* |
| Aulnage | 4½*d* |

[b] [1395-6]

Wakefield.  Emma Erle, 48 whole cloths, etc. Subsidy 16*s*. Aulnage 2*s*.
[6 other male names, total of 173½ cloths accounted for]
...
Barnsley.  [5 male names]
Ellen Wyld, 4 half cloths and 6 yards, etc. Subsidy 9*d*.
Aulnage 1½*d*.
[total of 26 cloths and 6 yards accounted for]

## 22. Customs of wines, Exmouth.

Language: Latin. Translation by Kowaleski in M. Kowaleski, *The Local Customs Accounts of the Port of Exeter 1266-1321*, Devon and Cornwall Record Society, XXXVI, 1993.

Ship called 'la Langbord' of Exmouth
Master: William Slegh
Docked: 16 April 1318
Cargo: 72 tuns, 5 pipes of wine. of which:
Philip Lovecock: 38 tuns, 3 pipes (free)
Thomas de Tetteborne: 1 tun (free)
Henry de Hugheton: 1 tun (customed)
Clement de Hampton: 7 tuns (customed)
William Dyne: 7 tuns (customed)
The shipmaster: 2 tuns for portage
Robert de Stanbrigg: 4 tuns, 1 pipe (free)
Thomas le Barbour: 2 tuns (free)

Richalda de Toppysham [widow of Robert Irlond of Topsham, near Exeter]: 1 tun (free)
William de Criditon and William Edmound: 1 tun (free)
Walter de Hugheton: 7 tuns, 1 pipe (free)
Edith Gyrard:[14] 1 tun (free)
Henry de Hugheton: 4 quintals iron
William Golloc: 2 quintals iron
Philip Lovecok: 2 quintals iron
Custom: wine, 5s of which 2s 8d in the pyx; iron, 2d.

## 23. Customs' accounts, Hull.

Language: Latin. Date: 1466. Translated from W. R. Childs, ed., *The Customs Accounts of Hull 1453-1490*, Yorkshire Archaeological Society Record Series, CXLIV, 1986.

Robert Stevenson's ship called 'Anne' of Hull, departed 10th day of
                    November
. . .

Denise Holme        9 sacks, 16 stones, 1 half stone of wool in 4 sarplers and
                    1 pocket
. . .

Robert Thornton's ship called 'Trinity' of Hull, departed the same day
. . .

Denise Holme        15 sacks, 6 stones of wool in 6 sarplers and 2 pockets
. . .

John Maister's ship called 'Christopher' of Hull, departed the same day
. . .

Denise Holme        4 sacks, 2 stones of wool in 2 sarplers
. . .

Thomas Kyrgan's ship called 'Mary' of Hull, departed the same day
. . .

Denise Holme        2 sacks, 2 stones, 1 half stone of wool in [3] pockets
. . .

The same Denise Holme       349 woolfells

14 Probably the widow of John Gyrard of Topsham.

## 24. Guild ordinances, York.

Translated from M. Sellers, ed., *York Memorandum Book*, 2 vols., Surtees Society, CXX, CXXV, 1912-15.

[a] Founders' guild. Language: French. Date: ?1390-1.

...

Firstly it is ordained and agreed that none of the said masters instruct anyone in their said craft save only their wives and their apprentices...

...

Also that no one of the said craft shall have an apprentice for less than a term of seven years and not several at a time, but only one apprentice, except that the said Giles [de Bonoyne] can have two apprentices at a time because he has no wife...

[b] Dyers' ordinances. Language: French. Date: late fourteenth century.

These are the ordinances and constitutions made in the craft of dyers of the city of York by the agreement and counsel of all the masters of the aforesaid craft, that is to say Thomas de Kelfeld ... [15 male names] ... Annis de Rudstan ... [6 male names] ... Annis de Helmeslay ... [32 male names] ... Agnes, who was the wife of Stephen Littester, Agnes de Meburn, John de Useburn.

...

Also that no woman of the said craft shall occupy the said craft after her husband's death longer than a whole year unless her servant who shall occupy the said craft is put by her of the franchise of the city...

[c] Language: Latin. Date: 1417.

There follows the constitution of the saucemakers and vendors of Paris[15] candles.

And because a serious complaint had been made here in the council chamber by the saucemakers of the city ... that, granted in respect of the constitution used hitherto the folk of the saucemakers' craft and also all the candlemakers without the Shambles who sell Paris candles in their homes and windows together should sustain with their dues and expenses the pageant in the feast and play of Corpus Christi ... yet while the skinners and other artisans of this city of York make and presume to sell through their wives in great number, who are not saucemakers, Paris candles in their houses and windows, however, when asked, they refuse to be contributory to the maintenance of the

15 I.e. tallow.

aforesaid pageant... Whence ... it is ordained that each and every artisan of the city, whosoever he is, who is not a butcher or the wife of a butcher, and sells by retail Paris candles by himself or by his wife within the city of York and the suburbs of the same, be henceforth a contributor with the saucemakers of this city, to the third penny, to maintaining the aforesaid pageant in the feast and play of Corpus Christi.

[d] Stringers' ordinances. Language: Latin. Date: 1420.

Also that no man or woman of the aforesaid craft shall occupy as a master within this city until he [or she] is received into the liberty of this city and is examined that he [or she] is able to work in the aforesaid craft...

## 25. Girdlers' ordinances, London.

Language: French. Date: 1344. London probably suffered from a saturated labour market prior to the Black Death. Translation in Riley, ed., *Memorials of London*.

Also, that no one of the said craft shall set any woman to work other than his wedded wife or his daughter.

## 26. Weavers' ordinances, Shrewsbury.

Language: English. Date: 1448. These ordinances occur alongside provision for a local monopoly on linen cloth and for only one apprentice per weaver. They thus represent a response to a declining market and employment opportunities. Translated from A. R. Myers, ed., *English Historical Documents*, IV, London, 1969.

Also that no woman shall occupy the craft of weaving after the death of her husband except for one quarter of the year, within which time it shall be lawful to her to work out her stuff that remains with her unworked, so that she be ruled and governed by the wardens and stewards of the said craft during the said terms as for the good rule of the said craft.

...

Also if any man of the said craft happen to be defamed that he should have two wives and so live in adultery, and that it may be so proved as the wardens and stewards of the said craft by their wisdoms can in short time be advised for the welfare of the said craft, that then none of the said craft, whether he be master or journeyman, have anything to do with him, nor help him until such defiance be duly amended...

## 27. Weavers' ordinance, Bristol.

Language: English. Date: 1461. Translated from Bickley, ed., *The Little Red Book of Bristol,* II.

Also, it is agreed, ordained, and assented by William Canynges, mayor of the town of Bristol, Thomas Kempson, sheriff of the same, and all the Common Council of the said town of Bristol held in the Guildhall there the 24th day of September in the first year of the reign of King Edward the Fourth after the Conquest, that for as much as various persons of the weavers' craft of the said town of Bristol direct, employ, and engage their wives, daughters, and maids, some to weave on their own looms and some to engage them to work with other persons of the said craft, whereby many and various of the king's subjects, men liable to do the king service in his wars and in defence of this his land, and sufficiently skilled in the said craft, go vagrant and unemployed, and may not have work for their livelihood, therefore that no person of the said craft of weavers within the said town of Bristol from this day forward set, put, or engage his wife, daughter, or maid to any such occupation of weaving at the loom with himself or with any other person of the said craft within the said town of Bristol, and that upon pain of losing ... 6s 8d to be levied, half the use of the Chamber of Bristol aforesaid and half to the contribution of the said craft, always provided and except that this act does not pertain to the wife of any man of the said craft now living at the making of this act, but that they may employ their wives during the natural life of the said women in the manner and form as they have done before the making of this said act etc.

## 28. Poll tax returns, Oxford.

Language: Latin. Date: 1381. The 1381 tax was levied at a variable rate on lay persons over the age of sixteen, though there is much evidence, both internal and external, to suggest that numbers of such persons were in fact overlooked. Usually only heads of household are identified by occupation. Translated from Thorold Rogers, ed., *Oxford City Documents.*

...

| | |
|---|---:|
| From John Lepere, baker, and Isabel his wife | 6s |
| From William Whitewonge, servant of the same | 12d |
| From Thomas Hulle, servant of the said John | 4d |
| From Nicholas Bonde, servant of that John | 4d |
| From John Pokyncherche, servant of the said John | 12d |

From John South, servant of the said John Lepere                          12*d*
From Agnes, servant of the aforesaid John Lepere                          4*d*
From John Bray, miller, and Felicity his wife                             2*s*
From Maud, servant of the same                                            4*d*
From William Combe, the baker's servant, and Joan his wife                2*s*
From John Hickes, spicer, and Alice his wife                          13*s* 4*d*
From John Dobbe, his apprentice                                           12*d*
From John Dorchestre, servant of the same John Hickes                     12*d*
From John Grove, servant of that John Hickes                              12*d*
From William the Brewer, servant of the said John Hickes                  12*d*
From John Trustone, maltman, servant of the same John Hickes 12*d*
From Maud, servant of that John Hickes                                    4*d*
From Margaret, servant of the aforesaid John Hickes                       4*d*
From John Dadynton, cutler, and Joan his wife                             12*s*
From Richard Haclitt, his apprentice                                      4*d*
From John, servant of the same John Dadyntone                             4*d*
From Rose, servant of the aforesaid John Dadyntone                        4*d*
From John Heuxseye, baker, and Agnes his wife                             2*s*
From Isabel, servant of the same                                          6*d*
From Henry Freman, sheather, and Alice his wife                           3*s*
From Thomas Couyntre, hosier, and Joan his wife                           16*d*
From Isabel, servant of the same                                          4*d*
From Juliana, mother of the aforesaid Joan                                4*d*
From Alice Gyngmere, kempster                                             4*d*
From Juliana, servant of the same                                         4*d*
From John Prince and Cecily his wife, servants of Richard
    Mayhew                                                                12*d*
From John the fuller and Margaret his wife                                12*d*
From Walter Burnham, draper and Felicity his wife                         4*s*
From William Wardale, servant of the same                                 12*d*
From William, servant of the aforesaid Walter                             12*d*
From Alice, tapster of that Walter                                        4*d*
From Richard Wakeman, brewer and Alice his wife                           2*s*
From Stephen Wynard, tailor and Joan his wife                             2*s*
From John Clyne, servant of the same                                      4*d*
From David, servant of the aforesaid Stephen                              4*d*
From John Charles, shearman, and Joan his wife                            8*d*
From Joan, tapster of Hamo Croxstone                                      6*d*
From John Appulford, draper, and Alice his wife                           4*s*
From Joseph [Josepo] the shearman                                         4*d*
From Joan Spinster                                                        4*d*

| | |
|---|---:|
| From Maud Spinster | 4*d* |
| From John Couyntre, ironmonger | 12*d* |
| From Edward Cordwainer and Joan his wife | 12*d* |
| From Thomas Love, taverner, and Elizabeth his wife | 8*d* |
| From John Bukyngham, draper, and Margaret his wife | 3*s* 4*d* |
| From John Irysshe, servant of the same | 12*d* |
| From Alan, servant of that John Bukyngham | 12*d* |
| From Clarice, servant of the said John Bukyngham | 4*d* |
| From Alice, servant of the aforesaid John Bukyngham | 4*d* |
| From Matthew the tailor | 2*s* 6*d* |
| From William Bristowe, tailor, and Alice his wife | 6*s* 8*d* |
| From John, servant of the same | 4*d* |
| From Alice, servant of that William | 4*d* |
| From Joan, servant of the said William | 4*d* |
| From Agnes Westhodd, servant of the aforesaid William | 8*d* |
| From Juliana Leigh, servant of the aforesaid William | 4*d* |
| From Thomas Smart, cordwainer, and Alice his wife | 2*s* |
| From John Asshewelle, shearman, and Christina his wife | 12*d* |
| From Nicholas, servant of the same | 4*d* |
| From William the chandler and Isabel his wife | 2*s* |
| From John, servant of the same | 4*d* |
| From Agnes, servant of that William | 4*d* |
| From Isabel, tapster of William Bristowe | 6*d* |
| From William Palmere, ironmonger, and Sarah his wife | 5*s* 8*d* |
| From John, servant of the same | 4*d* |
| From Thomas, servant of that William | 4*d* |
| From Elena, servant of the aforesaid William | 4*d* |
| From William Bergeveny, skinner, and Alice his wife | 6*s* 8*d* |
| From Margaret, daughter of the same | 4*d* |
| From John Fretewell, sheather, and Maud his wife | 12*d* |
| From Joan the ironmonger | 7*s* |
| From William the ironmonger and Agnes his wife | 3*s* 4*d* |
| From William servant of the same | 4*d* |
| From Margery, servant of the said William | 4*d* |
| From Christine, servant of the aforesaid William | 4*d* |

...

## 29. Borough records, Nottingham.

Language: Latin. Translated from Stevenson, ed., *Records of the Borough of Nottingham*, II.

[a] [1414–15] Foreign Fines.

Nicholas de Hill gives for fine to have a licence to buy and sell within the liberties of the town of Nottingham for the time as above [Michaelmas 2 Henry V to Michaelmas 3 Henry V], 8d.

Alice Pynkston for the same period, 6d.

...

Isabel Burgesse, 6d.

...

Alice Squyer, 6d.
Alice Pygot, 12d.
John Hornyngwolde, 12d.
William Smyth, 6d.
Isabel Mote, 6d.
Robert Heryger, 12d.
Alice Warde, 6d.
[34 males in total, 6 females]

[b] [1463–4]

Margaret Curwyn gives fine for a licence to trade, 4d.
William Baume gives for the same, 4d.
Agnes Baker gives for the same, 4d.
[Twelve further males]
Alice Bey gives for the same, 4d.

...

## 30. Borough court rolls, Newcastle under Lyme.

Language: Latin. Translated from T. Pape, *Medieval Newcastle-Under-Lyme*, Manchester, 1928.

[1376–7] William Felys, chaplain, is received into the liberty of the aforesaid town under the condition that he shall be resident in the same town and shall pay 10s at the feast of the Purification of the Blessed Mary, and he finds pledges Thomas Bower and John Prestbury.

...

Margery Slayomegrene is received into the liberty of the town under the same condition, 8s [at] Martinmas, pledge the mayor.

Agnes le Graye is received into the aforesaid liberty under the same condition, half a mark, [at] Christmas and the Annunciation.

...

[1378-9] Margaret Bodgehewer is received [into] the liberty under such condition and shall pay 6s 8d, viz. at Christmas 3s 4d and at Easter 3s 4d, and [she finds] pledge Adam Prestburye.

## 31. Borough ordinance, Bristol.

Language: Latin. Date: 1344. Translated from F. B. Bickley, ed., *The Little Red Book of Bristol*, I, Bristol, 1900.

23. Also it is ordained and agreed that if any woman being of the liberty, whether she is the daughter of a burgess or was previously the wife of a burgess, marries a stranger, unless he is of free status, respectable, and of upright conduct, and it is found that he is of servile status, then such women so marrying of their own will be of like status as are their husbands and in no manner enjoy the liberty, but they be entirely cast out and considered as strangers for the duration of the marriage.

## 32. Borough ordinance, Canterbury.

Language: English. Date: c. 1430. Translation in Myers, ed., *English Historical Documents*, IV.

Also if any man wed a freeman's daughter, freeborn, he may pay his dues in the chamber and become a freeman.

Also a freeman or freewoman of Canterbury may devise by testament his freehold within the franchise, both the husband to the wife and the wife to the husband, as well as to other persons.

...

Also every freeman of Canterbury is free of childwite, 'earesgeve', and brudtol,[16] and scot-ale, by charter.[17]

16 Merchet.

17 Myers suggests that 'earesgeve' was a gift paid to the sheriff at New Year. Scot-ale was another manorial levy.

# VII: Prostitution

See also 'Adolescence' [19], [26] deposition of Thomas Midelham;
'Widowhood, poverty, and old age' [17b].

### 1. Borough ordinances, York.

Language: Latin. Date: 1301. Translation in Prestwich, *York Civic Ordinances,*
1301.

Pigs and prostitutes.

No one shall keep pigs which go in the streets by day or night, nor
shall any prostitute stay in the city. If anyone finds a pig in the streets
he may kill it, and may at his choice cut off its trotters, or the bailiff
of York may let him have 4*d* for them, if it happens that a pig escapes
from someone's custody. If any prostitute keeps a brothel and resides
in the city, she is to be taken and imprisoned for a day and a night. The
bailiff who takes her shall have the roof timbers and the door of the
building in which she is lodged. None the less he who rents out houses
to prostitutes shall lose the rent of such a house for one term.

### 2. Borough ordinances, Bristol.

Language: Latin. Translated from Bickley, ed., *The Little Red Book of Bristol,* I-II.

[a] [undated, fourteenth century]

30. Also that no prostitute go about town without a striped hood.

[b] [1344]

11. Also it is ordained and agreed that henceforth no leper be resident
within the bounds of the town nor any common woman[1] living within
the walls.

12. And if such women should be found so living that then the doors
and windows of their houses be taken down and carried off by the
mayor's servants as far as the constable of the peace of that ward's
house and kept there, and such women be entirely removed.

---

1 A term used regularly to describe prostitutes since they were held to be common,
i.e. available, to all men.

### 3. Borough ordinance, London.

Language: French. Translation in Riley, *Memorials of London.*

[a] [1382] It was ordered by the mayor, and aldermen, and common council that all common prostitutes and all women commonly reputed as such should have and use hoods of striped cloth only, and should not wear any manner of budge, 'perreie', or 'revers' within the franchise of the City...

[b] [1393] Also, whereas many and various affrays, broils, and dissensions have arisen in times past, and many men have been slain and murdered by reason of the frequent resort of and consorting with common prostitutes at taverns, brewhouses of hucksters, and other places of ill repute within the said city and the suburbs therof, and more especially through Flemish women who profess and follow such a shameful and distasteful life, we do by our command, on behalf our lord king and the mayor and aldermen of the city of London, forbid that any such woman shall go about or lodge in the said city or the suburbs thereof by night or by day, but they are to keep themselves to places thereunto assigned, viz. the stews on the other side of the Thames and Cock Lane, on pain of losing and forfeiting the upper garments that she shall be wearing, together with her hood...

### 4. Borough ordinance, Southampton.

Language: Latin. Date: 1413. Translated from A. B. Wallis Chapman, ed., *The Black Book of Southampton*, I, Southampton Record Society, XIII, 1912.

At the court, commonly called Assembly, held at Southampton before Henry Holewey, mayor, on Friday the morrow of the Exaltation of the Cross in the first year of King Henry the Fifth after the Conquest, it was ordained and ruled by the aforesaid mayor, aldermen, bailiffs, and community of the said town, then assembled for the election of officers, that all prostitutes holding the common lodging in East Street be entirely removed from the said street, and that neither they nor any other women of their kind of life be admitted to live in or hold from anyone else any tenement or cottage in the same street, and especially on account of the continence of those passing through the said street or setting out from home to the churches of St Mary, Holy Trinity, and St Andrew. So that the above ordinance be held and observed in perpetuity they had it enrolled in the Black Book of the said town.

## 5. Borough ordinance, Leicester.

Language: English. Date: 1467. Translated from M. Bateson, ed., *Records of the Borough of Leicester*, II, London, 1901.

For brothels. Also that if any brothel or illicit sex operates, or procuress dwells within this town, then the burgess living nearest to them is to report them to the court, and that they be expelled at the first warning on pain of imprisonment and fine and ransom to the king.

## 6. Borough ordinances, Coventry.

Language: English. Date: 1492. This is part of a wider set of ordinances drawn up in the face of severe economic recession and designed to reform society from the top down. Thus the first of the ordinances provided that civic officers found guilty of fornication be stripped of office. Translated from M. D. Harris, ed., *The Coventry Leet Book*, Early English Text Society, original ser. CXXXIV-V, CXXXVIII, CXLVI, 1907-13.

For tapsters and harlots.

Also that no person within this city from henceforth keep, hold, receive, or favour any tapster, or woman of evil name, fame, or condition with whom any contact is inclined to be sinful, pertaining to lechery, upon the penalty that every such household lose 20s for evry offence. And that every person that has such a tenant, keeping such suspect persons within his house after such warning by an officer, unless he evicts such a tenant, is to lose 40s.

For receiving of apprentices and men's servants.

Also that no tapster or other person from henceforth receive or favour any man's apprentice or servant of this city in their house to spend any money there or keep company with any woman of evil name or other person of unsteady disposition or other defamed person against the will of his master, upon pain of losing on each offence 6s 8d.

For single women that they take no rooms.

Also that no singlewoman, being in good health and strong of body to work, under the age of fifty years, take or keep from henceforth houses or rooms to themselves, nor that they take any room with any other person, but that they go into service. And that every such person that receives any such persons or allows them to rent any house or room, at the first default 20s. ...

## 7. Borough records, York.

Language: English. Translated from L. C. Attreed, ed., *York House Books 1461-1490*, 2 vols., Stroud, 1991.

[a] [1482] And further, that the common women and other mis-governed women shall live in the suburbs outside the walls of this city and not within.

[b] Cherrylips. Memorandum that 12th day of May in the year of Our Lord God 1483, the whole parish of St Martin in Micklegate came before my lord the mayor and complained of Margery Gray, otherwise called Cherrylips, that she was a woman ill disposed of her body to whom ill disposed men resort to the annoyance of her neighbours.

## 8. Coroners' rolls, Oxford.

Language: Latin. Date: 1299. Translated from Thorold Rogers, *Oxford City Documents*.

It happened that on Sunday before the feast of the Apostles Philip and James in the 27th year of the reign of King Edward that Margery de Hereford died in a house in the parish of St Aldate, Oxford, and was viewed the same day by the coroner John de Oseneye and she had a wound next the left breast an inch wide and five inches deep, and the same day an inquest was held... And all the aforesaid jurors say on their oath that on the previous Friday a clerk, whose name is not known, took the aforesaid Margery about the time of lighting lamps to King's Hall[2] and there lay with her carnally, and because she asked her fee from him, he drew his knife and wounded her next the left breast whence she died as said before, but she had all ecclesiastical rites, and the said clerk immediately escaped from her so that he could not be arrested nor his name be discovered.

## 9. Coroners' rolls, London.

Language: Latin. Calendared translation in Sharpe, ed., *Calendar of Coroners Rolls of the City of London*.

[a] On Monday the morrow of St Edmund the King in the 29th year of King Edward,[3] information given to John the Clerk, coroner, and

---

2 Subsequently Brasenose College, the vicinity of which was apparently a red light district.

3 20 November 1301.

the sheriffs of London that a certain Christine de Menstre lay dead of
a death other than her rightful death in the churchyard of St Mary of
Woolchurch Haw in the ward of Walbrook. Thereupon they proceeded there and having summoned good men of the ward and of the
three nearest wards ... they diligently enquired how it happened. They
say on their oath that when on the preceding Sunday in the twilight
of evening a certain William le Sawiere of Carshalton met the said
Christina at the eastern corner of the said churchyard and asked her to
spend the night with him, and she refused and endeavoured to escape
from his hands. The said William, moved with anger, drew a certain
Irish knife and struck the said Christine under the right shoulder
blade, causing a wound an inch broad and six inches deep, of which
wound she then and there died...

[b] Monday the morrow of St Valentine the same year [1339],
information given to the aforesaid coroner and sheriffs that Alice
Warde of York lay dead of a death other than her own rightful death
in the rent of John de Blackwell in the lane called Fetter Lane[4] in the
parish of St Andrew, Holborn in the ward of Farringdon Without.
Thereupon they proceeded there and having summoned the good men
of the ward and of the ward of Farringdon Within, they diligently
enquired how it happened. The jurors ... say that on the preceding
Sunday at dusk, Geoffrey le Perler, a groom of the craft of lorimers,
came to the rent where the aforesaid Alice was living intending to find
Emma de Brakkele, a prostitute, and to lie with her, but failing to find
her, a quarrel arose between the said Geoffrey and Alice, and
thereupon the said Geoffrey secretly drew his knife ... and therewith
struck the said Alice on the side under the right arm, inflicting a
mortal wound...

## 10. Borough court, London.

Language: Latin. Date: 1385. Translation in Riley, *Memorials of London.*

... Elizabeth, the wife of Henry Moring was brought before the mayor,
Nicholas Brembre, knight, the aldermen and sheriffs of London in the
guildhall because, both on the information of diverse persons and on
the acknowledgement and confession of one Joan, her servant, the
same mayor, aldermen, and sheriffs were given to understand that the
said Elizabeth, under cover of the craft of embroidery which she
pretended to follow, took in and retained the same Joan and various

4 A name that derives from the Old French 'faitour' = imposter, deceiver etc.

other women as her apprentices, and bound them to serve her after the manner of apprentices in that craft, whereas the truth of the matter was that she did not follow that craft, but that, after so retaining them, she incited the same Joan and the other women who were with her and in her service to live a dishonourable life and to consort with friars, chaplains, and all other such men as desired to have their company both in her own house in the parish of All Hallows near the Wall, in the ward of Broad Street in London, and elsewhere. She used to hire them out to the same friars, chaplains, and other men for such stipulated sum as they might agree upon, both in her own house and elsewhere, retaining the sum so agreed in her own possession. And in particular, on Thursday the 4th day of May last, by the contrivance and procuring of the said Elizabeth and of a certain chaplain, whose name is unknown, she sent the same Joan and ordered her to accompany the said chaplain at night that she might carry a lantern before him to his room (but in what parish is likewise unknown), it being her intention of their own contriving that the said Joan should stay there the night with the chaplain, while the said Joan, as she says, was herself completely ignorant of it. She remained, however, with that chaplain there the whole of that night, and when she returned home to her mistress the next day, this Elizabeth asked her if she had brought anything with her for her labour that night, to which she replied that she had not. Thereupon the same Elizabeth used words of reproof to her and ordered her to return to the chaplain on the following night and take for her labour whatever she could lay hold of and bring it to her. Joan at her command accordingly went back the following night to the chaplain at his aforesaid room and again spent the night there, and the next day she got up very early in the morning and, bearing in mind the words of her mistress and fearful of returning without taking something to her said mistress, took a portable breviary that belonged to the chaplain and carried it away (the chaplain himself knowing nothing about it), which portable breviary she delivered to the said Elizabeth who took it, knowing well how and in what way the same Joan had come it. Afterwards the said Elizabeth pledged this portable breviary for eight pence to a man whose name is not known.

And many other times this Elizabeth received similar base gains from the same Joan and her other female servants, and retained the same for her own use, living thus abominably and damnably, and inciting other women to live in like manner, she herself being a common prostitute and procuress. Whereupon, on the same day, the said Elizabeth was asked by the court how she would acquit herself thereof, to which she made answer that she was in no way guilty, and she put herself upon the country as to the same. Therefore the sheriffs were instructed to summon twelve good man of the aforesaid district to appear here on the 28th day of the same month to make a jury thereon, and the said Elizabeth was committed to prison in the meantime. On which day the good men of the aforesaid district appeared, by Robert Tawyere and eleven others etc., who said upon their oath that the same Elizabeth was guilty of all the above matters of which she was accused, and that she was a common prostitute and common procuress. And because many scandals had befallen the said city through such women and like deeds, and that great peril might in future arise through such doings, therefore, in accordance with the custom of the city of London provided in such similar cases, and in order that other women might beware of so acting, it was ruled that the said Elizabeth should be taken from the aforesaid guildhall to Cornhill and put in the 'thewe',[5] to remain there for one hour of the day, the reason therof being proclaimed publicly, and afterwards to be taken to some gate of the city and there be made to forswear the city and liberty thereof...

## 11. Borough court, London.

Language: Latin. Calendared translations by Thomas and Jones in A. H. Thomas and P. E. Jones, eds., *Calendar of Plea and Memoranda Rolls of the City of London*, 6 vols., Cambridge, 1926-54.

[a] [1344] The jury further found that the beadle [of Farringdon Without] took bribes from disorderly women in his ward to protect them in their practices.

[b] [1422] Also they say that Alice, wife of John Cheyney, and Isabel Cobham on 20 September and on many other occasions committed fornication with two priests and afterwards with various other unknown men, and that they are common whores.

[c] [1439] The jurors said that a certain Margaret Hathewyk often ... in the parish of St Edmund in Lombard Street procured a young girl named Isabel Lane for certain Lombards and other men unknown, which Isabel was deflowered against her will in the said Margaret's house and elsewhere for certain sums of money paid to the said Margaret, and further the said Margaret took the said Isabel to the

---

5 A pillory used specifically for the punishment of women.

common stews on the bank of the Thames in Surrey against her will for immoral purposes with a certain unknown gentleman on four occasions against her will.

The jurors likewise say that a certain Margery went to the house of Joan Wakelyn in the parish of St Katherine Colman, and by agreement took her to the house of a certain important Lombard, the said Joan receiving 12d for her wicked and unlawful behaviour and paying the said Margery 4d therefrom, and that in turn the said Joan procured the said Margery, taking her at dark to the house of a very prodigal Venetian, and that both women for a long time, taking no thought for the safety of their souls, had carried on this base and detestable manner of life.

## 12. Fair court, St Ives.

Language: Latin. Translated from Gross, ed., *Select Cases Concerning the Law Merchant.*

[a] [1287] It is presented by the jurors of Bridge Street that Avenand received prostitutes, therefore he is in mercy. He is pardoned because poor.

... [Ten similar presentments]

Ralph de Armeston, his companion, and all the bailiffs are ordered to take the bodies of all the said prostitutes and the bodies of all the other prostitutes, wherever they are found within the bounds and perimeters of the fair, and bring them to the court and guard them securely until etc.

[b] [1287] Of Douce de Oxonia, an attainted prostitute, 6d, William Mauger and Hugh de Swineford pledges, and they are also pledges that she will behave respectably.

[c] [1295] Emma Hauteyn complains of Richard Burdun in that she rented a house from him for 21d for the length of the present fair on condition that Richard should receive no prostitute in his row, but Richard defaulted in this agreement with her and received prostitutes. As a consequence, Emma left the house before her term after she had paid the rent on her house. Afterwards the said Richard struck Emma in Geoffrey de Hylton's house on Sunday after Ascension day last, struck her with his feet, and ill used her to her great damage. Therefore the hue was raised by Emma. Richard, present [in court], denied the words of the court, the assault, the battery, and all the

things that are against the peace, and says that he never assaulted, beat, or ill treated Emma, nor did he break the agreement with her about the house which she had rented from him. That this is so he asks etc. [that inquest be made]. The inquest comes and says that there never was such a condition between Richard and Emma, but Richard could lawfully let his houses to whoever he wished, and that Emma held [the house] fully until the end of the term agreed between them through a certain female servant. It was judged, therefore, that Richard is quit and Emma is in mercy 6d for a false claim, Hugh Bakun pledge. They say also that Emma justly raised the hue on Richard because he hit her, therefore [he is] in mercy 6d, pledge his body, damages 2d.

### 13. Borough records, Southampton.

Language: English. Translated from R. C. Anderson, ed., *The Assize of Bread Book 1477-1517*, Southampton Record Society, XXIII, 1923.

[a] [1482] Also, for a fine of a priest from the Isle of Wight who was taken at the stew side with a common woman in Lent, 3s 4d.

[b] [1511] Also, of a wench of the stews for coming into town without her token, 8d.

### 14. Visitation to Bardney Abbey.

Language: Latin. Date: early fifteenth century. Translated from Hamilton Thomson, ed., *Visitations of Religious Houses in the Diocese of Lincoln*.

Also we will, direct, enjoin, and command under the penalties written above and below that seculars in no circumstances make their way through the cloister whereby the quiet of those studying or engaged in meditation be impeded or disturbed, and that absolutely no women, and especially Joan Martyn and her daughter, enter the cloister or other inner places such as the refectory, dormitory, or infirmary or its hall, unless they are the mothers or sisters of monks...

### 15. Visitations, diocese of Lincoln.

Language: Latin. Translated from Hamilton Thomson, ed., *Visitations in the Diocese of Lincoln*, I.

[a] [1518] Church of St Peter, Leicester. They say that Helen Gylbert and Alice her servant are public fornicators. Also they say that Robert

Botylmaker promotes illicit sex in his home, and John Melborn promotes illicit sex.

[b] [1519] Ellesborough... Stephen Sydall promotes illicit sex in his home. Two women gave birth in his home and he will not reveal the names of the fathers of these women's children.

[c] [1519] Semperingham... Joan Sothyll of Pointon was made pregnant by Thomas Sturdy of Pointon. The same Joan is known as a common whore.

[d] [1519] Wrangle... Agnes Millns promotes illicit sex. John Barrett, apparitor, keeps suspect company, viz. 'liule pretty Jane'. Roger Ingleby, butcher, promotes illicit sex having two wives. The same Roger made a woman pregnant.

John Harre promotes illicit sex with the same woman.

William Wasshyngboro promotes illicit sex with a woman in Agnes Millns' house.

[e] [1518] Bicester... Emma Wolmerst and Margaret Wilson are thought of as prostitutes.


## 16. Visitations, archdeaconry of Buckingham.

Language: Latin. Translated from Elvey, ed., *The Courts of the Archdeaconry of Buckingham.*

[a] [1492] Burnham. Isabel Dell there because she is a common prostitute. She appeared and did penance and was dismissed.

[b] [1496] Iver. Margery Tubbe because a procuress between her own daughter and various men. She appeared and purged herself and was dismissed.


## 17. Church court, York.

Language: Latin. Translated from BIHR, CP.F.111. Alice Russell c. John Skathelok.

[The following depositions are dated July 1432.]

Joan Semer of York, aged 40 and more, of free status and good standing, the blood relative, affine, servant or household member of neither party, admitted as witness, sworn, and diligently examined on the present attached articles. Examined and questioned on the first and second articles put separately to her, she says that she believes the articles contain the truth since she heard Alice Rassell, about whom this cause is concerned, often say and relate as is contained in these. Examined and asked on the third, fourth, and fifth articles put to her separately, she says that these articles contain the truth because she says that after the common hour of dinner one day around the time of Lent two years ago (asked, she does not remember at this time otherwise of this day, so she says) this witness, Isabel Herwod, Joan Bank, Joan Laurence, Isabel Grymthorp, Joan Tunstall, Margaret Bell, her fellow witnesses, and none others, met together in a certain upper room in John Bulmer's house in Fishergate, located in the city of York, to examine John Skathelok, about whom this cause is concerned. John was there in person in the presence of this witness and in the presence of the other women, her fellow witnesses, his clothes removed down to his tunic called 'petycote' and his hose and breeches unfastened and taken down to his knees. He was warming his penis at a large fire burning there and eating cakes called 'maynekakes' and drinking ale with this witness and the others, her fellow witnesses. Asked, she says that at the time that they were warming and refreshing themselves this witness displayed her bared breasts to the said John, embracing John around the neck, kissed him often and with her hands warmed at the said fire, fondled and held the said John's penis and testicles. The said witness raised her clothes as far as the navel and made John put his hand under and feel this witness' belly and said to John that for shame he should display his manhood and find out whether there was any harness[6] there that could please him and prove himself a man. She says by reason of her oath that the whole time she was speaking these sort of words and feeling the said penis, the said penis was scarcely four of this witness' fingers in length of her certain knowledge so she says, and it would not and was not able to become erect as if empty skin having no substance in it. It hung down at the end and was not able to become erect, nor did it become erect, for which reason this witness says knows well and dares on peril of her soul to say just as she will reply before the Supreme Judge on Judgement Day that John never knew the said Alice his wife carnally, nor was he able to know her or any other woman carnally, nor is he in any way able now. Asked, she says that the said Alice is a young woman, scarcely 26 years of age as she believes, sufficiently well formed, strong, and willing to be a mother and have children if the husband joined to her in marriage were sufficiently

6 A Middle English euphemism for genitals.

potent as she heard Alice often say and swear by her faith...

Joan Tunstall of York, aged 36 years...

[This and the remaining depositions are substantially the same as Joan Semer's.]

Joan Bank of York, aged 26 years...

Isabel Herwod of York, aged 30 years...

... this witness and the other women, as she says, then present cursed with one voice the same John and his penis because he should presume to take to wife any young woman by cheating her unless he were better able to serve and please her...

Margaret Bell of Swinegayle, York, aged 50 years...

... this witness and the aforesaid other women, having warmed their hands at the said fire, each in turn fondled and held [John's] penis and testicles, and displayed their breasts to the same John and, embracing the same John around the neck, kissed him and spoke various jestful words to the same John telling him that he should for shame show these women his manhood if he were a man...

Joan Laurence of York, aged 36 years...

... one of the women, whose name she does not now know to tell for certain, lay on a bed of straw which was in the same room and, with her bosom [bared] and her clothes raised almost to the navel, said to and instructed the said John that he should come hither and see whether there was anything between her legs that could please the same John and gladden his heart...

Isabel Semester, alias Grymthorp of York, aged 40 years...

... and the more attractive of the said women, as she says, took and held the said John's penis and testicles in their hands, warmed at the said fire, and, lying on a bed of straw which was in the same room and with their clothes raised to the navel, they made the same John lie between them and feel their private parts and, by raising their shins and lying upon him, they put his penis to their bared bellies telling the same John that he take to himself part of the harness that was there and show himself for shame a man...

[There are three further depositions dated March 1429-30 which relate to the marriage of John and Alice *in facie ecclesie* at the chapel of

Leppington on the Wednesday before the feast of St James two years earlier. The deponents are:

Sir William Menethorp, chaplain, celebrating divine [office] in the chapel of Leppington, aged 70 years...

Richard Parke of Leppington, aged 40 years...

William Collom of Leppington, aged 40 years and more...]

[The court dissolved the marriage on the grounds of impotence.]

# VIII: Law and custom

## Villeinage and custom

*See also 'Adolescence' [39], [42], [43] for merchet and leyrwite.*

### 1. Court of King's Bench.

Language: Latin. Date: 1334. Translated from Arnold, ed., *Select Cases of Trespass.*

... And John [parson of the church of Newbold Pacey] comes and denies force and wrong... And he truly denies that he ever ravished the aforesaid Agnes, wife of the aforesaid Richard [atte Green] or abducted her with the same Richard's goods and chattels as the same Richard complains. He says, however, that the same Agnes is a bondwoman of this John by right of his church of Newbold Pacey, and because the same Agnes refused to submit to John her lord in doing the things that he instructed her to do by reason of her servility, he took Agnes as his bondwoman whilst she was single in the sixth year of the reign of the present king, and took and carried away the goods and chattels found in the same Agnes' possession as his own goods and chattels as he was fully entitled to...

### 2. Manor court, Halesowen.

Language: Latin. Translated from Wilson, ed., *Court Rolls of the Manor of Hales.*

[a] [1276] Thomas Colling gives (6d) to have judgement whether he ought to have the principal utensils because he had married the senior heiress. He named a mare, a brass pot, a large vat etc. The court says that all the sisters, like a single male heir, ought to divide amongst themselves all the principals that pertain to them, and that his new wife will have a half share in the said mare.

[b] [1279] Amice Bonde found pledges that she will conduct herself faithfully in all matters towards the lord and towards all the men of the manor and will do a day's service to the lord in autumn. William the

young and Thomas Walreven pledges. The said woman will be under the lord's protection so long as she conducts herself well.

[c] [1300] William Marmion gives twelve pence to the lord to have an inquisition concerning his wife's right in two strips of land in Warley. Let therefore there be an inquest for the next court.

### 3. Manor court, Ingoldmells.

Language: Latin. Date: 1319. Translation in Massingberd, trans., *Court Rolls of the Manor of Ingoldmells.*

The township present that the custom of the manor is that if any freeman begets any [child] by a bondwoman of the lord that it ought to remain servile for ever. And they say that William, son of Sarah atte Crambes of the same condition was ordained without licence of the lord, therefore is in mercy (3*d*).

### 4. Consistory court, York. Deposition of Thomas son of Ydonson of Rillington.

Language: Latin. Date: 1366. Translated from BIHR, CP.E.92.

... Also, he says that Alice was procreated of a servile father of servile status who was a villein of Lord Latimer, but Alice's mother was a freewoman from her birth until the marriage contracted between her and Alice's father. This Alice was afterwards manumitted by charter or the court rolls and made free, that is three years ago, by Sir Clement Chamberlayn who had special authority granted him for this by Lord Latimer as this witness says.

# Transgressions against customary law.

### 5. Manor court, Halesowen.

Language: Latin. Translated from Wilson, ed., *Court Rolls of the Manor of Hales.*

[a] [1276] Isabel, daughter of Alan of Oldbury, who holds of Thomas, son of Richard of Oldbury, is wont to destroy fences on the lands of the abbot and of her neighbours.

[b] [1281] Godiva de Cackemor is distrained for harbouring Alice at

the Gate, an evildoer. She lives yet at the house of William Burnet, who is likewise to be distrained.

[c] [1299] John Thedrich is summoned to answer for harbouring Margery the weaver.

[d] [1300] Also they say that William de Tewenhale (6d) lodges two women in his house at Oldbury who take sheaves and other items from lord's household and especially from the carter of Blakeley. Therefore they are to be summoned and to find pledges.

[e] [1300] Agnes Dones is in mercy because she said that Thomas the clerk enrolled in the court other than he had in fact enrolled in the court, therefore she is in mercy. She is to make amends to Thomas which are assessed by the court at twelve pence and a fine to the lord. Henry Oniet and Henry Lovejoy pledges.

[f] [1301] Distraint. Maud de Edwineshull is not yet distrained and remains at her mother's house. She is consequently to be distrained if anything can be found by which she can be distrained. It is forbidden that anyone lodge her on pain of the lord's amercement until she comes to answer the lord.

[g] [1294] The inquest made by the jurors concerning the wrong-doers in the lord's wood reports that Maud of Kenelmstowe (3d), the daughter of Richard of the same (3d), and Margery the daughter of John of the same are accustomed to carry off the lord's wood and to burn the lord's and neighbours' fences.

## 6. Manor court, Tottenham.

Language: Latin. Translation in Oram, trans., *Court Rolls of the Manors of Bruces, Dawbeneys, Pembrokes (Tottenham)*, II.

[a] [1385] [Bruces] And that Christine Fuller (2d) entered the lord's close and took away the lord's hay out of the lord's grange, therefore in mercy.

[b] [1378] [Pembrokes] That Maud Taillour (2d) is a common malefactor in the fields and meadows, therefore in mercy.

That Joan Barbour (2d) is a common malefactor in the same and likewise in mercy.

**7. Manor court, Wakefield.**

Language: Latin. Translation by Walker in J. W. Walker, ed., *Court Rolls of the Manor of Wakefield*, V, Yorkshire Archaeological Society Record Series, CIX, 1945.

[a] [1326] Court held at Wakefield on Friday, tenth of October, 20 Edward II.

Essoins. William de Totehill by Thomas de Totehill. Pledge, John son of Robert.

...

Ellen de Rastrick by William Cussing.

...

[b] [1324] Wakefield...

Robert Couper's servant girl, 1*d*, Ibbot Sparow, 2*d*, Ibbot Chapman, 2*d*, William Bull's servant girl, 2*d*, Ralph Bate's servant girl, 2*d*, for dry wood.


# Disputes between neighbours

**8. Manor court, Halesowen.**

Language: Latin. Translated from Wilson, ed., *Court Rolls of the Manor of Hales.*

[a] [1276] Thomas the dyer gives 6*d* to the lord abbot to have the court's decision concerning the ditch between himself and Julia of the Green. The court gave judgement that if the said Julia closes her fence then the said Thomas will receive damage in respect of the said Julia's draught animals, but she will not in respect the draught animals of the said Thomas. The said Julia is to have the herbage of her said ditch both beyond the fence and beyond the ditch by half a foot, but the said Thomas is not bound to keep his draught animals from the said ditch.

[b] [1276] It was presented by William de Rugacre that the hue was raised at Vimark's house because Alice de Schiselhurst stole a measure of corn and half a measure of pease, set fire to her house, and afterwards fled outside the county so that she could not be arrested. It was ordered that she be arrested as soon as she can be found.

[c] [1279] Roger de Aula appeared against Philip de Hull concerning five pence that the said Roger's wife sent him to take to Shrewsbury

and which he retained and still keeps. The said Philip denied all wrong against Roger and his family and waged law.

### 9. Manor court, Littleport.

Language: Latin. Date: 1318. Translated from Maitland and Baildon, eds., *The Court Baron.*

It is found by inquest that John Brokenhorn sold a carpet which Isabel Launce had pledged to him for 1*d* to her loss adjudged at 9*d* which the court awards. The said John is in mercy...

### 10. Manor court, Ingoldmells.

Language: Latin. Date: 1422. Translation in Massingberd, trans., *Court Rolls of the Manor of Ingoldmells.*

William German complains of Joan Tant of a plea and demands 14*d* for his labour in going to harrow etc.

# Fornication

### 11. Church court, York.

Language: Latin. Date: 1370. Translated from YML, M2(1)f, fo. 10.

Sir Roger of Lincoln, a chaplain celebrating mass in the church of St Crux in King's Court, fornicated with Margaret de Keldesyke living with Alice the widow of Peter Scherman in Petergate. The woman appeared. She denies the article and has Tuesday after Holy Cross Day to purge herself twelve-handed. Afterwards she purged herself sufficiently.

### 12. Church court, diocese of Lincoln.

Language: Latin. Translated from Bowker, ed., *An Episcopal Court Book for the Diocese of Lincoln.*

4 September, 1516 the lord bishop sitting in judgement in the chapel of his manor of Liddington ordered Amy Martynmasse of Sharnford in the county of Leicester, who was appearing before him in person and had confessed that she had been known carnally by Thomas Westmorland the curate of Uppingham within the rectory of Uppingham ... on the following Wednesday to go round the market

of Uppingham publicly during market time wearing only her chemise,
her head, feet, and ankles bare, holding a burning candle in her hand
and to do like penance on the next two Sundays in front of the
procession in the church of Uppingham and also on the third Sunday
to perform a like penance in Liddington.

# Defamation

### 13. Church court, archdeaconry of Buckingham.

Language: Latin. Translated from Elvey, ed., *The Courts of the Archdeaconry of Buckingham.*

[a] A commission was issued addressed to master Thomas Tymeut,
vicar of the parish church of Donnington, and Thomas Cottebery,
notary public, to receive the expiation of Katherine Walrond, the wife
of Thomas Walrond of Waddeston concerning and in respect of that
she is accused first and foremost of having defamed master Roger
Denham by saying that he holds the wife of his servant Edmund in
adultery. A summons was made to all who should have been called by
right because they thought themselves to be concerned in this matter,
and in particular Sir Nicholas Barton, rector of one part of the rectory
in the aforesaid church of Waddeston. On the 27th day of the month
of May in the year of the Lord 1489 in the parish church of Waddeston
a proclamation was made by the aforesaid commission sitting judicially if anyone wished to object against the commission or the persons
to whom it was entrusted that they declare it in legal form, and
because no objector to the aforesaid commission appeared, they ruled
in respect of their jurisdiction and took upon themselves the burden of
their commission. When the said Katherine had been called and
appeared in person, she said that the aforesaid rector had obstructed
the compurgators by threats made to them. The rector was called and
he denied Katherine's purgation and said that Katherine first and
foremost defamed master Denham. The aforesaid commissaries gave
the rector the date of Monday next following to prove this before the
official of the lord archdeacon of Buckingham in the parish church of
Waddeston. That Monday, viz. the first day of June in the aforesaid
year of the Lord, having arrived, the aforesaid Sir Nicholas Barton
appeared in the parish church of Waddeston before master Richard
Spekynton the official of the lord archdeacon of Buckingham for the
tribunal sitting there and produced Thomas Walrond, John Grene,

John Clement, and John Andrew as witnesses. When these had been admitted and sworn, the aforesaid Katherine Walrond appeared and declared against the witnesses speaking and their words. The judge then assigned the plaintiff a time shortly to present witnesses a second time. On which shortly following day, viz. the last day of the month of June in the aforesaid year of the Lord, the plaintiff renounced the last production of witnesses...

...

[Visitation of 1495] Waddesdon. Elizabeth Godday called Katherine Walrond a whore alleging that she incited Sir Thomas Couley, chaplain, to commit adultery. She appeared and denied the charge. She purged herself and was dismissed.

[b] [1491] Burnham. Alice Walter widow because a common defamer of her neighbours. She appeared. She is let off and dismissed.

[c] [1494] Hartwell. Richard Hayle, Joan Hayle his daughter, and William Hayle are publicly defamed because they consented to the murder and death of one Agnes Hayle on which charge they sought to be purged...

[d] [1505] Agnes Horton of the parish of Brill and Joan Whitescale of Brill. Summoned ex officio reputed as common scolds each calling the other 'Thou art a strong whore' and vice versa.

[e] [Chesham, 1521] Agnes Yve the wife of Thomas Yve alias Clement is reported because she is a common defamer of her neighbours calling various honest women whores and many other scandalous words and sowing discord between the aforesaid parishioners. The said Agnes appeared and many other honest women of the parish up to the number of forty women who had good knowledge of Agnes and who all collectively and individually confirmed before the judge sitting for the tribunal the aforesaid report and that the said Agnes Yver is a common defamer of her neighbours and sower of discord among the aforesaid parishioners. And because the said Agnes was unable to purge herself concerning this report, the judge held her attainted and compelled her by swearing an oath to do penance in the following manner, viz. that she immediately seek pardon from the parishioners in the manner of a penitent and that from henceforth she desist from such scandalous words...

## 14. Church court, York.

Language: Latin. Date: 1422. Translated from CP.F.153. Agnes, wife of
Robert Popilton, cook of York c. Emma, wife of John Lylle.

Sir Ralph Amcotes of the parish of Holy Trinity, King's Court,
chaplain, aged 50 years...

Asked on the first article he says that he knew Agnes, about whom this
cause is concerned, for the past twelve years and more and that during
that time he never told or heard say other than that Agnes was a
trustworthy woman of good reputation and of honest conversation...

Asked about the second, third, fourth, fifth, sixth, seventh, and eighth
articles read out to him separately, he says that on Sunday last of the
present month, immediately after vespers had been sung in the aforesaid
parish church of Holy Trinity and at the time when the parishioners of
the same church were returning to their homes in great number, this
witness was present in person in the cemetery of the parish church. He
heard Emmot, about whom this cause is also concerned, publicly and in a
loud voice call out and name the said Agnes as she was going from the
vespers and the cemetery to her own home in Colliergate, York, which
was right by the cemetery and the church, 'old whore of monks and
friars', in English 'ald munkhore and ald frerehor', and 'thief and
attainted thief', in English 'ald rank tayntydthefe'. The said Emmot at
that time and place in the presence, as he believes, of sixty men and women
returning from the parish church and vespers, as stated before, and
other men and women of other parishes and places present there in
many various places repeated and publicly proclaimed these words with
great spirit and great malice out of wickedness and hatred with the
intention of publicly defaming Agnes, so that by the pronouncement of
these words and Emmot's malice all who heard and saw Emmot knew and
would clearly be able to know that Emmot, although she appeared
somewhat infirm in body, had a tongue flexible and vigorous for
articulating her talkativeness, and a spirit full of malice and irascibility
because Emmot purposed and desired to hit the same Agnes with a club
which she then had and held in her hand had she not gone back into her
home more quickly. Because of the defamatory words, Agnes' character
was besmirched and her standing, esteem, and reputation gravely and
abusively defamed and injured. Because of these defamatory words to
the knowledge and hearing of this witness, certain of Agnes' neighbours
refused [ ... ] with Agnes as they used to, and the husband of the same
Agnes would have driven her from his society and his home were it not
for the special request and entreaty of his neighbours...

[Three further depositions offer similar accounts.]

William Baker of the parish of Holy Trinity, King's Court, tailor, aged 50 years and more…

[Knew Agnes sixteen years.]

Alice, wife of John Rode, goldsmith, of the parish of Holy Trinity, King's Court, aged 20 years and more…

[Knew Agnes ten years and more.]

Isabel Cooke of the parish of Holy Trinity, King's Court, aged 40 years and more…

[Knew Agnes sixteen years and more.]

### 15. Borough ordinance, Preston.

Language: Latin. Date: twelfth century. Translation by Bateson in Bateson, ed., *Borough Customs*, I.

Also, if anyone calls a married woman a whore and an outcry arises as a consequence and witnesses are present, they shall purge themselves single handed. If, however, they are unable make their oath, they shall pay a fine of three shillings, and to the woman to whom they spoke, they shall do this justice, namely that they shall take themselves by the nose and say that they had lied, and they shall be reconciled. The same rule applies in the case of the widow.

### 16. Fair court, St Ives.

Language: Latin. Date: 1302. Translated from Gross, ed., *Select Cases Concerning the Law Merchant.*

Christine de Derlington complains of Adam the bursar of Bury St Edmunds and says that when she was in Hugh de le Fertre of Ely's tavern in a certain boat of the same Hugh in the vill of St Ives on Wednesday last this year, the said Adam came there and assaulted her with vile words calling her a whore, seductress, and other insults, saying that she had advised and abetted Richard de Salop's wickedness at the moment when the same Richard took and wrongly carried away a certain maple-wood bowl[1] from Peter the parmenter of Stamford's house on Wednesday before Palm Sunday this year, and afterwards he

---

1 I.e. a mazer.

charged the same Christine with having sold the said bowl at the tournament of Kingston, by which defamation she lost credit with a certain male friend for six quarters of wheat to her serious loss, £40 etc. The said Adam, present, denies etc. and sought judgement concerning this Christine and her account, which is, he says, defective. He ought not reply to this account because she told of a certain Wednesday last this year when she ought to have specified in the 29th or 30th year of the reign of King E[dward] as is customary in any court, and in respect of this he puts himself on the judgement of the merchants. And the said Christine says that she accounted adequately... And afterwards they agreed by licence [of the court] and Adam puts himself [in mercy], 6d, [which] he pays.

### 17. Manor court rolls, Tottenham (Pembrokes).

Language: Latin. Date: 1395. Translation in Oram, trans., *Court Rolls of the Manors of Bruces, Dawbeneys, Pembrokes (Tottenham)*, II.

Also they present that Alice Ederych has maliciously spoken against John Ederych in the presence of the steward and says in full court that he is untrustworthy, therefore in mercy (4d).

### 18. Manor court rolls, Ingoldmells.

Language: Latin. Date: 1292. Translation in Massingberd, trans., *Court Rolls of the Manor of Ingoldmells*.

Maud, wife of Alan Rumfar complains of Agnes, wife of Walter Bogg because on Thursday after the Assumption of the Blessed Mary last she defamed her by calling her a thief for carrying off her beans, to her damage half a mark. The said Agnes comes and defends the whole and demands it is inquired into and Maud likewise... [The jurors] say on their oath that the said Agnes neither called Maud a thief, nor defamed her, therefore let the said Agnes go free, and Maud is in mercy (6d)...

## Scolding and other subversive and anti-social activities

### 19. Visitations, diocese of Lincoln.

Language: Latin. Date: 1518-19. Translated from Hamilton Thomson, ed., *Visitations in the Diocese of Lincoln*, I.

[a] Hartford... The wife of the same John Kareles arouses discord between neighbours and parishioners there and resorted to the vicar with tales and flattery.

[b] Church of St Leonard, Leicester... Also, Margaret Stanton is a common slanderer. Also Elizabeth Whythrop, Margaret Frost, Margaret Watkyn, Joan Walker, and Agnes Slytpeny, and the same Agnes receives suspect persons.

[c] Thornton. The parishioners say all is well. The rector there has in his home a certain woman, Joan Thakham. The parishioners, however, suspect nothing ill of her, except that the woman is too proud and speaks haughtily to the parishioners there. And the said Joan Thakham is a common whore and lives in the rectory and keeps a common tavern there. Also the same Joan is a common scold. The rector lives with her incontinently.

[d] Surfleet... Item, the wives of John Austyn, Robert Carter, and William Hebburn keep public taverns which many use at time of divine service and, for that reason, absent themselves from divine service, especially John Robert, Thomas Barret, Edward Laborer, John Robynson, James Tailour, Richard Dalley, Robert Bacheler, and Thomas Tofte.

[e] Hemingby... Robert Grene [and] Richard Wyrth committed fornication with Alice Waytt. Thomas Norcotes and Alice Waytt defamed their neighbours. William Maltby does not live with his wife. Alice Waytt forged a false will of someone who had died.

[f] Haugh. The vicar keeps a girl in his house. The same vicar and the girl labour in the fields.

[g] Willoughton... Margaret Fraunces is a common scold... One Margaret Spynk is a common scold. The same Margaret Spynk and Margaret Fraunces are fornicators... Margaret Fraunces is lodged in the home of Richard Frauncis and he is a promoter of the same Margaret Fraunces' wickedness.

[h] Sandy... The wife of John Clark always has players at dice in her house at time of divine service to the bad example of everyone else.

[i] Sutton. John Alen and Agnes his wife receive servants and labourers to drink in their house at time of divine service.

## 20. Visitations, diocese of Lincoln.

Language: Latin. Date: 1530. Translated from Hamilton Thomson, ed., *Visitations in the Diocese of Lincoln*, II.

[St Ebbe, Oxford] The wife of one Elyott lives in a manner that arouses suspicion. Joan Coper lives in like manner. Widow [*uxor*] Hall lodges suspect persons in her house.

## 21. Borough ordinance, Hereford.

Language: Latin. Date: 1486. Translated from Bateson, ed., *Borough Customs*, I.

Also, concerning scolds, it was agreed that through such women many ills in the city arose, viz. quarrelling, beating, defamation, disturbing the peace of the night, discord frequently stirred between neighbours, as well as opposing the bailiffs, officers, and others and abusing them in their own person, and often raising hue and cry and breaking the peace of the lord king, and to the disturbance of the city's tranquility. Consequently, whenever scolds shall be taken and convicted, they shall have their judgement of the cuckingstool without making any fine. And they shall stand there with bare feet and the hair of the head hanging loose for the whole time that they may be seen by all travelling on the road, according to the will of the lord king's bailiff, and not that of the bailiff of any other fee whatever. And afterwards when judgement has been made they shall be taken to the lord king's gaol and shall stay there until they make fine at the will of the bailiff whoever's tenants they be. And if they refuse to be punished by such a judgement, they shall be thrown out of the city...

## 22. Borough court, Wellington.

Language: Latin. Date: 1361. Translation in Humphreys, trans., *Materials for the History of the Town and Parish of Wellington*.

And that Reginald Brid is a common gossip and disturber of the peace, therefore he is in mercy. And Lucy, wife of John Cory (3d) and Alice Lacok are common gossips and quarrellers to the disturbance of the peace, and because the aforesaid Alice has been many times here convicted hereupon, therefore it is ordered that she shall have judgement of the stoup [cuckingstool], and aforesaid Lucy in mercy.

## 23. Borough court, Nottingham.

Language: Latin. Translated from W. H. Stevenson, ed., *Records of the Borough of Nottingham*, I, III, Nottingham, 1882-5.

[a] [1395-6] John de Mampton and Gilbert Walker, decennaries of Hungate, present that Beatrix Matther is a common scold in the street of Hungate where she lives against her neighbours and against the peace of the lord king etc., whence she is attached etc. And therefore the same Beatrix comes, and puts herself upon the mayor's mercy and pays 6*d.*

[b] [1496] And they say that Joan Hunt of Nottingham aforesaid, spinster, on the twelfth day of July in the eleventh year of the reign of King Henry the Seventh and on various other days and places at Nottingham aforesaid, is a common receiver of servants of inhabitants of the town of Nottingham with their masters' goods in her houses at night time, and they keep a disorderly house there and make disturbances so that her neighbours and other subjects of the said lord king are unable to rest in their beds, to the serious annoyance of the said king's subjects and against his peace.

## 24. Manor court rolls, Wellington.

Language: Latin. Date: 1421. Translation in Humphreys, trans., *Materials for the History of the Town and Parish of Wellington.*

Werdesford. Alice Ryche (6*d*) unjustly and against the peace gossiped with Joan Bole, and Joan Papejayes (6*d*) unjustly and against the peace gossiped with Joan Bole and many others of their neighbours, and the said Alice and Joan are common scolds and disturbers of the peace to the nuisance, therefore they are in mercy... John Ryche (4*d*) on Monday next before the feast of St Matthias the Apostle, 7 Henry V, unjustly and against the peace came to the house of John Bole and broke and entered into the same house and took and carried away his hay found there to [his] damage and against the peace of the said lord king, therefore he is in mercy. And Alice, wife of the same John Ryche at various times for three years past, unjustly and against the peace, came and went down into John Bole's chamber and there took three busshels of malt and carried them away to the damage etc., therefore in mercy...

John Bole, by pledge of John Chilmely, is at law etc. against John Ryche and Alice his wife that he neither unjustly and against the peace made assault on the same Alice, nor struck her and maltreated her in the past year in the king's highway to her damage of 40*d*, because they had agreed in full concerning the same.

The same John Bole is at law etc. against the same John Ryche that he did not unjustly and without leave enter his garden, nor took and carried away a wallplate of timber there, to his damages of 12*d*.

## Casting spells

### 25. Visitation, diocese of Lincoln.

Language: Latin. Date: 1519. Translated from Hamilton Thomson, ed., *Visitations in the Diocese of Lincoln*, I.

Scothern. One Agnes Dowson there is a caster of spells.

### 26. Church court, London.

Language: Latin. Date: 1481. Translation in Myers, ed., *English Historical Documents*, IV.

St Sepulchre. Joan Beverley, or Lessell, or Cowcross, is a witch, and she asked two accomplice witches to work together, so that Robert Stantone and another gentle-born of Gray's Inn should love her and no other, and they committed adultery with her and, as it is said, fought for her, and one almost killed the other, and her husband does not dare stay with her on account of these two men. She is a common whore, and a procuress, and she wants to poison men...

### 27. Church court, archdeaconry of Buckingham.

Language: Latin. Date: 1495. Translated from Elvey, ed., *The Courts of the Archdeaconry of Buckingham*.

Colnbrook. Katherine Martyn the wife of Richard Richemounde *ex officio* concerning unlawful spells contrary to the teaching of the universal Church. She appeared and submitted herself to the mercy of the office and was beaten three times through the church and dismissed.

# Age of majority

## 28 Borough court, Southampton.

Language: Latin. Date: 1435. Translated from A. B. Wallis Chapman, ed., *The Black Book of Southampton*, II, Southampton Record Society, XIV, 1912.

To this court comes Katherine, daughter of Peter Jamys and Joan his wife, which same Katherine was the wife of Andrew Payn, commonly called Drewet Payn, formerly burgess of the town of Southampton, in her lawful widowhood and in her own person, and she declared herself to be fifteen years and more, viz. that she was seventeen years at the feast of St Lawrence last, and she asks that she be allowed to prove her age aforesaid acording to the custom of the aforesaid town. This was granted to her by the aforesaid court... And then the aforesaid men, sworn to speak the truth there on the aforesaid matters according to the custom of the aforesaid town, say on their oath that the aforesaid Katherine is fifteen years of age and more because they say that the said Katherine was seventeen years on the feast of St Lawrence the martyr last ... [that she was born] in the aforesaid town on the feast of St Lawrence in the fourth year of King Henry the Fifth, father of the lord king, and was baptised in the parish church of Holy Cross in the aforesaid town on that feast day by Thomas Halughton, lately vicar of the aforesaid church, and her godfather was Walter Fetplace and her godmothers were Isabel, widow of William Soper and Katherine, widow of William Nycoll, and each of the said twelve burgesses says separately that he was then living in the aforesaid town...

# Prison

## 29. Will of John Skirpenbek, cordwainer, York.

Language: Latin. Date: 1437. Translated from BIHR, Prob. Reg. 3 fo. 497.

Also to the prisoners in the Womankidcote, 12*d*.[2]

## 30. Borough records, London.

Language: Latin. Date: 1320. Translation in Riley, ed., *Memorials of London*.

Emma, daughter of William the wiredrawer of York, was taken by

---

2 I.e. the women's prison for the city of York located on Ouse Bridge. This is the earliest reference to a separate women's prison at York.

William the official, sergeant of the ward of Cheap, and put in the Tun[3] on the night of the Sunday next before Martinmas in the 14th year of King Edward because she was found wandering about after curfew rung at the place assigned, viz. at St Martin le Grand, together with a certain bundle of cloths. Afterwards on Tuesday, the feast of St Martin she was brought to the Guildhall before the mayor and was told that she must find surety as to keeping the Peace, and she was accordingly delivered to the said William the official that he might take pledge of her for doing so.

### 31. Letters patent.

Language: Latin. Date: 1353. Calendared translation in *Calendar of Patent Rolls, 1350-54.*

Pardon to Joan, late wife of John de la Berwe for breaking out of the prison of Worcester Castle, wherein she was detained by process before the justices of the Bench at the suit of the prior of Worcester because she abducted John, son and heir of the said John, whose keeping pertained to the prior as he pretended, on condition that she answer the prior if he proceed against her.

# Sanctuary

### 32. Sanctuary register, Beverley.

Language: Latin. Date: 1511. Translated from *Sanctuarium Dunelmense et Sanctuarium Beverlacense*, Surtees Society, I, 1837.

12th day of March in the second year of the reign of King Henry the Eighth, Elizabeth Nelson of Pollington in the county of York, spinster, came to the peace of St John of Beverley for felony and the murder of her child killed at Hull, and she was admitted and sworn.

### 33. Eyre roll, Kent.

Language: Latin. Date: 1313-14. Translated from F. W. Maitland, L. W. V. Harcourt, and W. C. Bolland, eds., *Year Books of Edward II*, V, Selden Society, XXIV, 1910.

A woman condemned for larceny and found to be pregnant was committed to prison until she gave birth. Afterwards she broke prison

---

3 A prison, so called from its large barrel shape.

and fled to a church and was extracated from the church by the gaolkeeper and taken before the justices. It was decided that she be taken back to the church and afterwards she abjured the realm and the keeper [was put] under judgement.

# Women before the law

### 34. Year book, 1313-14.

Language: French. Translated from Maitland, Harcourt, and Bolland, eds., *Year Books of Edward II*, V.

[a] Note, a man is outlawed and a woman waived, and the reason the woman cannot be outlawed is that she is sworn neither to the law nor to the peace.

[b] ... a woman can only sue an appeal against a man in three cases: for the death of her husband killed in her arms [or] her child aborted; for rape; and for chattels where the man is taken with such stolen goods in his possession and suit of this matter is straightaway made and the felon and his suit straightaway prosecuted and the felon and his suit straightaway attached ... the reason why the appeal of a woman ought not be allowed in as many cases as the appeal of a man [is] that women are changeable by nature and, on the other hand, a man does not have the same advantage of defending himself by his body in an appeal against a woman as he has against a man...

# Debt

### 35. Church court, York.

Language: Latin. Translated from BIHR, CP.F.174. Robert Lascelles, citizen and merchant c. Margaret Harman, chandler.

[The following three depositions are dated 13 May 1430.]

Agnes, wife of John Crispyn of York, cutler, aged 26 years, of free status and good standing...

Examined and asked on the first, second, third, and fourth articles put to her one at a time, she says that on Monday before the feast of St Mary Magdalene last year, Robert Lascels, about whom this cause relates, Isabel his wife, Margaret Herman, about whom this cause also relates, and the then husband of the same Margaret (since deceased) and this witness, and others whose names she does not recall at present as she says, dined together within Robert Lascels' home in the street called Petergate in the city of York, in which the same Robert then lived and still lives. And she says that at the time of the aforesaid meal the aforesaid Margaret related, told, and publicly acknowledged to her aforesaid husband in the presence of the said Robert Lascels, Isabel his wife, this witness, and the others aforesaid that the same Margaret before that time bought of the aforesaid Robert Lascels a certain quantity of wick called candlewick, for which, as she claimed, she owed the same Robert the sum of twenty-three shillings and ten pence sterling, and she said that she would pay the same Robert this sum of twenty-three shillings and ten pence at the Michaelmas then following without further delay. Examined and questioned on the fifth, sixth, and seventh articles put to her, one at a time, she says that she believes for certain that these articles contain the truth since, just as is contained in them, she heard the aforesaid Robert Lascels often say and acknowledge. Examined and asked about the eighth article, she says that she believes that this article contains the truth by those things that she deposed above. Examined on the last article, she says that the aforesaid matters deposed by her above were and are publicly known and manifest in the aforesaid city of York...

Joan Scharp, servant of Robert Lascels about whom this cause relates, 20 years of age, of free condition and good standing...

Examined and questioned on the first, second, third, and fourth articles put to her one at a time, she says that between three and four o'clock in the afternoon of Monday before the feast of St Mary Magdalene last year, this witness was personally present in her said master's shop in the street called Petergate in the city of York together with her master, Isabel his wife, and Margaret Herman, about whom this article relates, and no others so far as she remembers at present, so she says, where and when the same Margaret bought from the same Robert a certain quantity of wick, commonly called candlewick, extending to the value of twenty-three shillings and ten pence sterling. And she further says that this witness saw and was present at that time when the same Robert and Margaret weighed this wick. And she says that immediately after weighing this and after the value of the same was given, Alice Bawmburgh, at that time and still the aforesaid Robert's servant and one Margaret, then servant of the same Margaret Herman, carried the same wick from the aforesaid shop at the home of the said Margaret and her husband and there they left it. Then, as she says, the same Robert, Isabel his wife, the same Margaret, Agnes Crispyn, the fellow witness of this witness, and this witness, came together in a small summer hall located within the said Robert's home and they sat there, eat, drank, and relaxed together. At the time of this recreation, so she says, Thomas Herman, the said Margaret's then husband, entered the same summer hall and sat and eat and drank with them thus recreating at which time, so she says, the same Margaret in the presence of this witness, the said Agnes, her fellow witness, and the aforesaid Robert, Isabel his wife, and the wife of William Warde of York, tailor, and no others so far as she recalls at present so she says, told and publicly informed the said Thomas her husband how she bought the same day a quantity of wick, in English 'Candilweke', reaching to the value of twenty-three shillings and ten pence. She promised then and there and swore by her faith to pay the same Robert the which sum at the feast of St Michael the Archangel next following, or sooner, without further delay. The aforesaid Robert then replied and said that he believed for certain that the same Margaret wished to do so. Examined and asked on the fifth, sixth, and seventh articles put to her one at a time, she says that one day, which she does not remember for certain at present, but it fell, as she says, between Michaelmas and the following Martinmas, this witness was sent by the said Robert, her master, to the said Margaret to ask for this sum. When she actually asked for this sum in the name of her master from the same Margaret, she replied that she did not then have such a sum ready, but as soon as she were able, she wanted to arrange, as she asserted, for the same Robert to have that sum. Otherwise on these articles examined and questioned she says she knows not to depose. Examined and asked about the eighth article, she says she believes this article contains the truth for the reasons deposed by her above. Examined on the last article, she says that the aforesaid matters deposed by her above were and are publicly known and manifest in the city of York and all surrounding places...

John Crispyn of York, cutler, 40 years of age and more, of free status and good repute...

Examined and asked on the first, second, third, fourth, fifth, sixth, and seventh articles put to him one at a time, he says that one day, which he does not remember for sure at present, [but] this day fell then, as he says, last summer time, Robert Lascels, about whom this cause relates, came to this witness and told him that he had been summoned

to the sheriffs' court of the city of York at the instance of the Margaret
Herman in question by force of a certain obligation of six marks, which
sum, as he stated, he owed the same Margaret, and he further said to
this witness that the same Margaret also owed the same Robert the
sum of twenty-three shillings and ten pence for wick, that is
candlewick, bought from him, for which reason he asked this witness
if he would go with him to the same Margaret to hear the reckoning
to be made and had between him and the said Margaret. And he says
that this witness, at the same Robert's request, went with him to the
home of the aforesaid Margaret in the street called Peter Lane Little
in the city of York. At that time the same Robert, so he says, said to
the aforesaid Margaret, being in the same house, that he did not resent
that he had been summoned on account of the aforesaid sum of six
marks owed by him since he was always ready to pay her that sum of
twenty-three shillings and ten pence which Margaret owed him, which
she had been allowed in the first place. The same Margaret then said
that she did not want to make any allowance in that respect because
she had been advised to the contrary, but she said and swore by her
faith that if Robert would pay her the entire aforesaid sum of six
marks, Margaret would immediately pay him the sum of twenty-three
shillings and ten pence owed by her to the same Robert. The aforesaid
Robert then said he would freely do so. And he says that then Robert
and this witness went to the aforesaid Robert's home and, when they
had got together the sum of six marks, returned to the aforesaid
Margaret and paid and actually handed over to the same Margaret this
sum of six marks in the porch of the parish church of St Peter the
Little, in the city of York, in the presence of this witness, Henry
Rothwell, citizen and merchant of York, Robert Trewlofe, late of
York, deceased, William Warde of York, tailor, and the parish clerk of
the said church, and one other man whose name and surname he does
not remember at present so he says. After this sum was thus paid and
handed over, the same Robert then asked the same Margaret to pay
the same Robert the aforesaid sum of twenty three shillings and ten
pence which she owed him and honour her pledge and promise given
in this respect. She replied that she would not pay him one penny since
she had been advised not to as she said. Otherwise he says, examined
and questioned on this article, he knows not to depose. Examined and
asked about the eighth article, he believes this article to contain the
truth for the reasons stated by him above. Examined on the last article,
he says that the aforesaid matters deposed by him above were and are
publicly known and manifest in the aforesaid city of York and in

surrounding places and public voice and report has long circulated there about these matters and circulates still. He is not bribed, instructed, corrupted, or informed to depose as he deposed above...

### 36. Borough court, Chester.

Language: Latin. Date: 1317. Translated from A. Hopkins, ed., *Selected Rolls of the Chester City Courts*, Chetham Society, 3rd. ser. II, 1950.

Juliana Coty complains of Thomas le Skriven in a plea of unlawful detention of a cloth price 16d. Wherefore she complains that he unlawfully detains from her the aforesaid cloth pledged to him for four pence which she offered him and offers him still to her loss, 12d...

# Theft

### 37. Peace rolls, Lincoln.

Language: Latin. Date: 1351. Translated from E. G. Kimball, ed., *Records of Some Sessions of the Peace in the City of Lincoln 1351-1354 and the Borough of Stamford 1351*, Lincoln Record Society, LXV, 1971.

[a] Also they say that Alice the daughter of Robert Skynnere on Monday after the feast of St Bartholomew in the twenty-fourth year of the reign of King Edward III after the conquest entered the house of Cecily Skynner in the parish of St Botolph in the suburbs of Lincoln by night and secretly took and carried away a purse with twenty-eight shillings from one John de Shaftesbury sleeping in the aforesaid house.

Also they say that the aforesaid Alice ... went to the home of one Emma de Sleford and entered the said Emma's home with the aforesaid twenty-eight shillings stolen in this way and gave them to the said Emma to receive and the Emma received the twenty-eight shillings knowing of the theft.

[b] Margaret de Staynrop ([to be] hung, no goods, denies guilt, is returned to prison) is indicted because around Martinmas in 26th year [of Edward III] she stole at Lincoln a brass pot worth 4s.

### 38. Peace rolls, Lincolnshire.

Language: Latin. Date: 1375. Translated from Sillem, ed., *Records of some Sessions of the Peace in Lincolnshire*.

The jurors ... present that Maud, wife to William Wyne of Stow St Mary, on Monday after Epiphany in the 48th year of the king at Stow St Mary feloniously stole three bushels of malt worth 2s 3d from John Smyth of Stow at Stow.

## 39. Peace rolls, Lincolnshire.

Language: Latin. Translated from Kimball, ed., *Records of some Sessions of the Peace in Lincolnshire.*

[a] [1383] They say that Maud the widow of Richard son of Robert of Great Limber on Thursday after the feast of St Andrew the apostle in the 5th year of the reign of King Richard II ... at Great Limber secretly stole six shillings in cash from Henry de Meltynby of Limber, John son of Richard of the same, and William Warn of the same.

[b] [1387] They say that Joan Leveryk of Sibsey and others on Tuesday after Michaelmas last feloniously stole at night 18 geese worth 3s from Joan at Lathe of Sibsey at Sibsey. She is a common thief of oxen and horses.

[c] [1387] Also they say that Denise, wife of the said John on Wednesday after the feast of the nativity of St John the Baptist ... at Alford in John Wadster's house stole a new sheet worth 12d and a piece of velvet worth 2s from Walter Tipscheh. She is a common thief of shoes in the markets of Alford and of poultry in Bilsby.

[d] [1381] They say on their oath that Juliana, William Burreth of Hainton's wife on Tuesday after the feast of All Saints in the fourth year of the reign of King Richard II at Hainton feloniously broke the home of John Byddes of Hainton and stole a quarter of John's malt worth three shillings. They say further that she is a common thief.

[e] [1381] They say on their oath that Maud, the wife of Thomas Donz of Grimsby is a taker-away and remover from houses she enters, namely of vases, spoons, and other items. In this way she stole from the home of Richard Couper of Grimsby a platter, a pewter salt, and a kerchief worth 6d on Tuesday after the feast of St Luke the evangelist in the fourth year of the reign of King Richard II.

[f] [1381] Also they say that Isabel, the daughter of William de Dou of Worlaby on Sunday after Michaelmas in the fourth year of the reign of King Richard II stole at Worlaby five wool pelts of Robert Scotte worth 3s.

[g] [1381] Also they say that Alice Taliour of Epworth came to the house of William Coke of the same place on Thursday before the feast of the Purification of the Blessed Virgin Mary in the fourth year of the reign of King Richard II and there stole a bushel of beans worth 6*d.*

## 40. Peace rolls, Bedfordshire.

Language: Latin. Date: 1358. Translated from Kimball, ed., *Sessions of the Peace for Bedfordshire.*

They say further that Isabel le Pipere and Margery le Faucommer of Wyboston in the twenty-eighth of the reign of the present king took away a brass pot and a plate worth 3*s* from Maud Astwode at Bedford against the peace and a cloak worth 4*s* from a stranger at Cauldwell...

## 41. Peace rolls, Yorkshire.

Language: Latin. Date: 1362. Translated from Putnam, ed., *Yorkshire Sessions of the Peace.*

The soke of Pocklington – present that Thomas de Estryngton, servant of John del Flete took and feloniously carried away five stones of linen cloth, price 20*d,* and one blanket, price 12*d,* and other necessaries, price 18*d,* on Monday before the feast of Pentecost ... from Agnes le Milner of Beleby.

## 42. Trailbaston, Wiltshire.

Language: Latin. Date: 1280. Translation in Pugh, trans., *Wiltshire Gaol Delivery.*

Denise, wife of Roger Godyng and Roger Godyng, taken in Mere hundred with Agnes the kempster of Knoyle for suspicion of burgling Maud le Hopere's house at Mere, plead not guilty. The jurors say that Denise is guilty and the others are not guilty. So one hanged, two quit.

## 43. Manor court.

Language: Latin. Translated from Maitland and Baildon, eds., *The Court Baron.*

[a] 'Modus Tenendi Curias' [view of frankpledge, Weston 1340].

Also they say that Maud Suty is accustomed to steal her neighbours chickens. Therefore let her abjure the vill, and it is ordered that nobody receives or lodges her on pain of 2*d.*

[b] [Littleport, 1324] It is found by inquest that William le Foulere of Marchford made trespass against Walter Albyn and carried off his goods and chattels from his house on various occasions with his wife's consent, but against her husband's will, by frequently kicking her...

### 44. Letter patent.

Language: Latin. Date: 1352. Calendared translation in *Calendar of Patent Rolls, 1350-54.*

Pardon of special grace to Isabel, late wife of Richard Godefray of Carlton, Bedfordshire, of the king's suit for the larceny of goods of Henry le Hunte and Athelina Godefray, to the value of £10 and of twenty-four swine of Richard de Wodeford, whereof she is indicted or appealed, and of any consequent waiver.

### 45. Letter patent.

Language: Latin. Date: 1376. Calendared translation in *Calendar of Patent Rolls, 1374-77*, London, 1916.

Pardon to Agnes Cherlwordiswode in the county of Somerset of the king's suit for the theft of a brazen pan, three pecks of wheat, and a loaf of bread, whereof she is indicted or appealed, and of any consequent waiver.

# Receiving

### 46. Peace sessions, Lincolnshire.

Language: Latin. Date: 1373. Translated from Sillem, ed., *Records of some Sessions of the Peace in Lincolnshire.*

... they present that Katherine, the wife of Wiliam de Whityn is a receiver of John de Thorlay of Barton knowing him to have committed theft.

### 47. Peace sessions, Bedfordshire.

Language: Latin. Date: 1363. Translated from Kimball, ed., *Sessions of the Peace for Bedfordshire.*

The jurors of the town of Bedford present that Thomas Pichard who was outlawed for felony was received at the house of Isabel his wife against the peace and the will of the men of Bedford...

**48. Peace sessions, Shropshire.**

Language: Latin. Date: 1410. Translated from E. G. Kimball, ed., *The Shropshire Peace Roll, 1400-1414*, Shrewsbury, 1959.

And that the aforesaid Agnes Lynley on the aforesaid day in the aforesaid year received William Lynley and Roger Lynley at Haughton knowing that William had committed the aforesaid felony [theft and house-breaking].

# Arson

### 49. Peace sessions, Shropshire.

Language: Latin. Date: 1409. Translated from Kimball, ed., *The Shropshire Peace Roll*.

The jurors say that Margery Welshwoman on Monday after Michaelmas ... at Acton Pigot feloniously burned two barns of Hugh Burnell, knight, full of different kinds of grain.

# Assault

### 50. Peace sessions, Lincoln.

Language: Latin. Date: 1351. Translated from Kimball, ed., *Records of Some Sessions of the Peace in Lincoln and Stamford*.

Also they say that William de Langton ... butcher on Monday after Michaelmas in the twenty-fourth year of the reign of King Edward III after the conquest entered the home of Cecily Spacy in the parish of St Mark in the suburbs of Lincoln against the same Cecily's will and assaulted the said Cecily by force of arms and, finding ten marks in a purse hanging in her bosom, secretly took and carried them away.

### 51. Peace sessions, Lincolnshire.

Language: Latin. Date: 1387. Translated from Kimball, ed., *Records of some Sessions of the Peace in Lincolnshire*.

They say that John Beldge, chapman of Bilsby on Sunday in the feast of the translation of St Thomas the martyr in the aforesaid year [1387] by force of arms assaulted in the field of Bilsby Margaret de

Cane of Alford, beating her and wounding her such that her life was despaired of … and robbing her of a sheet worth 8*d*. He is a common thief of shoes in markets and poultry.

## 52. Peace sessions, Bedfordshire.

Language: Latin. Translated from Kimball, ed., *Sessions of the Peace for Bedfordshire.*

[a] [1356] They say further that Adam Ace, vicar of the church of Oakley, on Thursday in the vigil of St John the Baptist, the thirtieth year of the reign of King Edward III, assaulted Agnes, the wife of Adam le Bere of Oakley, beat and wounded her, and broke her left arm in two places against the peace. Adam was attached to answer the lord king and made fine. He gives the lord king 40*s* by pledge of William Baxtere, chaplain and John Pikel.

[b] [1357] … they say on their oath that Roger Mayn of Bedford and Juliana his wife came by force of arms on Friday after the feast of St Peter ad vincula in the thirty-first year of the reign of King Edward III in Bedford and assaulted Joan Holle of Bedford, beat wounded, and ill treated her against the peace…

[c] [1358] … they say on their oath that Maud Dolle on Sunday night before the feast of St Valentine in the thirty-third year of King Edward III at [Eaton] Ford assaulted Agnes Pitosfrei and broke her head against the peace. Richard le Sawere of Incomb came to the help of the said Maud and struck one William Sacomb junior against the peace. Maud and Richard were attached to answer the lord king the said Maud made fine and gives to the lord king 2*s* by the pledge of Robert Dolle and Henry Abbot…

[d] [1358] … they say on their oath Athelina Flemyng on Wednesday before the feast of All Saints in the thirtieth year of King Edward III after the conquest assaulted Isabel, wife of John Steke, beat her, and dragged her into a ditch against the peace…

## 53. Peace sessions, Yorkshire.

Language: Latin. Translated from Putnam, ed., *Yorkshire Sessions of the Peace.*

[a] [1361] And that William de Lydell of Cottingham on Tuesday after the feast of St Thomas the Martyr in the 32nd year of the reign of the present King made assault by force of arms on Ellen de Waghen

of Beverley at Cottingham and beat, wounded, and ill used him against the king's peace etc.

[b] [1361] John de Middleton of Driffield beat and ill used Ellen atte Brigg of Little Driffield there on Tuesday in Pentecost week...

[c] [1361] John Berier of Westhall and Agnes Broun of Cotom on Thursday on the vigil of St Barnabas the Apostle ... at Cottam made assault on Alice the wife of Henry Andrew and beat, wounded, and ill used her such that her life was despaired of against the king's peace etc.

[d] [1362] Also they present that Henry de Birkenshagh, vicar of the prebend of Barnby by Howden beat and ill used Emma, the wife of Arnold Cliff of Howden, that is on Tuesday before the feast of Pentecost at Howden...

Also they present that the same Henry beat and ill used Margaret the widow of Thomas Whitsid on Sunday before the feast of Pentecost ... at Howden.

Also they present that the same Henry beat Alice Daughdoghter the same day against the peace etc.

[e] [1363] And that Joan de Brigg, formerly the wife of Thomas Dand of Acklam entered by force of arms the house of William Gauge of the same and beat, wounded, and ill used Matillis, daughter of the aforesaid William, to her great loss and against the peace etc.

## 54. Visitation, archdeaconry of Buckingham.

Language: Latin. Date: 1495. Translated from Elvey, ed., *The Courts of the Archdeaconry of Buckingham.*

Langley... Isabel Squyer laid violent hands on Helen Gilham, which same Helen lifted a child of the same Isabel from the holy font... She admits the charge. She did penance and was dismissed.

## 55. Borough court, Nottingham.

Language: Latin. Date: 1395-6. Translated from Stevenson, ed., *Records of the Borough of Nottingham*, I.

[a] John de Mar and John Koo, decennaries of Frenchgate, present an affray made without blood on Agnes, servant of William de Torlarton, because the aforesaid Agnes came to Robert Brinkkelowe's house

against his will and there nearly throttled the aforesaid Robert's wife against the peace of the lord king etc., whence she is attached etc. And therefore the same Agnes comes, and puts herself upon the mayor's mercy and pays 6*d.*

[b] Walter Fletcher, decennary of Moot Hall Gate, presents an affray with blood against Joan de Bawtry of Moot Hall Gate on Maud Donne because the aforesaid Joan was disturbed and threw her on the pavement so that blood issued from her arm, and against the peace of the lord king etc., whence she is attached etc. And therefore the same Joan was put in prison. 6*d.*

[c] Walter Fletcher, decennary of Moot Hall Gate, presents an affray without blood against Maud, the wife of John Boyn, because the aforesaid Maud, the wife of the aforesaid John, of her own will and wrongdoing threw down and beat Agnes de Lenton with her fists against the peace of the lord king etc., whence she is attached etc. And therefore the same Maud was taken to the Common Hall by the mayor's bailiff and she broke the key of the Common Hall and escaped from there without leave of the mayor and bailiffs of the aforesaid town etc. She is forgiven because poor.

## 56. Fair court, St Ives.

Language: Latin. Translated from Gross, ed., *Select Cases Concerning the Law Merchant.*

[a] [1288] Maud, daughter of Richard Ledman, complains about Thomas the barber that when she was in a certain street which is called Cross Lane in the vill of St Ives opposite the house of the said Richard Ledman, her father, late last Sunday, the said Thomas came there against the peace of the lord abbot and his bailiffs and assaulted Maud with vile words and afterwards he took her by the shoulders and threw her into a pond and cruelly trampled her to her damage two shillings, and she produces suit. The aforesaid Thomas, present [in court], denied everything that there was to be denied...

[b] [1291] From Elsworth with Grove because the watchmen went away before the middle of the night on Sunday after the feast of St John before the Latin Gate, whence one Isabel the nurse of Cambridge was badly wounded and many other damages were done on that night through their absence, 12*d*...

## 57. Trailbaston, Wiltshire.

Language: Latin. Date: 1305. Cf. [34b] above, 'Widowhood, poverty, and old age' [18]. Translation in Pugh, trans., *Wiltshire Gaol Delivery.*

Walter Botevylayn for beating Isabel, daughter of William le Taylour at Market Lavington so that she brought forth a dead child.

## 58. Manor court, Halesowen.

Language: Latin. Translated from Wilson, ed., *Court Rolls of the Manor of Hales.*

[a] [1299] John Fille and Denise his wife complain of Roger de Hulle that on Monday in the feast of St Bartholomew the Apostle in the 27th year of the reign of King Edward, Roger assaulted and beat Denise to Denise's damage worth half a mark, and hence he brings suit. Roger came and says that he struck her because of abusive words. Amercement. Judgement was consequently given that Roger should make amends to them and amercement to the lord. Thomas atte Pirie and John de la Hethe pledges.

[b] [1299] Also, they present that Maud de Depsclou is in mercy because she drove out Elice de Rugacre who justly raised the hue. John her husband is in mercy because he contradicted the verdict of the vill. Pledge, the beadle.

[c] [1301] Amercement. The vill of Oldbury present that Alice the daughter of Philip Robines of Oldbury unjustly drew blood of Felicity the daughter of John Walter.

## 59. Manor court, Tottenham (Pembrokes).

Language: Latin. Date: 1395. This is part of a wider feud between the two men. Translation in Oram, trans., *Court Rolls of the Manors of Bruces, Dawbeneys, Pembrokes (Tottenham),* II.

The same John Sawndur complains of the same John Absolon in a plea of trespass, and therein complains that the son of the said John Absolon beat his daughter to his damage 40d, and the said John admits it, therefore in mercy (2d), and he seeks assessment of damages.

# Abduction

### 60. Peace sessions, Lincolnshire.

Language: Latin. Date: 1374. Translated from Sillem, ed., *Records of some Sessions of the Peace in Lincolnshire.*

Also they say that William Yue, goldsmith of Grantham on Thursday after the feast of St John at the Latin gate in the 48th year of the reign of King Edward III by night took Margaret, daughter of John de Repynghale, butcher at Grantham, abducted her, and held her in a secret place for twenty days against the will of Maud, the mother of Margaret and against the peace.

### 61. Peace sessions, Yorkshire.

Language: Latin. Date: 1362. Translated from Putnam, ed., *Yorkshire Sessions of the Peace.*

Also they present that Thomas de Wartre, chaplain, on Monday after the feast of Pentecost ... at Pocklington feloniously ravished Agnes, the wife of William Webbester of Pocklington against the will of her husband and against the peace of the lord king and consumed and wasted the goods and chattels of the same William to the value of forty pence.

# Rape

*See also [34b] above; 'Childhood' [6c]; 'Prostitution' [11c]; 'Widowhood, poverty, and old age' [12].*

### 62. Peace sessions, Lincolnshire.

Language: Latin. Date: 1374. Translated from Sillem, ed., *Records of some Sessions of the Peace in Lincolnshire.*

Also the jurors ... present that one John de Gernesaye, lately keeper of the Humber passage, on Wednesday after Michaelmas in the 48th year of the present king at Barton on Humber entered by night the close of John de Feribi and feloniously seized Emma, the said John's daughter, drew her into her house, and lay with her against her will.

## 63. Peace sessions, Lincolnshire.

Language: Latin. Translated from Kimball, ed., *Records of some Sessions of the Peace in Lincolnshire.*

[a] [1388] Also that Robert, lately servant of John Salt of Cold Hanworth on the feast of St Thomas the martyr in the 11th year of the reign of King Richard II by force of arms at Hanworth raped, lay with, and violated Margaret, the wife of William Lenyng against our peace.

[b] [1381] They say on their oath that one Robert, servant and carter of Henry the rector of the church of Aylesby, on Thursday after Michaelmas in the third year of the reign of King Richard II seized one Agnes, lately Robert Dyon of Laceby's servant, aged twelve years, cut her with his knife at Laceby and there raped her and knew her carnally against her will.

[c] [1395] Also they say that John Helwell, tailor, lately staying in Frodingham on Tuesday after the feast of the nativity of St John the Baptist in the 18th year of the reign of King Richard II at Asbby by Brunby bound Alice, the daughter of Robert Couper of Asackby, feloniously raped her there and violated her body.

## 64. Peace sessions, Bedfordshire.

Language: Latin. Translated from Kimball, ed., *Sessions of the Peace for Bedfordshire.*

[a] [1356] They say that Robert Basset is a common breaker of the peace and that on Monday after the feast of St Luke in the twenty-eighth year of the reign of the present king the said Robert and Roger Corbat entered Alan Muleward's close against his will and dragged his maidservant out of the close against the peace. Henry Muleward, chaplain came to help the said maidservant and the Robert and Roger would have beaten Henry if he had not made fine, viz. 6s 8d, and he paid the fine to the said Robert and Roger...

[b] [1358]... they say on their oath that Richard Cristemasse and his wife Agnes on Friday after Michaelmas in the thirty-second year of the reign of King Edward III at Keysoe entered the close of Henry Daye against the peace and the said Agnes assaulted Eve, wife to the said Henry and beat her against the peace...

They say further that John Pozoun of Keysoe on Sunday after the feast of the Invention of the Cross in the thirty-third year of the reign of

King Edward III at Keysoe entered the close of Henry Daye and seized
Eve, Henry's wife and attempted to rape her against her will. John was
attached to answer the lord king and made fine and gives to the lord
king 2s...

## 65. Peace sessions, Yorkshire.

Language: Latin. Translated from Putnam, ed., *Yorkshire Sessions of the Peace.*

[a] [1363] The jurors ... present that Elias Warner of Malton on
Monday after the feast of the Invention of the Holy Cross ...
feloniously raped Ellen Katemayden of Malton at Norton by Malton
and lay with her against her will and assaulted her and so battered her
that she died within the next three days...

... Elias, brought by the sheriff, came before the justices. The jurors
came likewise, who, chosen, tried, and sworn for this, say on their oath
that the aforesaid Elias is in no way guilty of the aforesaid felony...
Therefore it is judged that the aforesaid Elias is quit thereof etc.

[b] [1363] The jurors ... presented that John de Warter of Pocklington, tailor, on Monday after the feast of Pentecost ... broke by night
the home of Agnes de Wilton at Pocklington and assaulted the
aforesaid Agnes there and feloniously raped her.

Also the same jurors presented that the same John de Warter on
Monday after the feast of the nativity of St John the Baptist ... by force
of arms broke by night the door and windows of John Smyth of
Pocklington and assaulted, wounded, and feloniously raped Joan, the
wife of the said John Smyth and against the peace etc.

Also the same jurors aforesaid presented that the aforesaid John de
Warter on Monday before Christmas ... feloniously raped Ellen,
daughter of John de Welburn of Pocklington etc.

... the aforesaid John, brought by the sheriff, came before the justices.
The jurors came likewise, who, chosen, tried, and sworn for this, say
on their oath that the aforesaid John is in no way guilty of the aforesaid
felonies... Therefore it is judged that the aforesaid John may go quit
thereof etc.

## 66. Peace sessions, Shropshire.

Language: Latin. Translated from Kimball, ed., *Shropshire Peace Roll.*

[a] [1400] And that John Knylle and Alianor his wife, John Surgennel, and Roger Bele on Thursday before the feast of the assumption of the Blessed Mary ... by conspiracy made between them took and led one Adam Osberne, parson of the church of Chetton to the house of the said John Knylle and they said that the aforesaid Adam had wanted to rape the same Alianor against her will and they wanted to murder Adam there and they took forty pence from him on the aforesaid day by extortion against the peace of the Lord King.

[b] [1405] And that Isabel the wife of Ieuan Gronowessone, Joan daughter of the same, and Petronilla, sister of the same Joan, on Monday in Pentecost week in the sixth year of Henry IV lay in ambush in the field at Ightfield and they made assault on Roger de Pulesdon and held the same Roger and tied him with a cord around the neck and cut off his testicles. And that the same Isabel, Joan, and Petronilla on the aforesaid day and in the aforesaid place feloniously snatched and plundered the same Roger of a horse, price 23s, and after made away by that means.

### 67. Visitation, archdeaconry of Buckingham.

Language: Latin. Date: 1495. Translated from Elvey, ed., *The Courts of the Archdeaconry of Buckingham.*

Waddesdon. John Lome because he wanted to rape Lucy Glover of Ham so that she dared not come to church to hear divine services for fear of the said John. He appeared and denied the charge. He purged himself and was dismissed.

### 68. Trailbaston, Wiltshire.

Language: Latin. Date: 1306. Translation in Pugh, trans., *Wiltshire Gaol Delivery.*

Henry Hawys of Chitterne raped the virginity of Alice Godhyne in William Lyngener's house.

...

... Henry Hawys of Chitterne, indicted and taken because he raped Alice Godhyne in William Lyngener's house and carnally knew her. ... and Henry pleads not guilty. The jury of New Salisbury city say ... Henry [is] not guilty.

## 69. Year book, 1313-14.

Language: Latin. Translated from Maitland, Harcourt, and Bolland, eds., *Year Books of Edward II*, V.

[a] Joan sued an appeal of rape against one E. who was present and the aforesaid Joan counted against him that he had lain with her in the 13th year etc. and she spoke of no rape.

. . .

Justice: For a count to be good it is proper to count the year, the day, the place, and the deed so that the appeal can be duly made, and if one finds any of these wanting, abatement for the default may be asked in the count such as the sergeant ought to have done.

The justice directs the court that Joan go to prison for her bad count and E. is quit of the appeal in regards her suit, but he answers to the suit of the king. Sheriff, put him in irons.

Justice: And you answer to the king that you raped the maid Joan who is thirty years and carries a child in her arms.

The woman was asked whose the child was and she said it was E.'s, and it was said that this was a wonder because a child could not be engendered without the will of both, and it was returned that [E. is] not guilty.

[b] An Alice appealed a John of rape and of breach of the peace of our lord the king and said that on a certain day, in a certain place, in a certain town he had raped her maidenhood by force against the peace etc. John came and defended all manner of felony and whatever was contrary to the peace and the dignity of the crown etc. and said that he was culpable of nothing etc. whereby etc. And because it was found by inquest that he was guilty and that the deed had been done before the statute, unless Alice had on advice withdrawn her appeal, it would have been adjudged that she should tear out John's eyes and cut off his testicles because he was married, but if he had been single, the judgement would have been that he marry her or have the same punishment etc.

## 70. Letter patent.

Language: Latin. Date: 1350. Calendared translation in Calendar of Patent Rolls, 1348-50, London, 1905.

Pardon, in consideration of good service in a late conflict at Calais, to Nicholas de Bolton of the king's suit for the rape of Eleanor de Merton, wherewith he is indicted or charged, as well of any consequent outlawry.

# Homicide and petty treason

*See also 'Husband and wife' [23c].*

## 71. Peace sessions, Lincolnshire.

Language: Latin. Kimball, ed., *Records of some Sessions of the Peace in Lincolnshire.*

[a] [1382] Item they say that Richard Demyld of Hardwick and Isabel his wife feloniously killed John de Cotum of Hardwick at Hardwick with a club worth 1*d* on Wednesday after the feast of the Circumcision in the fifth year of the reign of King Richard II.

[b] [1395] They say on their oath that John Elmesale of Gainsborough and Diota, wife of William Baker of the same on Friday before the feast of St Andrew the apostle in the 18th year of the reign of King Richard II murdered at night in the said John Elmesale's house Alice, the wife of the said John Elmesale and fled as felons of the lord king.

## 72. Peace sessions, Shropshire.

Language: Latin. Translated from Kimball, ed., *Shropshire Peace Roll.*

[a] [1401] The jurors say that John Motlowe and John Stathum, late servant of John de Wolley on Friday before the feast of the purification of the Blessed Mary ... feloniously murdered and killed Roger Chelmeleye, Alice Motlowe, [and] William, servant of the aforesaid Alice at Ash and feloniously burned the house of the aforesaid Alice against the peace of the lord king on the aforesaid day. And that the same John and John on the aforesaid day in the aforesaid place feloniously stole animals and other goods and chattels of the same Alice to the value of twenty pounds.

[b] [1412] And that Margaret, daughter of Robert Passeuant on Saturday in the feast of St Lucy ... feloniously killed and murdered William Stocton, her husband at the vill called Meadowtown.

## 73. Coroners' rolls, Essex.

Language: Latin. Date: 1371. Translated from C. Gross, *Select Cases from the Coroners' Rolls A.D. 1265-1413*, Selden Society, IX, 1896.

[a] It happened there that Agnes, the wife of John Dryvere of Little

Baddow was found dead on Thursday in Easter week in the 45th year
of the reign of King Edward the Third at Little Coggeshall, and that
John Growel first found her dead and told the four nearest neighbours,
viz. Edmund Fullere, Walter Trewe, John Sterre, and Richard
Heyward, who told Thomas Pecok, the king's bailiff of the aforesaid
hundred, which bailiff informed John de Gestnyngthorp, one of the
coroners of the aforesaid county. He came to Coggeshall on the
following Friday in that week to view the body of the aforesaid Agnes.
And the aforesaid John Growel, the finder, showed him the body,
which he saw and he felt, and he made inquest concerning the aforesaid
death on the oath of Thomas Lavender ... [and eleven other named
men]. They said on their oath that John Dryvere, the son of Emma de
Badewe, the aforesaid Agnes' husband, took the aforesaid Agnes, his
wife, on Palm Sunday in the aforesaid year to a certain field called
Westfield in Coggeshall to a certain water-filled pit in that field and
there beat her on the head and neck, and so ill treated her that he
almost killed her. And when John Dryvere believed that Agnes was
dead, he threw her into the said pit so that the whole body of Agnes
was in the water except the neck and the head. In like manner the same
Agnes lay there in the water until the following Good Friday, on
which day the aforesaid John Growel found her still alive lying in the
aforesaid manner, and he told the neighbours there who retrieved her
from the aforesaid pit and carried her to Margery Rush's house in the
aforesaid vill. There she lay still alive and she lingered until the
following Thursday in Easter week, on which day she died by reason
of the aforesaid injury. And thus the aforesaid John Dryvere feloniously killed the aforesaid Agnes.

[b] It happened there that Alice Cherles of the same vill [Maldon] on
Wednesday after the feast of the Apostles Peter and Paul in the 45th
year of the reign of King Edward the Third was found dead at Maldon
and that John Rakyere first found her dead. He told the four nearest
neighbours, viz. Robert Peper, John Tras, William Bew, and William
Arundel, who notified Geoffrey atte Wode, the bailiff of the lord king,
which baliff informed John de Gestnyngthorp, one of the coroners of
the aforesaid county. He came there on Saturday following the
aforesaid feast to view the body of the aforesaid Alice. And the
aforesaid John Rakyere, the finder, showed him the body, which he saw
and felt, and he made inquest about the aforesaid death on the oath of
Thomas Bretewell ... [and eleven other named men]. They said on
their oath that on Wednesday after the aforesaid feast in the aforesaid

year, one Katherine Ronges of Messing, unsound of mind, met the said
Alice at the Heath in the aforesaid vill and there struck the same Agnes
on the head with great tiles and sea coal and afterwards threw her into
the sea there by which she came to her death.

## 74. Eyre roll, Kent.

Language: Latin. Date: 1313-14. Translated from Maitland, Harcourt, and
Bolland, eds., Year Books of Edward II, V.

Hundred of Blengate. It is found in the rolls of the coroner that it was
presented before the coroner by the whole of that hundred except the
borough of Beltinge [Kent] that an unknown woman was killed in the
borough of Beltinge on Sunday before the feast of St Alphegus in the
thirtieth year of the reign of King Edward the father of the present
lord king, was despoiled, and was buried beneath the seashore in front
of Beltinge by Robert Godestrey, who has died, and John Waryn
without view of the coroner. And because the same John and Robert
had a robe of green cloth which belonged to the said woman and other
chattels, and because Helewis, the said John's wife, gave one of her
own chemises in order to cover and bury the aforesaid woman, and
that all this was done with the assent of the borough of Beltinge and
concealed by the same. Therefore the aforesaid John and Helewis were
taken and it was inquired more fully on this matter. Afterwards it was
inquired by the jurors of this hundred except the jurors of the borough
of Beltinge together with the jurors of the hundreds of Rislo,
Downhamford, and Whitstable which are next adjacent the aforesaid
borough of Beltinge concerning the aforesaid deed. [They found] that
no such unknown woman was discovered or killed in the aforesaid
borough of Beltinge as was found in the coroner's rolls etc. In fact the
aforesaid story was contrived to injure the aforesaid Robert, who has
died, and therefore nothing is to be done about arresting the aforesaid
John and Helewis etc.

## 75. Letter patent.

Language: Latin. Date: 1352. Calendared translation in *Calendar of Patent
Rolls, 1350-54.*

Pardon of special grace to Alice, daughter of Richard of Holyns of the
king's suit for the death of Margery, daughter of John le Smyth of Derle,
whereof she is indicted or appealed, and any consequent waiver.[4]

4 Waiver is the equivalent of outlawry. See [34a] above.

# Suicide (*felo de se*).

*See also 'Husband and wife' [23]; 'Widowhood, poverty, and old age' [19].*

## 76. Eyre roll, Kent.

Language: Latin. Date: 1313-14. Translated from Maitland, Harcourt, and Bolland, eds., *Year Books of Edward II*, V.

Agnes, daughter of Thomas Rolf of the borough of Womenswold [Kent] was at a certain well in the town of Womenswold and by jumping in she drowned herself of her free will. Judgement of suicide, and Robert le Wyne the first finder and likewise three neighbours came and are not suspected, and Ralph the smith, a neighbour, came not, but is not suspected, and he was attached etc. Therefore they [his pledges] are in mercy. The aforesaid Agnes' chattels [are worth] 5s 6d, for which the sheriff answers...

# IX: Recreation

*See also 'Adolescence' [23] for wrestling contests, the sport of 'shooting at cock', and also patronising alehouses. For eating as recreation see 'Law and custom' [35] deposition of Joan Scharp. Pilgrimage (see 'Devotion' [17]) can also be regarded as a form of recreation. For various constructions of women's conversation see 'Childhood' [3] deposition of Eufemia the wife of John; 'Law and custom' [21], [22], [23a], [24].*

## 1. Household accounts.

Language: English. Translated from Stevenson, ed., *Report of the Manuscripts of Lord Middleton.*

[1521] Also, the Thursday, the 2nd day of April [sic] to the women that gathered for Our Lady's light at Middleton, 4*d.*
...
Also, for your reward to the maids of Polesworth, 2*d.*
...
Also, to the women of Wollaton that gathered for Our Lady's light, 4*d.*
...
Also, for your reward to a maid that gave you a garland of St Peter's eve at the bonfire, 1*d.*
...

[1526] Also in reward to the women of the town that gathered for St Stephen, 4*d.*

## 2. Banns of the Chester Corpus Christi play cycle.

Language: English. Date: ?1467. Translated from P. Happé, ed., *English Mystery Plays*, Harmondsworth, 1975.

> The worshipful wives of this town
> Find of Our Lady the Assumption;
> It to bring forth they be bound
> And maintain with all their might.

### 3. Churchwardens' accounts, St Ewen's, Bristol.

Language: English. Translated from Masters and Ralph, eds., *The Church Book of St. Ewen's, Bristol.*

[a] [1467-8] Receipts of dancing money:

In the first place, of Margaret Nancothan, 20*d*.
Also, of William Tayllour, 6*d*.
Also, of Margaret Wolf, 15*d*.
Also, Laurence Wolf, 13*d*.

[b] [1473-4] Receipts of the sale of ale the same year towards the said vestments[1] as follows:

In the first place, of Joan Brown and Margaret Edwards, 18*s* 10*d*.
Also, of Joan Pekok and Emmota Chestre, 24*s*.
Also, of Isabel Gillam and Christine Leche, 14*s*.
Also, of John Gryffith and Alison his wife, 8*s*.
Also, of Margaret Nancothan, 3*s* 6*d*.

### 4. Churchwardens' accounts, Andover.

Language: English. Date: Easter, 1472. Translated from Williams, ed., *The Early Churchwardens' Accounts of Hampshire.*

Of Philpot Morant and William Sadeler for a 'kyngale', £1 3*s*. 0*d*.
Of Thomas Hode and Agnes Maynsak for a 'kyngale', £1 4*s* 0*d*.
Of William Plomer and Alice Fewar for a 'kyngale', £1 3*s* 0*d*.
Of Richard Nutkyn and Agnes Waterman for a 'kyngale', £1 6*s* 0*d*.

### 5. Churchwardens' accounts, St Mary at Hill, London.

Language: English. Translated from Littlehales, ed., *The Medieval Records of a London City Church.*

[a] [1498-9] Also, for 3 ribs of beef to the wives on Hock Monday, and for ale and bread for them that gathered. Total, 16*d*.

[b] [1514-15] Received of the gathering of the women on Hock Monday. Total, 14*s* 8*d*.

Received of the gathering of the men on Hock Tuesday, 4*s* 5*d*.

---

1 A new set of blue velvet to which Alice Chestre contributed £6 13*s* 4*d* and Elizabeth Sharpe 26*s* 8*d*.

**6. Borough records, London.**

Language: French. Date: 1406. Translation in Riley, *Memorials of London.*

Let proclamation be made that no person of this city or within the suburbs thereof, of whatever estate or condition such person may be, whether man or woman, shall in any street or lane thereof take hold of or constrain anyone, of whatever estate or condition such may be, inside house or outside, for hocking on Monday or Tuesday next called Hock Days, on pain of imprisonment and making fine at the discretion of the mayor and aldermen, and that every constable, sergeant, beadle, and any other officer of the said city shall have power to arrest any person whatever who shall do or practise such hocking, and to take the same to prison to remain there according to the judgement of the said mayor and aldermen.

**7. *Fasciculus Morum.***

Language: Latin. Date: ?early fourteenth century. Translated from Wenzel, ed., *Fasciculus Morum.*

Fourth, I say do not take pride in power and position. For he who glories in these things is like the very poor girl who in the summer in a girls' game is made queen, putting on the trappings borrowed from others. When she looks about in such estate, having forgetten her former rank, believes herself truly to reign and disdains the other girls...

**8. *Memoriale Presbiterorum*, anonymous English pastoral manual.**

Language: Latin. Date: 1344. Translated from quotation in P. P. A. Biller, 'Marriage patterns and women's lives: a sketch of a pastoral geography', in P. J. P. Goldberg, ed., *Woman is a Worthy Wight*, Stroud, 1992, n. 147-8, p. 106.

First, whether they have used superfluous, pompous, monstrous, and inordinate apparel of their heads because they walk about horned and in monstrous manner, which is a form of pride... Also whether they have anointed their own faces by besmearing with colour or unguent so that they appear more red or more white to men...

**9. Pageant play of the Judgement.**

Language: English. Date: ?first half of fifteenth century. Translated from G. England, ed., *The Towneley Plays*, Early English Text Society, extra ser. LXXI, 1897.

Tutivillus: [Speaking of 'females a quantity'] ...

> If she be never so foul a dowd   with her nets and her pins,
> The shrew herself can shroud   both her cheeks and her chins.
> She can make it full proud   with tricks and contrivances,
> Her head as high as a cloud,   but no shame of her sins
>                   They feel.
> When she is thus painted,
> She makes it so quaint,
> She looks like a saint,
>                   And worse than the devil
>
> She is horned like a cow...

## 10. Borough records, London.

Language: French. Translation in Riley, *Memorials of London.*

[a] [1281] It is provided and commanded that no woman of the City shall from henceforth go to market or in the king's highway, out of her house, with a hood furred with other than lambskin or rabbitskin, on pain of losing her hood to the use of the sheriffs, save only those ladies who wear furred capes; the hoods of these may have such furs as they may think fit. And this because regratresses, nurses and other servants, and women of loose life dress themselves excessively and wear hoods furred with great vair and miniver in guise of good ladies.

[b] [1351] Whereas the common sort of women who live in the city of London or who come to the same city from other foreign places have now of late from time to time assumed in unreasonable manner the fashion of being dressed and attired in the manner and dress of good and noble ladies and damsels of the realm, it is provided and ordered by the mayor, sheriffs, aldermen, and commons of the said city that no such common sort of woman now being in the said city, or who shall hereafter come to the aforesaid city, shall be so bold as to be attired either by day or night in any kind of clothing trimmed with fur, such as miniver, badger fur, close-trimmed winter squirrel, spring squirrel, 'bys' of rabbit or hare, or any other kind of noble budge, or lined with sendal, buckram, samite, or other noble lining either in winter or summer, nor yet be clothed in either coat, surcoat, or hood set off with fur or lining after the feast of St Hilary next, on pain of forfeiting the same clothes, but let every common sort of woman, going about the city by day or night after that feast of St Hilary, go openly with a hood

of unlined, striped cloth and clothes neither trimmed with fur nor yet
lined with lining, and without any kind of decoration, so that
everybody, natives and strangers, may know what rank they are, on
pain of imprisonment etc.

## 11. 'Impossible to Trust Women'.

Language: English. Date: later fifteenth century. The unsubtle irony of this
poem, typical of this genre of antifeminist verse, may still tangentially reflect
social practice. Translated from Davies, ed., *Medieval English Lyrics.*

. . .

> To the tavern they will not go,
> Nor to the alehouse never the more,
> For, God knows, their hearts would be woe
> To spend their husbands' money so.

. . .

# X. Devotion

## Female religious

### ① Prologue to the English register of Godstow Abbey.

Language: English. Date: c. 1460. Translated from A. Clark, ed., *The English Register of Godstow Nunnery, near Oxford,* Early English Text Society, original ser. CXLII, 1911.

The wise man taught his child to read books gladly and understand them well, for, in default of understanding, negligence, hurt, harm, and hindrance are frequently brought about, as experience proves in many places. And, in so far as women of religion in reading books in Latin are excused great understanding since it is not their mother tongue, consequently, although they want to read their books of remembrance and their muniments written in Latin, for lack of understanding they frequently took great hurt and hinderance. And, what for lack of truly learned men that are always ready to instruct and advise, and also very great fear of openly showing their evidences (regularly a cause of regret), it is very necessary, as it seems to the understanding of such women religious, that they should have some writing in their mother tongue from their Latin books whereby they might have better knowledge of their muniments and more clearly give information to their servants, rent collectors, and receivers, in the absence of learned counsel. For this reason a poor brother and wellwisher to the good abbess of Godstow, Dame Alice Henley, and all her convent, who are for the most part well versed in books in English, heartily desiring the worship, profit, and welfare of that devout place, that, for lack of understanding of their muniments, should not hereafter incur any damage to their livelihood ... the sense of the greater part of their muniments contained in the book of their register in Latin ... have purposed, with God's grace, to render ... from Latin into English...

### ② Visitations of the bishop of Lincoln.

Language: Latin. Translated from Hamilton Thomson, ed., *Visitations of Religious Houses in the Diocese of Lincoln,* I.

[a] Elstow Abbey, 1421-2.

Richard by divine permission bishop of Lincoln to our beloved in Christ the abbess and convent of the monastery of Elstow of the order of St Benedict, of our diocese, greeting, grace, and blessing. On our last visitation of you and the said monastery both in head and in members we discovered several transgressions and offences notoriously in need of correction, and lest the dark shadow of such transgressions and offences hereafter obscure the light of religion in this house ... we send you by these presents certain injunctions and orders of ours written below...

First, since we have discovered from the evidence of inference and of the certainty of observation that because of the stay of visitors in the said monastery, especially of married persons, the purity of religion, the sweetness of honest conversation and conduct ... have suffered grave shipwreck and may, as is likely, suffer more gravely in future, we direct, instruct, and command you the present abbess, and all those who will in the future be abbesses in the said monastery, under pain of loss of office besides the other penalties written below ... that henceforth you do not admit or permit to be admitted or received any males or females over twelve years of age, however honest they may be, to visit or stay within the claustral enclosure, nor anyone else within the precinct of the said monastery, and especially not married people, unless you have in such cases specifically obtained our special permission or that of our successors who shall be bishops of Lincoln at the time.

Likewise, we enjoin you as abbess ... that you neither grant nor sell liveries, pensions, yearly payments, fees, or corrodies for a life term or for a fixed time...

Likewise, we direct that every nun of the said convent have one dish of meat or of fish appropriate to the season each Monday, Wednesday, and Saturday, each dish worth a penny.

Also that each nun have five measures of superior ale every week, and that there be no distinction between the bread of the abbess and the bread of the convent, and that bread is to be 60 shillings' worth in weight.

Also that henceforth suitable persons be received as nuns, for whose reception or entrance let no money or anything else be taken, but let them hereafter be admitted without any illicit agreement or settlement of any sum of money or of other things which used to be done by the wicked deed of simony... And if they should be clothed at their own or friends' expense, nothing at all should be demanded or sought other than their clothes or the just price of their clothes.

Also that two prudent nuns from among the more senior nuns be chosen and appointed treasurers or bursars of the monastery by the common counsel and assent of the abbess and sounder part of the convent, to whom we will that all monies coming to the monastery be paid faithfully without any sort of detraction to be placed and kept securely in a certain common chest under three keys, of which the abbess shall have one and the treasurers the other two. We will that these monies be paid to be directed to purposes of the monastery according to the direction of the abbess and the sounder part of the convent as the use and need of the monastery shall require.

Also that the collectors and receivers of rents and profits pertaining to the monastery, and the other servants deputed and to be deputed for this purpose, shall take a corporal oath that to the best of their abilities they shall faithfully levy and collect the money arising from rents and profits, and pay it wholly to the abbess and the aforesaid treasurers using indentures or tallies made between them.

Also let the aforesaid treasurers, the cellaress, the sacrist, and the other nuns of the monastery holding office in the same and ministering in temporal matters, render a full account of their administrations at least once a year before the entire convent and other persons deputed for this purpose. And she who is found negligent or at fault in this respect shall be gravely punished as the office holder and absolutely expelled from that office.

Also that a competent nun of unblemished behaviour be deputed to the office of sacrist that she may honestly receive everything that pertains to your office and to the best of her ability see that satisfactory provision is made regarding the same office in respect of light and other requirements.

Also that a more suitable nun be deputed and ordained precentress, and that the senior nuns be preferred to the lesser if they be capable and suitable for such offices.

Also that no nun convicted, publicly defamed, or obviously suspect of the crime of incontinency be appointed to any office within the monastery, and especially to that of gate keeper, until it is sufficiently established concerning the purgation of her innocence.

Also that the nun infirmaress visit her invalid sisters twice or three times a day, or more often if need dictates, that she see that the infirm are adequately and suitably ministered to in regard those things that they need according to the monastery's resources, and that a suitable priest be provided who is to celebrate mass daily in the infirmary chapel before the infirm nuns.

Also that the abbess invite to eat with her those nuns whom she shall know to have greater need of refreshment, and that she change her chaplains each year.

Also that the abbess does not surrender or demise at farm appropriated churches, pensions, portions, manors or granges belong to the monastery, nor do anything else so important without the specific agreement of the greater and sounder part of the convent.

Also we direct you the abbess and each of your successors in the said rank, under pain of suspension from the administration of the goods of the monastery, to show and return a full and true account of your and their administration of the goods of the monastery every year in the weeks after Michaelmas before the whole convent or the sounder part thereof in the monastery's chapter house. We will that these same rolls of account be placed and safely and securely kept in a recognised and sufficiently strong chest under three keys, of which the abbess shall have one, the prioress another, and the precentress the third, together with other muniments and the common seal of the house, so that, when needed, easier access may be had to any of them.

Also that the abbess shall observe carefully what secrets of the chapter are in any way made known, and punish severely those who transgress in this matter according to the rule.

Also that each nun returning from distant parts be provided, as far as the resources of the house permit, for four horses for the whole day or, if she comes after nones, for the remainder of the day and the following night.

Also, when the bell has been rung competently for divine service and the canonical hours and masses according to the rule, all the nuns who are not infirm or lawfully prevented are to come together in the choir at the proper time, and devoutly chant and fulfil together divine office at the proper hours both day and night, and that no one leave before the end without good cause or having first asked and gained the permission of the abbess, prioress, or other president.

Also that each and every one of the nuns of the said monastery, not known to be infirm or lawfully prevented, lie the whole night together in the dormitory, and that two scrutineers, without exception senior nuns, be appointed in the said monastery, who are to observe night and day whether all the nuns, at least those who are able, come to masses and the canonical hours at the proper and accustomed times according to the rule, and that they are settled in their beds in the said dormitory at the proper hours before and after midnight, and if they find any defaulters to disclose and reveal them to the abbess without respect of persons. Let her punish and correct such defaulters according to God and the rule such that their correction and punishment serves as an example to the others.

Also that no nun make any secret conventicles or say or imagine anything by way of insinuation or slander by which charity, unity, or the good name of religion in the convent may be impeded or disturbed.

Also that the novices and other young nuns be diligently and religiously instructed and taught in the observances of the rule so that they may be humble in bearing, conversation, and devotion, and given to holy works.

Also that the prioress or subprioress sit and stay in the cloister more often to watch over and see that those in the cloister conduct themselves religiously there and keep and observe silence.

Also that from now on, after the time the doors of the claustral precinct are closed, no secular or any man of religion be allowed to enter these parts unless he is a great and noble personage, and this for a very good, obvious, proper, and significant purpose.

Also that no nun secretly admit any seculars or other men of religion into her chamber, nor, if admitted, keep them there too long.

Also that the gates be opened and shut at the proper times according to demands of the rule.

Also that no nun have access to the town of Bedford or to the vill of Elstow or other villages or places thereabouts, nor let her eat outside the monastery unless from clear and unavoidable reason to be approved by the abbess and her permission first sought and obtained.

Also that no nun go outside the claustral precinct unlicenced by the abbess unless she has first obtained special permission for the most pressing reason and she be accompanied by at least one nun of mature years and discretion and of good repute who may be witness to her conversation. However, that permission to walk in seemly, enclosed places at appropriate times be not denied the nuns provided that the younger go in the company of the more senior and be ruled by them.

Also that silence be kept by all without distinction at the due times and places, viz. the oratory, the cloister, and the dormitory, on pain of fasting on bread and water on the Wednesday and Friday following...

Also we enjoin and direct that no nun presume to wear silver pins on her head, or silk gowns, or numerous rings on her fingers, but only the one of her profession, under the penalty written below.

Also that no writing nor any letter be sealed with the common seal of the house, particularly if it concerns anything important, unless a consultation about this business is held in the chapter for two days by the sounder part of the convent, and so at length on the third day let it be ratified by the common seal if by diligent consultation it seem expedient.

Also that each and every one of the above injunctions be published and read publicly in the common mother tongue eight times a year, that is twice in every quarter of the year, in the chapter house before the entire convent assembled together in chapter, lest any nun or lay sister be able to pretend ignorance of them...

[b] Godstow Abbey, 1434.

Also that Felmersham's widow [uxor] with her entire household and other mature women be removed entirely from the monastery within the coming year since they are disturbing for the nuns and the occasion of bad example by reason of their dress and their visitors.

Also that the present bailiff of the monastery has no private conversation with any nun since he says that there is not any good woman in the monastery.

Also that there be no parties or drinks after compline, but when it is over all the nuns go together to the dormitory and lie there the night other than the abbess, if she be infirm or impeded by strangers to the profit and honour of the monastery, and except the infirm who then shall be lying in the infimary.

...

Also that the beds in the nuns' lodgings be entirely removed from their rooms other than those for the children, and that no nun receive any secular for any recreation in their rooms under threat of excommunication. For the scholars of Oxford say that they can have whatever entertainment with the nuns they wish to desire.

...

Also that the access of the scholars of Oxford to the monastery be altogether checked and curbed.

Also that there be but three households [*familie*] of nuns besides the household of the abbess. There shall be at six, seven, or eight nuns in each of these three households according to the number of nuns in the convent.

Also that the neither monastery's gatekeeper nor any other secular person convey any presents, rewards, letters or tokens to any Oxford scholars or any other secular persons from the nuns...

### 3. Visitations of the bishop of Lincoln.

Language: Latin. Translated from Hamilton Thomson, ed., *Visitations in the Diocese of Lincoln*, II.

[a] Ankerwyke Priory, 1519.

Dame Alice Hubbard had abided there for four years in nun's habit and had then gone away in apostasy and married one Sutton, a blood relative of Master Richard Sutton, steward of Syon. She lives with him in adultery in Sutton's part of the world.

[b] Burnham Abbey, 1521.

Dame Anne Belfeld complains somewhat because these days they do not have a fixed allowance as they used to have, but everything in common...
...
The nuns now sleep two to a bed until the dormitory is repaired and made ready. The bishop directed that from now on they do not lie together, but in separate beds.
...
The abbess ought by the monastic rule to sleep in the dormitory and eat in the refectory with the nuns. The present abbess, however, does not do this, but sleeps in her chamber and has another nun in her bed with her and she eats in her chamber. The bishop commanded the abbess that she eat at all times in the refectory and that she never have anyone in bed with her.
...
There are several children in the convent, viz. Margaret Restwold, Anne Bogar, Michael Bovington, and Margaret. They pay nothing for their commons [i.e. meals, but perhaps also clothing] to the convent's loss. One Katherine is there also. The bishop ordered the abbess to put

this right.

...

The abbess does not make an annual account and if such an account were made it is not revealed to the nuns so it follows that the nuns are unsure of the state of the house. The bishop directed the abbess always to make an account every year.

...

The treasurer and the other officials did not render account. The bishop instructed that they always make accounts.

...

The abbess is not impartial in her manner towards all the nuns, but shows greater affection to some than to others,[1] viz. Dame Elizabeth Woodford, Dame Margaret Moosse, and Lucy Paget...

...

There are some nuns within the convent who are unable to read and sing.

...

Dame Alice Collis says that Dames Elizabeth Woodford, Margaret Moosse, and Lucy Paget do not go to the dormitory immediately after matins, but wait longer. Anne Nores says the same. Margaret Browne says likewise.

...

Dame Elizabeth Woodford complains that secular women come to the convent and talk there with the nuns and the nuns talk with them which is not right.

...

Dames Anne Belfeld, Margaret Brown, and Alice Nores do not eat in the refectory, but usually have their meals in their own rooms. The bishop ordered that this henceforth be corrected.

...

Dame Joan Twiford, the gatekeeper, frequently allows lay women to go into the cloister although it is not allowed.

...

The bishop directed that from henceforth no children should sleep within the dormitory.

...

Silence is not observed other than in the cloister.

1 The text is damaged, but the sense of it is reproduced here.

[c] Greenfield Priory, 1525.

Newcome. She had been made pregnant by Sir William Wharton who now lives in the diocese of London it is said. She was corrected by the prioress. Dame Agnes Graunde is light-minded character and is in some way associated with James Smyth. Agnes Kettill does not seem suitable to be a nun.

[d] Elstow Abbey, 1531.

Dame Alice Erdes says that my lord [the bishop] did not command us to take my lady Snawe as prioress, but he said, 'If you will not take her as prioress, I will make her prioress myself.' She says that she was one of those who walked out of the chapter house because my lady Snawe is not able to be prioress, saying that they were accustomed to have the prioress chosen by the abbess and convent, and not by my lord, according to the rule of St Benedict...

## 4. Church court, diocese of Lincoln.

Language: Latin. Date: 1517. Translated from Bowker, ed., *An Episcopal Court Book for the Diocese of Lincoln.*

Dame Katherine, prioress of Littlemore appeared in person and was examined on various articles, some made against her on oath, others made by her on oath on the gospels.

To the first article she replied and acknowledged [that as prioress she was subject to the jurisdiction of the bishop of Lincoln]. To the second article she says that seven years ago she was known carnally and made pregnant by one Richard Hues, by whom, as she claimed, she had a girl child. This witness confessed that she fed and cared for this child within the priory for three years up until the time of the child's death. She says further that Richard Hues was domestic chaplain to the prioress serving in her own house and that for six months seven years ago he kept company with the prioress and held her in incestuous embrace for that six months. To the third article she says that before and after the feast of the Purification of Mary last Richard was with this witness in the priory and resided there the whole time. This witness confessed that by admitting Richard to her house she had done wrong and set a bad example to her sisters, but she was not known carnally by him on that date. To the fourth article she responded that Dame Juliana Wynter gave birth to a girl child in the said nunnery begotten by one John Wikesley, a servant in the house... She replies to the fifth article and denies it. To the sixth article she acknowledges that she lent Richard Hues a feather bed with a bolster, a pair of sheets, a surplice, and a silver chalice, all of which items Richard still has in his possession. To the seventh article she denies that she wasted the assets of the monastery. She says, however, that a hundred pounds would not suffice to make adequate repairs to the priory. The prioress finally submitted herself to correction by the lord bishop of Lincoln...

## 5. Bishop's register, Salisbury.

Language: Latin. Calendared translation in Horn, ed., *The Register of Robert Hallum.*

[a] [1412] Mandate to the abbess and convent of Shaftesbury forbidding the nuns to leave their house except for good cause, approved by the superior, and in the company of senior nuns of proved character. It has been reported that several nuns have often been wandering outside the house in various places longer than is seemly and for frivolous reasons. The abbess and prioress are enjoined to consider the punishment that overtook Dinah the daughter of Jacob for yielding to the desire to go abroad, so that the bishop is not forced to impose punishment himself.[2]

[b] [1414] Mandate to the prioress and convent of Bromhall to receive Alice Boyton, nun of Kingston St Michael, who is to be transferred on account of her bad behaviour. She is to be in the special custody of a mature, God-fearing nun and is to be kept from communication with secular or religious people except in the presence of this guardian. She is not to go outside the monastery until further notice. The house will be paid for her stay by the priory of Kingston St Michael.

[c] [1408] Letter to abbess and convent of Shaftesbury nominating as nun Katherine, daughter of John Brombelegh of Sherborne, a young girl, in accordance with the bishop of Salisbury's customary right of appointment. She will be sent by the bishop and is to be received and put into the company of Agnes Poney, who is to instruct her in the regular disciplines. They are to notify the bishop of the action taken...

[d] [1410] Commission to the abbot and convent of Cirencester, diocese of Worcester, to act as collectors of the tenth and a half in the

---

2 Dinah, according to the account in Genesis 34, 'went out to visit the women of the land' and was raped by Sechem. Sexual violence, or the threat of violence, was thus justified as 'punishment' for nuns' (and other women's) disobedience in going abroad of their own volition. Cf. also 'Husband and wife' [16].

archdeaconries of Wiltshire and Berkshire. The benefices of the following are exempted: the poor nuns of Lacock and Kingston St Michael in Wiltshire archdeaconry, and of Bromhall in Berkshire archdeaconry...

## 6. Papal letter.

Language: Latin. Date: 1368. Calendared translation in *Calendar of Papal Letters*, IV.

To the archbishop of York. Mandate, on petition of William, master general of the order of Sempringham, to summon those concerned and make order touching Alice, daughter of John de Everyngham, of Birkin, Gilbertine nun of Haverholme, who, having left her order, and having refused to obey the master's monition, was excommunicated by him, and then lived incestuously with James de Huthulle, layman of the same diocese, as if they were man and wife. On her refusing to appear before the said master, papal letters were obtained to the dean of Lincoln, who commissioned Geoffrey de Scrop and Raynold de Belvero, canons of the same, to hear the cause. The canons absolved Alice, under caution, from the sentence of excommunication, upon which the master appealed to the pope.

## 7. Clerical poll tax returns.

Language: Latin. Nuns were regularly named after their place of origin rather than by any family name. Consequently the modern form of the place name has been used here where this was easily identifiable and 'of' has been preferred over 'de' used elsewhere. Translation by McHardy in A. K. McHardy, ed., *Clerical Poll-Taxes of the Diocese of Lincoln 1377-1381*, Lincoln Record Society, LXXXI, 1992.

[a] [1377] Nuns of Bullington: Katherine Pigot [prioress], Amy of Alington, Isabel of Lincoln, Mabel of Beseby, Felicity of Prestwold, Pernell Sleygh, Lucy of Freskenay, Agnes Bussy, Margery of Helyng, Alice of Barkeworth, Joan Towers, Mabel of Holing, Agnes of Dautre, Amice of Schepay, Maud of Fulnetby, Julia of Waltham, Eleanor of Heling, Elizabeth Brews, Helen Brews, Rose of Prestwold, Katherine Belers, Alice of Lincoln, Joan of Wells, Alice of Scremby, Joan of Crosholm, Iseult Roos, Margery of Wynceb, Lora of Dysterby, Alice Roos, Isabel of Boston, Elizabeth of Beckingham, Hawis Cressi, Joan of Sibthorp, Alice of the same, Alice of Brigg, Agnes of Leek, Mary Sallow, Alice Sallow, Beatrix of Birketon, Alice Levelaunce, Joan of Prestwold.

Sisters of Bullington: Audrey of Paunton, Joan of Redmerthowe,

Margery of Skeldinghop, Constance of Barkworth, Alice of Wynwold, Joan Burdet, Agnes of Fulnetby, Muriel of Bolington, Margery of Fulnetby, Joan of Raund.

[b] [1379] Priory of Markyate. Prioress for all her goods, spiritual and temporal, worth £50, paying 13s 4d.

Nuns paying 12d each: Sibyl Attleborough, Margaret Cresy, Margaret Fauxwelle, Maud Senescal, Mary Bardulf, Denise Pevere, Agnes Cheddington, Sarah Lorynge, Agnes Somersham.

Chaplain: John.

[c] [1381] Priory of St Leonard, Grimsby. Agnes of Humberston, prioress; Agnes of Helyng, Margery of Helyng, Elizabeth Pouchler, Agnes Bryan [canonesses] paying 3s 4d each.

[d] [1377] House of St Katherine [Lincoln]. Brothers John of Whatton, prior, William of Ness [and nine other named canons].

Lay brothers: Brothers Thomas, John, Robert.

Sisters: Adeline of Bultham, Katherine of St Botolph, Alice of York, Isabel of Green, Isabel of Whatton, Margery Gray.

[e] [1381] Priory of St Katherine, Lincoln. Dom. John Watton, prior, William Nesse [and nine other named] canons.


## Anchoresses

### 8. Wills, diocese of York.

Language: Latin.

[a] Will of Alice Haukesworth, York. Date: 1430. Translated from BIHR, Prob. Reg. 3 fo. 373.

Also I leave my niece Isabel the anchoress of Fishergate 2s.

[b] Will of John Gray, York. Date: 1474. Anchorholds were usually associated with parish churches, but sometimes, as here, with nunneries. In such instances they probably provided for former nuns. For both these points see also [10] below. Translated from BIHR, Prob. Reg. 4 fos. 215-15v.

Also I leave to Dame Alice Derby, anchoress in the house of St Clement by the city of York [i.e. St Clement's nunnery], 12d.

### 9. Household accounts.

Language: English. Date: 1522. Translated from W. H. Stevenson, ed., *Report of the Manuscripts of Lord Middleton*, Historical Manuscripts Commission, LXIX, 1911.

Also, in reward to the anchoress [of Polesworth] the same day, 8*d.*

### 10. Commission by bishop of Lincoln to Abbot John of Thornton.

Language: Latin. Date: 1436. Translated from Hamilton Thomson, ed., *Visitations of Religious Houses in the Diocese of Lincoln*, I.

... We came to the aforesaid parish church of Winterton on the 21st day of the aforesaid month [January] to examine according to the authority, form, and effect of your reverend commission Beatrix Franke, a nun of Stainfield, who was awaiting our arrival there, about her retreat from the communal life to the solitary, the length of time [she was] so minded, and the dangers of choosing such a life and afterwards regretting it. When the examination was over, finding her in no way either hesitant or wavering, but wanting unfailingly the life of an anchoress almost from the time of her youth, sticking the whole time to that purpose, we absolved her and caused her to be released from the yoke of obedience to her prioress of Stainfield. On St Vincent's day, reading openly and clearly, she publicly made a new profession before the high altar of the aforesaid church during mass, and furthermore promised obedience and chastity to us, in your place, and your successors.

After the mass had been, as is the custom, solemnly performed and celebrated, with the assent of the common people among whom she today resides and the consent had before, enclosing the aforesaid sister Beatrix in a certain house and enclosure built on the north side of the said church, and fastening the door thereof with locks, bars, and keys, we left her, as is believed by many, in joy of the Saviour, in peace and quiet of spirit...

## Hospital sisters

### 11. Ordinances for hospital of St James, Northallerton.

Language: Latin. Date: 1244. Translated from J. Raine, ed., *The Register, or Rolls, of Walter Gray*, Surtees Society, LVI, 1872.

... There are also to be three sisters who should likewise have the

habit and rule of sisters, two of whom should take care of the infirm
in their beds when it is night, and at other times look to the other
needs of the house...

## 12. Presentments under the Statute of Labourers, Oxford.

Language: Latin. Date: 1390. Translated from H. E. Salter, ed., *Medieval
Archives of the University of Oxford*, Oxford Historical Society, LXXIII, 1921.

And Alice Deye and Alice Mey say that they serve the infirm being in
the said hospital [of St John] and watch and labour about them much,
and they say that each of them takes 10*s* a year...

# Lay piety

*See also 'Adolescence' [23]; 'Widowhood, poverty, and old age' [12]
depositions of Roger Marschall and Agnes Kyrkeby.*

## 13. Wills, diocese of Carlisle.

Translated from R. S. Ferguson, ed., *Testamenta Karleolensia*, Cumberland and
Westmorland Antiquarian and Archaeological Society, extra ser. IX, 1893.

[a] Will of Agnes de Denton, Thursby nr. Carlisle.

In the name of God, amen. I, Agnes, the wife Sir Richard de Denton,
of sound mind, on Friday after the feast of St Giles the Abbot in the
year of our Lord 1356 make my will in this manner. In the first place
I leave my soul to God and the blessed Mary, and my body to be buried
in the parish church of Thursby before the altar of the blessed Mary,
and my best animal to the said church for mortuary and my second
best animal to the church of Denton for mortuary. Also, I leave in wax
to burn about my body three stones of wax. Also, I leave in oblations,
one mark. Also, I leave for almsgiving to the poor, 30*s*. Also, to the
friars minor of Carlisle, 10*s*. Also, to the friars preachers of Carlisle,
10*s*. Also, to the Austin friars of Penrith and Appleby, half a mark to
divide between them. Also, I leave to the nuns of Armathwaite, 10*s*.
Also, I leave to John de Kirkbride two oxen and two cows and two
heifers. Also, to Dame Cecily of Armathwaite, two cows. Also, I leave
to my cousin Christiana, two cows. Also, to Robert Linok, two cows.
Also, to Robert Linok, two shillings. Also, to John del Hall, two
shillings. Also, to Thomas his brother, two shillings. Also, to Adam his

brother, 12d. Also, I leave to Dame Cecily a best brass pot and to my cousin Christiana a brass pot. Also, I leave 6 marks [£4] for the use of a chaplain saying mass for my soul in the said church of Thursby. Also, I leave the residue of my goods pertaining to me to my lord, Sir Richard de Denton. I appoint these my executors to carry out faithfully my will, viz. my lord, Richard de Denton and his brother John and William de Denton, rector of the church of Ousby. Given at Ousby the aforesaid day and year.

[b] Will of Christiana de Briswode, Dalston nr. Carlisle.

In the name of God, amen. 21 day of January 1367 was proved the will of Christiana, the wife of William son of Gilbert de Briswode of the parish of Dalston made nuncupatively in these words. In the first place she left her soul to God, the blessed Mary, and all the saints, and her body to be buried in the cemetery of the parish church of Dalton with her best draught animal by way of mortuary. Also, she left the vicar of the same church 6d. Also, she left her sister Agnes a cow, half a basket of malt, and half a basket of flour. Also, she left her sister Alice a tunic. She gave the remainder of her goods to the said William, her husband, and directed him to dispose of the said goods for her soul. She made her said husband her executor.

## 14. Wills, archdeaconry of Buckingham.

Translated from Elvey, ed., *The Courts of the Archdeaconry of Buckingham*.

[a] Will of Agnes Umfrey, widow, Edlesborough. Language: Latin.

In the name of God, amen. In the year of the Lord 1484, 24th day of March. I Agnes Umfrey, late wife of John Umfrey now dead, of sound mind, make my testament in this manner. In the first place I leave my soul etc. Also, I leave to the high altar of the same [church] two measures of wheat. Also, to the light of the crucifix, 4d. Also, to the eight greater lights of the same, 8d. Also, to the light of the image of the Blessed Mary of Pity, 1d. Also, for the repair of the torches, 4d. Also, I leave for the chapel of Dagnall a measure of wheat. Also, for the purchase of a set of vestments for the church of Edlesborough, if such happen to be bought, according to the will of my executors. Also, to the church of Little Gaddesden, 12d. To the fraternity of the church of Great Gaddesden, 20d. Also, I leave for the maintenance of a priest to celebrate in the church of Edlesborough, if the parish happens to provide such, 6s 8d. If not, however, the same sum is to be disposed for other pious uses by my executors as seems to them most expedient for the salvation of our souls. Also, to each godson and goddaughter of mine, 4d. Also, I leave to Agnes Merston an acre of wheat to be assigned at the will of my executors. Also, to the same a pair of sheets and a brass pot. Also, I leave to Hugh my servant an acre of wheat according to the assignation of my executors. Also, that my messuage together with the lands pertaining to it be sold and one half of the price be disposed for the salvation of the souls of those from whom it descended. Also, that my obit and those of my husband and other of our blood kin be observed yearly in the church of Edlesborough. I will that the second half of the price be divided equally between my sons, viz. Thomas and George, and I will that Thomas' part be paid to him or his assigns by my executors within the space of four years. The residue of my goods I give and bequeath to my son George and to William Billyngdon senior whom I make and ordain my executors to dispose for the salvation of my soul.

[b] Will of Jane Kegyll, widow, Edlesborough. Language: English.

In the name of God, amen. The 30th day of the month of December the year of our Lord 1518. I Jane Kegyll, late wife of John Kegyll, with a whole mind make my testament in this manner. First I bequeath my soul to Almighty God and to Our Lady St Mary and my body to be buried in the churchyard of Edlesborough. Also, I give and bequeath to the mother church of Lincoln, 2d. Also, I give and bequeath to the high altar of Edlesborough, a quarter of malt. Also, I give and bequeath to the eight lights of Edlesborough, a quarter of malt. Also, I give and bequeath to the same, a new towel of four ells. Also, I give and bequeath to the rood light, two busshels of malt. Also, I give and bequeath to everyone of the small lights in the same church, 1d. Also, I give and bequeath to Sir Thomas Amyes, 20d. Also, I give and bequeath to Agnes Hartley, my best gown. All the residue of my goods I give and bequeath to John Geffray otherwise called John Hartley and to Agnes his wife, which two persons I make and ordain my executors and to keep my children. And if it happen that my children pass away and die, that then the said John Hartley and his wife shall hire an honest priest to read and sing in the parish church of Edlesborough for all Christian souls as long as the goods may extend. These witnesses: Thomas Sowthyn, Richard Sowthin, and Sir Thomas Amyes.

[c] Will of Joan Ingrame, widow, North Marston. Language: English.

In the name of God, amen. In the year of Our Lord 1519, the 12th day of December. I Joan Ingrame, widow, of the town of North Marston within the county of Buckinghamshire, whole of mind with good deliberation have made this my present testament containing my last will in the manner and form following. First I bequeath my soul to Almighty God, to our blessed Lady, and to all the company of heaven, my body to be buried in the church of North Marston near my husband. Also, my best good for my mortuary. Also, I give and bequeath to the mother church of Lincoln, 4d. Also, to the high altar for my tithes forgotten, a cloth of diaper. Also, to St Sunday's altar in that church, a sheet with a seam of black silk. Also, to the rood light, half a pound of wax. Also, to St Katherine's light, as much. Also, to St Christopher's light, a quarter of a pound of wax. Also, to St Thomas' light, as much. Also, to St Margaret's light, as much. Also, to St Anne's light, as much. Also, to Master John Schorne's light, a pound of wax. Also, for burial in the church, 6s 8d. Also, to Thomas Baker, a horse with a black collar and one ear, also a speckled cow calf, and two silver spoons, and £3 6s 8d. Also, I give and bequeath to Isabel Baker, the wife of the foresaid Thomas Baker, a feather bed with two patches, a pair of blankets neither of the best nor of the worst with a coverlet and a pair of sheets in like manner, two silver spoons, two platters, two dishes, two saucers, and a heifer, the eldest of five. Also, I give and bequeath to the church of North Marston two silver pieces to drink wine in order to make silver cruets and a little bell of silver if possible. Also, I give to William Gyllot the next best horse to Thomas Baker's and a calf. Also, I give to Joan Kyng a brass pot next to the best. Also, I give to St Peter's church Worminghall an ox being in the keeping of William Browton. Also, I give to Katherine Browton my best gown. Also, I give to the sepulchre light in the church of North Marston, a pound of wax. Also, I give to William Sevys the younger an iron bound cart. Also, I bequeath to the highway in the parish of North Marston, five marks. Also, I give to a priest to sing for my soul in the parish of North Marston, eight marks. Also, I give to Katherine Awdley my best kirtle, my best apron, and my best cap. Also, I give to every godson that I have in the parish of North Marston, 4d. Also, I give to Nicholas Hall the house that I dwell in with all the land and closes pertaining to it so that he bestow every year 13s 4d – 6s 8d for a dirige and 6s 8d among poor people. The residue of my goods ungiven I would that master Simon Gadd and Nicholas Hall should have to bestow for my soul, whom I make my executors. Witness hereto: Edmund Paratt, John Awdley, Thomas Baker, William Pede with various others.

### 15. Manor court rolls, Ingoldmells.

Language: Latin. Date: 1387. Translated in Massingberd, trans., *Court Rolls of the Manor of Ingoldmells.*

John Smyth and Maud his wife demised to Robert, son of the said John 11 acres of land and pasture with a messuage in Ingoldmells to have after the death of the said John for 20 years under condition that the same Robert shall pay in the first 10 years each year 2 marks in works of charity for the soul of the said Maud by the view and direction of the parson of the church of Ingoldmells who for the time shall be...

### 16. 'Italian Relation'.

Language: Italian. Date: c. 1497. Translation in Sneyd, trans., *A Relation ... of the Island of England.*

Although they all attend mass every day, and say many Paternosters in public, the women carrying long rosaries in their hands, and any who can read taking the office of our Lady with them and with some companion reciting it in the church verse by verse in a low voice after the manner of churchmen, they always hear mass on Sunday in their parish church and give liberal alms...

### 17. Church court, York.

Language: Latin. Date: 1366. Scarborough had a hospital dedicated to St Thomas of Canterbury. This is a brief extract from a longer series of depositions in a disputed marriage case. Translated from BIHR, CP.E.92. Alice Roding c. John Boton.

...

[Deponent examined 14 October, 1366.]

Robert son of Philip of Scampston, living there, and so resident since his birth...

... asked about the first article, he says that on St Thomas the Martyr's day last but one, and not before, he heard a rumour going about concerning a contract of marriage made between the parties in question. On that day the parties were at Scarborough on pilgrimage and a dispute arose between them there, but about what this witness does not know, and when they returned that day from Scarborough to Scampston the contract of marriage between the parties was advertised publicly, but he did not notice whether by the friends of one party or the other.

John Emmotson of Scampston, aged 30 years, of free status, a blood relative of John Boton, but in what degree he does not know, sworn and examined on the aforesaid articles. Asked about the first, he says that the report about the contract had its origin, as this witness knows, on the day of the translation of St Thomas last with Alice, so this witness says. Asked whether this witness heard this, he says no, but he well remembers and believes that on that St Thomas' day before the hour of vespers and after nones men and women to the number of twenty, who had come with the said Alice on her pilgrimage made to Scarborough, were sitting in a house at Scampston drinking, and there this witness heard for the first time report of the contract...

### 18. Wills, diocese of York.

Language: Latin.

[a] Will of Alison Hudson, Brodsworth. Date: 1509. Translated from BIHR, Prob. Reg. 8 fo. 22.

Also I owe my pilgrimage to the Holy Rood of Chester, to St Saviour, to St Sitha of Eagle, and to St Sebastian, and the said John Hudson shall perform them...

[b] Will of Thomas Bardolffe, woolman, York. Date: 1432. Translated from  BIHR, Prob. Reg. 2 fo. 604v.

And to Margaret Erysacre to go on pilgrimage for me to Canterbury on her own feet, 13s 4d.

### 19. Churchwardens' accounts, St Ewen's, Bristol.

Language: English. Translated from Masters and Ralph, eds., *The Church Book of St. Ewen's, Bristol.*

[a] Inventory of goods. Date: 1455 and later.

Also, a pair of vestments of red damask of the gift of Elizabeth Scharpe with other things thereto according.

...

Also, one coat to St Katherine[3] of satin of Cypress with one piece of coral capped with silver of the gift of Katherine Gylys.

[b] [1454-5] Receipts of bequests and gifts to the said cross from various members of this church:

3 I.e. an image of St Katherine.

In the first place, of Thomas Lumbard, 6s 8d.

…

Also, of Isabel Gyllard, one pot[crok'] sold for 4s 10d.
Also, of Maud Hopkyn, 6s 8d.
Also, of Dame Margaret Leche, 12d.

…

… of Agnes, George Roche's wife, 3s 4d.

…

Receipts from broken silver for the aforesaid cross

…

Also, of Alice Sylkwoman, one ring of silver weighing a half quarter
and one farthing gold weight
Also, of Thomas Fyssher, one spoon weighing one ounce
Also, of Lucy Thomas, one ounce

…

Also, of the executors of Edith Blays, one spoon weighing one ounce
Also, Dame Margaret Leche, a half ounce and one farthing gold
weight
Also, of Joan Hoper, widow, one ounce, a half, and two pennies weight

[c] [1464] Memorandum that on Sunday, 8th January in the third year
of King Edward IV, our said mistress Sharp 'full womanly' brought the
cake with candles unto this church, her maid bearing the same after
her, and a fair twill towel, embroidered at both ends and in one piece.
After she had offered up the cake and candles with her prayers as is the
custom in such acts, called unto her our said parson William Sampson,
John Wolf, Robert Core, Robert Jonettes, our parish clerk, and various
others, both men and women, being there and then present a little
before the hour of seven before matins, and said these words:

Father parson and my spiritual father and all who are present here, I
am  right pleased and glad of this good end that is had and concluded
between my husband and you and this church. And in token whereof,
after my decease, I give you this same towel. And … because this same
church has stood destitute of a long towel to serve the parishioners of
an Easter Day, unless by joining three or four small towels together as I
see well yearly, I will that the clerk of this church fetch this towel every
Easter Day only in worship of the sacrament, and after my decease
without any condition it shall remain unto this church to the said use.

[d] [1474-5] Also, of the maidens' collection for Our Lady light taper,
2s 6d.

[e] [1454-5] Receipts for the sale of seats:

In the first place, of Richard Batyn, goldsmith, procurator [i.e. church-warden], for his seat and his wife's, 12d.
Also, of Robert Core, procurator, for his wife's seat, 6d.
Also, of Laurence Wolf for his seat and his wife's, 12d.
Also, of John Wolf for his seat and his wife's, 12d.
Also of James Swetman for his seat, 6d.

[f] [1459-60] Receipts for the sale of seats:

In the first place, of John Chetcorn, tiler, for his seat and his wife's, 16d.
Also, of William Tayllour for Agnes his daughter's seat, 6d.
Also, of Maud, Robert Core's mother for her seat, 6d.
Also, John Forbour, [living] with Rotur, for his wife's seat, 8d.
Also, of Alice, wife of John Capper, for one seat behind the new enterclose [a type of screen], 6d.

[g] [1489-90] Also, for nails to repair the wives' seats, 2d.

## 20. Churchwardens' accounts, St Mary at Hill, London.

Language: English. Translated from Littlehales, ed., *The Medieval Records of a London City Church.*

[a] [1514-15] Received of Mr Doctor of the good charity of certain women in the parish which they gave towards the altar cloth of white and red cloth of gold and the curtains for the same of white and red sarsenet, that is to say of Ingleby's wife, £5, and of various others, the total of £4 10s. Total received, £9 10s.

[b] [1512-13] Paid for making of 3 men's pews, for the poppies [i.e. the carved finials on the bench ends] and other stuff, 20s.

Paid for underpinning of the men's pews and the women's pews...

## 21. Wills, diocese of York.

[a] Will of John Gray, York. Language: Latin. Date: 1474. Translated from BIHR, Prob. Reg. 4 fos. 215-15v.

Also I leave Elizabeth Morton, widow, in the house of St Leonard's, York [i.e. St Leonard's hospital] an image of the Trinity.

[b] Will of Cecily Giry, widow, York. Language: Latin. Date: 1388. Translated from BIHR, Prob. Reg. 1 fo. 5v.

And I will that the three feather beds with the sheets pertaining to them in the guest chamber remain there to serve as a hospice for the needy poor.

[c] Will of Gilemota [Wilmot] Carrek, York. Language: Latin. Date: 1408. Translated from BIHR, Prob. Reg. 3 fo. 585v.

Also to Alice, daughter of William Bows an English book of 'The Spirit of Guy' and a French book of 'Barlaham and Josephath'.

[d] Will of Agnes Stanssal, widow, Doncaster. Language: Latin. Date: 1430. Translated from BIHR, Prob. Reg. 2 fo. 633v.

I leave to the wives of the town of Doncaster, 6s 8d.[4]

[e] Will of Agnes Poost, widow, Doncaster. Language: English. Date: 1505. Translated from BIHR, Prob. Reg. 6 fo. 206v.

Also I bequeath all my wood and coals to be divided among poor people hastely after my death.


## 22. Guild of St Katherine, Norwich.

Language: English with heading, preamble, and end note Latin. Date: 1389. Translated from J. Toulmin Smith, ed., *English Gilds*, Early English Text Society, original ser. XL, 1870.

Norwich. To the most excellent prince and lord, our lord Richard, by the grace of God King of England and France, and his council in his chancery, his humble liege subjects, the wardens of the same guild of St Katherine virgin and martyr in the church of Saints Simon and Jude in Norwich, all obedience, reverence, and honour. By reason of a certain proclamation lately made at the royal mandate by the sheriff of the county of Norfolk at Norwich, we certify to your excellency according to the form of the aforesaid proclamation that our aforesaid guild was begun in the year of Our Lord 1307 by some parishioners of the said church and others devoted to God, for the honour of the Holy Trinity, the Blessed Virgin Mary, St Katherine virgin and martyr, and All Saints, and to sustain the augmentation of the lights in the aforesaid church, under certain ordinances made and published by the common consent of the brothers and sisters of the aforesaid guild. The substance of these ordinances follows in these words:

In the beginning, with one assent it is ordained that all the brothers

---

4 Wives here may imply widows and hence suggest a charitable bequest, but it could also imply a women's 'guild' or more informal collectivity (cf. 'Recreation' [2]).

and sisters of this guild shall come together in the parish church of Saints Simon and Jude in Norwich on the day of St Katherine in order to go in procession with their candles, which are borne before them, and to hear the mass of St Katherine in the aforesaid church, and that every brother and sister shall offer a halfpenny at that mass.

And also it is ordained that any brother or sister who is absent from the aforesaid procession or at mass or the offering shall pay to the goods of the guild two pounds of wax, but they may be excused for good cause.

And also it is ordained that whenever a brother or sister has died, every brother and sister shall come to the dirige and mass, and at the mass everyone shall offer a halfpenny and give a halfpenny for alms, and for a mass to be sung for the soul of the dead person, a penny. And at the dirige every brother and sister that is lettered shall say the placebo and dirige for the soul of the dead in the place where they shall come together, and every brother and sister that are unlettered shall say twenty times for the soul of the dead person the Paternoster with the Ave Maria, and there shall be of the goods of the guild two candles of wax of 16 pounds weight around the body of the dead person.

And also it is ordained that if any brother or sister dies within eight miles outside the city, that six of the brothers that has the goods of the guild in their care shall go to that brother or sister that is dead, and if it is lawful he should be carried to Norwich and in other wise be buried there. And if the body is buried outside Norwich, all the brothers and sisters shall be notified to come to the aforesaid church of saints Simon and Jude, and there shall be done for the soul of the dead person all services, lights, and offerings as if the body were present there. And if any brother or sister is absent at the placebo and dirige, or at mass, he shall pay two pounds of wax to the goods of the guild, but may be excused for good cause. And nevertheless he shall do for the deed as it is said before.

And also it is ordained that on the morrow after the guild day, all the brothers and sisters shall come to the aforesaid church and there cause to be sung a requiem mass for the souls of the brothers and sisters of this guild and for all Christian souls, and everyone there offer a farthing.

And also it is ordained that if any brother or sister falls into poverty through worldly misfortune, his livelihood shall be helped with a farthing in the week from every brother and sister of the guild.

And also it is ordained by common assent that if there is any discord between brothers and sisters, first that discord shall be shown to other brothers and sisters of the guild and accord shall be made by them, if it may reasonably be. And if he may not be so reconciled, it shall be lawful for him to go to the common law without any maintenance. And whoever acts against this ordinance shall pay two pounds of wax to the light.

And also it is ordained by common assent that whichever brother of this guild is appointed to an office and refuses it, shall pay three pounds of wax to the light of St Katherine.

And also it is ordained by common assent that the brothers and sisters of this guild shall have in worship of St Katherine a livery of hoods as clothing, and eat together on their guild day at their common expense. Whoever fails shall pay two pounds of wax to the light.

And also it is ordained by common assent that no brother or sister shall be received into this guild but by the alderman and twelve brothers of the guild.

And regarding the goods and chattels of the said guild, we likewise make known to your excellency that we, the aforesaid guardians, have in keeping for the use of the said guild 20s in silver.

## 23. Vow of chastity.

Language: Latin memorandum and English oath. Date: 1454. Widows who took such vows were known as vowesses. One such is observed from Agnes Kyrkeby's deposition (see 'Childhood' [3]). Translated from Clark, ed., *Lincoln Diocese Documents*.

Memorandum that on Sunday, that is the 10th day of November in the year of the Lord 1454, the reverend father in Christ and lord, John, by God's grace, Lord Bishop of Lincoln, dressed in pontificals in the chapel within his house at Old Temple, London, during the service of mass he received and acknowledged the oath of Isabel Maryone, read and made by her, and gave the veil and mantle of widowhood blessed by the reverend father and clothed her with them. There were present Masters William Wytham, doctor of laws, John Rudyng, Thomas Estyntone, and Thomas Whitfeld, the ministering priests, and others, and [John] Bugge [notary public]. The form of words of the vow that was uttered is:

In the name of the Father, the Son, and the Holy Ghost, I, Isabel Maryone, of your diocese, widow, promise and vow to God, Our Lady,

St Mary, and to all the saints, in your presence, reverend father in Christ Sir John, by the grace of God, Bishop of Lincoln, to be chaste and I determine to keep myself chaste from this time forward as long as my life lasts. In witness of this I here subscribe with my own hand, and she made a cross +

### 24. Visitation, diocese of Lincoln.

Language: Latin. Date: 1518. Translated from Hamilton Thomson, ed., *Visitations in the Diocese of Lincoln*, I.

Church of All Saints, Leicester... Also, Helen Brodbysum does not attend divine service.

### 25. Visitations, archdeaconry of Buckingham.

Language: Latin. Translated from Elvey, ed., *The Courts of the Archdeaconry of Buckingham*.

[a] [1489] Langley. Joan Mason and Thomas Mason because they do not keep the Sabbath holy. They are let off and dismissed.

[b] [1492] Penn. Isabel Bovyngton does not keep the Sabbath. She appeared and confesses the article and is beaten thrice through the church and is dismissed.

Thomas, John, and William the sons of the same Isabel for like cause. They appeared and confessed guilt. They did penance and were dismissed.

# Heresy

### 26. Trial of Margery Baxter of Norwich.

Language: Latin; reported speech in English where specified. Date: 1429. Translated from N. P. Tanner, ed., *Heresy Trials in the Diocese of Norwich, 1428-31*, Camden Society, 4th ser. XX, 1977. The translation, printed in Coulton, *Social Life in Britain*, from Foxe, *Acts and Monuments* is an abridged version of part of the text translated here.

Depositions against Margery, the wife of William Baxter, wright [carpenter]

On the first day of the month of April in the year of the Lord 1429, Joan Clyfland, wife of William Clyfland, living in the parish of St Mary the Less in Norwich, was summoned and appeared in person before the reverend father in Christ and lord, William by the grace of God the Lord Bishop of Norwich, sitting in judgement in the chapel of his palace. On the said lord's order, she swore by a corporal oath, herself touching God's holy gospels, to speak truthfully to all and everything that is asked of her concerning the matter of the faith.

When the oath had been thus taken, Joan Clyfland said that on Friday next before the feast of the Purification of the Blessed Mary last, Margery Baxter, the wife of William Baxter, wright, lately living at Martham in the diocese of Norwich, whilst sitting and sewing with this witness in her room next the fire place in the presence of this witness and of Joan Grymell and Agnes Bethom, servants to this witness, said and told this witness and her servants that they should in no way swear, saying in the mother tongue, 'Dame, beware of the bee, for every bee will sting, and therefore see that you swear neither by God, nor by Our Lady, nor by any other saint, and if you do to the contrary, the bee will sting your tongue and poison your soul.'

This witness then says that the said Margery asked her what she did in church every day. And she replied to her saying that first after her entrance into church, kneeling before the cross, she was accustomed to say five Paternosters in honour of the cross and the whole Ave Maria in honour of the Blessed Mary, mother of Christ. And then the said Margery said to this witness by way of rebuke, 'You do ill by so kneeling and praying before images in such churches because God never was in such a church, nor has ever departed, nor will depart from heaven; nor will he show or grant you more merit for such genuflections, adorations, or prayers done in such churches than a lighted candle screened beneath the lath cover of the baptismal font can give light to those in church at night time, because there is no greater honour to be shown to images in churches or images of the crucifix than is to be shown to the gallows from which your brother was hung,' saying in the mother tongue, 'Unlearned carpenters hew and shape such crosses and images from blocks of wood, and afterwards unlearned painters embellish them with colours, and if you are keen to see the true cross of Christ, I will show you it here in your own home.' And this witness said she would willingly see the true cross of Christ. And the said Margery said, 'Look', and she then stretched her arms out wide, saying to this witness, 'this is the true cross of Christ, and this cross you can and should see and worship every day here in your own home; and thus you labour in vain when you go to church to worship or pray to any dead images or crosses.'

And then this witness said that the said Margery asked her what she believed respecting the sacrament of the altar. And this witness, so she claims, replied to her saying that she believed that the sacrament of the altar after consecration is the true body of Christ in the form of bread. And then the said Margery said to this witness, 'you believe ill, because if every such sacrament is God and the true body of Christ, there are numerous gods, because a thousand and more priests make a thousand such gods and afterwards eat these gods and, having eaten them, discharge them through their posteriors into foul smelling privies, where you can find plenty of such gods if you want to look. Therefore, know for certain that that which you call the sacrament of the altar shall never by the grace of God be my God, for such a sacrament was falsely and deceitfully ordained by priests of the Church to bring simple people to idolatory, as that sacrament is but material bread.'

Then, asked by this witness, the said Margery said to this witness, as she says, that the Thomas of Canterbury that people call Saint Thomas of Canterbury was a false traitor and is damned in hell because he injuriously endowed churches with possessions, and he promoted and encouraged many heresies in the Church which deceive the simple people. Therefore if God was and is blessed, Thomas was and is accursed, and if Thomas was and is blessed, God was and is accursed; and those false priests lie who say that Thomas suffered his death patiently before the altar, because as a false, foolish traitor he was killed as he fled in the doorway of the church.

And then this witness said that the said Margery, asked by this witness, said to her that the cursed pope, cardinals, archbishops, bishops, and particularly the bishop of Norwich, and others who uphold and sustain heresies and idolatories, ruling generally over the people, shall have within a short time the same or worse punishment than had that cursed Thomas of Canterbury, for they falsely and cursedly deceive the people with their false idolatories and laws to extort money from simple people in order to sustain their pride, excess, and idleness; and know that without doubt God's vengeance will shortly come upon those who most cruelly killed God's most holy sons and teachers, that is holy father Abraham, William White, the most holy and learned teacher of divine law, and John Waddon, and others of the party of Christ's law...

Also this witness said that the said Margery said to her that no child or infant born, having Christian parents, ought to be baptised in water according to common use because such an infant is adequately baptised in its mother's womb, and thus that superstition and idolatory that those false and accursed priests do when they dip infants in fonts in churches, they do only to extort money from the people to support those priests and their concubines.

Also that the same Margery said to this witness then present that the consent of mutual love between man and woman alone suffices for the sacrament of marriage, without any exchange of words and without solemnisation in churches.

Also that the same Margery said to this witness that no faithful man or woman is bound to keep fast in Lent, on the Ember days, Fridays, and other days appointed by the Church, and that anyone may lawfully eat meat and all other kinds of food on such days and at such times, and that it were better to eat the meat remaining from Thursday's leftovers on fast days than to go to market and get into debt buying fish, and that Pope Sylvester ordained Lent.

Also that the same Margery said to this witness that William White, who was condemned as a false heretic, is a great saint in heaven and a most holy teacher ordained and sent from God, and that she prayed every day to that holy man William White, and she will pray to him every day of her life as he is worthy to intercede for her before God of heaven...

Also that the same Margery taught and instructed this witness that she should never go on pilgrimage to Mary of Falsingham[5] nor any other saint or place.

The same Margery also said that Thomas Mone's wife[6] is a woman most learned and an intimate follower in the doctrine of William White, and that the son of Richard Belward's brother was a good teacher and first instructed her in the doctrine and his beliefs.

This witness also said that the said Margery asked this witness that she and the said Joan, her servant, should come secretly by night to the said Margery's room and there she should hear her husband read the law of Christ to them, which law was written in a book which the said husband was wont to read to Margery at night. And she said that her husband is the best teacher of Christianity.

The said Margery furthermore spoke thus to this witness, 'Joan, it seems from your expression that you intend and purpose to report to

5 A parody of Walsingham, the most important Marian shrine in Norfolk and probably East Anglia.
6 Another Lollard suspect.

the bishop the counsel I have told you.' And this witness swore that she would never reveal her counsel in this matter unless Margery herself gave her occasion to do so. And then the said Margery said to this witness, 'and if you were to accuse me to the bishop, I will do to you as I did to a Carmelite friar of Yarmouth who was the most learned brother in the whole region.' This witness replied to her and asked what she did to the said brother. And Margery responded that she spoke with the said brother, rebuking him because he begged and because alms would not do or give him good, unless he would give up his habit and go to the plough, and in that way he would please God more than by following the life any other friars. And the friar then asked Margery was there anything else she wished to say to or teach him, and Margery, so this witness says, expounded the gospels in English to the said brother. And then this friar went away from Margery, as this witness says, and afterwards the same friar accused Margery of heresy. And Margery, hearing that the friar thus accused her, Margery herself accused the friar that he wanted to have known her carnally and because she refused to yield to him, the friar accused her of heresy. And Margery said that because of this her husband wanted to kill the friar and so, for fear, the friar kept quiet and retreated shamefaced from the locality.

The said Margery also said to this witness that she often made a sham confession to the dean of the Fields[7] to the effect that the dean thought her to be of good life, and for that reason he often gave Margery money. And this witness then asked her if she had not confessed all her sins to a priest. And Margery said that she never brought evil to any priest and therefore she never wished to confess to a priest nor to obey any priest, for no priest has the power to absolve anyone of their sins, and priests sin every day more than other men. And the same Margery further said that every man and every woman that are of Margery's persuasion are good priests and that Holy Church is such in the places where all those who are in her sect live. And therefore Margery said that one should confess to God alone and no other priest.

The said Margery also said to this witness that the people venerate the devils who fell from heaven with Lucifer, which devils after they had fallen to earth, entered into images standing in churches, and they continued to live and still live in them hidden; people worshipping them thus commit idolatory.

7 I.e. the college of St Mary in the Fields.

She said that the said Margery told this witness that blessed water and blessed bread are but trifles and of no worth, and that all bells are to be pulled down from churches and destroyed, and that all those who furnished bells in churches are excommunicate.

The same Margery also said to this witness that Margery ought not be burnt even if she were convicted of Lollardy as, so she told this witness, she had and has a charter of protection in her womb.[8]

Also, the same Margery said that she overcame in judgement the lord bishop of Norwich, Henry Inglese, and the lords abbots being with them.

Also, the said witness says that Agnes Bethom, a servant of this witness, was sent to the said Margery's house on the Saturday after Ash Wednesday last and, the said Margery not being in the house, found a brass pot standing on the fire, in which pot a piece of salt pork with oatmeal in the pot, so the said Agnes told this witness.

Joan Grymle, the servant of William Clyfland, aged 16 years and more...

[confirms Joan Clyfland's testimony]

Agnes Bethom, servant of William Clyfland of Norwich, aged fourteen years...

[confirms Joan Clyfland's testimony and adds]

... that the said Margery said around the feast of the Purification of the Blessed Mary last in the presence of this witness, Joan Clyfland, and Joan Grymle in the said Joan Clyfland's house, that the sacrament that priests elevate above their heads after consecration and show to the people is not the body of Christ as these false priests claim to the deception of the people, but is only a torte of bread baked by the baker... This witness said that on Saturday after Ash Wednesday last this witness, sent to the said Margery's house about a bench to be made by her master, saw a brass pot standing boiling and covered on the fire in the said Margery's house, the said Margery not being in the house. This witness uncovered the pot and saw a piece of bacon in it boiling in water with oatmeal.

8 Implicitly Margery was pregnant and so could not be executed before the delivery of the child.

# Bibliography

## Manuscript sources

Borthwick Institute of Historical Research (BIHR), St Anthony's Hall, York:
Probate registers, Prob. Reg. 1-9.

Cause papers, CP.E.82; CP.E.89; CP.E.92; CP.E.155; CP.E.159; CP.E.221; CP.E.241P; CP.F.36; CP.F.104; CP.F.127; CP.F.174.

York Minster Library, York:
Probate registers, D/C Reg. 1-2.
Consistory court book, M2(1)f.

## Primary printed sources

R. C. Anderson, ed., *The Assize of Bread Book 1477-1517*, Southampton Record Society, XXXIII, 1923.

M. S. Arnold, ed., *Select Cases of Trespass from the King's Courts 1307-1399*, I, Selden Society, C, 1985.

L. C. Attreed, ed., *York House Books 1461-1490*, 2 vols., Stroud, 1991.

W. P. Baildon, ed., *Select Cases in Chancery AD 1364 to 1471*, Selden Society, X, 1896.

M. Bateson, ed., *Records of the Borough of Leicester*, II, London, 1901.

M. Bateson, ed., *Borough Customs*, I, Selden Society, XVIII, 1904.

F. B. Bickley, ed., *The Little Red Book of Bristol*, I-II, Bristol, 1900.

M. Bowker, ed., *An Episcopal Court Book for the Diocese of Lincoln 1514-1520*, Lincoln Record Society, LXI, 1967.

*Calendar of Papal Registers*, IV, London, 1902.

*Calendar of Patent Rolls, 1348-50*, London, 1905.

*Calendar of Patent Rolls, 1350-54*, London, 1907.

*Calendar of Patent Rolls, 1374-77*, London, 1916.

W. R. Childs, ed., *The Customs Accounts of Hull 1453-1490*, Yorkshire Archaeological Society Record Series, CXLIV, 1986.

A. Clark, ed., *The English Register of Godstow Nunnery, near Oxford*, Early English Text Society, original ser. CXLII, 1911.

A. Clark, ed., *Lincoln Diocese Documents, 1450-1544*, Early English Text Society, original ser. CXLIX, 1914.

R. T. Davies, ed., *Medieval English Lyrics*, London, 1963.

R. B. Dobson, ed., *York City Chamberlains' Account Rolls 1396-1500*, Surtees Society, CXCII, 1980.

*Durham Halmote Rolls*, I, Surtees Society, LXXXII, 1882.

E. M. Elvey, ed., *The Courts of the Archdeaconry of Buckingham 1483-1523*, Buckinghamshire Record Society, XIX, 1975.

G. England, ed., *The Towneley Plays*, Early English Text Society, extra ser. LXXI, 1897.

R. S. Ferguson, ed., *Testamenta Karleolensia*, Cumberland and Westmorland Antiquarian and Archaeological Society, extra ser. IX, 1893.

A. T. Gaydon, ed., *The Taxation of 1297*, Bedfordshire Historical Record Society, XXXIX, 1959.

C. Gross, *Select Cases from the Coroners' Rolls A.D. 1265-1413*, Selden Society, IX, 1896.

C. Gross, ed., *Select Cases Concerning the Law Merchant*, I, Selden Society, XXIII, 1908.

A. Hamilton Thomson, ed., *Visitations of Religious Houses in the Diocese of Lincoln*, I, Lincoln Record Society, VII, 1914.

A. Hamilton Thomson, ed., *Visitations in the Diocese of Lincoln 1517-1531*, I-II, Lincoln Record Society, XXXIII, XXXV, 1940-4.

P. Happé, ed., *English Mystery Plays*, Harmondsworth, 1975.

M. D. Harris, ed., *The Coventry Leet Book*, Early English Text Society, original ser. CXXXIV-V, CXXXVIII, CXLVI, 1907-13.

P. Heath, *Medieval Clerical Accounts*, Borthwick Papers, XXVI, York, 1964.

R. H. Helmholz, ed., *Select Cases on Defamation to 1600*, Selden Society, CI, 1985.

A. Hopkins, ed., *Selected Rolls of the Chester City Courts*, Chetham Society, 3rd. ser. II, 1950.

J. M. Horn, ed., *The Register of Robert Hallum, Bishop of Salisbury 1407-17*, Canterbury and York Society, LXXII, 1982.

W. Hudson, ed., *Leet Jurisdiction in the City of Norwich during the XIIIth and XIVth Centuries*, Selden Society, V, 1892.

A. L. Humphreys, trans., *Materials for the History of the Town and Parish of Wellington in the County of Somerset*, London, 1910.

R. F. Hunnisett, ed., *Bedfordshire Coroners' Rolls*, Bedfordshire Historical Record Society, XLI, 1961.

R. F. Hunnisett, ed., *Sussex Coroners' Inquests 1485-1558*, Sussex Record Society, LXXIV, 1985.

E. G. Kimball, ed., *The Shropshire Peace Roll, 1400-1414*, Shrewsbury, 1959.

E. G. Kimball, ed., *Records of some Sessions of the Peace in Lincolnshire 1381-1396*, II, Lincoln Record Society, LVI, 1962.

E. G. Kimball, ed., *Sessions of the Peace for Bedfordshire 1355-1359, 1363-1364*, Bedfordshire Historical Record Society, XLVIII, 1969.

E. G. Kimball, ed., *Records of Some Sessions of the Peace in the City of Lincoln 1351-1354 and the Borough of Stamford 1351*, Lincoln Record Society, LXV, 1971.

J. L. Kirby and A. D. Kirby, 'The poll-tax of 1377 for Carlisle', *Transactions of the Cumberland and Westmorland Antiquarian and Archaeological Society*, new ser. LVIII, 1959, pp. 110-17.

M. Kowaleski, *The Local Customs Accounts of the Port of Exeter 1266-1321*, Devon and Cornwall Record Society, XXXVI, 1993.

J. Lister, ed., *The Early Yorkshire Woollen Trade*, Yorkshire Archaeological Society Record Series, LXIV, 1924.

H. Littlehales, ed., *The Medieval Records of a London City Church*, Early English Text

Society, original series. CXXV, CXXVIII, 1904-5.

A. K. McHardy, ed., *Clerical Poll-Taxes of the Diocese of Lincoln 1377-1381*, Lincoln Record Society, LXXXI, 1992.

F. W. Maitland and W. P. Baildon, eds., *The Court Baron*, Selden Society, IV, 1891.

F. W. Maitland, L. W. V. Harcourt, and W. C. Bolland, eds., *Year Books of Edward II*, V, Selden Society, XXIV, 1910.

W. O. Massingberd, trans., *Court Rolls of the Manor of Ingoldmells in the County of Lincolnshire*, London, 1902.

B. R. Masters and E. Ralph, eds., *The Church Book of St. Ewen's, Bristol 1454-1584*, Publications of the Bristol and Gloucestershire Archaeological Society, Record Section VI, 1967.

T. F. Mustanoja, ed., *The Good Wife Taught Her Daughter*, Helsinki, 1948.

A. R. Myers, ed., *English Historical Documents*, IV, London, 1969.

R. Oram, trans., *Court Rolls of the Manors of Bruces, Dawbeneys, Pembrokes (Tottenham) 1 Richard II to 1 Henry IV (1377-1399)*, Manor of Tottenham Series, II, London, 1961.

D. Oschinsky, ed., *Walter of Henley and other Treatises*, Oxford, 1971.

T. Pape, *Medieval Newcastle-Under-Lyme*, Manchester, 1928.

F. S. Pearson, ed., 'Records of a ruridecanal court of 1300' in S. G. Hamilton, ed., *Collectanea*, Worcestershire Historical Society, 1912.

M. Prestwich, *York Civic Ordinances, 1301*, Borthwick Papers, XLIX, York, 1976.

R. B. Pugh, trans., *Wiltshire Gaol Delivery and Trailbaston Trials 1275-1306*, Wiltshire Record Society, XXXIII, 1978.

B. A. Putnam, ed., *Yorkshire Sessions of the Peace, 1361-1364*, Yorkshire Archaeological Society Record Series, C, 1939.

J. Raine, ed., *Depositions and other Ecclesiastical Proceedings from the Courts of Durham*, Surtees Society, XXI, 1845.

J. Raine, ed., *Testamenta Eboracensia*, IV, Surtees Society, LIII, 1869.

J. Raine, ed., *The Register, or Rolls, of Walter Gray*, Surtees Society, LVI, 1872.

H. T. Riley, ed., *Memorials of London and London Life*, London, 1868.

R. H. Robbins, ed., *Secular Lyrics of the XIVth and XVth Centuries*, Oxford, 1955.

'Rolls of the Collectors in the West Riding of the Lay-Subsidy (Poll Tax) 2 Richard II', *Yorkshire Archaeological Journal*, VII, 1882, p. 30.

B. Rowland, *Medieval Woman's Guide to Health*, Kent, Ohio, 1981.

H. E. Salter, ed., *Medieval Archives of the University of Oxford*, Oxford Historical Society, LXXIII, 1921.

*Sanctuarium Dunelmense et Sanctuarium Beverlacense*, Surtees Society, I, 1837.

M. Sellers, ed., *York Memorandum Book*, 2 vols., Surtees Society, CXX, CXXV, 1912-15.

R. R. Sharpe, ed., *Calendar of Coroners Rolls of the City of London A.D. 1300-1378*, London, 1913.

R. Sillem, ed., *Records of some Sessions of the Peace in Lincolnshire 1360-1375*, Lincoln Record Society, XXX, 1937.

C. A. Sneyd, ed., *A Relation ... of the Island of England ... about the Year 1500*, Camden Society, XXXVII, 1847.

W. H. Stevenson, ed., *Records of the Borough of Nottingham*, I-III, Nottingham, 1882-5.

W. H. Stevenson, ed., *Report of the Manuscripts of Lord Middleton*, Historical Manuscripts Commission, LXVI, 1911.

R. N. Swanson, *Catholic England: Faith, Religion and Observance Before the Reformation*, Manchester, 1993, pp. 96-104.

N. P. Tanner, ed., *Heresy Trials in the Diocese of Norwich, 1428-31*, Camden Society, 4th ser. XX, 1977.

A. H. Thomas, ed., *Calendar of the Early Mayor's Court Rolls*, Cambridge, 1924.

A. H. Thomas and P. E. Jones, eds., *Calendar of Plea and Memoranda Rolls of the City of London*, 6 vols., Cambridge, 1926-54.

J. E. Thorold Rogers, ed., *Oxford City Documents*, Oxford Historical Society, XVIII, 1891.

J. Toulmin Smith, ed., *English Gilds*, Early English Text Society, original ser. XL, 1870.

J. W. Walker, ed., *Court Rolls of the Manor of Wakefield*, V, Yorkshire Archaeological Society Record Series, CIX, 1945.

A. B. Wallis Chapman, ed., *The Black Book of Southampton*, I-II, Southampton Record Society, XIII-XIV, 1912.

S. Wenzel, ed., *Fasciculus Morum: A Fourteenth-Century Preacher's Manual*, Philadelphia and London, 1989.

C. H. Williams, ed., *English Historical Documents*, V, London, 1967.

J. F. Williams, ed., *The Early Churchwardens' Accounts of Hampshire*, London, 1913.

R. A. Wilson, ed., *Court Rolls of the Manor of Hales*, III, Worcester Historical Society, 1933.

C. M. Woolgar, ed., *Household Accounts from Medieval England, Records of Social and Economic History*, new series XVII-XVIII, 1992-3.

T. Wright and J. O. Halliwell, eds., *Reliquae Antiquae*, 2 vols., London, 1841.

## Secondary works

K. Ashley and P. Sheingorn, eds., *Interpreting Cultural Symbols: Saint Anne in Late Medieval Society*, Athens, Geo. and London, 1990.

M. Aston, 'Lollard Women Priests?', *Journal of Ecclesiastical History*, XXXI, 1980, pp. 441-61.

M. Aston, 'Segregation in Church', in Sheils and Wood, eds., *Women in the Church*, p. 264.

W. O. Ault, *Open-Field Farming in Medieval England*, London, 1972.

C. M. Barron and A. F. Sutton, *Medieval London Widows 1300-1500*, London, 1994.

S. G. Bell, 'Medieval Women Book Owners: Arbiters of Lay Piety and Ambassadors of Culture', *Signs*, VII, 1982, pp. 742-68.

H. S. Bennett, *The Pastons and Their England*, Cambridge, 1932.

J. M. Bennett, 'Medieval Peasant Marriage: An Examination of Marriage License Fines in the Liber Gersumarum', in J. A. Raftis, ed., *Pathways to Medieval Peasants*, Toronto, 1981, pp. 193-246.

J. M. Bennett, *Women in the Medieval English Countryside: Gender and Household in Brigstock before the Plague*, New York, 1987.

J. M. Bennett, 'Misogyny, Popular Culture, and Women's Work', *History Workshop Journal*, XXXI, 1991, pp. 166-88.

J. M. Bennett, 'Conviviality and Charity in Medieval and Early Modern England', *Past and Present*, CXXXIV, 1992, pp. 19-41.

P. P. A. Biller, 'Birth-Control in the West in the Thirteenth and Early Fourteenth Centuries', *Past and Present*, XCIV, 1982, pp. 3-26.

P. P. A. Biller, 'Childbirth in the Middle Ages', *History Today*, XXXVI, 1986, pp. 42-9.

P. P. A. Biller, 'Marriage Patterns and Women's Lives: a Sketch of a Pastoral Geography,' in Goldberg, ed., *Woman is a Worthy Wight*, pp. 60-107.

A. Blamires, ed., *Woman Defamed and Woman Defended: An Anthology of Medieval Texts*, Oxford, 1992.

J. M. Carter, *Rape in Medieval England*, Lanham, Md., 1985.

A. Cheifetz, '"Spiritual Mansions": Female Space and the Privatisation of Piety in Late Medieval England', unpublished University of York M.A. dissertation, 1992.

E. Clark, 'Some Aspects of Social Security in Medieval England', *Journal of Family History*, VII, 1982, pp. 307-20.

E. Clark, 'The Quest for Security in Medieval England' in M. M. Sheehan, ed., *Aging and the Aged in Medieval Europe*, Toronto, 1990, pp. 189-200.

P. Clark and J. Clark, 'The Social Economy of the Canterbury Suburbs: The Evidence of the Census of 1563', in A. Detsicas and N. Yates, eds., *Studies in Modern Kentish History*, Kent Archaeological Society, 1983, pp. 65-86.

R. M. Clay, *The Medieval Hospitals of England*, London, 1909.

M. C. Cross, '"Great Reasoners in Scripture": The Activities of Women Lollards 1380-1530', in D. Baker, ed., *Medieval Women*, Studies in Church History, Subsidia I, 1978, pp. 359-80.

P. H. Cullum, 'Vowesses and Veiled Widows', paper given at conference on Medieval Women: Work, Spirituality, and Patronage, York, 1990.

P. H. Cullum, '"And Hir Name was Charite": Charitable Giving by and for Women in Late Medieval Yorkshire', in Goldberg, ed., *Woman is a Worthy Wight*, pp. 182-211.

P. H. Cullum, '"For Pore People Harberles": What was the Function of the Maisondieu?', in D. J. Clayton, R. G. Davies, and P. McNiven, eds., *Trade, Devotion and Governance: Papers in Later Medieval History*, Stroud, 1994, pp. 36-54.

P. H. Cullum, *Hospitals and Charity in Medieval England*, Manchester, forthcoming.

K. Dockray, 'Why did Fifteenth-Century English Gentry Marry?', in M. Jones, ed., *Gentry and Lesser Nobility in Late Medieval Europe*, Gloucester, 1986, pp. 61-80.

C. Donahue, Jr., 'Female Plaintiffs in Marriage Cases in the Court of York in the Later Middle Ages: What Can We Learn from the Numbers?', in Walker, ed., *Wife and Widow*, pp. 183-213.

E. Duffy, *The Stripping of the Altars: Traditional Religion in England c. 1400- c. 1580*, New Haven and London, 1992.

A. M. Dutton, 'Harley 4012: Devout English Noblewomen and Clerical Authority', paper given at Seventh York Manuscripts Conference, 1994.

C. Dyer, *Standards of Living in the Later Middle Ages*, Cambridge, 1989.

C. Dyer, 'Gardens and Orchards in Medieval England', in idem, *Everyday Life in Medieval England*, London, 1994, pp. 116-27.

A. Finch, 'Parental Authority and the Problem of Clandestine Marriage in the Later Middle Ages', *Law and History Review*, VIII, 1980, p. 196.

R. Gilchrist, *Gender and Material Culture: The Archaeology of Religious Women*, London, 1993.

P. J. P. Goldberg, 'Female Labour, Service and Marriage in the Late Medieval Urban North', *Northern History*, XXII, 1986, pp. 18-38.

P. J. P. Goldberg, 'Urban Identity and the Poll Taxes of 1377, 1379, and 1380-1', *Economic History Review*, 2nd ser., XLIII, 1990, pp. 194-216.

P. J. P. Goldberg, 'The Public and the Private: Women in the Pre-Plague Economy', in P. R. Coss and S. D. Lloyd, eds., *Thirteenth Century England III*, Woodbridge, 1991, pp. 78-80.

P. J. P. Goldberg, ed., *Woman is a Worthy Wight: Women in English Society c. 1200-1500*, Stroud, 1992.

P. J. P. Goldberg, *Women, Work, and Life Cycle in a Medieval Economy: Women in York and Yorkshire c. 1300-1520*, Oxford, 1992.

P. J. P. Goldberg, 'Women', in R. Horrox, ed., *Fifteenth Century Attitudes*, Cambridge, 1994, pp. 112-31.

P. J. P. Goldberg, 'Girls Growing Up in Later Medieval England', *History Today*, June, 1995, pp. 25-32.

H. Graham, '"A Woman's Work...": Labour and Gender in the Late Medieval Countryside', in Goldberg, ed., *Woman is a Worthy Wight*, pp. 136-44.

B. A. Hanawalt, *The Ties that Bound: Peasant Families in Medieval England*, New York, 1986.

B. A. Hanawalt, *Growing Up in Medieval London: The Experience of Childhood in History*, New York, 1993.

R. H. Helmholz, *Marriage Litigation in Medieval England*, Cambridge, 1974.

R. H. Helmholz, 'Married Women's Wills in Later Medieval England', in Walker, ed., *Wife and Widow*, pp. 165-82.

D. Herlihy and C. Klapisch-Zuber, *Tuscans and Their Families: A Study of the Florentine Catasto of 1427*, New Haven and London, 1985.

R. H. Hilton, *The English Peasantry in the Later Middle Ages*, Oxford, 1975.

M. C. Howell, 'Citizenship and Gender: Women's Political Status in Northern Medieval Cities', in M. Erler and M. Kowaleski, eds., *Women and Power in the Middle Ages*, Athens, Geo. and London, 1988, pp. 37-60.

A. Hudson, *The Premature Reformation: Wycliffite Texts and Lollard History*, Oxford, 1988.

A. M. Hutchison, 'Devotional Reading in the Monastery and in the Late Medieval Household', in M. G. Sargent, *De Cella in Seculum: Religious and Secular Life and Devotion in Late Medieval England*, Cambridge, 1989, pp. 215-27.

R. Hutton, *The Rise and Fall of Merry England: The Ritual Year 1400-1700*, Oxford, 1994.

R. M. Karras, 'The Regulation of Brothels in Later Medieval England', *Signs*, XIV, 1989, pp. 399-426.

C. Klapisch-Zuber, *Women, Family, and Ritual in Renaissance Italy*, Chicago and London, 1985.

M. Kowaleski, 'Women's Work in a Market Town: Exeter in the Late Fourteenth Century', in B. A. Hanawalt, ed., *Women and Work in Preindustrial Europe*, Bloomington, Ind., 1986, pp. 149-59.

M. Kowaleski and J. M. Bennett, 'Crafts, Gilds, and Women in the Middle Ages: Fifty Years after Marian K. Dale', *Signs*, XIV, 1989, pp. 474-88.

A. Kussmaul, *Servants in Husbandry in Early Modern England*, Cambridge, 1981.

J. S. Loengard, '"Legal History and the Medieval Englishwoman" Revisited: Some New Directions', in J. T. Rosenthal, *Medieval Women and the Sources of Medieval History*, Athens, Geo. and London, 1990, pp. 210-36.

P. C. Maddern, *Violence and Social Order: East Anglia 1422-1442*, Oxford, 1992.

M. K. McIntosh, 'Local Change and Community Control in England, 1465-1500', *Huntington Library Quarterly*, XLIX, 1986, pp. 219-42.

S. McSheffrey, 'Women and Lollardy: a Reassessment', *Canadian Journal of History*, XXVI, 1991, pp. 199-223.

L. Mirrer, ed., *Upon My Husband's Death: Widows in the Literature and Histories of Medieval Europe*, Ann Arbor, 1992.

J. Murray, 'On the Origins and Role of "Wise Women" in Causes for Annulment on the Grounds of Male Impotence', *Journal of Medieval History*, XVI, 1990, pp. 235-49.

T. North, 'Legerwite in the Thirteenth and Fourteenth Centuries', *Past and Present*, CXI, 1986, pp. 3-16.

M. Oliva, 'Aristocracy or Meritocracy? Office-holding Patterns in Late Medieval English Nunneries', in Sheils and Wood, eds., *Women in the Church*, pp. 197-208.

I. and P. Opie, *The Singing Game*, Oxford, 1985.

L. L. Otis, *Prostitution in Medieval Society: The History of an Urban Institution in the Languedoc*, Chicago, 1985.

S. A. C. Penn, 'Female Wage-Earners in Late Fourteenth-Century England', *Agricultural History Review*, XXXV, 1987, pp. 1-14.

L. R. Poos and R. M. Smith, '"Legal Windows onto Historical Populations"? Recent Research on Demography and the Manor Court in England', *Law and History Review*, II, 1984, pp. 128-52.

J. B. Post, 'A Fifteenth-Century Customary of the Southwark Stews', *Journal of the Society of Archivists*, V, 1977, pp. 423-8.

J. B. Post, 'Ravishment of Women and the Statutes of Westminster', in J. H. Baker, ed., *Legal Records and the Historian*, London, 1978, pp. 150-64.

E. Power, *Medieval English Nunneries c. 1275 to 1535*, Cambridge, 1922.

Z. Razi, Life, *Marriage and Death in a Medieval Parish*, Cambridge, 1980.

J. E. T. Rogers, *A History of Agriculture and Prices in England*, 8 vols., Oxford, 1866-1902.

L. Roper, *The Holy Household: Women and Morals in Reformation Augsburg*, Oxford, 1989.

J. Rossiaud, *Medieval Prostitution*, trans. L. G. Cochrane, Oxford, 1988.

W. Scase, 'St Anne and the Education of the Virgin: Literary and Artistic Traditions and their Implications', in N. Rogers, ed., *England in the Fourteenth Century*, Harlaxton Medieval Studies, III (Stamford, 1993), pp. 81-96.

M. M. Sheehan, 'The Formation and Stability of Marriage in Fourteenth-Century England: Evidence of an Ely Register', *Medieval Studies*, XXXIII, 1971, pp. 228-63.

W. J. Sheils and D. Wood, eds., *Women in the Church*, Studies in Church History, XXVII, 1990.

R. M. Smith, 'Hypothèses sur la Nuptialité en Angleterre aux XIIIe-XIVe Siècles', *Annales: Economies Sociétés Civilisations*, XXXVIII, 1983, pp. 107-36.

R. M. Smith, 'Some Thoughts on "Hereditary" and "Proprietary" Rights in Land under Customary Law in Thirteenth and Early Fourteenth Century England', Law and *History Review*, I, 1983, pp. 95-128.

R. M. Smith, 'Women's Property Rights Under Customary Law: Some Developments in the Thirteenth and Fourteenth Centuries', *Transactions of the Royal Historical Society*, XXXVI, 1986, pp. 165-94.

R. M. Smith, 'Coping with Uncertainty: Women's Tenure of Customary Land in England c. 1370-1430', in J. I. Kermode, ed., *Enterprise and Individuals in Fifteenth-Century England*, Stroud, 1991, pp. 43-67.

R. M. Smith, 'The Manorial Court and the Elderly Tenant in Medieval England', in idem and M. Pelling, eds., *Life, Death, and the Elderly: Historical Perspectives*, London, 1991, pp. 39-61.

S. Sutcliffe, 'The Cult of St Sitha in England: an Introduction', *Nottingham Medieval Studies*, XXXVII, 1993, pp. 83-9.

J. H. Tillotson, *Marrick Priory: A Nunnery in Late Medieval Yorkshire*, Borthwick Papers, LXXV, York, 1989.

B. J. Todd, 'The Remarrying Widow: a Stereotype Reconsidered', in M. Prior, ed., *Women in English Society 1500-1800*, London, 1985, pp. 54-92.

S. S. Walker, ed., *Wife and Widow in Medieval England*, Ann Arbor, 1993.

S. S. Walker, 'Litigation as Personal Quest: Suing for Dower in the Royal Courts, circa 1272-1350', in eadem, *Wife and Widow*, pp. 81-108.

A. K. Warren, *Anchorites and their Patrons in Medieval England*, Berkeley and London, 1985.

D. M. Webb, 'Woman and Home: the Domestic Setting of Late Medieval Spirituality', in Sheils and Wood, eds., *Women in the Church*, pp. 159-73.

# Index